Derek E
3249 W
Vancouver, B.C.
V6L 1L3
604 736 1194

MW01222360

Developing Quality Metadata

Developing Quality Metadata

Building Innovative Tools and Workflow Solutions

Cliff Wootton

AMSTERDAM • BOSTON • HEIDLEBERG • LONDON
NEW YORK • OXFORD • PARIS • SAN DIEGO
SAN FRANCISCO • SINGAPORE • SYDNEY • TOKYO
Focal Press is an imprint of Elsevier

Acquisitions Editor: Angelina Ward
Publishing Services Manager: George Morrison
Project Manager: Paul Gottehrer
Assistant Editor: Doug Shults
Marketing Manager: Christine Degon Veroulis
Cover Design: Eric DeCicco
Book Production: Borrego Publishing (www.borregopublishing.com)

Focal Press is an imprint of Elsevier
30 Corporate Drive, Suite 400, Burlington, MA 01803, USA
Linacre House, Jordan Hill, Oxford OX2 8DP, UK

 Recognizing the importance of preserving what has been written, Elsevier prints its books on acid-free
paper whenever possible.

Library of Congress Cataloging-in-Publication Data

Wootton, Cliff.
  Developing quality metadata : building innovative tools and workflow
solutions / Cliff Wootton.
     p. cm.
  Includes bibliographical references and index.
  ISBN-13: 978-0-240-80869-7 (pbk. : alk. paper)
  ISBN-10: 0-240-80869-X (pbk. : alk. paper) 1. Metadata. 2. Database
design. 3. Computer software--Development. 4. Knowledge
management--Data processing. I. Title.
  QA76.9.D26W65 2007
  025.3--dc22
                            2006101915

British Library Cataloguing-in-Publication Data
A catalogue record for this book is available from the British Library.

For information on all Focal Press publications
visit our website at www.books.elsevier.com

07 08 09 10 11   5 4 3 2 1

Printed in the United States of America

Dedication

Kisses and hugs to my girls: Jul, Han, Lyd, Roo.

Now will you 'pack-it-in!'

Contents

Acknowledgments

There are so many people who help you when you write a book. Some willingly, some not. Some wittingly, some unwittingly. I would like to say a personal thank-you to a few who have 'been there' when I needed them.

First off, thanks to the team at Focal Press for giving me an opportunity to work with them again. Thanks to Angelina Ward who has managed the project from Focal's perspective and Joanne Tracey who has always been an encourager and leads a really great team.

It has been a joy to get to know Eric Schumacher-Rasmussen as he edited my manuscript into a sensible shape ready for publication. Grateful thanks to Becky Fulker who has done a magnificent job of typesetting the book and getting it ready for print. Thanks also to Paul Gottehrer and Doug Shults at Focal for project managing the production.

I'm also grateful to people in the broadcasting industry who have helped me out with advice. In particular Neil Dunstan at Metaglue, Russell Merryman at Al Jazeera International, Julie Foster at the BBC, Rob Freeman and John Angeli at the Press Association. Thank you also to Tony Cleverley and his team at Marketpipe.

As ever, my team 'back at the ranch' have supported me through the long dark night hours as I toiled over the manuscript and wrestled with my prose and beat it into submission. My girls all laugh at my jokes even when they aren't funny and keep my feet on the ground.

Cliff Wootton
Crowborough
October 2006

Part 1

Introduction

"How to Bash the Bits and Beat the Bytes into Shape"

Data and metadata drives the TV production and broadcast scheduling systems. Metadata helps to manage content and when you examine a broadcast infrastructure, a lot of what is happening is to do with the manipulation of nonvideo data formats. Interactive TV and digital text services also require data in large quantities. Managing it, cleaning it, routing it to the correct place at the right time and in the right format are all issues that are familiar to data management professionals inside and outside the media industry.

While I wrote this book, I spent a little time working with some developers who build investment-banking systems. Interestingly they face identical problems to my colleagues in broadcasting. I suspected this was the case all along because I have frequently deployed solutions in broadcasting that I learned from projects in nonbroadcast industries. Spend some 'sabbatical' time in another kind of industry. It will teach you some useful insights.

Workflow in an organization of any size will be composed of many discrete steps. Whether you work on your own or in a large enterprise, the processes are very similar. The scale of the organization just dictates the quantity. The quality needs to be maintained at the highest level in both cases. The Data and Metadata Workflow Tools you choose and use are critical to your success.

The key word here is Tools. With good tools, you can "Push the Envelope" and raise your product quality.

There has been much discussion about metadata systems and data warehouses. Systems used as data repositories are useful but if you don't put good quality data in there you are just wasting your time. We need to focus on making sure the data is as good as possible—and stays that way.

Raw data is often in somewhat of a mess. There are a series of steps required to clean the data so it can be used. Sometimes even the individual fields need to be broken down so that the meaning can be extracted. This book is not so much about storage systems but more about what gets stored in them.

There are defensive coding techniques you can use as avoidance strategies. There are also implications when designing database schemas. Data entry introduces problems at the outset and needs to be as high quality as possible or the entire process is compromised. The book describes risk factors and illuminates them with real-world case examples and how they were neutralized. Planning your systems well and fixing problems before they happen is far cheaper than clearing up the mess afterwards.

This book is designed to be practical. If nontechnical staff read it, they will understand why some of the architectural designs for their systems are hard to implement. For people in the implementation area, they will find insights that help solve some of the issues that confront them. A lot of the advice is in the form of case studies based on genuine experience of building workflows. Some explanation is given about the background to the problem and why it needs to be solved.

The material is divided into two parts. Part 1 deals with theory while Part 2 provides many practical examples in the form of tutorials.

We lay a foundation for further projects that look inside the media files and examine audio/video storage and the various tools that you can build for manipulating them. Before embarking on that, we need to manage a variety of data and metadata components and get that right first.

1

Framing the Problem

About this Book

This book is about designing better workflows that will lead to creating good quality metadata (and essence data). You still might not create perfect metadata but it should be significantly less flawed than it could be without a well-designed workflow in place. The quality of input to systems that are designed to be inherently stable and reliable requires a singleness of purpose from the outset.

This applies equally to large-scale enterprises or small one-man outfits trying to leverage systems as labor saving devices.

We need to be pragmatic and practical in our approach to workflows and metadata systems. The high-level structures are helpful when organizing the big-pieces of our infrastructure, but the rubber hits the road when we manipulate a numeric value and forget to deal with byte ordering as the value is moved from a PowerPC to an Intel system. This book is more about the little pieces than the big pieces.

Try to think laterally and use the tools at your disposal in nontraditional ways. A new and original solution can profoundly affect the efficiency of your workflow. Use commodity GUI-driven applications in script-based wrappers. They can contribute to your automation. Good ideas can save time and money. Sometimes, you will have a bad idea. The consequences of that can be painful and long-term. Cultivate the ability to divine which is which:

- Think first.
- Design carefully and diligently.
- Prototype and test new ideas.
- Build components.
- Test them.
- Integrate the system.
- Test again.

Notice that the word "test" occurs in several places. That's because you can never test too often.

This book is divided into two main parts. The first part is more philosophical and describes why metadata systems need to be carefully constructed. It contains some case history along the way, but you'll find many more examples collected as tutorials in Part 2.

Part 2 is the practical application of the theory we discuss in Part 1. This works well, because we can cover theoretical concepts in Part 1. The real world is not as neat and tidy.

We take our inspiration from many different sources as we solve a problem. Transferring technologies from one industry to another is particularly useful. What one industry perceives as a problem, another industry has already solved, but the connection may not be obvious at first.

The chapters in Part 1 are organized according to a natural progression starting with the most basic data components. They deal with increasingly complex architectural concepts to describe a toolbox of ideas and technologies for building workflow infrastructures:

- Metadata.
- Systems design concepts.
- Conversions.
- Data formats from raw to highly structured.
- Rights issues.
- Enterprise issues.
- Tools and API layers.
- Platform-by-platform scripting and automation techniques.
- Integrating the components to build systems.
- Conclusions.

The task-based Part 2 aggregates some of the theoretical material into useful solutions built around real-world content creation and processing scenarios.

Where it is useful, a reference to a numbered tutorial in Part 2 will direct you to relevant discussions.

Why the Basic Stuff is Still Important

In these modern times, too many software engineers believe that if they make their systems read and write XML, they can get any application to exchange data with any other. The truth is that systems need to share a common and compatible understanding of the document type definition (DTD) if they are going to communicate properly, and that's the tricky part.

A similar oversimplification is being rolled out again, this time with metadata suggested as the universal panacea to systems integration problems. If only it were that easy. The trick is to make sure that the metadata schemes being used at each end are compatible.

Whatever level of abstraction and technology is applied, the software engineer is still faced with the same problems of data truncation, information float, and incorrect mapping of character sets. The new technologies don't really solve the fundamental problems of deploying untested software and allowing it to be used by lazy operators who have no stake in entering high-quality data.

Systems designers and implementation engineers have lost sight of how to solve basic software integration problems. Instead, we take it for granted that the large blocks of software that hurl huge XML files around with ease are foolproof. They may be powerful, but we can still misuse them. Nothing happened during the evolution of XML that absolved us of the responsibility as engineers to take care with the quality of our software implementation and pay attention to the low-level code.

What Is a Workflow?

A workflow describes the movement of documents or tasks through a sequence of processing steps during which work is performed on the content. It is the operational aspect of a work procedure and controls the way that tasks are structured. It also determines where and who performs them, and in what order. The synchronization of tasks might be controlled with auxiliary information flowing in to support the activity. The system tracks the work as it is done, and a journal of who did what, as well as when and how they did it, is maintained.

The information recorded in the journal may be analyzed later on to calculate throughput as a measurable value. This has evolved from the "time and motion" studies that measured the performance of the people staffing and operating manufacturing plants since the industrial revolution.

Workflow might also describe a production process in an industrial context; it is not necessarily always an audiovisual- or information-based process. It might describe a sequence of algorithms that are applied in a scientific or numerical analysis system. This is particularly useful when studying genetics, due to the sheer bulk of information needing to be processed. Business logic can be embodied in a workflow to control and manage a commercial enterprise. In other words, an organization may have multiple workflows all running concurrently in different parts of the business.

About the Task

Metadata is often used to control the workflow. Data and metadata are covered in more detail in Chapter 2.

Workflow is the process that surrounds a content management system. It is worth taking a few moments to examine each of those three words—content, management, and system—separately.

The *content* is up to you. It is whatever you want to create, edit, collate, and deploy. It might be movies, text, pictures, or graphics. It could be physical assets in the real world represented by objects in the system.

The "M word" (*management*) means you are controlling and operating on something. You probably want to:

- Make a new one.
- Edit an old one.
- Delete one you don't want anymore.
- Give a copy of one to someone else.

Distribution may include some conditional access, possibly with some residual control remaining in your hands.

Something that is *systematic* is planned, regulated and controlled in a predictable way. Systematizing the content management means, you have planned how it is going to work.

It is not a process that works correctly on an occasional and random basis. Some systems are like that. They don't merit being called systems because they are probably informal processes with no well thought-out design.

It is up to you to choose the content, decide what you need to do to manage it, and design a set of tools that allow your users to operate on that content systematically.

High-quality metadata makes it all work consistently and reliably.

Driving Forces

Designing large content systems is no small feat. It is always a challenge to construct something that is streamlined, efficient, cost-effective, and easy to manage. These are often multimedia systems that manage textual, spatial, temporal, and abstract data. In major deployments, several hundred users will simultaneously access content in a repository in which several million items are managed. At the other end of the scale, the system may be used by only a handful of users and manage a few thousand assets. Aside from their size, the two extremes are amazingly similar in many respects, and the same problems crop up in both.

 The data quality must not be compromised to make the system easier to build. The most highly engineered system cannot deliver high quality output if the input material is of inferior quality.

The Meat of the Problem

In the past, the entire system would be built from scratch. Now, significant parts of the system are available "off the shelf" as turnkey components, and the engineering task concentrates on integrating the large modular system blocks together. That is sometimes difficult, because different suppliers may have used different—and incompatible—data formats or interfaces.

This book focuses some attention in this "glue-ware" area. Ultimately, the quality of the service offered by your web site, TV channel, video-on-demand, IPTV, PVR, or DVD sell-through business depends on how well integrated your systems are. The same applies to other business areas whether they are in banking and finance or energy and exploration.

Problems exist in the spaces between systems. It may require ingenuity and careful software engineering to successfully connect two incompatible systems. Your suppliers may help, but they won't want to be responsible. To them, this is a support overhead.

It is much easier to implement this glue-ware correctly in the first place than to throw something together in a hurry and spend a long time debugging it. You need to understand both sides of the connection and exactly what transformations are necessary. Then implement the glue carefully.

Simply disregarding something like a time-zone offset and not storing it at all during the ingest process may not cause a problem most of the time. After all, your video journalists may all be shooting within the same time zone as the play-out system is broadcasting to. You might assume that a time-zone value wastes space in your database. Wrong!

Later on, a foreign data item arrives, and the time signature is incorrect because the time zone adjustment cannot be applied. You could be faced with a difficult and complex upgrade that needs to be applied urgently to your system. That is the wrong time to be thinking about changing a fundamental part of your data and metadata storage model because the knock on effects could be serious. A fix like this might have to be applied to an ingest process and have consequences throughout the entire system.

Take It in Small Steps

Breaking down the problems into smaller tasks is important. Something simple like counting how many pages are in a PDF file can become quite complex due to the different ways that a PDF file can be constructed.

The obvious approach is to open the PDF and parse it with your own application. This is not necessarily the best solution. The same is true when dealing with other complicated formats like video, audio, and image data. If the information you need is trivial and likely to be in the file header, then it will be quicker to access directly by opening the container as a raw file and reading in the first few bytes. If you want to analyze the image content in more detail, you could gain additional leverage by using other tools and controlling them externally.

That approach operates indirectly on the data by remotely controlling another application.

Think Differently

The solutions to many recurring problems can be explained more effectively with tutorials. The tutorials often solve these problems by using hybrid techniques. Sometimes they enclose applications or tools in script wrappers; I prefer to let the operating system and scripting tools take the strain.

I spent a long time trying to make Adobe Illustrator export an image file as text. The scripts I wrote at first never worked completely satisfactorily, because there would be a point at which I would have to step in and click a mouse button to continue. This immediately prevents the solution from being deployed in automated workflow systems.

Sometimes, a solution that appears unusable or unnecessarily labored suddenly gives way to a much simpler answer. In this case, after I stepped away from the problem and approached it in a different way, I found a workable solution that consisted of barely three lines of AppleScript and one UNIX pipe with several simple commands.

Don't always select the apparently obvious first solution. It is tempting to go straight for an XML interchange format. Yes, XML is powerful and ubiquitous, but what did we use before XML came along? Sometimes those old-fashioned techniques are faster, more compact, and easier to publish or manipulate. For some legacy applications, they might be the only way you can import or export data in a way that those applications can understand.

I like XML solutions because you can do a lot with the output. Since XML is well covered in other books, I am going to focus here on alternatives to XML, other technologies or approaches you may not have thought of using. The "road less traveled," if you will.

Creative Artists vs. Geeks

As a rule, creative people come from an arts background and they often think of a computer as a tool without any degree of built-in intelligence. To many of them, it is just a different kind of canvas on which to draw or paint and appears to be a tool that depends almost exclusively on manual operation. As such, they often fail to exploit the intelligence that the computer offers them.

I come from a technical background and developed my creative skills through some of the work I did earlier in my career as an illustrator. I often think of technical, automated ways to accomplish repetitive creative tasks. That provides me with useful leverage to improve my creative productivity. It also speeds up my throughput by an order of magnitude at least.

It is important to get the maximum value from your computing resources, whether they are small and limited to a single machine or of a grander scale, perhaps serving several hundred users. In the context of creating, storing, and managing metadata in any kind of workflow, let's push the envelope a little in order to get the maximum leverage from the systems at our disposal.

Platforms

The computing platform on which any of us works is irrelevant. There are certain pros and cons to any given platform.

On the Mac OS X platform, I use several different kinds of scripting to speed up all the things I do. This is usually accomplished with short fragments of labor-saving code. The Spotlight desktop searching technology is also a great assist, and I use this to search an electronic archive of over 500 gigabytes of technical reference literature that I keep online and close at hand.

On Windows, the things you need may be built-in, like they are on Mac OS X, or you may need to purchase third-party solutions and download shareware.

On Linux (and all the other UNIX variants), the solutions are more likely to be open source and—more importantly to some users—free. However, "free" also implies that the software is "supported by your own efforts." You don't have a supplier company you can go to for help with fixing a bug, but you do have the source code to fix it yourself—if you can. This is not always attractive to the corporate user. Hence, there is some potential revenue to be earned by creating a proprietary solution. There may also be business opportunities in providing support to people using these open source applications. As they say in the East London vernacular, "Ya pays yer money—ya takes yer choice."

You can build powerful solutions in any operating system. If you prefer Windows and you want to add a little UNIX seasoning to it to get the best of both worlds, then install Microsoft Services for UNIX.

Scripting Languages

We all have our favorite platforms and languages. It is important that you don't look at my examples and decide they aren't useful solutions because they are coded in a language that you don't know or built on a platform you don't use. Most of my examples are implemented in AppleScript and UNIX command line shells. Those technologies just happen to be convenient for creating workflows and what I have been using predominantly in recent times.

If you are thinking about building workflows on Windows, you have access to all of the same scripting tools except AppleScript (you can use the Windows equivalent, PowerShell). Earlier Windows scripting languages are useful as well. All of the other shell programming languages like Perl, Python, and Expect—as well as the UNIX command line environments—are open source and available on all platforms.

Look at the philosophical approach I use in my AppleScript examples and then translate that into your own favorite language or platform.

For example, sometimes you can't get an application to open a file directly. Instead, you can ask the operating system (Mac OS X Finder or Windows Explorer) to open the file with that application. I am sure that approach would work on Windows with PowerShell, but the syntax would certainly be different.

Labor-Saving Search Tools

There are substantial gains to be made by implementing simple tools with scripts.

I fashioned a specialized search tool that helps me find keywords in the 50 or so component Microsoft Word document files and 250 or so illustrations that comprise a typical book manuscript. By using AppleScript and Automator, it is feasible to have a GUI tool into which you can type a keyword and it will open every chapter in Word and every illustration in Adobe Illustrator that contains that keyword.

The alternative would be to open all of the chapters and pictures and inspect them manually one by one, an extremely boring and time-consuming task, to say the least. About 75% of the open-and-search operations on the document collection would be pointless, because the keyword would not be in those files. Automation is the answer. It avoids the boredom and reduces the chance of human error.

Check out Tutorial 59 for the details of how to build a script-based tool that searches Word documents like this.

In Mac OS X, the Spotlight application programming interface (API) and software development kit (SDK) give access to this kind of searching at an altogether more powerful level (if you are a software developer), but most of the time you can accomplish what you need with some simple shell scripts.

When It All Goes Wrong

Many of the topics I address are to do with where things can go wrong—sometimes quite badly wrong. Be careful not to take your data sources for granted and assume that they are always accurate. There will be some spurious errors eventually. You need to build in the necessary coping mechanisms.

There may be mistakes and inaccuracies in the data, quite separate from any purposely hidden information that the owner might have put in there. Some data items might technically be wrong, but hide "fingerprints" in the data. We discuss this copyright protection mechanism later.

Processing data in a workflow needs to be considered carefully, whether you are building tools or operating as a user. Video journalists shooting video will need to know the implications of entering badly formatted or incorrect data. They may not realize that the comments they enter could end up on the viewer's TV screen with no editorial monitoring in between. That is a worst-case scenario, but it could happen.

About the Standards

During the research for this book, a consistent picture started to emerge regarding metadata standards. This was also evident after I investigated several Media Asset Management (MAM) systems for clients.

Although there are many standards to choose from, some are more complete or rigorously defined than others. Many MAM software manufacturers claim to support one or more of the metadata standards. In only a rare few cases does the system come pre-configured with a schema based on one of these standards. Even then, the suggestion was that most of the schema definitions could be removed for performance reasons.

The consensus seems to be that a deployment of a MAM system would involve installing the system first and then configuring it with those parts of the schema that apply to your business model. Indeed, you may even find that the system vendor suggests selecting parts of different schemas and constructing a pick 'n' mix schema of your own.

This is a somewhat pragmatic approach. You should be able to export to any other standardized metadata scheme that you need to, provided you understand the concepts of data loss through truncation and mapping. Then define your schema's containers to hold a superset of the properties. In such a situation, the metadata standards facilitate the interchange between systems rather than describe a form of storage.

Refer to Appendix B for a summary of some useful metadata standards.

Multimedia Workflows

Although we have many standards already being used to work with multiple kinds of media, the available choices for containment and aggregation into interactive packages are fewer. Perhaps this is because interactivity is a much more complex model to understand than simple spatial images, linear video and textual content. Interactivity requires that you model connectedness between time and space across all the different media being used. Events need to be described with a level of detail that describes buttons being pressed down, released and clicked multiple times as discretely different things.

We need a mechanism that translates from one format to another. Similar to the way that QuickTime works as an interchange node for converting audio, video, and graphics. We don't yet have that centralized concept for interactive multimedia presentations.

QuickTime works as well as it does as an interchange point because it understands a superset of the functionality contained within all the hosted video, audio, and graphic media formats. This makes the mapping between one format and another much easier to accomplish.

To build the same transformation architecture for our interactive content requires that we develop an open model based on a superset of all the interactive formats that we want to use. This is something that I have worked on as a developer and systems designer for some time and we are getting closer to a solution. However, we aren't there yet and the progress is glacially slow.

One reason why I wrote this book was to try to crystallize some of that thinking and open a dialog with anyone who cares to discuss the architectures in order to move the ideas forward.

I think that process all starts with creating good metadata. To do that, we need to build well-conceived systems. Then we can move on to powerful asset publishing tools and end up by building a multimedia aggregation system that will do a great job.

Conclusion

We learn more from our mistakes than our successes. Taking all of these ideas into consideration and reflecting on the things that did not work optimally when I have built systems provides a solid foundation on which to build this book.

I learned many of these ideas from other people as we worked together and by reading about disciplines other than computing, media, and information technology systems. You can solve spatial problems in broadcast and media systems, for instance, with algorithms that are well known in the oil and gas industry for drawing maps. It is also possible to solve oil exploration problems by applying broadcasting technology. Lossless audio compression could be used to reduce the disk space occupied by well logs which are essentially a multitrack audio recording of an underground explosion.

In the next chapter we will examine what metadata is and how it is distinguished from essence data. They are quite different. You sometimes need to think carefully about whether a value is metadata or essence data. It is not always obvious and it might qualify as both.

Metadata

Knowledge Is Power

Metadata is sometimes seen as the magic bullet that will save us all and provide some order to the chaos that is hidden behind the walls of every media organization. It is not going to accomplish a solution unless we use it thoughtfully.

This chapter looks at metadata from several angles and examines how it might be used in the production process and beyond.

Standards

Standards are developed because of a need to connect systems together. It is a search for compatibility between the systems. There are many standards available, and many more that are in development. Choosing the best ones for your system can be a challenge, because there are so many alternatives. It is sometimes difficult to select standards that are compatible with systems and technologies you already have in place. The standards continue to evolve whilst your systems might be deployed and running for years.

A standard is usually developed by a group of like-minded people who may operate commercially in competition with one another. Standards create business relationships and drive commercial activity. That may mean agreeing with one of your competitors to deliver consistent output from each of your competing products. This is driven by the hope that the overall marketplace will grow larger, and your own competitive slice of the cake will be bigger even if your market share remains the same.

Suppliers use standards to make their systems more flexible and capable of integration. Purchasers like standards because it helps them to avoid lock-in. We all need standards to ensure systems and software are interoperable.

What Is Metadata?

Metadata is "data about data." It may come as a surprise that metadata is not a recent invention by the broadcasting industry. It has been around for thousands of years. It hasn't been formalized until relatively recently—in the last few hundred years that is.

An index that collates references to information contains metadata. It can be implemented physically with a set of handwritten record cards such as you might find in a library. It is more convenient to use an online system, but both are metadata systems. Information professionals describe the information that adds value to the underlying essence data as metadata. The essence data is created, collated, organized, described, tracked, and maintained by the system with any auxiliary information being stored as metadata. Information objects that are wrappers or containers represent external essence data in a way that can be understood by a workflow system.

Why is Metadata Useful?

Metadata describes the information necessary to locate a document or other media object in a consistent way. A metadata *scheme* is a minimum set of metadata that is well understood and used by everyone. It should be unambiguous. A metadata scheme provides these facilities:

- A standardized way to locate network-accessible material.
- A consistent descriptive framework to store properties of the material.
- Facilitates queries that are more precise.
- A degree of fuzziness for queries (near, like, similar to).
- Groups objects into sets.
- Provides an order by which objects can be ranked.
- Access control.
- Commercial value and business logic support.
- Conversion and reuse for other purposes.
- Industrial strength workflow automation.

The Difference Between Data and Metadata

It is natural (but wrong) to assume that essence data and metadata are the same thing even though they may look similar. The simplest explanation is that essence data is the actual information product while metadata is the data about that essence data.

A collaborative task force assembled by European Broadcasting Union (EBU) and Society of Motion Picture and Television Engineers (SMPTE) members addressed the question and decided that some clarifying definitions were required (See Table 2-1):

Table 2-1 Terminology definitions

Terminology	Description
Essence data	Describes the text, pictures, sound or moving images
Metadata	Describes the properties of the essence data
Content	Combining Essence data and Metadata together
Asset	An asset is some content plus its rights-management properties

In the context of a digital video file, the information that comprises the actual pictures you see is essence data. The file name and the count of the number of frames in that sequence, as well as the copyright information, are not part of that presentation but describe the essence data in some way. It is metadata.

Metadata can be multilayered. As well as describing the essence data, it can describe the containers in which the essence data is stored. Higher levels of abstraction can describe combinations of essence data and metadata as *content*.

The data itself is called *essence data* because it is the true essence of the information being stored. The essence data is that which you have some proprietary rights over and which has commercial value, while the metadata helps you find, manage, and distribute that essence data in order to monetize your asset value. You may also have rights that pertain to the metadata, which may be separate to the rights you have to the essence.

Metadata Management

When building a system, get the metadata management working robustly. This book is about improving the quality of metadata. It is the very foundation of the system. If we do this right, subsequent stages of the process can build on it in the knowledge that there is a secure underpinning.

If we make the process of improving metadata quality easier through effective use of automation, then it is likely that the quality of our metadata won't be compromised so easily through laziness or omission. We must never assume that automation can take the place of a human being. Content is created for consumption by human beings. It makes sense that it is authored and qualitatively checked editorially by a human.

The Information Science Viewpoint

Information Science deals with the philosophy and semantics involved in metadata. Standard approaches to its organization are:

- Taxonomies.
- Vocabularies.
- Dictionaries.

These are all tools that describe structural relationships between different aspects of the data.

Designing the metadata structures should happen long before any essence data is created or ingested into your repository. This is analogous to an architect designing a house where the software engineer is equivalent to the builder. Both have their skills and have to work together to build a house correctly. The builder may have insights about the practical process that the architect needs to assimilate and vice-versa. The same applies to information design and software engineering a system according to that plan.

The Engineering Viewpoint

From an architectural point of view, essence data is quite different from metadata (information that describes the essence data). When we start to engineer a solution, the distinction is much less obvious. We use the same kind of containers and store similarly formatted information for both.

An image pixmap is clearly essence data, while its modification date is metadata. An event in a calendar might also have a modification date, but the essence data is a date value too. For calendars, we might have two date values represented identically, but one is essence data and one is metadata.

 The engineering problems and quality issues regarding accuracy and formatting apply equally to metadata and essence data.

This book is about considering metadata quality and how it helps you to design and build better systems. The practical advice is directly applicable to both essence data and metadata.

We want to deliver the best quality we can for both essence data and metadata.

Separating Content and Style of Presentation

Metadata fits with the concept we have developed around web sites where the information content and presentational style are separated from each other. If the layout and appearance is maintained separately, then repurposing for a different form factor is much easier to do.

The typical HTML vs. CSS proposition can be applied to interactive TV and multimedia presentations. The HTML page is essence data and a CSS style sheet describes how that content appears. It isn't quite metadata, but the relationship is similar.

In an interactive TV scenario, we might have a collection of assets that need to be aggregated into an interactive package (MPEG-4 BIFS, wired QuickTime, SMIL or Flash). The assets are manufactured independently of each other, but the metadata describes how they can be combined into a package that can be viewed interactively. By changing the metadata, the content can be reshaped to work on a different platform without affecting its meaning.

Where Do We Use Essence Data?

In a digital TV workflow process, the essence data is the footage that might be cut and edited on your video editing desktop computer. Perhaps you are using Apple's Final Cut application, Avid Xpress, or Adobe Premiere. These applications might store the data in different kinds of project containers, but the essence data they are manipulating is the same. They might perform the editing operations in completely different ways and use different algorithms. The result is always a playable video clip.

In multimedia and broadcast systems, those video clips may have been edited together from a variety of different sources. For public broadcast purposes, we need to know where they came from and who owns them. They are (usually) not owned by the person who edited the clip together. This provenance information is metadata, and it must be maintained at the highest quality and accuracy.

The provenance chain is shown in Figure 2-1 for a quite simple two-generation edit.

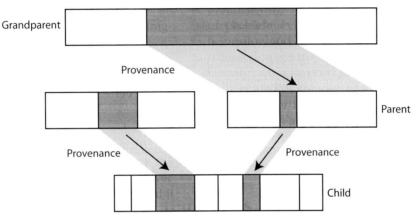

Figure 2-1 Inheritance via provenance metadata

Tracking that provenance is of vital importance, because the rights issues surrounding the use of video clips are extremely limiting and complex. A broadcaster may have permission to broadcast a goal in a soccer match only six times. An additional usage fee is due if it is broadcast a seventh time.

A scene in a studio with a TV set showing an old episode of a TV program would be even more complex. The broadcaster must clear the rights for the picture and sound on that TV set in addition to what is being filmed in the foreground.

In the past, this was managed with massive amounts of paperwork, but now computerized databases make the job much easier. Those databases need to be carefully integrated with the workflow process, and the provenance may need to be nested with parent and child relationships between clips having to be maintained through some complex duplication, cutting, and redistribution mechanisms. Clearly, this is a nontrivial thing to get right. If the data is inaccurate or missing then you have wasted your money investing in a computerized system.

Standardization

Content systems work best when the essence data and metadata is standardized and many people agree to use the same structure, format, and meanings for the values being exchanged. Anything you can do to eliminate conversions between one format and another will help to maintain the quality of your metadata. The conversion processes are often where some of the most subtle data corruption takes place.

The meshing and intersection of standards is complicated because they don't all support the same entities and properties. Some are strictly hierarchically organized, while others are not much more than a vocabulary. This makes the harmonization more difficult. You should choose the smallest set of standards that do what you need and design your own object model as a superset of them so that you don't truncate fields, records, properties, or objects.

Be careful how you implement extensions. Often the comment fields can be used as additional storage locations with some careful formatting of what you embed there. You shouldn't rely on them being stable after any export/import operations. Comments are routinely stripped off and discarded. It is because they are (disposable) comments. Genuine structures containing real data should remain intact.

Profiles can be used to reduce the complexity of a standard and impose some range limits on the values being stored. This is helpful, but make sure that you remain compatible with the profile and not just with the standard in its nonprofiled form.

Table 2-2 lists some relevant standards for metadata and essence data formats. This list is not exhaustive and a more complete description of metadata standards is provided in Appendix B.

Table 2-2 Metadata and essence data standards

Standard	Description
ATSC	Advanced Television Standards Committee is the U.S. equivalent to DVB for standardization of digital TV services.
DTV	Digital TeleVision services describe packaging of data into a broadcast stream. Your metadata will end up here *en route* to the viewer.
DCMI	The Dublin Core Metadata Initiative delivers a range of standard descriptors to assist in searching for material across systems.
DVB	Digital Video Broadcasting consortium. Primarily European standards-oriented. Some DVB standards work is applicable in the U.S.
DVB-SI	The DVB equivalent to PSIP for carrying EPG metadata and service information.
EBU P/META	The P/META standard defines a set of Names and Identifiers that are organized as a vocabulary.

Table 2-2 Metadata and essence data standards (continued)	
EPG	Electronic Program Guides are available as embedded data streams that you can extract from the broadcast signal or as online services that can be downloaded. There are standards for the format and structure, but some data is available in nonstandard ways.
ISAN	ISO Audio-Visual Number.
MPEG-7	The MPEG-7 standard describes a "Multimedia Content Description Interface."
PDC	Program Delivery Control as specified by ETSI also describes a genre-tagging scheme.
PSIP	The Program and System Information Protocol standard describes how metadata is carried in an ATSC transmission.
SMEF	Standard Media Exchange Framework, an "Enterprise Semantic Data Model," designed to cope with large data sets.
SMPTE 335M	The SMPTE Metadata Dictionary Registry.
TV-Anytime	The TV-Anytime standard describes a mechanism for discovering programs using metadata-searching techniques.
V-ISAN	Version controlled ISO Audio-Visual Number.

Exchange File Formats

We are all familiar with file formats such as Windows Media, Real Video, Flash and QuickTime. They are ubiquitous and well supported within certain platform constraints that are driven by commercial imperatives.

 Choose your formats wisely to avoid being locked in to a format that prevents you doing things in the future. Always go for openness and avoid proprietary choices when you can.

For industrial-strength workflow design, we cannot afford to be painted into a corner by one format or another. The emerging nonplatform-specific formats are more attractive.

That is not to say we wouldn't use QuickTime or Windows Media, but their limitations need to be weighed carefully. QuickTime has an advantage in that it is generally as well-supported on Mac OS X and Windows, and it is, after all, a platform that plays open standard and proprietary formats without prejudice one way or the other and it is not only a video/audio player but a multimedia platform. By comparison, Windows Media is a less attractive option because it is well-supported on Windows but barely supported on Mac OS X—and then only by virtue of a third-party plug-in (Telestream's Flip-4-Mac). Where it uses open standard media, it doesn't always support it correctly (e.g., open standard MPEG-4 video with proprietary audio). Neither Windows Media nor QuickTime are supported properly on Linux although some third-party solutions and hacks help deal with playback.

Table 2-3 lists some useful exchange formats for file-based content.

Table 2-3 Exchange file formats	
Format	*Description*
AAF	Advanced Authoring Format.
AFXP	Authoring Format eXchange Profile. An enhanced version of DFXP for authoring subtitle content once and mapping it to many other outlets. Still in development, and expected to support graphics as well as text.
ASF	Advanced Systems Format.
DFXP	Distribution Format eXchange Profile.
DPX	Digital Picture eXchange Format. Designed to transport moving image representations in a file per frame structure.
EXIF	EXIF stands for EXchangeable Image File Format, and is a standard for storing interchange information in image files, especially those using JPEG compression. Favored by digital camera manufacturers.
GXF	The General eXchange Format was originally conceived by Grass Valley Group for the interchange of simple camera shots over data networks, and for archival storage on data tape. Now standardized as part of SMPTE 360M.
MXF	Pro-MPEG Material eXchange Format. Also favored by the P/META group.
TT AF	The W3C Timed Text Authoring Format represents text media for interchange between authoring systems. Timed text is textual information that is associated with timing information such as subtitles.

Where Do We Use Metadata?

The metadata will facilitate many of the commercial processes involved in production, editing, and broadcast. We discussed editing earlier, but here are some more opportunities for metadata to provide assistance:

- Researching, developing and planning the program ideas.
- Commercial planning, budgeting, and control.
- Managing resources.
- Technical systems management.
- Paying the correct cameraman to go out on a shoot.
- Paying a stock footage company only for the footage being used.
- Capture, ingest, and logging.
- Postproduction.
- Publishing/marketing.
- Promotion planning for advertising and media sales.
- Ensuring that programs are broadcast to the correct territories.
- Ensuring programs are broadcast at the right time.

- Controlling whether, when, and for how long a program may be stored on a PVR.
- Driving interactive services with embedded and synchronized content.
- Linking programs to enhanced and interactive functionality and supporting web sites.
- Compliance recording (FCC and other international bodies).
- Feeding location data through so that programs can be found via end-user searches.
- Audience research and feedback after broadcast.

Editing Metadata—Accidentally

Manufacturers of nonlinear editors (NLE) advertise that their systems will maintain embedded metadata when cutting video content together. Avid MetaSync shows how metadata editing is infiltrating the whole NLE editing workflow. Final Cut supports exchanges via an XML interface.

If your video editing is wired into a workflow system, as might be commonplace in a news environment, the metadata might be maintained outside of your NLE tools but within the content management system. The BBC News organization has a project to implement this sort of capability on a massive scale.

The NLE will edit sound and video clips and place them in any order taking them from a variety of sources that might all have a different provenance. If the NLE also copies metadata from those sources and embeds it in the edited output you should check that the metadata is correct as well as the audio and video cutting. This can be classified as an accidental and potentially erroneous edit because the metadata is usually invisible. The operator may be completely unaware that they have edited it along with the sound and picture.

Depending on your system, the maintenance of the metadata might be done manually or automatically. It is likely that if a significant manual process is involved, many errors and omissions will occur.

Automation significantly reduces the likelihood of problems happening but it needs to be capable of responding in a benign way to unexpected situations. Problems that could be attributed to human error might be caused by:

- Tiredness.
- Laziness.
- Negligence.
- Carelessness.
- Lack of training.
- Lack of supervision.
- Lack of postproduction quality auditing.

Your automation and business process logic needs to guard against all of these possibilities, as well as cope with purposeful acts of malice.

Metadata Dictionaries

Metadata dictionaries are quite big. When you combine several metadata schemes for different aspects of your system (technical, commercial, content genre-specific), you can have a large dictionary to manage (see Table 2-4 for examples).

Table 2-4 Dictionary sizes

Standard	Scale (approximate)
SMPTE Metadata Dictionary	1000 terms
Automation and control systems	150 commands
Traffic management	100 terms
Genre thesaurus/vocabulary	2500-5000 terms per genre

While you wouldn't expect to use all of these dictionaries, you need to ensure your name spaces are free of any clashes, and you need to know about them all.

In 2001, the SMPTE Metadata for Broadcast and New Media conference highlighted more than 70 ongoing metadata standards-related activities. That number must be significantly higher by now. Many initiatives are aware of each other. Some standards have merged. Some standards have edited out the duplication and refer to other standards documents instead.

For example, country codes are usually represented using an ISO standard whenever they are referred to in other standardized schemes. Provided each individual standard is maintained separately and does not encroach on areas covered by other standards—we can develop a healthy ecology using whichever standards are necessary for our systems design.

Metadata Tagging

Tagging is the process of attaching keywords to programs so that they can be located by genre or content. The tagging might be hierarchical or a simple list of keywords. If a hierarchical method is used, you need to be careful how you define the precedence of each keyword.

Let's take an outdoor religious celebration event that is comprised primarily of musical performances. Should that be categorized and tagged as a "Music" or "Religion" genre item? Whichever you choose, the other will likely be attached as a secondary tag. The fact that it takes place outdoors is probably not worth a high-priority tag, but might be added as a useful keyword.

Within the category of "Music" in the context of "Religion," many sub-categories are needed to further classify the musical style. There are probably 25 quite distinct Contemporary Christian Musical styles. Some of those are applicable to secular music, too. This is large enough industry sector to qualify as a genre category in its own right (CCM). There are CCM music charts and CCM sections in major record stores.

Categorization and tagging requires us to attach multiple hierarchies if we want to use anything other than a list of relevant keywords. Figure 2-2 shows how that might be done in our object model.

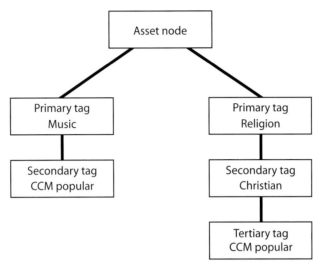

Figure 2-2 Alternative tagging chains

The P/META standards working group has begun to publish some useful tagging vocabularies on the EBU web site. There are many categories of data that would benefit from a tag vocabulary. An EBU standard describes the different roles that people contribute to a production.

One approach is to use the tagging as search keys regardless of whether they are arranged hierarchically or not. Then the hierarchical organization can be used to rank the results. It is a useful compromise that works with all kinds of tagging.

Organizing Metadata Elements

Metadata elements might be better understood and managed by your workflow if you group them into sets or categorize them. Table 2-5 illustrates how the BBC Standard Media Exchange Framework (SMEF) data model organizes some Dublin Core Metadata Initiative elements into groups.

EBU role codes: http://www.ebu.ch/en/technical/metadata/specifications/role_codes.php

Table 2-5 Grouping of Dublin Core elements in SMEF

Content	Ownership	Containment
Coverage	Contributor	Date
Description	Creator	Format
Type	Publisher	Identifier
Relation	Rights	Language
Source	Commercial details	Storage
Subject		Ingest process
Title		
Included material		
Participating actors		

Metadata Roles and Duties

There are many roles and responsibilities. Who does what? The answer depends on your business model and what industry you are working in.

Consider the roles shown in Table 2-6 as a starting point. Several roles are listed with the connotations describing what those roles might mean.

Table 2-6 Metadata roles and responsibilities

Role	Description
Creator	The author of the original content. The author would provide any original and authoritative source form, but the delivery format may be derived from that source form. The first entry in the change history would denote the creator.
Owner	Someone who receives monetary rewards for fee-based deployment of the content. The metadata contains the owner's name in the copyright message.
Editor	The person responsible for making changes as opposed to having editorial authority. Often the custodian or curator as well, but the duties may be split in large organizations. Any change history records would denote the editor.
Curator	The agent of the owner who administers and looks after specific content on a day-to-day basis. The contact person for inquiries about the asset controlled by the metadata.
Librarian	A person whose general duty is organizing assets and keeping a collection neat and tidy. Metadata describing the collection as a whole might provide contact details for the librarian.
Custodian	The person who has official or technical responsibility for making sure a system works or content is available. Any metadata related to the storage, schema, or architecture might be addressed to the custodian.

The roles described in Table 2-6 are generic. Your business might identify some other specific roles and duties not listed here that relate to metadata that is unique to your company or industry.

Metadata Evolution Over Time

Roles and responsibilities, and the metadata for which they are responsible, will change over time. Consider some metadata that relates to a news story. At what point does today's news become tomorrow's historical archive? Bear in mind that news has a tendency to come back into the foreground when an event later on evokes some earlier issue. Perhaps a war zone flares up again, or a very important trial commences the prosecution of a criminal who committed a crime some years earlier. We need to consider when a news story reverts from being historical archive to a live story again. Does that alter the ownership from information and archives back to an editorial responsibility?

Dark Metadata

You may import a file, which contains metadata entities, and essence data for which you have no corresponding storage designed into your repository. This is called *dark metadata*, and you might be able to safely ignore it, but beware. Provided you are only ingesting and never intend to forward that metadata package, you could discard the things you don't need.

If you have to turn the content around and send it onwards, then you must ensure that all of the metadata is safely preserved for onwards delivery.

This can happen when new properties are added to a standard you are already using. Upgrading standards requires some diligence on your part to ensure that your system is able to cope correctly with the new information.

You should watch out for numerical and namespace clashes when dark metadata is present and you are creating your own properties. If you choose a property name and that then later on shows up in some dark metadata, unpredictable things may happen.

The MXF file format standard has some special header support called a Primer Pack. It describes how user-defined tags that are represented as 16-bit values are mapped to the global key structures that are 16 bytes long. This is designed to alleviate the pain and grief that dark metadata can cause.

There are some mechanisms where special tags can be embedded to carry dark metadata. In web pages, we might use **<DIV>** and **<SPAN>** tags and set their display attribute to "none" or perhaps hidden **<INPUT>** fields in a **<FORM>** structure.

Black Metadata

Dark metadata is syntactically and semantically correct and may conform to the standard even if your application doesn't support it. The term *black metadata* is occasionally used to describe dark metadata but describes something quite different.

The documents that mention black metadata describe mechanisms for appending nonstandardized metadata to existing storage formats after the logical end-of-file (EOF). This would allow software to read the file in the normal way and totally ignore anything following its end-of-valid-data marker. Black metadata-aware applications could then continue reading onwards to access the additional data. This takes advantage of the fact that file buffers are block structured, and all kinds of garbage might be tagged onto the end of a file when it is closed.

 Don't break the standards purposely. Extending the standard with your own ideas and to make it incompatible with the rest of the world is a bad idea.

Storing black metadata in your files and implementing mechanisms to support it in your application is a very bad idea! It compromises the integrity of the file format by adding what might appear to be spurious data to the end of the file.

If you need to carry metadata that is not described as part of the standard, then you should explore the proper extension and escape mechanisms provided by the standards and use them as they were intended. Purposely breaking a file structure with proprietary extensions is completely unsupportable.

Hijacking tags for the wrong reason, storing data in nonstandard ways, and creating *de facto*, application-specific ways to transport metadata is the sort of dirty trick that companies use to lock you into their software, and it should be challenged at every opportunity.

 Just when you thought you had learned the jargon, along comes a weird inconsistency in nomenclature. XSL stands for eXtensible Stylesheet Language. CSS stands for Cascading Style Sheets. When you refer to an XML styling mechanism, use the single word 'stylesheet'. Separate it into two words when you describe the styling used with HTML. Consistency? Pah!

Cross-walking the Standards

Cross-walking between different metadata standards can be accomplished with eXtensible Stylesheet Language (XSL) if you are operating in an XML-based environment. XSL is useful because it describes how to format and transform the target data. The transformation converts one XML tree into a different XML tree or a plain text form. XSL provides a method for selecting, reordering, and outputting specific nodes from the tree. The ability to move data from one XML representation to another makes XSL an important tool for building XML-based workflows.

How is Metadata Created?

At almost every stage in the lifecycle of a program's creation, and often long afterwards, there are opportunities to add metadata.

Some of the metadata may be created automatically by the equipment being used. Other data may be the result of something that an operator does. Perhaps some metadata is created through an editorial process. The lifecycle of the metadata goes on indefinitely for many years after the essence data itself has been completed.

Creating Metadata on Location

The earliest opportunity to create new metadata is when the footage is shot, with the camera inserting information about the type of camera, the exposure settings, the lens type, and the GPS location. Beware of what the camera (or camera operator) puts into the metadata records. At this point, the tape cartridge being used should already have been logged with the master librarian system. Although, that could be done as the tape is ingested for the first time.

Metadata becomes important at this point. It can help to avoid overwriting valuable original footage. Add descriptive electronic metadata to that tape before you take it out of the camera. When you send it back to base by courier, and the sticky label falls off, at least there is some information recorded on the tape to describe what is on it. If there is no label on the case and no metadata on the tape, you can't rely on the automation systems preventing it from being recycled inadvertently.

Other important information needs to be recorded aside from the GPS. Date and time are obvious candidates. The location of the subject matter may be some distance away from the observer's position. The GPS location of the camera may be less relevant than the location of the subject being filmed. The distance might be some tens of feet or several miles. Figure 2-3 shows how a very long-range shot can be incorrectly logged when relying on GPS by itself.

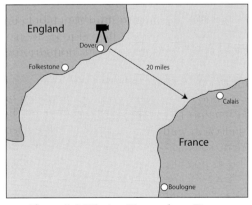

Figure 2-3 Filming France from Dover

The distance between camera and subject could be thousands of miles—from the earth to the moon.

Here are some potential metadata tags and properties that could be entered on location:

- Camera operator name and details.
- Date.
- Time.
- News slug.
- Story.
- Location.
- Tape/reel number.
- Tape format.
- Shot list.
- Shot location on tape.
- Type of shoot.
- Details of cut away shots, vox pops, and stock shots.
- Shot flagging (good, not good).
- Names of participants.
- Contact details of participants.
- Description of the key action.
- Times and time codes.
- Crew list.
- In and out words.
- Transport method (courier or online).
- Working hours logged for chargeback.

Creating Metadata in the Studio

Camera-based metadata generation may be a useful part of your workflow when shooting on location. It is less useful in the studio, because the recordings would likely not be done by a handycam with its own built-in recording mechanism.

Studio-based cameras may still have some useful data to be recorded. Motion tracking is useful when creating virtual studio sets. Knowing the zoom factor of the lens and its focus setting, as well as its aperture, all helps to provide insights that a virtual reality studio system can use to accurately match-move the presenter against 3D-generated environments.

Here are some potential metadata tags and properties that could be added in the studio:

- Camera operator name and details.
- Date.
- Time.
- News slug.
- Story.
- Studio location.
- Server file name where recording is stored.
- Shot list.
- Shot quality flagging (good, not good).
- Names of participants.
- Contact details of participants.
- Description of the key action.
- Times and time codes.
- Gallery crew list.
- In and out words.

Creating Metadata During Ingest

When the material arrives back at the studio from an outside broadcast or is fed from an external service, it will be ingested through processors that extract meaning and metadata. The operator has the opportunity to add more metadata about whom, when, and where. Proxy copies may be created at this time. They need to be noted in the content system and tracked back to the parent via appropriate provenance metadata links. The proxy copies will be used for desktop browsing and possibly editing.

Some ingest systems, such as Virage VideoLogger, will create huge amounts of additional metadata. Virage performs optical character recognition, facial recognition, and voice recognition, all of which add to the value of the ingesting process.

Telestream FlipFactory is an alternative that is strong on its technical capabilities to convert many different formats of incoming video, but does not apply as much analysis as VideoLogger. It won't deliver as much metadata for you to load.

Here are some potential metadata tags and properties that could be added to the metadata at ingest time:

- Frame rates.
- Aspect ratio.
- Tape details.
- Source format.
- Clip details.
- Extracted metadata.
- Picture size.
- Aspect ratio.

Creating Metadata with Speech Recognition

Fast-Talk is a useful voice recognition tool for ingesting audio feeds. It performs a clever phonetic analysis that is resilient when ambient noise interrupts the audio. This is useful when you are searching audio archives.

Voice recognition is not quite good enough to publish directly as a transcript for sub-titles. It is evident that broadcasters are using it that way when you watch some programs though.

If you have the script available, then the speech recognition tools can marry up the text with the video and synchronize the two. The open-source Thistle speech recognition system has been demonstrated by BBC research engineers as a way to synchronize an Autocue to the spoken audio track. The Autocue script can have embedded lighting controls and camera moves. We can close the loop on studio automation systems by combining audio, metadata, and speech recognition together.

Emerging standards such as the W3C Timed Text Authoring Format (TT AF) are an obvious candidate for output file formats for these systems.

Here are some potential metadata tags and properties that can be added as the audio is analyzed:

- Length of recording.
- Audio format.
- Number of tracks (stereo/mono).
- Length and duration of clips.
- Time codes, etc.
- Date and time.
- Location.
- Names of participants.
- Sound recordist.
- Equipment used.

Creating Metadata During Postproduction

Editing a proxy produces an edit decision list (EDL) that can be applied to the full-quality video in a craft editing workstation. The NLE must also preserve any metadata and store it in or with the EDL.

The editing process should be nondestructive. Cropped versions of the video become child clips that are created as references to the original footage. There is no need to render this footage again until we are conforming the final program. Several child clips can be joined together with transitions and other source materials (titles and graphics) to create a completely new material item. This is related to the source clips, and their provenance needs to be maintained. Because of the transitions, the clips are not a direct image copy. Metadata needs to propagate through this system and will be added to and enhanced along the way.

Eventually, the program is finished and more metadata, such as production team names and duties, is added to describe it. Copyright stamping for the compilation and production branding could happen here. Some rights control relating to commercial issues might be added at this stage too. Then, the program can be added to a catalogue of products for sale.

This is an opportunity to apply quality assurance and check that any surviving metadata that made it through the editing process is genuinely needed. I would classify this is a vital piece of editorial checking at this point. **Tutorial 51** addresses this issue as a use case study and illustrates what could happen accidentally.

Here are some potential metadata tags and properties to add during post-production:

- NLE system.
- Location of master copy if proxy used.
- Location of EDL file.
- Provenance relationship to parent clips.
- Music details.
- Frame rates.
- Compression method used.
- Noise reduction.
- Color correction applied.
- Dubbing details.
- Aspect ratio.

Creating Metadata for Traffic Scheduling

Metadata can be embedded into the program material and used during the broadcasting process. Storing a reference to a subtitle data file within the video container is an example. Directly embedding the subtitle data into a text track means that everything you need at broadcast time is readily at hand.

Here are some tracks containing data that could be added:

- Additional enhancements.
- Interactivity.
- Game play.
- Linked content.
- Hint tracks.
- URL tracks cross-links.

Here are some potential traffic scheduling metadata tags and properties:

- Scheduled airtime for broadcast.
- Channel to be broadcast on.
- Location of master tape/server containing video file.
- Contact in case of emergency.
- Producer/director.
- Tagging info.
- Interactive event data.
- Interactive spool file for carousel loading.
- Subtitle data.
- URL crosslink data.

Creating Metadata During Play-out

At broadcasting time (sometimes referred to as play-out), we want to store the airdate, channel (or portal), and other information about how the program is presented.

Some useful metadata can be embedded into the transmission stream. All users who receive the broadcast can access and store the information and use it to make some decisions about how to access the essence data.

Here are some potential metadata tags and properties to note during broadcast:

- Actual time the program was broadcast.
- Actual channel.
- Person controlling the play-out.
- Compliance information.
- Report of any technical issues during play-out.

Creating Metadata During Deployment

For Internet-delivered content, the equivalent to scheduling a broadcast is the deployment of the content on a public-facing web server. Then it is ready for demand-driven consumption.

You might publish metadata describing that content to a static file on a server that your end users can access. RSS feeds can be used to detect new metadata automatically.

Here are some potential metadata tags and properties to note when publishing to the Internet:

- URI style location of published file.
- Time taken to process publication.
- Master ID of story in database.
- List of related pages that point to this asset.
- Date of publication.
- Date and time when last checked for access.
- HTTP status result from last access check.
- Access time measurement for performance metrics.
- Feedback from log analysis on asset popularity.

Creating Metadata in the Receiver

Eventually, an end-user receives and watches a program but may also record it on a PVR, computer or iPod on a temporary or permanent basis. More metadata could be added here to uniquely identify that copy so that piracy issues can be addressed.

Here are some potential metadata tags and properties for implementation inside the consumer device:

- Date recorded/downloaded.
- Unique ID of material.
- Tagging info.
- Channel or portal the content was recorded from.
- Broadcaster whose portal it was recorded from.
- Other metadata that came packaged with the program.
- File name on local storage.
- Embargo details.
- Rights of access.
- Rating of content.
- Links to other media (IMDB, CDDB, etc.).
- Compression format.
- Aspect ratio switch.
- Surround sound settings.

Creating Metadata After Broadcast

Sometimes a community of users develops around a program, and collectively they add more information that is potentially useful metadata. This clearly happened with *Star Trek*, *Star Wars*, *Lord of the Rings* and *Doctor Who*. It can happen with any programs with additional and useful related content becoming available long after the program was completed, especially where there is a cult or community developed around the program.

Perhaps some production notes come to light long after production is finished. It is not unusual for directors to house all their papers in an archive and donate them to a college or museum as a lasting legacy. These need to be collated together, carefully preserved, and linked with the original movie or TV program that they directed—possibly some tens of years previously.

Here are some potential aftermarket and post-broadcast metadata tags and properties. Some of these may be generated by a community of interested fans rather than the production company. That can present some interesting rights issues because the fan created metadata describes the essence that the production company owns. The fans own the rights in the metadata that they produce but they must be creating genuinely new intellectual property:

- Links to fanzines and web sites.
- E-commerce links for merchandizing.
- Actor biographies.
- Crew biographies.
- Season episode listings.
- Stills gallery.
- Filmographies.
- News of follow-up or otherwise related programs.
- Recommended other viewing.

Recycling and Repurposing

Recycling of previously used material may add to or alter certain aspects of the metadata. Should we preserve the previous information so there is an audit trail? Journaling the changed data is worthwhile and useful, especially considering that the differences are probably textual and might only occupy a small amount of the available storage capacity. It seems a worthwhile trade off to make in return for being able to trace the provenance more effectively and to track down some later changes if that becomes necessary.

Referencing back to earlier material means that you need to consider the long-term scale and scope of your repository. We should have learned that much from the millennium bug, which was the consequence of trying to save a few meager bytes of memory in some computer systems developed in the early part of the information revolution.

Forward thinking needs to happen when examining the data model for your metadata in order to allow the system scope to increase significantly beyond what might seem to be the expected range of values.

Further Study

There are a bewildering and increasing number of metadata standards, profiles, exchange file formats, and *de facto* implementations for you to consider. The list is increasing all the time. You cannot hope to stay abreast of every new development. Table 2-7 lists some places where you can look from time to time for some useful new technologies.

Table 2-7 Further study opportunities

Organization	Relevant work
Adobe Labs	Public trials of research prototypes of its image-editing tools, some of which will make it into production. You can test these when they are at a prototype stage. The Lightroom metadata controls a nondestructive picture editor.
EBU	The European Broadcasting Union publishes new standards documents all the time.
ETSI	European Telecommunications Standards Institute.
ISO	The International Standards Organization's standards steering process usually operates in collaboration with working groups belonging to other bodies.
DVB	The Digital Video Broadcasting project does European digital TV standards work.
SMPTE	The Society of Motion Picture and Television Engineers does primarily US-based film and television standards work.
W3C	The Worldwide Web Consortium's web-based standards work is published here.
ATSC	Advanced Television Standards Committee.
Google	Scan the Google database occasionally when you come across an unfamiliar term.
Wikipedia	The content is provided by the public and not always considered authoritative. Political and commercial material needs to be weighed carefully, but technical information is rich and deep and appears to be mostly of a high quality. A good jumping-off point for further investigation.

Boiling It Down

We have toured around the metadata world, briefly looking at some of the processes involved in multimedia production. There are many alternative standards in other industries, but the problems that engineers face are very similar.

Bear in mind that some metadata schemes are highly organized while others are not much more than a collection of tag values. There is a big difference between a hierarchy and a vocabulary.

The quality of the service you deliver depends on how well you implement the software that processes the values stored in a metadata scheme. The next chapter looks at modeling the system design before we begin to implement anything.

Object Modeling Your Data

Plan First—Code Second

This chapter is about designing your system. There are many design methodologies to choose from, some old and some new. Often, you will find that the choice of methodology is already made for you by corporate policy or historical precedent. All design methodologies have strengths and weaknesses. The important thing is that they all make you think about your design before you start coding. The pragmatic approach exploits the useful aspects of all of the different methodologies, adopting and adapting parts of them that are useful to your needs.

Before You Start

Before you begin any coding, you should properly design your data and object model for the metadata. This also applies to the essence data, and when we get into the engineering phases of a project, many of the pitfalls and design processes are the same for both essence and metadata. As far as the software is concerned, it is all data. Essence data happens to be classified as something different to metadata because it is the content rather than the description of the content. Deciding whether something falls under the essence data or metadata heading is a normalization process similar to that used when designing relational database schemas.

Object-oriented design is a way to build the systems with efficient coding and lower maintenance overheads. It is particularly well suited to building content and metadata repositories because the processing operations are similar for many different kinds of assets. The physical structure of the data is replicated as a set of object containers that inherit common functionality from a super-class.

 Think before you build. One hour of planning avoids several hours of debugging. It can save several days or a nasty experience for your customers. Not to mention your telephone help line staff.

Without this inheritance capability, the same functionality needs to be implemented for every kind of asset and this was the bane of many programmer's lives when a linear approach was used. Some degree of reuse is possible with linear programming, by using includable code modules and libraries. Much of that complexity is hidden with an object-oriented approach and our internal mental model of a system is much easier to come to terms with.

Some conceptual aspects of the modeling process are listed in Table 3-1 under the general headings of Vocabulary, Ontology, Taxonomy, Schemas and Schemes:

Table 3-1 High level concepts

Term	Description
Vocabulary	Used to describe a genre-tagging scheme. It is a collection of key words or phrases but not necessarily organized or connected to anything else.
Taxonomy	An organized collection of data. Often arranged into a tree structure with a parent object at the top and increasing numbers of children added at each level. Inverse trees are also possible, with a child object belonging to more than one parent. Networks of nodes can also be referred to as taxonomies.
Ontology	Ontology describes a collection of objects with some insights into their unique identity, existence, and classification.
Schema	This describes the model that we build in the data context. It can describe the design of a relational database management system (RDBMS) or a collection of related XML documents.
Scheme	A metadata scheme collects the model, vocabulary, and taxonomy together into a standardized structure.

Workflow Sequence

The workflow has several important phases:

- Initialize the workflow.
- Detect some content to process.
- Ingest some content.
- Process the content.
- Output the content.
- Repeat the processing loop as called for.
- Close down in an orderly fashion.

Various applications, components and people are be involved in the processing of data through the workflow. Consider a purchase order that moves through various departments for authorization and eventual purchase. The orders may be treated as messages, which are put into various queues for processing. A workflow process involves constant change and update. You can introduce new components into the operation sometimes without changing any code but changes should always be planned carefully and thought through.

Data Models

Your data model represents the data definitions and business logic rules that determine the relationships between items and groups of data. Data models are built from three main component types:

- Entities.
- Attributes.
- Relationships.

These are connected together and operated on by the workflow software systems. We will examine these briefly from a data modeling point of view. Later we will look at them in more detail as components of our object model.

Your model defines whether you are building a simple vocabulary-driven tagging system or a more complex hierarchical design. Hierarchies are more powerful but harder to implement.

Data Entities

An entity is a "thing" that your system maintains some metadata to describe. Broadcasters would consider an entity to be a video program. A news organization would describe a story as an entity. A 3D special effects company might describe a scene and some of the rendered elements within it to be entities.

A media asset management system would maintain program, clips, stills, text blocks and other assets as discrete entities. Some of those entities would be contained within others either explicitly or implicitly.

Attributes of Data Entities

Entities have attributes. These correspond to properties in the object-oriented world. These attributes are the metadata that we need to maintain in the system. We must focus on maintaining the quality of values stored in these attributes.

Relationships Between Data Entities

The relationships between entities are managed by using attributes to link things together or make decisions. This is where the business logic for your workflow resides. Careful attention is required here, as this will fundamentally alter the way your system works. Bad design or relationship choices could degrade system performance, reduce reliability, and compromise security.

Primary Keys and Identifiers

One of the attributes will be the primary key or identity of the entity to which it is attached. This value must be unique within the system. It should be unique within the organization. It ought to be unique across all participating organizations, and it can be unique on a global basis. Note how the qualifiers for the uniqueness of an identifier are slackened as the degree of control is reduced. This is because, from a pragmatic point of view, it becomes increasingly more difficult to ensure uniqueness as control and ownership decreases.

Some architecture designs will compensate by using multiple key values as they attempt to keep an asset unique. Some of those identifiers might represent departments, organizations, or global locations of assets. These are effectively creating a name space within which the uniqueness can be maintained. Responsibility for uniqueness is then easier to delegate.

Combining keys during queries is no problem, but using compound keys to generate indexes and manage table structures is a severe performance inhibitor and indicates poor architectural design.

Database Schemas

The schema for a database is a plan for storing data in a collection of tables. You may in fact decide to partition things into multiple databases and within each of those have many tables.

Relational databases are an excellent way to store object data in a persistent way. Instead of serializing the object and storing it in a resource file, you can write the property values to database fields with one record corresponding to a single object instance.

- Each table in an RDBMS corresponds to an object class.
- Each column corresponds to a property of the objects.
- Each row corresponds to an instance object.

When designing a schema, we are only concerned with the database. The schema is consistent with our object model design and may look quite similar to it. In this aspect of our systems design, we consider auxiliary columns of our database tables such as indexes that will help us to access the data more quickly. Extra columns will aid the collating and sorting or ranking of items within the tables, and those columns may not appear in our object model as properties of the corresponding object. They exist to help make the database run more efficiently.

Normalization

An IBM research technologist named Edgar F. Codd invented this methodology of organizing the data content to reduce duplication. In the 1970s, many useful techniques were invented because memory was expensive and scarce. Had computers been invented with massive memory from the start, we might not have benefited from some of these ideas.

Normalization is quite straightforward and is based on some simple rules. The major benefit of normalizing is to improve the consistency of the data you manage.

Step 1 is to move the data into its First Normal Form. This is sometimes called *1NF*. This ensures that each field only contains one data item.

A text box containing a multiple line address is not in 1NF. Use separate fields for house number, street name, town, county and postcode. This is how you achieve 1NF. You may need additional fields for some addresses. Figure 3-1 shows the First Normal Form for a simple UK-based name and address.

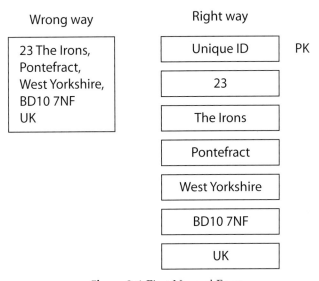

Figure 3-1 First Normal Form

At this point, we would also identify a field we can use as a primary key. For an accounting system, it might be an invoice or transaction number. For a video catalog or workflow, it would be the unique ID of that piece of material.

Now that the data is in the First Normal Form, we can move onto the Second Normal Form (*2NF*). First, we should look for duplication. Inspect each field in the table and see whether there is a possibility that it might show up more than once. A film catalog would list the director. This might be repeated for several movies. We need to separate the directors to a table of their own.

After splitting the components into separate tables, we need to make sure each table has a primary key column. That key is used to join the tables together using the relational links that an RDBMS provides. We can traverse those joins in our object model. This fits perfectly with an implementation in an OOP language like Objective-C, C++, or Java.

To form a primary key, we could use a genuinely unique value such as the director's social security number and the film's Motion Picture Association of America (MPAA) or British Board of Film Classification (BBFC) certificate number. We might include the IMDB identifier that would provide a linkage to an external data system as well.

Classifications like this must be aware that different territories will classify movies differently for cultural reasons. An MPAA certification might be broadly equivalent to BBFC ratings but the nomenclature is different and the age ranges may not be quite the same. Both censoring organizations may differ in their view of the rating as well. A film will only be granted a certificate if it is released in the territory covered by that organization. The MPAA may classify more films than BBFC (this is certainly evident for region 1 vs. region 2 DVDs) but not every film may be certified by the MPAA. A primary key needs to be unique but also globally—all encompassing in its scope.

Now we move on to the Third Normal Form (*3NF*). Making sure the tables are 3NF requires that we check once more that everything belongs where it should. A 3NF database must already be 1NF- and 2NF-compliant. We may have satisfied the uniqueness criteria but still not have some fields in the correct table.

Consider the design of an invoice. You have contact details for invoice queries. Those might not yet have been moved with the name and address. Contact details should belong to people, not invoices. This is a last refinement that ensures the database is as robust and flexible as possible.

Now there are some useful normalization tips that you should remember:

- If it could duplicate information, it is not 1NF.
- If the content is from several entities, it is not 2NF.
- If a table has many to many relationships, it may not be fully 2NF structured.
- If some fields are still not in the correct table, it is not 3NF.
- You can test whether your normalization schema meets this criteria in a spreadsheet.
- Database software (such MySQL) may enforce this on your data.
- The **ENUM** and **SET** data types are not recommended for use as they undermine the normalization of the database.

There are also upsides and downsides to using normalization:

- Normalization helps to organize your data better.
- It helps you reuse data.
- It connects multiple systems of data together.
- Unfortunately, it adds complexity to your system.
- For large tables, it may slow the performance.
- For enterprise applications, you should get the most powerful database engine you can for fully normalized databases.

When you normalize your database design, you should pay special attention to how you describe media items. Unique Material Identifiers (UMIDs) must be truly unique. You may use a primary key within your database that is unique within your system, but a UMID must be genuinely unique worldwide.

Data Structure Components

We build our data models with components such as numbers, strings, fields, and records. Sometimes collecting these together into organized groups means we can describe our model with fewer components. Where these components are in a form that cannot be broken down into smaller parts, they are sometimes called primitives or atoms. Table 3-2 lists some higher-level constructs.

Table 3-2 Higher level data structures

Structure	Description
Array	A collection of objects that is accessible by index number. The ordering may be according to how the objects were added or specified in the array declaration or because of a sort.
Dictionary	A vocabulary that is organized with connected objects associated with each entry. Not necessarily ordered but able to be rapidly searched. This is sometimes called an associative array. In that case, the array is accessed using keywords instead of index numbers.
Thesaurus	Like a dictionary. Can be implemented with dictionary and array code. Its purpose in an asset management and workflow context is to map keywords to alternative keywords.

Object Models

An object model is a description of content and metadata broken down into component parts that are joined (or related to one another) using the data model as a starting point. By abstracting the metadata into an object-structured system, we gain some potential for reuse. Developing the software that operates on metadata becomes much easier.

While object-oriented programming might appear complex at first if you are used to a more linear or procedural approach, it pays huge dividends and isn't difficult to learn about—at a basic level. Indeed, it never becomes hugely complex, because everything is broken into objects that conceptually remain quite small.

Objects are described as belonging to a class, which is family of identical objects whose functionality is described in the definition of the object class. Any objects that are members of that class are merely containers for data values. Any processes or actions that might be carried out on them happen using code that is maintained within the class definition. The class also defines what values belong to the object. This might be based on a unique and stand-alone object or one that is a modified version of an already-existing class.

Some of the values (or properties) of an object are often references to other objects. These correspond to the relational joins that occur in a database. You will often find that Structured Query Language (SQL)-based RDBMS systems are used as object storage silos.

We need to consider those two aspects of our system separately for engineering but together when architecting. Their structural design is interdependent and changes to one will result in changes to the other.

Object Modeling Tools

We plan databases by designing a schema and object models with an entity relationship diagram. If we are extremely fortunate, our supporting frameworks and SDK tools will provide diagramming tools that directly translate a graphical model we can draw on the screen and automatically create the database schema and SQL scripts from the entity relationship diagram.

The Enterprise Objects Framework that ships with Apple's WebObjects tools is an example. This tool goes back to 1994 and was introduced to work with the NeXT operating system. Although it is powerful, it has fallen out of favor with the introduction of new technologies. Other tools include the CoreData tools built into Xcode, and similar tools are available for Windows and Linux. Table 3-3 lists some potentially useful tools although this list is by no means exhaustive:

Table 3-3 Data modeling tools

Tool	URL
Poseidon	*http://gentleware.com/*
MDA tools	*http://www.sparxsystems.com/*
Select Enterprise	*http://www.selectbs.com/*
ERwin/ERX	*http://www3.ca.com/smb/solution.aspx?ID=5290*
Visual CASE	*http://www.roguewave.com/*
Stingray	*http://www.roguewave.com/products/stingray/*
Rational Rose	*http://www-306.ibm.com/software/rational/*
Visual UML	*http://www.visualuml.com/*
First Place tools	*http://www.infogoal.com/fpg/fpgres01.htm*
Others	*http://www.databaseanswers.com/modelling_tools.htm*

These tools don't all do the same thing. They each have strengths and weaknesses when compared with each other and you need to examine their capabilities carefully before selecting the best one for your project design process.

Their capabilities might be grouped under one or more categories like this:

- Data modeling tools.
- Process modeling tools.
- Object modeling tools.

Interfacing via a Persistence Framework to an RDBMS

The glue-ware that put objects into the database or creates them as the result of a query is called a Persistence Framework. There are several alternate frameworks you can use, depending on the object-oriented language or tools you are using. Table 3-4 lists some of the popular alternative languages and frameworks.

Table 3-4 Some persistence frameworks

Language	Framework/Interface
Objective-C or Java on Mac OS X	Enterprise Objects Framework (EOF) or CoreData
Java	Hibernate, OJB, JNDI, JDBC, JDF
Windows	.NET and its derivatives/descendants
Generic	ODBC

This is an area where many open source solutions are available. There are at least 20 alternatives if you develop Java applications. Proprietary solutions offer another dozen possibilities.

These persistence frameworks are designed to help you build your application without having to implement database access code to query the database and manufacture objects. The models you build to interact with your database via a persistence framework become part of your business logic and can be recycled on many future projects. This is useful to almost every developer, and it is normal to find the support for the database already provided by the operating system.

You can concentrate on the design of your product and focus on the code that makes it unique. Building modern applications with integrated development environments like Xcode and Visual Studio is much easier than it used to be. Now, it is an exercise in writing plug-in modules, since the major part of the application can be built from the UI design tools. Xcode provides document save, load, print, and many other basic functional capabilities of an application without writing a line of code. You can build and test most of the user interface (UI); only needing to implement the handlers for when the user clicks on a button or selects a menu item. The menu drawing and mapping of mouse positions to onscreen controls is no longer something you have to be concerned about.

Database access is also easy to implement now that the tools are mature. The persistence framework or glue-ware that binds your application to the database takes care of many things like fetching the records and converting them into a useable form. You request some data and a collection of pre-packaged objects are returned ready to use. If you designed the application properly, those objects belong to classes that you created and have methods and properties that will exploit your code. All you have to do is define the object shape and provide the code to implement the methods.

It is not exactly effortless, but much of the boring drudgery is removed. You can focus on the interesting aspects of implementing your business logic around the entities that are retrieved from the database. Add a small amount of controller code to connect your logic to the UI, and soon you will have a finished application.

Abstracting Information and Representation

Abstracting the information content and presentation format from each other is important, because it helps you to author once and deliver everywhere. This has been a holy grail of content management systems for a long time. Reducing the authoring and editorial costs and monetizing your assets across multiple platforms is a key incentive for businesses.

This is related to the concept used by software engineers when building the content model. They use an abstraction called Model-View-Controller (MVC), which separates the underlying object model from the view that the user sees. The linking is done by the controller. We will look at that in more detail shortly.

Changes that are enacted in the view are propagated into the model by the controller. Other views on that same model are updated through a key value-observing mechanism. This is how sophisticated user interfaces reflect a single edit change across multiple open windows and dialog boxes.

Abstracting our content and the delivery platform gives us advantages relating to content creation, letting us focus on what is being said rather than how it is going to look typographically on any one specific device.

How are Objects Stored?

Objects are maintained in the memory of your computer system as a block of structured data. You don't need to know how this is done, because you don't operate on them directly. Instead, you call the methods for an object and those methods store or retrieve values in the object to which the instruction is addressed.

Resource File Structures

When objects are stored in files, they need to be serialized. That is, the properties are arranged like beads on a necklace. The serialized data is packaged as binary information and written to a file. A collection of objects in such a file usually has additional information surrounding it. Then, individual objects can be located and edited. These are sometimes called resource files, and they are like an additional layer of directory or folder structure but are contained within the file. Internally some kind of rudimentary directory structure is maintained so that any object within the file can be quickly located.

Atomic File Structures

The structures inside a resource file are sometimes called atoms or chunks.

Deleting objects is accomplished by removing the directory pointer to the object. Appending new objects is done by adding them to the end of the file and updating the directory pointers. Likewise, replacing an object with one that occupies more space requires a delete-and-append to take place as a single atomic action.

You may not realize that many of the files you use on a routine basis are structured in this way. QuickTime movie containers are a prime example. Sometimes the physical storage mechanism of a resource file is used without the content being serialized objects. It is a useful way to manage and edit complex data structures without having to rewrite an entire file.

Occasionally, after some editing, you can save some disk space by writing a fresh copy of the file that omits any dead space. This process is usually done when you "save-as" or "save-a-copy." It becomes particularly necessary if you are performing a large number of edits in an interactive session. Soon the pointers become hopelessly tangled. This happens in Microsoft Word and you need to save the document every now and then to clean it up. You'll know when this is necessary. It is indicated when the application crashes after only editing a file for a few minutes.

Model-View-Controller Concepts

During the essence data or metadata repository design process, using a Model-View-Controller (MVC) paradigm may help you build a better system.

 Careful factoring of your application pays dividends at every stage. It is easier to build and maintain. Many parts of the implementation can be reused more efficiently. This saves time money.

The model and the view are completely independent of each other. They are connected via the controller. A view might be a web page but it could also be a GUI application or a printed summary. It should be possible to create these views without altering the model in any way. The model is a complete description of the data system including the business logic required to make it work.

This model has an interface that the controller understands. The view is able to talk to the controller and tell it that it wants to know about changes to the model if they are triggered by a different view. This mechanism is called Key-Value-Observing (KVO), and it ensures that things are updated when necessary.

Open a folder window in the Mac OS X Finder and in the terminal application. Then, in the terminal window, create a new text file at the directory location that corresponds to that Finder folder. KVO ensures that the file appears in the Finder window immediately because that window has registered an interest in that directory. The controller mechanism is triggered by a change to the directory contents by a hook inside the OS. This then informs any interested and registered observers that they should update their view.

Changes that are caused by a user interaction with the view are passed to the controller that enacts them on the model. The required business logic will be invoked automatically.

The beauty of this approach is the functional separation of the different kinds of activity. There is a sense of ownership about different aspects of your overall implementation, and MVC makes sure that the view logic is not polluted by any model implementation or its business logic. Likewise, the model remains devoid of any view code and can be used with any controller and view that needs to connect to it as a client.

Abstracting your system like this is an object-oriented way of thinking and leads to significant productivity gains and reuse of your models and view code.

Entities and Relationships

An entity relationship diagram is a plan for your object relationships. This differs from the database schema that shows much more detail of how the joins are implemented. We mark the connecting "wires" with a symbol to indicate whether the relationship is one of the classic four types:

- One to one.
- One to many.
- Many to one.
- Many to many.

This is referred to as the *cardinality* of the relationship.

Figure 3-2 is a hybrid class and entity relationship diagram that shows a story object and three child objects associated with it. This illustrates connections at the class level. The class is a template for the objects that are manufactured with it. Their relationships will not be completely resolved at the object level until a journalist has created a story object and associated two text objects and an image object with it.

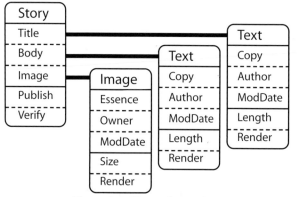

Figure 3-2 Class relationships

These classes are purposely simple. They all have a class name at the top, three properties, and two methods. The properties in the **Story** object are references to child objects. The properties in the **Text** and **Image** objects are references to essence data.

The **Story** object can be published or verified with its methods. The verification might check that all the objects have been associated with it and are available. This could be called by the **Publish** method as a safety check to ensure that it can be published.

Some entities remain constant because they contain static reference data. Lists of country codes, video formats, etc. Other data related to ingesting new content will change all the time. Some values or objects might change frequently for a while and then remain static. All of this can be noted on your architecture plans and diagrams.

Entity Relationship Diagrams

In Figure 3-2, the classes are illustrated as well as the entity relationships. Sometimes these are shown as completely separate diagrams. Figure 3-3 is an entity relationship diagram without the internal details of the classes.

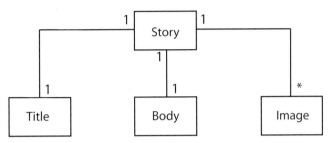

Figure 3-3 Entity relationships

The one-to-one mapping is shown by placing a 1 at each end of the association. In the case of the Image object, many images could be associated on a one-to-many basis. If the classes are shown as a collection of unconnected boxes merely to illustrate their properties and methods, then it is a vocabulary diagram. This is similar to a data dictionary that database designers use. The idea is to collect all of the classes for the project so they can be viewed in one place.

Figure 3-4 shows a completely different diagram style that describes the same relational joins.

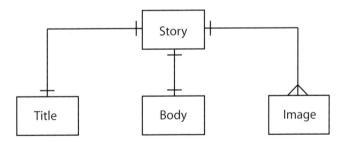

Figure 3-4 Entity relationships (alternate version)

Additional detail can be added to the diagram to indicate whether items are optional.

The cardinal relationships can be extended to include the case where zero, one, or many connections are possible. The class diagrams merely illustrate the possibilities. You can also indicate that a relationship is mandatory, whether one object owns another, the dependency, and whether the means of uniquely identifying an object depends on its relationship to a parent.

The object instantiations realize those possibilities in a concrete form. You can draw object instantiation diagrams that are the hard-wired versions of the class diagrams but this is not normally necessary.

Inheritance Trees

The image and text objects have some similar properties. They might belong to a common parenting super-class that would implement the functionality that they both share. They would then only have to implement the new functionality. Figure 3-5 shows how two sub-classes are based on a single parent super-class.

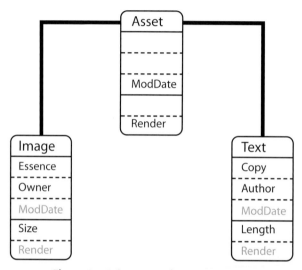

Figure 3-5 Inheritance from super-class

The **Render** method and **ModDate** property are defined in the super-class. Both the **Image** and **Text** sub-classes inherit those items. The **Image** sub-class defines **Essence** and **Owner** properties while the **Text** sub-class defines **Copy** as a holder for the body text and **Author** as the person who edited the text. Those properties could be moved into the super-class too.

The **Size** and **Length** values could be rationalized too. They could be defined in the super-class as an extent rectangle. An extent rectangle is that smallest rectangle which would just completely enclose the object. It is described as left, right, top and bottom values. Often it is represented by a pair of X-Y co-ordinates for diagonally opposite corners of the rectangle. The **Image** sub-class could then omit the **Size** property while the Text sub-class might still support a **Length** property.

The **Render** method is inherited here, but it might require some local overriding. That could be done via some private methods that are not published in the entity model. The **Render** method could be defined as a super-class method. The **Render** method in each sub-class would call some additional specialized code by referring to the **self** object when it is executed.

Think about and draw inheritance charts for your classes and how they are sub-classed from one another. It is a similar thought process to database normalization.

State Transitions

Entity relationship diagrams only show classes. They are also static and don't show how things change over time. You need state transition diagrams for that. Figure 3-6 shows a state diagram for a process observing a watch folder.

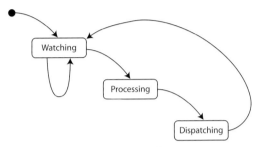

Figure 3-6 State diagram

Think about changes over time and draw state transition diagrams. You can add more annotations to each of the state transition arrows if it makes the state change clearer.

Workflow Charts

Workflow charts take the state transitions and organize them so that a time sequence is described. Time proceeds down the page and various activities are arranged into horizontal columns labeled boxes represent activities in the workflow. These are sometimes called state transition diagrams. They can get quite complex with branches and alternative routes being shown. This is a simple linear flow. Figure 3-7 shows an example:

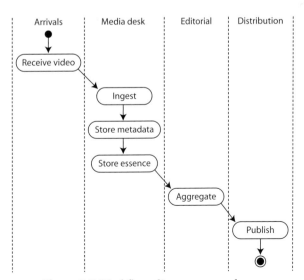

Figure 3-7 Workflow diagram example

State transition diagrams are useful for identifying what is known as *race hazards* in your software. Race hazards happen when the process divides into multiple streams of execution. Some of those streams may be processed more quickly and complete sooner than the others. You need to identify the slowest ones and make sure that the next stage in the workflow that depends on all of these multiple threads having been completed already is not triggered too soon. This is all about triggers and dependencies.

Attaching the trigger action to a process that completes too soon means that the next stage is initiated before all of the inputs are available. It might run but miss some data, or you might have to code it so that it goes into a hold state pending the arrival of late data. Abstracting the hold logic and making sure that the triggers are asserted at the right time and from the object that is being depended on leads to more reliable systems.

State transition diagrams can be drawn in a variety of ways. You may prefer that time proceeds down the page or across the page in a left to right direction. The preferred orientation may depend on how many items are being considered and how many state transitions occur.

A project plan or Gantt chart drawn in a project management tool such as Microsoft Project is a state transition diagram of sorts. You can clearly see the dependency of one part of a project on another. Identifying the critical path through the project plan allows you to estimate the overall project duration.

Looking at the state transition diagram and identifying the slowest processes and their dependencies means you can see the same critical path through the workflow process.

Node-Based Workflow Design

Workflow design is beginning to be formalized with a disciplined approach based on identifying and applying certain patterns or templates for their behavior. This leads to a component-based approach.

Each stage of a workflow can be defined as shown in Figure 3-8, with an input description, transformation rules, algorithms and an output description:

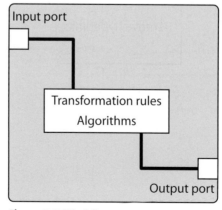

Figure 3-8 Workflow process component

The illustration shows one input and one output port. There might be more than one of each.

Systems built around this approach can have an interesting GUI connection systems built as a control surface so the workflow can be organized graphically.

For this to work, the components must have compatible inputs and outputs. You can't plug a text stream output into a video input. The Quartz Composer editor in the Apple developer tool kit is an interesting example of a workflow editor, albeit one that works in a constrained way to build graphical workflows.

Scientific visualization and image processing tools have used this approach since the 1980s.

Workflow Connection Diagrams

Designing interchange and conversion sequences for content should start with a survey of the data you have in its source form and knowing exactly where it needs to be sent as its final destination. This should start you thinking clearly about joined-up modular workflow connection diagrams. Boxes in those diagrams should represent the applications, and the connecting lines are the data formats that used for exchange between them. Working from a diagram like this should help to clarify your planning. You can see exactly what you need to do. Figure 3-9 illustrates a simple example that takes documents and separates URLs and text to generate two inputs to the document metadata databases. One feed appends items to the URL database and the other adds potential keywords to the candidate keywords for the index file.

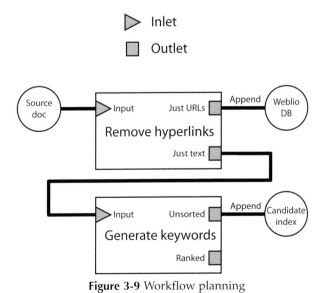

Figure 3-9 Workflow planning

Constructing libraries of diagram components that represent the different applications and adding inlets and outlets to the modules to represent the different data formats will give you a tool kit that is ready to use.

Clearly labeling those connection nodes will speed up your diagramming process. You might even be able to install those libraries into your diagramming software. Check out the Visio and OmniGraffle applications for examples of the sort of diagramming software you could use. This could be done in any drawing program in an unstructured fashion. Visio and OmniGraffle give you some additional help with maintaining the structure of the diagram.

Transformation Maps

If you have a collection of documents that you need to convert from one format to another, you need to work out the best way to do this. Drawing some diagrams that represent the applications that can operate on those documents might help to visualize the transformations. You can draw these maps as document centric or application centric.

Figure 3-10 is an application centric view of Excel.

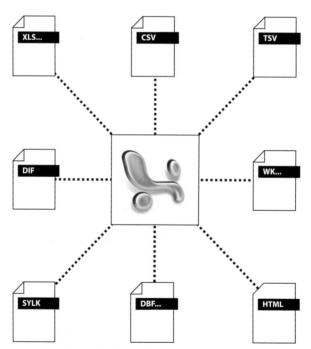

Figure 3-10 Application centric view

Visio: http://office.microsoft.com/en-us/visio/FX100487861033.aspx

OmniGraffle: http://www.omnigroup.com/applications/omnigraffle/

If we have these maps for other applications, we can plug them together where they share a common document format for import/export (or save as).

If we look at this from the document perspective, we get a similar kind of diagram. Figure 3-11 illustrates the RTF file format the diagram has been extended in Figure 3-12 to show transformations from Word documents to Open Office ODT.

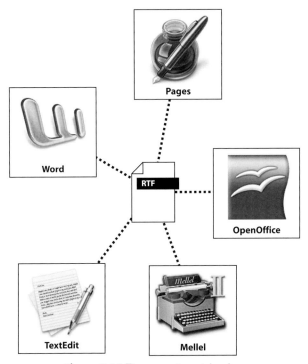

Figure 3-11 Document centric view

Once you map the transformations out like this, you can identify the best route from source format to destination format. The simplest path would be the one with the least hops but this may not yield the best quality. You need to test the transformations to ensure no data is lost along the way. By combining these two maps with others you have created for different applications and document types, your workflow path becomes clear. Figure 3-12 is an example that takes documents produced in several word processors into a DocBook format for processing to make other formats for embedded help files.

These diagrams are quite easy to construct. Documents can only connect to applications and applications can only connect to documents.

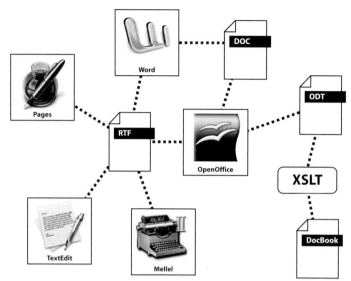

Figure 3-12 Document workflow map

The Value of Diagrams

Apply some rigor to your design. Draw diagrams that show the relationship of objects, one to another.

In addition to the diagrams that help you plan your software architecture, don't forget to document your network infrastructure and hardware rack installations. The network planning helps you identify where access controls might need to be addressed and the hardware planning is important for capacity planning and allocating sufficient space, air-conditioning, and uninterruptible power supplies (UPS).

Object Patterns

Many standard solutions can be deployed when designing architectures. A profoundly useful approach was developed by Erich Gamma, Richard Helm, Ralph Johnson, and John Vlissides. Their book *Design Patterns: Elements of Reusable Object-Oriented Software* (1995) contains a collection of basic designs for object models that address problems that frequently arise. Those models are great starting points and way of describing what you want to build. Some of their names are obvious, such as Adapter or Bridge, but others such as Facade or Decorator require some study.

In building a workflow, we would make great use of the patterns described in Table 3-5. These are a few selected examples from those described in *Design Patterns*.

Table 3-5 Useful object patterns

Pattern	Description
Abstract Factory	Manufactures new objects whose class is not defined until a subclass of the Abstract Factory is created.
Factory Method	A well-defined interface for creating objects but with no actual code inside. Subclass this and add the code to create your own factories.
Adapter	Makes classes compatible between models that normally could not be joined.
Composite	Used for building tree structures.
Decorator	Add new responsibilities to a class without sub-classing. This is useful for creating user databases with different roles.
Facade	Builds a user interface to front a complex system.
Proxy	Use this is a placeholder for an object. The Proxy knows how to replace itself with the genuine object when necessary. This is useful for attaching object models to databases. A Proxy can act as a database fault. When a reference is made to it, the fault will fire some intercept code that can fetch the data and create the real object. This reduces the amount of database access and hence improves the system performance.
Behavioral Patterns	A whole group of useful patterns for handling commands, building queues, etc.
Memento	Takes a snapshot of the current state of an object so it can be reused. Useful for storage, backup, and undo support.
Observer	Watches for changes and routes alerts to interested objects. Used for building Model-View-Controller scenarios.

Unified Modeling Language (UML)

There are many different and competing methodologies and diagramming styles for describing object-oriented designs. Probably the most popular is Unified Modeling Language (UML), but it is not your only choice.

You should choose a methodology and notation that fits with your working patterns and try to use it consistently across your organization. Try to keep to the same notation within a single project. UML is helpful for new projects. Older projects may use a legacy modeling language and methodology. You might update the methodology used by a project to be UML-compliant at a major upgrade stage, but it is not necessary to discard your old models and convert everything to UML just to carry out some maintenance.

Modern design tools should all be UML-compliant. They may be able to import your old style diagrams and models and convert them for you.

Planning Tools

Tools for developing workflow allow us to construct the system in a pictorial or textual way. This is analogous to the source code of an application. Later on, this model needs to be executed in a run-time environment. If we can abstract the conceptual design from the implementation, both aspects can be engineered independently.

A variety of new languages, paradigms and platforms are emerging to use for workflow systems design:

- Business Process Modeling Notation.
- Workflow Open Service Interface Definition (OSID).
- Job Definition Format (JDF).
- Windows Workflow Foundation (WF).
- AppleScript Automator on Mac OS X.

Web Service Composition Languages (WSCL) are emerging to describe how a web-based system will operate on data being passed to it:

- Business Process Execution Language (BPEL).
- Yet Another Workflow Language (YAWL).
- Business Process Modeling Language (BPML).
- Web Services Flow Language (WSFL).
- Web Services Description Language (WSDL).
- XLANG—Extended WSDL.
- Semantic Web Services Language (SWSL).
- XML Process Definition Language (XPDL).

Capacity Planning

Processing images and video requires some careful thought about the choice of format used for storage. In a production pipeline, you should avoid any kind of compression. This implies that input to output processing will increase the storage capacity required at each process step.

You might clean up temporary files at the end of the process but your capacity planning needs to consider this intermediate storage.

Elsewhere, in one of the case studies, we talk about using multiple threaded queues.

Let's say we have a collection of 5-GByte video sequences that go through five steps of processing. However, we might have five simultaneous processes running. It's not just a simple multiplication because we don't want to do the clean up until the jobs are all completed and dispatched. A single pipeline might have five intermediate files for a finished job but the unfinished jobs all have earlier staged files too. A single five-stage pipeline might have 20 intermediate files in flight at once. If we have a five lane processing farm, that could be 100 GBytes just for work in progress.

It is a fact of life that you can never have enough CPU power to get the work done quickly enough. Networks never have sufficient bandwidth, and you cannot have too much disk space.

Capacity planning needs to be done carefully and should always be pessimistic and take into account the worst case scenarios. It should also make predictions that assume growth factors are higher than you might expect them to be. Only then will you have made sufficient provision. Nevertheless, it is still inevitable that you will run out of disk and network capacity.

Summary

If we consider a systematic plan, building our workflow out from a data model is a sound approach. The object model can be derived from that data model. After that, we can construct our business logic and then attach a user interface.

It all sounds simple, and the approach is rigorous and we must still be diligent in how we go about the implementation to avoid building a smart system that manages and stores corrupted metadata. In the following chapters, we will dig down into the basics of the system and examine ways in which we can avoid such a scenario.

Transfer and Conversion

Limiting Your Problems

When you build a workflow, whether it is managing metadata or any other kind, you often have to reinvent the wheel—at least for some of the functionality. You should aim to recycle some components or applications that you have used before or tools that are built and maintained by other third parties where you can. They will usually require alteration, enhancement or some kind of glue-ware to augment or integrate them with your system.

Essentially, you need to build the overall structure of your system from scratch and gradually incorporate those reusable components one at a time. The components you can work with are getting larger and more capable and it is becoming easier to build workflows.

While all the participants might agree on which application programming interfaces (APIs), standards, or import/export formats to use, these are not usually profiled.

You might have an API call that passes a string value, but two systems that share this API may allow the maximum length to be quite different.

Profiling a standard defines a set of ranges or limits on the values that control the scope of variability. For instance, if a standard defines that a user's name is stored in a text string, it might not indicate the maximum length. A profile would define that maximum length and possibly a limited range of valid characters that may be used.

You should examine the tools you have available to see what format conversions you have available. Even then there are some fine points with different vintages and variants of these formats.

A Workflow Taxonomy

The design of a metadata-controlled workflow breaks down into several important parts. These components are based on increasingly complex aggregations of data. Starting with a single Boolean flag, we build up our physical structure as shown in Table 4-1.

Table 4-1 Workflow taxonomy

Component	Description
Boolean flag values	Values that can be true or false. Conditions based on evaluating a function or expression. The result of testing something for validity.
Characters	Individual character glyphs mapped into one of many alternative character sets. The glyph means very little by itself. The mapping into a character set provides context and meaning.
String	A collection of characters that can be organized to mean something such as a financial value or a person's name.
Numbers	Numbers come in a variety of different formats. They can be represented as a binary value or a string of characters.
Fields	Strings of data with semantic meaning such as dates. Some content may be represented in a variety of forma. Dates could be represented as a text string or a numeric value.
Records	A collection of related fields. Sorting and processing must preserve the integrity of the collection. Fields must not be randomly associated with other records.
Tables	A table collects multiple rows together. Each row is distinct but formatted identically to its siblings.
Databases	A database containing many tables can have relationships constructed between the tables. These relationships are called joins and translate well into object-oriented structures.
Systems	A system is a connected set of applications that might operate on the databases and communicate with one another to delegate tasks to a specialized unit that is optimized to process a particular kind of material.
Data centers	A data centre might be shared across an entire enterprise with multiple systems connected together passing work from one to another. Certain systems are designated as gateways, often operating as ingest or output but not usually both.
Ecologies	A collection of enterprises collaborating for mutual benefit. They may interconnect at the data center level or from one system to another in a different enterprise. This is the level at which commerce and security become paramount.

Standards-Based Numeric Values

Search for any relevant open standards that apply to the system you are building. This provides a firm foundation on which to build your system and helps to make it much clearer to any of your customers what the values in your data mean. If you all adhere to the same standard, then you can assume a minimal level of quality in the exchange because the values you are sharing are maintained in a consistent way.

The IEEE standardized numeric computation in the 1980s. Two standards apply: IEEE 754-1985 and IEEE 854-1987. These standards describe numeric computation and number conversion, respectively. You probably use these standards every day without realizing it, because they have become an integral part of most operating systems.

 Make sure you have adequate error trapping and handling set up to take advantage of the capabilities of your numeric system and maintain the accuracy of any computed results.

Some of the most useful aspects of the IEEE numerics standards are how they define values that are out of range. When you divide a value by infinity or zero, you will get an error. The values are represented as "Not-a-number" (NaN) and can be effectively trapped by the application.

Type Coercion

Type coercion is tricky and sometimes prone to data loss. There is a limited range of available data types. Within each of those types, there are a few variations (see Table 4-2).

Table 4-2 Data types	
Type	*Sub-types and description*
String	Quoted, Pascal, C language. Character data is stored as a sequence of characters collected as a string. We can perform useful text manipulations of string values. They are also a convenient way to transport other data types whose internal representation may be different on the target system.
Integer number	Integers are considered separately from floating-point values because they are a simpler data type. For small numbers, integers can be stored in a compact form.
Floating-point number	Floating-point values can represent a wide range of values, much larger than the range available to integer values.
Other number types	Fixed, financial, scientific octal, hex and other number bases (radix values).

IEEE 754 numerics: http://grouper.ieee.org/groups/754/

Table 4-2 Data types (continued)	
Boolean	Represented as either **TRUE** or **FALSE**. Boolean values help us evaluate conditions and make decisions when we need to provide branching in our business logic. The values '**TRUE**', '**Yes**', '**on**', '**1**', positive-values and nonzero values might all mean the same thing in different contexts but they are clearly not represented in an identical way. We need to test the semantic meaning of a Boolean value, not its representation.
Date	Date, time, religious calendars, time zones, daylight savings. Date and time are usually represented internally by a tick count resolved to millisecond accuracy. Humans are presented with formatted dates and times when viewing this kind of data. Dates can be moved between systems of an identical type as UTC values, but you should consider transporting as strings to other operating systems or for long-term archives.
Object	Unlimited range of possibilities.
NaN	Various special values.

You need to be careful when transforming data from one type to another. Test your system by transforming your value forwards, and then reverse the transformation back

 Convert to a target format and convert back again to test the accuracy of the coercion. Any variability will require attention to your code to correct or provide additional handling.

to the original format, storing the value in another variable and comparing the two. If the conversion is truly bi-directional, no data loss will occur and the values should be identical. This is the ideal that should always aim for. You should test with values covering the extremes of the range, as well as all boundary conditions such as zero-crossing values. Test for accuracy, number of characters in the result, and illegal values.

Information Float

Information float is what happens when you move data from one system or environment to another and the receiving container does not maintain the same resolution.

Consider the banking system. If you store financial values to two decimal characters of accuracy, often a percentage calculation will yield a value with four or more decimal places. If your receiving container can only resolve two decimal places, you have just lost a few hundredths or thousandths of a penny in the system. By rounding these values down we lose some accuracy. For all real-world intents and purposes, the value may be accurate enough but it is not precise.

Be sure that any rounding is not compromising your computations. Beware of the effects of compounding the effects of rounding errors. Be careful when using the rounded value in subsequent computations.

For visual effects, avoid cutting fragments out of finished programs. Instead, trace the provenance of the clips and cut from the originally ingested rushes. The same applies to audio editing.

For images, try to use an uncompressed source master image. Avoid recompressing images, and work from the largest copy you can find. Never scale an image up if you can avoid it.

This might seem to be of no consequence for a single transaction. If you can harvest these errors across the billions of transactions in the banking system, you can generate a considerable income stream from it.

This effect can be seen visually as noise or missing content. In the multimedia and broadcasting industries, we see this kind of problem evidenced as lost frames at the beginning and end of a clip if they have been trimmed to get rid of a dissolve when extracting clips from finished programs. Information float is also evidenced in graphic images as contouring or blocky artifacts resulting from scaling down and scaling up again later.

Truncation

Truncation happens most often with string data. Strings are a sequence of characters, and some applications will provide a buffer of a finite size in which to store and work on the string.

It's important to ask two questions here:

- How large is that buffer?
- What is a reasonable length for that buffer?

If the standard being applied by the exporting and importing applications does not define what the string length should be, then software developers or database administrators must decide this for themselves. The size chosen and defined in the model likely will be dependent on the developer's own experience. If the developer is from a cultural background where family names are quite short, they might allow only 32 characters for a name field. Another developer from a different cultural background where names are often much longer might allocate 64 or 128 characters. Moving to the application with the longer buffer is fine. Moving data back the other way will truncate some fields.

Oddly, we always naturally assume string length values should be a power of two—why is that?

Sometimes we can control these buffer sizes; sometimes we can't. If the software is well-documented, the value should have been

Make sure you know all the buffer capacities and string lengths. If necessary, run some tests to find out. This is quite easy to do. Store a value, then read it back and compare. If it is complete, make it one character longer and test again. When you get a truncation, you know you have reached the buffer size limit. Refer to Tutorial 16 for more details about this technique.

described in a manual or specification. If it hasn't been, then run some tests to determine where the strings get truncated.

Coordinated universal time (UTC) values hit a critical threshold at 1:46:40 on September 9th, 2001. At this moment, the UTC value on many systems rolled over and carried a digit that made the value 10 characters long, where it previously had been nine. Boundary conditions like the 99-to-100 transition will cause truncation problems. Any incrementing value that might be displayed in a textual form could be subject to this. Make allowances by extending the buffer length accordingly, but be sensible about it. Document the problem in the support manual, assuming you have written a support manual in the first place.

Numeric Values

Numeric values are portable when rendered as text. Unless you are constraining the target platforms, you run into difficulties when moving binary representations between computers of different types and architectures.

Integer Values

Integer values are strictly whole numbers. No fractional part after the decimal place is allowed. Integer values come in a variety of sizes, with 1, 2 and 4-byte values being the most common. The number of bytes will dictate the range of available values.

Truncation and information float occur if you move the value to a smaller container.

Integer values might be unsigned ranging from zero to the maximum value permitted by the available bits. The alternative is signed, which reduces the potential magnitude to half and uses the most significant bit to indicate a negative value. Table 4-3 lists the value ranges for each size of value.

Table 4-3 Integer value ranges

Data size	Sign	Value range
1 Byte	Signed	−128 to +127
2 Bytes	Signed	−32768 to +32767
4 Bytes	Signed	−2147483648 to +2147483647
1 Byte	Unsigned	0 to 255
2 Bytes	Unsigned	0 to 65535
4 Bytes	Unsigned	0 to 4294967295

If the value ranges are undocumented, run some tests to establish the size and whether the values are signed or not.

Beware of the endianness of the values when moving data from one system to another. The endianness describes whether the bits are ordered left-to-right or the other way. It can also affect the byte ordering in multi-byte values. Transporting binary files from PowerPC to Intel architectures requires that bytes be rearranged. If you want more reliable and unambiguous transporting, then render out as a numeric string and convert back again on ingest (assuming that the receiving container is big enough).

 Floating-point storage values may not be compatible between operating systems or architectures. Using IEEE numerics may solve this, but always be aware that OS and computer manufacturers might change something in a way that causes incompatibility. When in doubt, print the values as a string and then scan them back in at the receiver.

 Beware of incompatible storage formats across different systems.

 Run some tests to establish the maximum and minimum values. They may be system dependant. Transfer between different systems using a text string format.

You can run similar range tests for numeric fields as you can for string data to examine undocumented systems and work out what kind of storage is being used.

Float Values

Floating-point numbers allow a larger range of values to be expressed than an integer, including fractional parts. A straightforward notation places the decimal point where required, in the way a human being would normally write the number.

Floating Point—Scientific

Scientific notation uses a mantissa and an exponent. The mantissa is limited in its range of values, while the exponent moves the decimal point to multiply the value into the correct range. A common limitation here is that you have a fixed number of digits. Although the values are accurate to this number of digits, for larger magnitudes a long string of zeros is effectively placed at the right of the value. The errors are small but might compound. This is principally an import/export format. Internally the numbers are represented as floating point. The loss of accuracy only happens when interchanging the data.

Fixed-Point Numbers

Fixed-point numbers allow a fractional part but the decimal point cannot move. This is useful for financial values and also sometimes for geographic data. Computationally, the behavior is like an integer with a known placement of the decimal point.

NaN and Friends

The **NaN** concept was introduced when the IEEE was developing the standards for numeric representation. The idea is that it is a legal value within the numeric framework, but it represents a value that is Not a Number. Various **NaN** results are summarized in Table 4-4.

Table 4-4 Special numbers in IEEE 754

Operation	Result
Any value divided by ±Infinity	**0**
±Infinity multiplied by ±Infinity	±Infinity
±Nonzero divided by zero	±Infinity
Infinity plus Infinity	Infinity
Zero divided by zero	**NaN**
Infinity minus Infinity	**NaN**
±Infinity divided by ±Infinity	**NaN**
±Infinity multiplied by 0	**NaN**

You may want to argue with some of these special cases:

- Should infinity divided by zero still yield infinity?
- Would infinity multiplied by zero equal zero?
- Infinity minus infinity could equate to zero, provided both values for infinity are the same. They should be the same, because they are both infinity. The experts might argue that they may be equal but are not identical.

Refer to IEEE 754 for details. Check the result codes from evaluating a numeric computation and provide handlers for invalid results.

These issues are bound to be up for debate as the IEEE 754 standard is examined and revised by a panel of experts.

String Values

Strings are usually delimited (marked at each end), either with single or double quotes. Beware of the possibility that you may have to deal with foreign quotes and typographical quotes, too.

In the computer memory, strings are represented in the C language as a run of characters terminated by a null or zero byte (or word).

The string representation for the Pascal programming language is implemented with a count value (byte or word) followed by that number of textual characters.

This is all complicated by using a mixture of byte organized code sets like ASCII and multibyte and word organized character sets such as Unicode.

Don't try to access the wrong kind of strings.

C language string routines might interpret the length value of a Pascal string as a control character if the string is shorter than 32 characters long. Any longer than that and the string appears to have an addition prefix character. The C language routines will continue reading until they see a null character that will likely be a long way away if you have a sequence of Pascal strings.

Pascal will see the first character of the C string as a length value and read that number of the following characters into its buffer. Very likely, it will include the terminating null somewhere in the middle. You'll also notice that Pascal has eaten the leading character.

For strict interchange between two systems, you should avoid the 'prettification' of numbers:

- **Don't place spaces or commas in as thousands separators.**

- **Don't add leading zeros or spaces.**

- **Omit the sign unless it is negative.**

- **Don't use the financial practice of enclosing negative values in brackets unless the target system understands that notation.**

- **Avoid scientific notation if possible.**

- **Be aware of range issues.**

Numeric-to-String Conversion

Expressing the values in text—so that numeric values are "spelled-out" using numeric characters—allows them to be scanned in when opened on the foreign system. The downside of this is that the data can balloon to a gigantic size, often growing by an order of magnitude.

This will generally present few problems. You might be rendering numeric values out for publication, or perhaps the target system with which you are exchanging cannot understand the binary representation of your number-storage mechanism and hence cannot accept a binary file.

Knowing as much about the target system as possible will help you make optimal choices about the way that numerics are formatted when they are rendered as strings. Introducing anything other than meaningful characters that convey part of the value increases the likelihood that the system decoding your string will have problems.

Formatting numeric values is primarily something we do for the benefit of human beings. We don't need to introduce any ambiguity when designing interchange mechanisms between systems.

String-to-Numeric Conversion

Converting from string to numeric seems to be a straightforward proposition, since it is something that we do all the time. Certainly, when moving data around using XML, the values contained within a marked-up entity block are going to be represented as a string of numeric characters.

Clearly, a numeric value can be stored in much less memory, and you can perform arithmetic with it directly. Attempting to apply arithmetic operators to strings may not perform a mathematical operation at all. The operators can be overloaded with additional functionality that is selected depending on the context of the operation.

The numeric value **1000** and the numeric value **100** can be subtracted to yield the value **900**. If the same operation is used in the context of a string in the old VMS DCL command line environment, the syntax that subtracts **100** from **1000** would search for the sub-string **"100"** and delete it if present in the target string. You would get the value **"0"** instead of **900**.

The moral here is to make sure you perform arithmetic computation on numeric values. Converting the string to a numeric value is typically called scanning. It might be called parsing in some programming environments. Scanning starts at the left and proceeds to the right until it encounters a nonnumeric or invalid character.

Beware of spaces, commas, and full stops used to format numbers. A well-designed scanner will happily accommodate all of the thousands separators and exponential notation as well, but you should test your numeric scanner to ensure it can cope properly with these.

 Test your scanner with some sample values. Attempt to break it in order to establish its failure modes and document the behavior. Implement checks for those failure modes in the code that calls the scanner and provide fallbacks and error handlers. It easier to do this as part of the design activity than to track down the cause of a corrupted database. By then the data is possibly corrupted beyond repair.

Note that thousands separators are an internationally localizable property and, depending on the locale, they may be full stops, spaces, or commas. Knowing your current locale as well as the locale in which the document being scanned was produced is important.

Western script proceeds from left to right. Eastern languages use different rules, but numbers may be westernized within a framework that is Eastern. Local custom and culture will dictate certain rules about how you scan numeric values.

Booleans Never Lie

Boolean values are either **TRUE** or **FALSE**. You will occasionally encounter some difficulties with them. There are many ways to represent Boolean values, and quite a few interpretive issues within systems.

Table 4-5 lists some corresponding values for **TRUE** and **FALSE** that I have encountered over the years.

Table 4-5 Boolean value representations

True value	False value
TRUE	FALSE
"TRUE"	"FALSE"
"YES"	"NO"
"OUI"	"NON"
1	0
1.0	0.0
"1"	"0"
-1	0
Any nonzero value	0
Any positive value, including zero	Any negative value
Any legal numeric value	NaN
One single bit within a byte	NaN
The computed result of a Boolean expression	NaN
The returned result of a function	NaN
The exit status of an application	NaN
A hardware switch is closed	A hardware switch is open
A light sensor is illuminated	A light sensor is not illuminated

You may feel that it is no longer necessary to consider some of the old formats, because the systems that produced them are obsolete. If you are importing archival data, you may encounter some of the more arcane varieties. Your modern systems still must continue to interpret them correctly and convert them to the right value.

 There are many ways that Booleans can be represented in an external storage format. Internally, your software only has one representation, but the way that you map that to the world outside your application is crucial.

In the case of Boolean values, the one thing we can be certain of is that you are either completely correct or you are completely wrong in your interpretation of a value. There is some leeway for rounding or clipping non-Boolean values.

Visual Basic represents **TRUE** as **-1** and **FALSE** as **0**. This is because its arithmetic is based on 16 bit values and it fills all 16 bits with 1's to make the **TRUE** value.

Date Parsing

Early computing systems stored year values as two characters instead of four to save memory. Because those systems were only expected to last a short time before being replaced, certain judgment calls were made as to whether to use a two-digit representation for a year number as opposed to a four-digit representation.

It seems to have completely passed everyone by that a binary representation of that date value instead of an ASCII representation could have stored a much larger range of year values in the same or even less memory capacity.

Nevertheless, two-digit year numbers were used, and as a result, much re-engineering became necessary as the millennium approached.

Today, we represent date/time values together in a single binary value that contains a millisecond-accurate clock value measured from some reference date. Our concern now is that the reference date is not always the same for every system. Date value exchanges are still most reliable when transferred as a clear text string.

String representations throw up some interesting issues having to do with the spelling of month names in different locales, as well as with differing time zone values. Daylight savings time kicks in on different dates in different locales and changes the offset of the time zone. Provided that it is referenced back to Greenwich Mean Time (GMT), we can still calculate an absolute value.

Bear in mind that date and time are stored together. When doing arithmetic to generate alarms, you need to make sure that any time value is zeroed when you are doing calculations only on dates. Imagine we create a "to do" alarm system. If we set the alarm time so that it also contains a time value of 3:00 p.m., our alarm may not trigger until that time of day. Setting the time value to zero means the event will correctly trigger an alarm just after midnight as the new day begins.

 Transfer dates as a string to avoid any errors due to binary representations, and reference a starting date being different between the source and destination systems.

If you need to store date values, use a 64-bit (4-byte) format even if the time value is currently only 32 bits. In the near future, it will be extended to 64 bits. Deal with it now as an avoidance strategy.

Date and time values require further discussion, and Chapter 9 is devoted entirely to the topic of calendars and clocks.

If you really want to know the most intricate detail about time and date computation, then check out Lance Latham's book entitled *Standard C Date/Time Library*. It is a wonderfully useful resource and covers all manner of unusual and interesting date and time issues.

Memory and Architecture

There are two principal areas of difficulty when moving binary data between systems. Bit ordering or endianness of the bits, which represent numeric values. Values, which need to be represented with multiple bytes, may also suffer from byte ordering issues.

Historically, programmers in some languages exploited the in memory organization to convert between one data type and another. It worked but it has been proven a problem for ongoing software maintenance.

Big Endian, Little Endian Math

The endianness of a binary representation of a numeric value comes from the fundamental design of the CPU chip. Some manufacturers decided that the bits were organized from left to right, while others decided that they should be organized from right to left.

In our context, where we might need to move work between different computing architectures, that makes a significant difference. Two byte values are swapped around, and storing binary information into files that must be exchanged between the two types of systems requires some special handling.

The shortcut is to render everything out as a string and parse it back in again through a string scanning function. XML becomes a useful format for these transfers.

Refer to the discussion about character encoding formats in Chapter 6 where the endian issue surfaces again when encoding Unicode character strings. Chapter 16 covers the same issue where it affects TIFF files.

Unions and Common Memory

Some software development languages allow you to define the physical location of data storage in memory. You can create a block of memory and organize it so that you know how the storage bytes are allocated to the values contained in a series of variables. This has been used in the past to convert between data types using zero computation.

The reason it uses zero computation is that it uses the knowledge that mapping those bytes to one variable of a particular type will organize them so that they can be viewed as a different type of value if a second variable shares the same memory storage location.

In the original Apple Mac OS Classic operating system, four character strings were used to represent file types or identities for the applications that own them. If they share a 4-byte memory storage cell with a long integer variable, you can use the integer comparison to check the values with a single compare instruction instead of a looped comparison, character-by-character through the string. This yields a more than 4X speed improvement.

Algorithmically, this is very clever, but in terms of software design, it is arguably a bad practice. That's because the values have multiple data types, which is not neat and tidy from a design point of view.

The problem with manufacturing binary values from memory-mapped groups of alphanumeric letters is that only the values that correspond to legal character codes in the string representation are used. This means that about three out of every eight bits are wasted, because the letter codes can be represented with only five bits each. That's 12 bits overall, meaning that 4,096 values are not available.

Another possible problem is that some of the remaining values are illegal because they use nonprintable characters. Even worse, perhaps, is that some numeric values may contain zero bytes; from the earlier discussion on C language strings, you should recall that a zero byte would terminate a character string. If we set a value from the numeric side and try to read it from the string-based angle, we might get a string that is too short.

 Be aware of the endianness of the architecture on which you are executing. Decide as part of your data modeling what kind of endianness you require. Consolidate all the endianness support (switch and convert functions) into one code module so you can conditionally compile for either endian architecture in one place.

This technique was used in the early days of computing. The Fortran language let us define common blocks to share data like this. Modern languages can still do this by virtue of using pointers and structure blocks to define what the byte organization is but now that we have the Mac OS X operating systems running on PowerPC and Intel chips, we have the added problem of endianness in the data to contend with.

Summary

In this chapter, we have examined conversions between primitive data components and how they need to be treated with some degree of respect in order to avoid data corruption problems. This applies to essence data as much as it does to metadata. It is an engineering problem.

We have begun to "look under the hood" of workflow systems, and already we are discovering some interesting and possibly nasty surprises. Don't worry about that too much at this stage, it gets much worse than this.

In the next chapter, we will discover what lurks inside the unformatted and unstructured garbage that is hurled into our workflow for us to mold into something beautifully structured and well organized.

Dealing With Raw Data

Garbage In . . .

Information feeds that are used as content sometimes arrive in raw, unstructured, and unformatted condition. Perhaps it is typed in on location when some video is being shot, or perhaps it is a scanned image of a rap sheet. Sometimes, there may be no data recorded at all, and you must rely on a debriefing session and conversations with crewmembers in order to extract the necessary information.

Ideally, information is gathered onsite when shooting footage, recording sound material, or taking photographs. If you are shooting plates to use as backgrounds for some later visual effects work, then the more you know about the location and position of the camera and the kind of lens being used, the easier it will be to match the moves back in the postproduction studio.

Many times, this information isn't recorded at all, and the postproduction team has to figure it out by deduction or even make it up. The consequence is that your postproduction process will cost more and take longer than you were expecting. While it might appear to save time and money during the production stage, it is really a false savings to avoid gathering as much raw source data as you can at the point of shooting.

This all sounds obvious, but it is quite rare to find data being recorded adequately in the field. Camera manufacturers are addressing this by adding GPS location equipment to cameras and recording its output as a data track on the media, but geographical location is but one of many components of quality metadata.

Ingesting Documents

An important source of metadata for multimedia and video is the paperwork that might have been used on the shoot. Scripts, call sheets, and various other bits of documentation all contain useful information, but usually in a form that cannot be conveniently searched.

 You can find plenty of example call sheets to look at by using the Google Images search engine with the search key "Call Sheet".

These should be scanned as document images and filed in your content system. Then you can create a metadata linkage between the images and the footage they describe. Then, some re-keying or OCR process can be run in a context that maintains that linkage. If you don't make the linkage early on, any keying or OCR of the data needs to be associated manually.

You need to scan, store, and connect assets together logically. The ideal situation is to have all that information in an electronic form in the first place. The paperwork used at the shoot might well have been originated in a Microsoft Word document, which your content system could store with an asset wrapper placed around it. Then the asset management system can keep track of it. Assets can then be collected together and parented to a common master node that might represent program or film being shot. Figure 5-1 shows how the object model connects a collection of assets to a parent node.

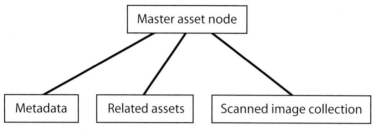

Figure 5-1 Source metadata linked to asset

The ideal entity-relationship model is to create a master asset node that represents this piece of content. That can then relationally join to any assets that are associated with it, including the footage itself. This allows complex relationships between one story and another to be made without those relationships being dependent on any one particular piece of media.

User-Entered Information

Making sure the metadata that your users enter is of the highest quality is a difficult challenge. Unless you can get them to buy into the process and the reasons for it in the first place, they aren't going to be very motivated.

At the BBC, we debated this aspect for some time and concluded that it might require threats that a program would not go to air unless the metadata was completed. This turned out to be far too draconian, and inevitably some compromises were made to allow the production staff some leeway in not entering metadata before content was publicly available.

The nature of those compromises unfortunately means that sometimes the data is not entered. If you are racing to get a piece edited to go on the air in ten minutes—and this is by no means unusual—putting in names and dates in a metadata form is not going to come high on your list of priorities.

In the longer term, this will likely have some knock-on effects when searching the archives for content. It is an example of how the cost driven short-term approach can affect your long-term business strategy.

You need to look at the larger picture, and it is likely that people who work in your archives department are appropriately skilled and have the right mindset to do that. You need someone with the attitude of a curator.

In BBC news, a workable solution was to pull the archives team from the end of the workflow process and place them at the start of it. By giving the archivists ownership of the ingesting process at the outset, they understood the implications of the value of metadata over the entire media lifecycle. Most importantly, they were able to convey that importance to others in the ingest process.

Because the systems made the media available to anyone who needed it immediately, there was little penalty for reorganizing the workflow in this way. People who needed to edit the footage could continue to do so, because the metadata was maintained in a separate but connected database. Indeed, several people could pull off proxy copies of the footage and make different cuts for their own news programs without affecting each other.

The digital revolution has made it possible to share the essence data between multiple simultaneous users. We sometimes miss the opportunity to delegate the metadata input and editing process along the way.

It is a question of looking again at the overall structure and what you need from the system and then examining whether there are opportunities to exploit by taking a radically different approach.

For instance, data entry processes are well understood. Data entry into transactional systems for finance and record keeping have been around since computers were first deployed on a large scale in the 1960s and 1970s. All of the usual techniques for ensuring data items are clean and of good quality and integrity can be applied:

- Input format templates.
- Mandatory field entry.
- Checksums.
- Bar code scanning.
- Field-end checks.
- Record-end checks.
- Spelling.
- Formatting.
- Relational lookups.

OCR-Scanned Documents

When working with paper documents, we can scan the whole document as an image. Perhaps that scanned document could be stored in a portable container such as a PDF file. That would allow it to be viewed on every platform it is likely to be required.

The next stage would be to start creating zones of interest on the scanned image area. Perhaps these might reduce the quantity of digitized pixels being stored and, while they aren't searchable unless some recognition takes place, the PDF files would shrink in size. This might be useful if you have many of them.

The information becomes much more useful if some OCR processing is done to extract the text. That won't work reliably on handwritten content, but anything that has been typed should yield some meaningful data.

Zoning the scanned image first allows some automation to be applied to the OCR process. Only the relevant zones need to be OCR-processed. The rest can be kept as pixel maps until it is necessary to scan them. That can take place as part of the reviewing process when a user calls up the document.

The important thing is that the refinement process gradually improves the quality of the metadata. There are still interim solutions that allow the document to be displayed or printed in a human-readable form even if the metadata extraction is not yet completed.

Legacy Text Files

Storing text in an electronic format in a way that ensures it is still readable many years in the future is a challenge, even if we ignore the question of the long-term viability of the physical media. A useful storage format guarantees that a user in the future can access the information without having to undergo a cryptographic exercise.

Consider whether you could decode a ZIP archive file without knowing the Lempel-Ziv-Welch algorithm. On the other hand, comma- and tab-separated ASCII files are easy to parse, although they lack the more complex structures.

XML files written using a Unicode code set would probably represent an optimal solution because there is structure in the XML markup, the code set is easy to understand, and the layout is somewhat human-readable.

If you have some older legacy files, there are issues you need to take account of as you decode them. ASCII code sets have many variations and are available in 7-bit and 8-bit variants. If the data is from a very old system, it may have been coded with EBCDIC or other code sets. Translating these to ASCII is not always straightforward, because there are character representations in some code sets that are not conveniently represented in others. This forces the use of some strange escape sequences. Converting to a Unicode character set should be the most reliable approach, but in going from a single-byte to multiple-byte representation, the size of the data may well increase significantly even though there's no net increase in its informational value. Capacity planning issues become important when this is being done on an industrial scale.

Some data capture happens by using software drivers to front-end a legacy system. This is sometimes called *screen scraping*. A virtual terminal is created, and the content displayed on a cellular grid of characters is translated to a GUI representation that the user sees. They may not realize that they are still talking indirectly to an ancient system.

Mainframe computers are still widely used in commercial situations. They process data in a batch oriented and record structured transactional manner. The results are carefully formatted and presented on a character cell terminal display. A graphical user interface (GUI) isn't called for.

If you go to a command-line environment on your workstation, you will use a character terminal application that is similar to the kind of display a mainframe has. The application maintains a buffer that contains the screen full of characters. When screen scraping, it waits for a trigger to indicate that the screen is full. Perhaps this is recognizable character appearing at a known location on the screen. The application can then pause any further screen updates while it parses the screen display to extract the data from it.

As a process, this is not much different to a framed transfer protocol, where data arrives in fixed format packets to be parsed by an input processor. We happen to have used a screen display buffer as a connection point in the API. See Figure 5-2.

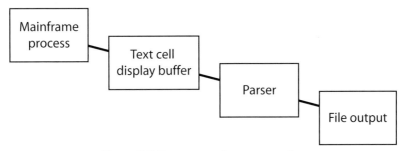

Figure 5-2 Screen scraping process steps

Capturing this data into a file is straightforward. In fact, you can do it yourself if you fire up a terminal emulator and log into a UNIX command line. Turn on the keystroke logger, which should also record any output to the screen as well.

You will record a mixture of useful data with escape character sequences interposed. These escape sequences may be necessary to turn on highlighting effects or change text colors. They might be used to position the cursor on the screen to update the display in a nonsequential way. If that happens, then your decoding process must take into account the escape control codes in order to reassemble the data into a coherent form for use in other systems.

In fact, you have this problem when parsing PDF files, because the text may not be written into the file in strictly sequential order. It is a set of drawing instructions, and little of the original textual content would retain its correct positioning within the narrative.

The solution is to push the PDF file through an OCR process, because while the characters are recognized accurately, you exploit the spatial organization capabilities of the OCR software. This approach might be useful for processing old terminal session recordings, too. You would have to honor the escape sequences in order to paint a virtual frame buffer with the text in its correct positions, but the OCR detection can then lift the text off the frame buffer in a coherent form.

Line Endings

Files arriving from different sources may have been composed on different operating systems. This can sometimes cause problems with text import. If the import routines are not aware of the variety of different line endings, the file can be misinterpreted as one single line with some unrecognized control characters embedded.

Table 5-1 summarizes the line endings for the three main operating systems you would be concerned with.

Table 5-1 Line ending characters

OS type	Line ending
Unix	**LF**
MacOS	**CR**
Windows	**CR LF**

Word Processor Integration

It is possible to extract the pictures from word-processed documents and replace them with some markup so they can be stored separately. We would also like to identify headings and treat them accordingly so that we can work on the structure of the document.

Unfortunately, many word processors will present you with a document where the only identifiable markup is the text style. This is analogous to the way web pages were constructed before XML and CSS became popular.

We need to represent the document in a clear text format for all the same reasons that we saw for spreadsheets not being accessible in a binary form.

Microsoft Office represents the most popular source of any document we would be interested in working on. Fortunately, it does have some useful automation hooks that can be accessed by AppleScript on Mac OS X. On the Windows platform, Windows Script Host and PowerShell support will provide ways to wrap the application in a scripting container so it can be plugged into a workflow.

Another major advantage for systems integrators is the variety of import/export formats Office supports:

- Plain text (TXT) files.
- Older versions of Word.
- HTML.
- XML (in the latest versions of Office for Windows).
- Rich Text Format (RTF).

Check your own copy of Office to see what is available.

All of these are supported to some extent by other word-processing software. Even the Microsoft Word document formats can be imported into competing products, although the latest version of Microsoft Office may support some formats that are not yet available in other programs.

Open Office imports Word documents and can help you solve some of these problems. Saving the document in the ODT format will burst out all the illustrations into a folder containing separate files that can be operated on directly.

Integrating text-based reports using a formatted presentation is useful as a management-reporting tool. While you might create an HTML page that Microsoft Word can understand, other formats offer document management capabilities that go beyond what HTML can accomplish on its own.

Plain text and RTF are quite useful for exchanging text and documents. RTF is a proprietary format created by Microsoft but it was designed to be a useful portable interchange format and is understood by many applications made by other manufacturers. You should check the vintage of the RTF file you are creating. You can usually load an older RTF file into a newer system, but it may not be feasible to load a more recent vintage RTF file into an older system.

Moving content in and out of word-processed documents and storing it in content management systems can be quite complex and cumbersome. The documents have a great deal of embedded styling, metadata, and dynamic field codes, and might carry embedded illustrations.

Data Mining

Search automation has applications in broadcasting because people always need to do data mining. Data mining is a process that extracts value from your archives. If you can make the business case for it, a huge amount of useful data could be mined from your archives. Collecting this data may not seem important at the time, but over a long period that data may take on a different value.

I collected the fuel prices every time I filled my car. This was important because I needed to account for the costs to claim my fuel expenses on my taxes. Because I did this for 25 years, I have fuel prices recorded in a spreadsheet over a very long time. These figures make an interesting and useful graph that shows how fuel has increased in price over that time.

When I stood at the pump noting the figures, I wasn't thinking in terms of a 25-year data collection exercise. It was a useful by-product that didn't cost anything to collect.

Another example is the BBC ENPS system, which has about 8 million stories in it, including the score for every major national and international cricket match over the last 25 years. That data set was discovered by accident, and could be mined with some data-gathering scripts to be turned into useful program input for commentators to use when covering matches on-air. Such a data-mining exercise could only happen if the funding is provided to facilitate it.

 Dig through your archives and you could find rare and valuable data that can be re-purposed or sold for a profit.

Lucene Text Search Tools

Apache Lucene is an open source high-performance, full-featured text search engine library written entirely in Java. It is suitable for a wide variety of applications that requires full-text search, especially cross-platform. It is, (for the moment), only available in Java but you could download the source code and integrate it via a bridge with other languages.

Lucene text searching library: http://lucene.apache.org/java/docs/index.html

Silk Purses Into Sow's Ears

Our aim is to clean up the unstructured, raw data and present it in a form that allows our metadata ingest process to store meaningful references to it. That probably means we want to create some XML from the input data.

Part 2 includes tutorials showing a variety of useful things you can do when processing data. Tutorial 21 shows how to manually convert tab-separated data to XML. You may already have closed-box solutions that perform this conversion automatically. Learning how to do it by hand might get you out of a hole when your normal tools are not available.

Add some structure to the data you are importing. Life would be great if that was all there was to it, but there are still some dragons to slay. The structure may be fine, but the character codes may mean different things in different countries. An 8-bit byte can represent a variety of different things. Some of them look similar but are not the same. We'll explore that in the next chapter.

Character Mapping and Code Sets

Lost In Translation?

Using mixed character sets can be hazardous to your health. Back in the 1970s and 80s, computer systems from different manufacturers were much harder to integrate into a single workflow. We had problems getting data moved from IBM to DEC computer systems. This is partly because the character codes were represented using different mapping schemes. On DEC VAX systems we used ASCII, while the IBM systems used EBCDIC that was completely different.

While mapping characters one-to-one wasn't difficult, dealing with missing characters presented a serious problem. In EBCDIC, we had a character for U.S. cents (¢). It occupied the same position as UK Pound signs (£). There was already an ambiguous meaning for that character code. In the standard ASCII 7-bit code set, there was no corresponding character for cents. Several other characters also presented difficulties.

Now we have the Unicode standard, which solves many problems. In the journey from ASCII to Unicode, we created many ASCII-based code sets that need careful consideration when they are imported into a workflow. The consequence is that you must use a substitute character that may be satisfactory when going in one direction but loses important data if the transfer needs to be reversed or some data is moved back to the original system.

Today, we might face some issues with mapping character codes when moving content between systems in different countries. The internationalization support for different locales is significantly better than it used to be, and there are mechanisms already built into the operating systems to help us. We should never be complacent about this issue, especially when importing legacy files.

ASCII

Most of the time, you won't experience any problems with ASCII files. Nevertheless, importing content from old archival material will still require careful checking.

ASCII was first published as a standard in 1967 and was last updated in 1986. The lowest group of 32 character codes and the highest-numbered character (127) are nonprinting control characters. Most of these were relevant when teletypewriters were used but are now obsolete. Table 6-1 lists some of the legacy ASCII codes that are still relevant.

Table 6-1 Important ASCII control codes

Character code	Decimal value	Mnemonic
Alarm bell	7	BEL
Back space	8	BS
Horizontal tab (tab)	9	HT
Line feed (new line)	10	LF
Vertical tab	11	VT
Form feed (new page)	12	FF
Carriage return (new line)	13	CR
Escape	27	ESC
Delete	127	DEL

The lower 128 characters of the Unicode standard also describe a compatible mapping of character codes to glyphs. Unicode also supports some extra character glyphs to represent the control codes in a visible form.

Beware of how legacy data files might set the eighth bit of a character code. It was used as a parity bit, but on some systems that did not support parity, it might have been forced to zero or 1. The safe option is to strip it off and use the lower 7 bits unless you know that the code-set is a genuine 8-bit format.

The latest authoritative specification is ANSI X3.4-1986 and ECMA-6 (1991). ISO 646 is also relevant, as is ISO 8859 in all its variants. Refer to Appendix D for a list of relevant standards.

Unicode (Versions 1–5)

Unicode is standardized as ISO 10646. The Unicode Standard, which is maintained independently, is the authoritative document. Both map characters in the same way, but the Unicode Standard published as ISBN 0321185781 offers much more detailed descriptions.

Character Glyphs

Unicode defines its range of character glyphs—more than a million—with the Universal Character Set (UCS), which is also covered in the ISO standard. Unicode adds collation rules and other contextual support, as well as encodings. Generally, a Unicode implementation as a font or editing system would be designed around the basic 65K two-byte subset. That subset is called the *Basic Multilingual Plane*, and most of our metadata work can probably be accomplished within it.

Because Unicode attempts to include all of the character glyphs from the other code sets, it becomes a useful way to represent documents. This solves the EBCDIC-to-ASCII problem, by mapping both code sets into Unicode. The downside is that characters must be expressed using the two-byte representation but since storage is so cheap, that is a trivial problem.

Unicode has a variety of encoding schemes. They all encode the character mappings according to the overall scheme, but the number of bytes per character determines whether the entire Unicode glyph set is represented with one, two, three, or four bytes. Historically, Unicode was a fixed-length 2-byte format, but this was considered quite wasteful when most characters in the Latin alphabet were within the ASCII character set.

Unicode Transformation Formats

Characters in the Unicode standards are encoded using one of the Unicode Transformation Formats (UTF). These are represented by the shorthand UTF-n where n represents the number of bits per character in the coding scheme. UTF-8 and the other UTF formats have been developed as the Unicode standard evolved, giving us a large range of glyphs within a compact storage scheme.

 Unicode does present issues regarding file sizes, and choosing the wrong format by accident can make your data files much bigger than they need to be.

These are the implications of using the different Unicode Transformation Formats:

- A document encoded in UTF-32 could be twice as large as a UTF-16 encoded version, because the UTF-32 scheme requires four bytes to encode any character, while UTF-16 only uses two bytes for the characters inside the basic multilingual plane. Characters outside the Basic Multilingual Plane are rare. You'll seldom need to encode in UTF-32.
- The character encoding in UTF-8 is a variable length format and uses between one and four bytes to encode a character. UTF-8 may encode more or less economically than UTF-16, which always encodes in 2 or more bytes. UTF-8 is more economic than UTF-16 when characters having a low (one byte) value predominate.
- UTF-7 encoding is more compact than other Unicode encodings with quoted-printable or BASE64 encodings when operated in a 7-bit environment but it is difficult to parse.

For most metadata applications, UTF-8 would be the most portable. If you use many foreign interchange processes, UTF-16 might be more suitable, and if you deal with Asian languages, you may need to use UTF-32.

During transfers between systems, data sometimes becomes corrupted. The UTF-8 format is the most resilient to any data corruption errors; UTF-16 and UTF-32 are less so. UTF-7 is not recommended for use with systems that require searching. It is useful as an interchange format but should be converted to UTF-8 on arrival and not used for storage, as it is cumbersome to work with. UTF-8 is much preferred and has become the dominant standard.

Beware that byte ordering within the file may change the binary layout for UTF encodings larger than UTF-8. UTF encodings are not straightforward binary expansions, and the tricks that you might use with ASCII to remove the eighth bit or possibly change the sign of the fifth bit to convert between upper and lower case may not work as you expect.

Table 6-2 lists the byte sizes of various character ranges for different encodings.

Table 6-2 Unicode encoding byte sizes

Range (hex)	UTF-8	UTF-16	UTF-32
000000 – 00007F	1	2	4
000080 – 0007FF	2	2	4
000800 – 00FFFF	3	2	4
010000 – 10FFFF	4	4	4

The Unicode character range from **0** to **10FFFF** (hex) is divided into 17 planes. These are summarized in Table 6-3.

Table 6-3 Unicode character planes

Plane	Range	Description
0	00000 – 0FFFF	Basic Multilingual Plane (BMP)
1	10000 – 1FFFF	Supplementary Multilingual Plane (SMP)
2	20000 – 2FFFF	Supplementary Ideographic Plane (SIP)
3	30000 – 3FFFF	Unassigned
4	40000 – 4FFFF	Unassigned
5	50000 – 5FFFF	Unassigned
6	60000 – 6FFFF	Unassigned
7	70000 – 7FFFF	Unassigned
8	80000 – 8FFFF	Unassigned
9	90000 – 9FFFF	Unassigned
10	A0000 – AFFFF	Unassigned
11	B0000 – BFFFF	Unassigned
12	C0000 – CFFFF	Unassigned
13	D0000 – DFFFF	Unassigned
14	E0000 – EFFFF	Supplementary Special-purpose Plane (SSP)
15	F0000 – FFFFF	Private Use Area (PUA)
16	100000 – 10FFFF	Private Use Area (PUA)

Unicode is currently undergoing a major revision from version 4 to version 5. The changes are detailed at the Unicode Consortium's web site (*http://www.unicode.org/* .

Charts of Unicode character assignments to international scripts are provided here (*http://www.unicode.org/charts/*).

Windows Code Pages

Windows code pages are the equivalent of character encodings in other operating systems. If you receive metadata or text-based essence data files that are encoded with these mechanisms and you don't want to deal with that complexity throughout your workflow, the ingest point is a good place to immediately translate all of these different formats into their Unicode equivalents.

In common usage, there are ten generic code page maps and thirteen that are used in character-based terminal windows. A study of the online sources of information on this topic reveals many other variants, some old, some relatively new, and some proposed for future use. They are all overlays on top of the ASCII code set, which is extended using the eighth bit, or by using 2-, 3- or 4-byte encodings. Trying to present this all on screen at the same time is challenging. If your viewer supports Unicode, then you have access to all of the code pages simultaneously

The lower 128 characters are compatible with ASCII. From character 128 upwards to 255, they are mapped to a variety of international characters, foreign alphabets, forms design glyphs, and mathematical symbols. A few characters are left unmapped in some code pages.

Appendix D lists many Windows code page numbers with the languages and locales where they are relevant.

Internationalization

Internationalization and localization is the process of adapting software for different foreign markets. The translation of text prompts in the user interface of an application is easier to maintain if all the text strings are collected together into one place. The user interface must be able to adapt to strings that might be longer in one language than another.

The same problem of text strings becoming longer in foreign translations also occurs with content storage systems.

Asian and Oriental Languages

Mapping some Asian and Oriental languages to a Latin representation is beyond the capabilities of anyone but the most specialized interpreter. There might be some Latin text and figures embedded within Asian text, and it might be possible to extract them. This needs to be examined on a case-by-case basis, and only those companies and individuals that are working with foreign content providers on a regular basis need worry about this.

Bidirectional Text

Bidirectional text is something you need to deal with if any of your content comes from countries that write their scripts from right to left. Latin-Roman scripting systems write from left to right, which is fine for the U.S. and other countries that may supply you with content that only needs to have its character mappings fixed. You may also need to translate the text.

You may need to scan the characters from right to left when you display them. Careful inspection of the data files will reveal whether the sequential ordering of characters is correct or whether you have to scan strings from the end towards the beginning.

You could delegate this problem to the operating system.

Escape Sequences

Escape sequences were invented to allow character sets to be extended with additional characters that could reuse existing codes. This is managed by using multibyte characters and executing the Unicode encodings in such a way that they don't need escape sequences at all.

Escape sequences were popular in the 1970s and 1980s with character-cell terminals. Tektronix implemented an escape control sequence system that supported complex high-resolution line drawing on graphics displays. This evolved into plotting languages like HPGL, CalPlot, and the codes used to drive large-format printers. The Digital Equipment Corporation (DEC) used escape sequences in its VT series terminals. These supported character attributes such as bold, color, and background/foreground support. Many terminal emulation applications that we use on Mac OS X and Windows continue to support escape sequences like these. If you capture console sessions or have an archive of plot files from Tektronix and Calcomp plotters, you may need to decode these escape sequences to remove the data you don't want and extract the text that you do.

Companies building graphics workstations in the 1980s advanced the state of the art to encode GKS display list models (such as metafiles) using very complex escape sequences. Although the syntax is different, these are like SVG files in that they are a spooled capture of a vector image. There could be quite a large archive of spooled vector data encoded with escape sequences. Many maps and engineering diagrams were created with systems using this technique. Converting this data to SVG is not overly complex, but it does require some special knowledge.

Byte Order Markers

We discussed big endian and little endian data in Chapter 4 when we looked at issues related to transferring data between systems. It surfaces again as an important subject when we look at character-encoding schemes in Unicode.

Unicode supports a special Byte Order Marker (BOM) character, using the character code for a nonbreaking space having zero width. This is a good character to select because it is a valid displayable glyph but it doesn't move the graphics cursor onwards and won't cause a premature line break. The character is coded at position **U+FEFF** (hex).

Table 6-4 lists the BOM byte sequences for UTF-8, 16, and 32 encodings.

Table 6-4 Unicode BOM encoding

Encoding	Byte order	BOM sequence
UTF-8	Irrelevant	**EF BB BF**
UTF-16	Big Endian	**FE FF**
UTF-16	Little Endian	**FF FE**
UTF-32	Big Endian	**00 00 FE FF**
UTF-32	Little Endian	**FF FE 00 00**

 Files composed of non-Unicode 8-bit character streams present no problem. They don't need to be converted, because they are written one byte at a time and read back in the same way. Endian issues don't occur.

Chapter 16 describes how this issue is dealt with in TIFF files. Refer to Tutorial 43 for details of how to detect BOM codes in your workflow.

E-mail Code Sets

Ideally, we would do most of our processing in what is called an *8-bit clean environment*. If any of our workflow processes transfer data via e-mail, this is going to cause a problem because Simple Mail Transfer Protocol (SMTP) was designed to cope only with 7-bit ASCII. SMTP can cope with 8-bit and larger data, but we need to format the messages carefully and might need to encode the data being transmitted.

Unicode can be put into e-mails using the variable length UTF-7 encoding, but you must make sure the code set is identified in the headers. Beware that UTF-7 is not particularly popular. A straightforward ASCII encoding may be preferable for portability.

HTML Document Encoding

HTML documents can define the character encoding in an HTTP header like this:

```
Content-Type: text/html; charset=ISO-8859-1
```

Or with a **\<META\>** tag in the **\<HEAD\>** block like this:

```
<meta http-equiv="Content-Type" content="text/html; charset=US-ASCII">
```

Or, if they are XHTML (valid XML documents), in the first line like this:

```
<?xml version="1.0" encoding="ISO-8859-1"?>
```

Web Page URL (Percent) Escaping

Percent coding is described in RFC 3986 and illustrated in Table 6-5.

Table 6-5 Percent encoding

Description	Character	Encoded form
Exclamation point	!	%21
Hash sign	#	%23
Dollar currency symbol	$	%24
Percent sign	%	%25
Ampersand	&	%26
Single quote	'	%27
Open bracket	(	%28
Close bracket	)	%29
Asterisk	*	%2A
Plus sign	+	%2B
Comma	,	%2C
Forward slash	/	%2F
Colon	:	%3A
Semi-colon	;	%3B
Equals sign	=	%3D
Question mark	?	%3F
Commercial "at" sign	@	%40
Open square bracket	[	%5B
Backslash	\	%5C
Close square bracket	]	%5D

Back slash (\) was included here although some sources do not always list it as an escaped character.

Web Page Character Encoding

Most of the text you want to put into an HTML document can be typed at the keyboard. There are certain characters that cannot be used without being escaped but escaping text in HTML is not done with the **ESC** character provided by the standard ASCII character set.

You can embed HTML character entities into the text of the document. Alternatively, with JavaScript code and URL references, you can use percent escaping. This is sometimes called *URL escape code*.

Character entities are represented by escaping them with an ampersand, hash, and either a mnemonic symbol or the Unicode code point decimal value of the character. Other code tables can be used, but Unicode is recommended for portability.

There are only a few characters that must be escaped in web pages. The context where you introduce character entities is different to that where you would use the percent encoding style, which is used for encoding URL values. You need to escape anything that would cause problems in HTML. The tag delimiters (**<** and **>**) and ampersand character (**&**) are obvious examples. A few bullets and symbols for **<UL><LI>**...**</LI></UL>** constructs and the foreign currency symbols are also candidates for being escaped with ampersand notation.

Mathematical formulae might be encoded with character entities, but positional locations of characters are important and some tricky CSS-style control is necessary. You should consider rendering complex formulae as an image or use SVG. MathML might be feasible, but rendering is still required through some kind of style transformation to deliver the correct visual appearance.

XML Character Entities

XML processes must support the five character entities described in the XML 1.0 specification. They may support others but these are mandatory.

Table 6-6 lists the mandatory XML character entities that are also supported by HTML and XHTML.

Table 6-6 XML character entities

Description	Character	U code point	Decimal	Name
Quotation mark	"	U+0022	34	&quot;
Ampersand	&	U+0026	38	&amp;
Apostrophe	'	U+0027	39	&apos;
Less-than sign	<	U+003C	60	&lt;
Greater-than sign	>	U+003E	62	&gt;

HTML Character Entities

Web browsers have different rules for displaying character glyphs in Unicode fonts. Table 6-7 summarizes the general behavior:

Table 6-7 International font handling in web browsers

Browser	Unicode glyph support
Mozilla	Intelligent selection of font on a character-by-character basis.
Firefox	See Mozilla.
Opera	See Mozilla.
Safari	See Mozilla.
Microsoft Internet Explorer (MSIE) on Windows	Characters must be present in the first designated font for the page or in the fall back font.
MSIE on MacOS	Asian language support sometimes OK, middle eastern languages not well supported.
Netscape Navigator	Only displays correct characters if they are present in the font specified for the page.

The document type definition for HTML defines 252 character entities. There is an excellent table listing them all in Wikipedia. Browsing the page will automatically prove that your browser displays the characters properly (or not).

Table 6-8 illustrates a few of the more commonplace entities. The five mandatory character entities that are supported by XML have been omitted but should be included as well. They were summarized in Table 6-6.

Table 6-8 Common HTML character entities

Description	Character	U code point	Decimal	Name
No break space		U+00A0	160	
U.S. cent currency	¢	U+00A2	162	&cent;
UK pound currency	£	U+00A3	163	&pound;
Copyright	©	U+00A9	169	&copy;
Registered trademark	®	U+00AE	174	&reg;
Bullet	•	U+2022	8226	&bull;
Euro currency	€	U+20AC	8364	&euro;
Trademark	™	U+2122	8482	&trade;

Search Wikipedia for: " HTML character entities"

Character entities can be represented with their numeric (decimal) equivalent. Therefore, the copyright symbol can be represented as **©** or **©** whichever is more convenient.

Summary

If you are moving data from one operating system to another, be aware of any unusual character encodings or document headers that could cause you problems with character mapping.

Working entirely in one character-encoding scheme such as ASCII or Unicode is ideal, but you cannot always control the format your suppliers will use to deliver information to you.

Refer to Appendix D for a list of code sets that might need to be filtered due to character remapping problems.

Now that we have the character mapping in some controlled environment, the next level of abstraction is field structures. We will look at those in the next chapter as we head towards record-oriented data tables for loading into databases.

Data Fields

Atoms

Now that we've dealt with character mapping, let's start to work upward through the storage architecture and head for our discussion of database storage. First let's look at field-level data.

We'll begin with primitives, then storage representations and finally examine some of the techniques that data entry systems from the 1970s can teach us.

Primitive Data Types

 Refer to Chapter 4 for discussions on how data values can be corrupted during the transfer between different systems.

Our primitive data types are few. It is quite amazing that everything we build can be described in simple terms using these primitives. We build increasingly complex data types from these basic components and re-use them at a higher level (as arrays and dictionaries and then linked lists, etc.).

Transporting Binary Values

Moving binary numeric values from one system to another might be subject to corruption due to the endian problems described in Chapters 4 and 6. If the receiving software is able to determine the endianness of the incoming data and compensate for it, you don't need to worry.

You could transfer a structured file in an XML container or a TSV file. Alternatively, encode the binary files in such a way that they will transfer unambiguously. Files containing a sequence of double byte, word, or long-word sized data (2-byte or 4-byte) can benefit from this technique.

The solution is to convert the binary values to a hexadecimal character-based form. A 2-byte value becomes four characters long and a 4-byte value becomes eight characters. The disadvantage is that the files will grow to twice their original size but we aren't proposing that you do this with GIF, JPEG, audio, or video files, all of which are already well-supported.

When the hexadecimal text is converted back into numeric values, each group of four or eight characters is repacked into a numeric 2- or 4-byte value, but this time, the endian problem is dealt with automatically.

The advantage to this approach is that you don't need to know the endian nature of any of the participating systems. It just works. You don't need to include a BOM code, because byte ordering is handled automatically. This will work provided the 2- or 4-byte cadence of the data is not compromised. You cannot mix the word-sized values with an occasional byte that would offset them.

Name–Value Pairs

It is quite common to encounter values stored in name-value pairs. The attributes in an HTML tag are stored as **`name="value"`** constructs.

Sometimes the name and value pair is passed as a pair of parameters, and maintaining the association between them requires some care. If they become separated, they no longer have any meaning. Here is an example:

```
(Name = "propertyname" Value = "propertyvalue")
```

Key, Length, and Value (KLV)

Name and value pairs can be presented to some interfaces as a Key, Length, and Value triplet. This is used by the MXF wrapper.

Earlier on, we discussed the difference between Pascal and C language strings. KLV coding is similar to Pascal strings with a key placed in front. In the MXF scheme, the key is either a short two-byte value that is called a local key or a 16-byte long-form SMPTE-defined value. When the short-form method is used, the mapping to a 16-byte key is done elsewhere.

KLV coded blocks can be nested. A first level of coding creates a collection of values contained in separate KLV wrappers. They are collected together into a contiguous block of memory and wrapped in another KLV block and then they can be exchanged as a whole set.

Variable-Length BER Coding

The length values used in KLV coded data for MXF files containing SMPTE metadata use a variable length scheme. It relies on the use of the most significant (eighth) bit to indicate an additional byte is needed. This is illustrated in Figure 7-1.

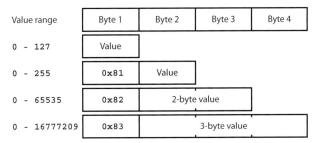

Figure 7-1 Variable-length BER coding

If the most significant bit is zero, then the remaining seven bits encode a value up to 127. Setting the sign bit to one means that the lower 7 bits are interpreted as a byte count for the value encoded in the subsequent bits.

This is used for the Length part of a SMPTE and MXF KLV value, which will be formatted as one of these alternatives:

- **XX**
- **81XX**
- **82XXXX**
- **83XXXXXX**

SMPTE KLV Packaging

Now we can illustrate the packaging of three metadata values into a KLV pack. This uses SMPTE Unique Labels (UL), which are described in Appendix B.

- Item 1 is the string **'AAAA'**.
- Item 2 is the numeric value **1000** stored in a 2-byte integer.
- Item 3 is the string **'0123456789'**.
- KLV pack 1 has a 16-byte SMPTE label, a 1-byte short-form length, and the data. It is 21 bytes in total. KLV 2 is 19 bytes long and KLV 3 is 27 bytes long.
- Packed together, they occupy 67 bytes. This means they can still be represented by a short-form length value. When wrapped in an outer KLV package the entire data set is 84 bytes long.
- The nested KLV wrapping echoes the tree-structured nature of the SMPTE metadata dictionary nodes. It also translates quite readily to an XML format.
- While this scheme is highly organized, it isn't very compact.

Tagged Containers

XML containers wrap individual fields in tags that provide semantic meaning to the contents. Our KLV wrapper would instead be implemented as a tag. The three KLV packages could be wrapped like this inside XML:

```
<container>
<one>AAAA</one>
<two>1000</two>
<three>0123456789</three>
</container>
```

Tag Attributes

Instead of wrapping the values in tags, we could use tag attributes, like this:

```
<container one="AAAA" two="1000" three="0123456789" />
```

Compared with the previous two examples, this looks quite compact.

Hierarchical Data Format

Scientific visualization systems often move data around using the HDF format. There are several varieties of these files. Most commonly HDF4 and HDF5.

HDF is designed for transporting large data sets and because they are organized Hierarchically, you can navigate through them to drill down to specific data items quickly.

Summary

The values we store in data fields correspond with literals that we define as constants in the source of our applications. They also correspond to variables where we can store and manipulate the fields with our scripts or application code.

The next stage in the development of our data architecture is to organize these fields into record structures. Chapter 8 takes us into that area.

Hierarchical Data Format *(HDF): http://www.hdfgroup.org/*

Fields, Records, and Tables

Molecules

In this chapter, we will look at field and record structures. These are directly related to database topics and object modeling, since the fields and records are normally written to an RDBMS as an alternative to saving things in a file. Objects are constructed from the RDBMS or serialized file data.

We won't be delving too deeply into database design, since that has been amply covered in other books. We will look deeply enough to uncover some potential pitfalls though.

Record Structures

Understanding different kinds of record-structured files and data helps to select the right storage mechanisms when we build databases into the workflow process. You may need to translate the data from TSV to an SQL format. It is helpful to understand why the different formats all exist. They didn't go away just because we started looking at everything through the lens of a web browser or decide to store the entire world in a collection of XML files. They receded into the depths of the system. They are still there, alive and well. Get to know them and you will have a useful set of additional tools to process your content.

For some of you, this might seem to be presenting information at a level too basic to be interesting, or even useful. Even experienced systems engineers have been caught out by a badly placed comma. It pays to go back and review the simple things sometimes, even if you have been doing this kind of work for years.

Fixed-Length Records

The good thing about fixed-length data is that you can traverse through a large collection of records quickly by jumping forward by a fixed byte count for each new record. Locating individual records is easy and fast. The downside is that it can waste memory or disk capacity. That is much less of a worry now, but you should still avoid structures like this on new projects. We will encounter this kind of data when processing legacy databases.

The modern counterpart is a variable-length storage structure with an index to the starting location of each record. First let's remind ourselves of why fixed length storage is such a bad idea (see Figure 8-1).

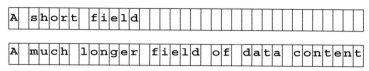

Figure 8-1 Fixed-length field containing variable-length data

Figure 8-2 shows fixed-length fields in a fixed-length record structure.

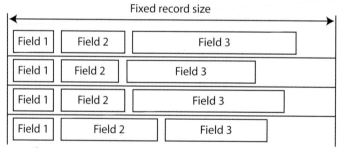

Figure 8-2 Fixed-length fields in fixed-length records

You also can have variable length fields in a fixed length record structure as shown in Figure 8-3.

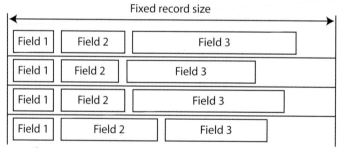

Figure 8-3 Variable-length fields in fixed-length records

The database software will usually find an optimal storage format. You only need to be concerned with issues like this as they relate to your external files.

Variable-Length Records

Variable-length records can reduce the storage requirements significantly but require an index to allow them to be traversed quickly. Scanning a variable-length record structure with millions of records from beginning to end in a linear fashion is an extremely time-wasting process.

SQL Databases

If you have old SQL script files, they will contain some data that you can extract. If you can create a dummy database, you can create a table and run the insertion scripts to reload the data. Likewise, if you have old exported database content, you may be able to reload it into a correctly defined schema. That is, provided you can reverse engineer the original schema or have access to the documentation that describes it.

Once the data is in the database, you can connect to it in other ways, perhaps with a hypertext preprocessor (PHP) or with an application that uses Open Database Compatibility (ODBC). Once you have a connection, the data can be extracted with tools that can access via those APIs. It would be feasible to construct a PHP extractor that could extract the data you loaded from an SQL script and save it into an XML file.

There are many ways to do this, and which is the easiest or fastest depends on the tools you have available. In the past, this would have been a nearly intractable problem that would have taken weeks to solve. Now, you can probably download and install some free software, write some scripts, and leave a process running that will accomplish the task overnight.

Primary Keys

 It is possible to construct a primary key from several components. However, these compound keys, as they are called, are hard to index and slow the performance of a database to a crawl because everything needs to be searched linearly. It is best to keep the keys numeric and unique.

Primary keys are fields (or columns in a table) that are handled specially by the database software. They must be unique within the table in which they are stored and should not be reused. They should be numeric to ensure high performance and are usually indexed for rapid access.

A primary key is the means by which any unique record is located and referred to from elsewhere. It also can be used as the unique ID of an object that is constructed from the row of data in the database.

Foreign Keys

A foreign key is a primary key value from another table stored as a field of data. Foreign keys may be duplicated in the column to satisfy a one-to-many relational join. This key is used to connect the selected record to another record in another table with the join taking place around the foreign-to-primary key connection. SQL queries can then refer to the columns in both tables as if they were a single joined table.

Relationships and Joins

Be careful when re-assimilating old data that might have had relational joins. You may have a database extract with primary keys in some tables and foreign key connections to them from other tables. If you can reload the data without having to restructure the tables, you may be able to use the old schema intact. This might not always be possible if you are importing old data into a new system. You can't reasonably change the names of primary key fields. If you edit the data to name the primary key fields so they are compatible with an existing schema, you then run into problems with auto generating sequences of primary key values or even accidentally generating duplicate keys. This compromises the integrity of your database.

The best approach is to let the system continue to allocate its primary keys as it needs to but have a column with the old primary key value stored in it. You can still use joining mechanisms in the SQL query syntax to join records together, but you use the old keys to make the joins. You can clean this up once the data is loaded without corrupting the database but you may have to edit some query scripts.

If this is a translation exercise, then you may be deleting this data eventually, and it will only be temporarily resident. If the intention is for it to be permanently resident, then the keys can be remapped and the joins made with the correct primary keys.

None of this is impossible or even difficult to do, but it does need to be carefully thought out.

Refer to Tutorial 13 to see how to implement many to many relationships.

Inserting New Data

Building workflows to insert data into the databases can use any of these techniques:

- Buy or build a GUI application and load it manually.
- Control that GUI application with AppleScript or PowerShell.
- Publish an SQL source file and load it through the command line interface.
- Write some PHP code and load the data via a web page driven manually.
- Use different PHP code to load text data from a flat file.
- Use PHP to load data from an XML file.
- Use an XML-to-RDBMS bridge application to load XML into the database.
- Use a spreadsheet application to import, clean, format, and store via an ODBC interface.
- Create a CGI gateway script into which you can upload a text file.
- Write an application that talks to the SQL gateway.
- Write an application that talks HTTP to a PHP-driven gateway.
- Write a command line tool that talks to the SQL gateway.
- Write a command line tool that talks HTTP to a PHP-driven gateway.

You can use any combination of these or other techniques built with C, C++, Perl, Python, or Java. Fundamentally, they all work the same. They read a text format, deduce the record structure, and create database-loading instructions. Wrapping the insertion process in script code lets you bind it into your workflow more easily.

Sorting and Indexing

Databases support indexing via more than one field. You can introduce extra fields to control the collating sequence. Be careful when designing collating sequences, as the following need special handling:

- Celtic clan names beginning with Mc or Mac.
- Foreign spellings.
- International character sets.
- Punctuation.
- Numbers used as part of a name.
- Tagged and marked-up content.

Searching

Searching a database does not always yield the results you expect. If the client misspells the key, you can introduce techniques based on phonetics to work round the problem. Tutorial 14 describes how to create phonetic search keys.

The indexing by different collating sequences is useful for ordering the results into some kind of ranking.

Formatting Control Characters

When you process old legacy data files, the first step is to discern the format within which the data is organized. Sometimes this is not easy; for instance, the data might have been line-wrapped. You need to find a record separator of some sort. Then within that record, a field separator will identify the individual fields.

Electronic files from legacy data systems may use control characters to separate these items. The character codes shown in Table 8-1 are used to delimit ASCII data even though not all of them have been designed specifically for this purpose. These are all taken from genuine examples encountered in a mixed collection of legacy and modern files.

Table 8-1 Common ASCII delimiters

Description	Name	Dec	Hex	Delimits
Horizontal tab	HT	9	09	Fields
Line feed	LF	10	0A	Records
Form feed	FF	12	0C	Incorrectly used for records
Carriage return	CR	13	0D	Records
New line	CR + LF	13, 10	0D 0A	Records
File separator	FS	28	1C	Incorrectly used for fields.
Group separator	GS	29	1D	Incorrectly used for records
Record separator	RS	30	1E	Records
Unit separator	US	31	1F	Fields
Space		32	20	Fields
Exclamation point	!	33	21	Fields
Double quote	"	34	22	String literal (whole field)
Single quote	'	39	27	String literal (whole field)
Round bracket	( )	40/41	28/29	String literal (whole field)
Comma	,	44	2C	Fields
Dash	–	45	2D	Sub-fields
Period	.	46	2E	Sub-fields
Forward slash	/	47	2F	Fields
Semicolon	;	59	3B	Last field in record
Caret	< >	60/62	3C/3E	String literal (whole field)
Square bracket	[ ]	91/93	5B/5D	String literal (whole field)
Backslash	\	92	5C	Fields but also escapes
Brace	{ }	123/125	7B/7D	String literal (whole field)

Some of these delimiters are misused as field separators. The **FS** control-code, does not stand for "field separator" but "file separator."

An XML file imposes a more organized structure, but the concept of records and fields still exists even though it might be expressed as Objects and Properties. These are implemented as outer and inner nested tag structures.

Line breaks are typically used as record separators and commas or tabs are field separators in plain text file storage. Files stored in PDF or RTF file structures can still be decoded, but considerably more work is required to remove the markup and, in the case of a PDF, to reassemble the text into the correct run sequence.

Using a word processor such as Microsoft Word within a script framework might be a simpler way to decode RTF files, although that is by no means the only solution.

PDF files can often be fed into OCR applications, which then parse the imaged text to extract the coherent, and correctly sequenced, data.

Be careful that you inspect the end of a line before blindly importing it into your database. Some trailing punctuation or white space is often present. This needs to be cleaned off. It won't cause the same problems as an embedded extra comma or tab character but it could cause an import routine to reject the record for having too many characters when exporting the data to another system.

Comma-Separated Value (CSV) Files

You will often find Comma-Separated Value (CSV) files listed as a potential import-export file type. It is quite simple; each record is placed on a line by itself with a terminating new line, carriage return, or line feed. Each field is separated from the next by a comma. That's it.

Issues with Commas

Consider what happens if one of your fields has a comma in it when you export. A poorly designed system will write that field out having placed a comma before and after it to separate it from its neighbors. You will not be able to re-import it without paying special attention to that record.

Our four field structure has a spurious comma:

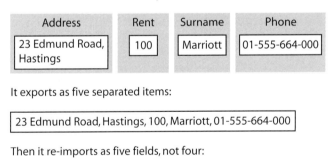

It exports as five separated items:

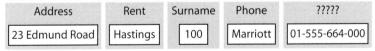

Then it re-imports as five fields, not four:

Figure 8-4 Spurious comma

That line has one more comma in it than is required. Consequently, it has too many fields. That should halt the import. If the import is lazy and imports fields without regard to counting them (which would be OK in a spreadsheet), you will see that all the fields after the offending one will be displaced.

The fix for this problem should be applied either at the export stage or by analyzing and cleaning the data tables before attempting to export or, preferably, at the input stage to avoid the comma being present at all.

We need an escaping mechanism to preserve a comma character at the right place if we do want one but we must do it without using a comma character. The simplest thing is to replace the comma with another character that isn't used anywhere else, but that is a hack rather than a proper solution.

Applying some escape rules such as placing a backslash character in front of the comma might work, but it requires a change to the importing routine as well. We also now need to escape the backslash character, but that's something we expect to do because backslash escapes are probably the most popular way to solve this problem.

A quite neat solution is to use a backslash but also encode the comma character using its numeric character code equivalent. This could be imported back into the database and would then be fine. The hex value is used, because this is normally a two-digit value with leading zeros and does not require further delimiting because it is a fixed length.

Figure 8-5 Escaped comma

This comma-separated problem is not as rare as you would imagine. A developer might not think to check that a user has entered two alternative (work and home) telephone numbers into a web form and submitted it to the server. There is nothing in the route into the database via web servers that would have a problem if the user entered a comma to separate their two phone numbers. Unless you put something there to intercept this, your database was clobbered and you probably won't notice until you need to integrate this system with another one.

Tab-Separated Value (TSV) Files

Tab-Separated Value files are almost the same as CSV files. Replace the comma characters with a **TAB** character instead. Records are still one per line, but fields are separated by a tab character. The benefit here is that a tab is a nonprinting character. It won't usually show up inside the field. We have fewer occasions (almost zero) where we need to place an escape inside the field to deal with embedded field delimiters.

This has its heritage in the ASCII character set that was originally developed for use with teletypewriters. The tab character was one of a special set of characters with values in the range **0** to **31**, reserved for use as control codes. They didn't print anything but caused something to happen in the communications link or at the receiving end. We looked at this in detail in Chapter 6.

Always be aware that someone out there is likely to do something that can break your workflow and if you skimp on the testing and fixing at the input stage, you are running the risk of breaking your workflow later—probably at a critical moment when you are faced with a deadline.

You'll see the ASCII characters mentioned throughout computer literature, and they have weird names based on this very ancient usage. They live on in modern character sets like Unicode because it is too risky to eliminate them and it helps to keep things interoperable. The lower 128 and 256 characters in Unicode (sometimes called UTF-8) are similar to ASCII codes and their derivatives.

From our point of view, these codes could be useful as escapes and delimiters because all the meaningful character codes are numbered 32 and higher. Some UI systems are beginning to sneak occasional character glyphs into those lower 32 characters.

Sometimes tab characters can be problematic, because you don't realize they are there. Your input routines should do some character-level data cleaning before importing the data. You should only have tabs where you really want a field separator. Exactly the same issues can crop up as arise with additional commas, except that in this case the gremlins are harder to see.

Data Entry Systems

Data entry systems have been in existence ever since computers were first deployed as office automation. Time-sharing systems had rooms full of keypunch operators entering data from handwritten forms with numeric keypads.

The data is entered into a forms-based interface that supports some useful capabilities. The data entry form is defined as a series of individual fields. Certain checks are applied at the field level, while others take place across the whole record.

Field content is determined by an input format that describes the length and legal range of permitted characters. On leaving each field and going to the next, a checking script is run that tests the field for validity. Different scripts can be applied to each field. Invalid data is rejected and the correct information must be re-keyed.

At the end of the record, another script is executed to crosscheck all the fields, perform some arithmetic, and ensure that the record structure is correct.

This combination of input formats, field-end checks, and record-end checks makes these traditional data entry systems extremely robust. Data errors did occur, but they were rarely the fault of an operator.

This level of input checking is almost never implemented on forms input. Occasionally a piece of JavaScript will check that all the mandatory fields have been completed. Occasionally, you will see a ZIP or postal code checked.

We can significantly improve the quality of our content if we implement the kind of rigor that the data entry systems of the 1970s used every day. Build this into your data ingest applications:

- Strict formatting of input fields.
- Field-end edit scripts.
- Strict mandates on the presence of fields in records.
- Record-end edit scripts.
- The use of normalization by-products to look things up.

Spreadsheet Integration

Spreadsheets are a two-dimensional grid of data cells, organized loosely into rows and columns somewhat like a database table structure. They aren't databases and while we can apply formats to columns, we could change those formats on a cell-by-cell basis, which would completely, break the database integrity.

Knowing that there is a correlation between a 2D cell structure and a database might offer us some ways to exchange the data between a spreadsheet and another application by saving the data into SQL tables and then accessing it via another means. This deals with the situation that arises when two communicating applications do not share any common data formats. Provided both can be made to access an SQL database, there might be a route for transferring the data.

Summary

It is unlikely you will invent anything new in the area of data entry, but don't reject techniques used by older systems just because they've been around for 30-odd years. They lasted that long because they had something to offer and worked. Robust data entry techniques and XML are not mutually exclusive. They work well together.

We have reached an important stage. Our data and object models are done, and we understand more about data structures, code sets, and how the physical storage of data can affect the quality of our content workflow systems.

Now we can look at some more complex data types. The next chapter begins that part of the workflow development by looking at date and time values.

Times, Dates, Schedules, and Calendars

Matter of Time

Time is not as straightforward to deal with as you might think, especially in broadcast systems. In this chapter, we will look at some time-related problems and discuss some potential solutions. You can find some sample solutions in Part 2 of this book in the tutorials.

Times and Dates

We often use dates and times separately. Computer systems find it most convenient to maintain a single time value that is measured from a reference date and time. The counter increments its value in milliseconds. By rounding the value to whichever unit we want to use and adding that to the reference value we can compute any date or time within the working range.

Dealing with Dates

Let's consider first how we deal with date values. They are formatted differently to time values and have some special considerations.

Date String Parsing

When dates are written out as a text string, a format is defined to set out how many characters the various parts of the date require and where they are positioned with respect to each other. If you know what that formatting string was, then using it to extract the fields is quite easy.

 Thankfully, the complexities of working with time and date values are well provided for in the library support. If you have a C compiler, the standard library supports many time-based routines to break down the system time into components.

Parsing dates is best explained as the reverse of using a date formatter, but you can still encounter problems. If the person creating the unstructured data used a nonstandard formatter and you don't know what that formatting configuration string was, you'll need to figure it out.

The process of parsing arbitrarily formatted date strings is a bit harder and involves a series of thoughtfully designed and structured checks to identify and extract the date components:

- Convert to a useable code set.
- Break into tokens using delimiters such as commas, dashes, slashes and spaces.
- Inspect the tokens looking for obvious values such as day of week or four digit year number and month names.
- Look at the remaining tokens considering where they appeared to deduce what they represent.
- Once all tokens have been identified, generate the UTC time value.

Provided all the dates are formatted the same, this is fine. Automatically recognizing the date layout and parsing it using an appropriate formatter adds a level of complexity that is often solved by introducing a human being into the loop.

If you consider all the possibilities, then there is a reasonably well-bounded set. You can apply some tokenization and deal with parts of the problem separately. Identifying both days and months by name, instead of using numeric values for months, might help to disambiguate the date string. Careful placement of punctuation and time zone values will also help reduce ambiguity.

Leading zeros and two- and four-digit numbers help to identify day, month, and year locations. Determining which of two values is the day and month might be difficult but combining this with the day name may allow a back conversion to compare two candidate dates to see which is the correct one. Date values will probably be separated by dash or slash characters. In most cases, time values will be separated by colons.

The parser algorithm might become somewhat sophisticated but not beyond most developer's capability. After all, you only need to write this parser once in order to deploy it in many different implementations. Getting this parsing logic right is definitely worth some effort. It is better to stick to some formatting rules in the first place, and international standards-based approaches are well-worth considering.

Relative Dates

We frequently need to calculate relative time and date values. By maintaining a single time quantity that includes the date values, you can perform useful arithmetic operations on the value. There are several obvious candidates:

- Yesterday.
- Today.
- Tomorrow.
- Next week.
- Next month.
- Next year.
- Last month.

Relative dates are used frequently when analyzing web site statistics. Any kind of metrics reporting is based on the recent past, and designing scripts that refer loosely to a recent day calls for representing specific dates with a symbolic name.

To solve this in a UNIX shell-scripting environment is very hard. The solution is to create a compiled application that is deployed as command line executable that calculates these relative dates for you. Then your scripts can refer to symbolic dates.

Schedule production for EPG and broadcast systems needs to look forwards in time and compliance systems need to look backwards but the same relative references are still useful.

Tutorial 35 shows how to write a small C language component that is used as a command line extension to compute relative dates. This works well in UNIX and could be implemented on Windows if PowerShell does not already provide sufficient relative date handling.

Special Dates

Several times a year, we have special dates. These upset our regular scheduling due to daylight savings time. Holidays and seasonal events would all call for special schedules.

Suppose we needed to know whether next Christmas Eve was a weekday, given that our script doesn't want to compute relative dates but needs the date for the previous Friday. How could we do that?

This problem crops up when building web statistics analyzers or building long-term broadcasting schedules. It shows up in project management metadata and asset management systems too, especially when trying to control release and embargo dates.

Doomsday Scenarios

Y2K wasn't the only date to give us severe headaches. Watch out for other key dates that might cause your systems some problems. We all worried about Y2K because of the ambiguity regarding the century number. These other possibilities are far more subtle and insidious.

Whenever a programmer uses the value 99 to mean a test or sample value or defines a date so far in the future that it won't affect things now—look out! When the future eventually arrives, as it inevitably will, that system will suddenly develop strange faults that no one anticipated.

Consider what might happen for the following example dates:

Table 9-1 Doomsday scenarios

Date	Problem
December 31, 2009	At midnight, New Year's Eve, 2009, the year number goes from 9 to 10. If you don't already use leading zeros or include the century, the year number will then add one extra character to all subsequent dates. That won't be a problem necessarily until both the day and month number both go to two digits each.
October 10, 2010	This is another critical date because all dates for the rest of that year will require more space than any date before that if you represent dates in character strings. Someone might have made an arbitrary decision to limit the length of a date field to only nine characters. If you include dashes, dates will suddenly require 10 characters. Truncation is going to happen somewhere. It might be the leading digit of the year number or the trailing digit of the day number. Wherever it is, you don't want it to happen.
January 1, 2028	7-bit binary year number values will have a problem. Because the value is added to 1900, the wrap around happens when the year number reaches the end of year 127 (**0x7F**). An 8-bit year value staves this off until the end of 255 years after 1900, when **0xFF** becomes zero. The problem could show up in the year 2156 as well.
February 7, 2036 06:28:16 UTC	The Internet clock described in RFC 1305 wraps to zero. UTC is a 32-bit unsigned integer number of seconds since Midnight, January 1, 1900.
January 19, 2038 03:14:08 UTC	The UNIX clock wraps to zero. This value is a 32-bit signed integer number of seconds since midnight, January 1, 1970. Extending the integer size to 64 bits cures the problem but introduces others where a 2-byte value needs to be replaced by a 4-byte value.
September 17, 2042 23:53:47 UTC	The present IBM Mainframe clock implementation wraps to zero. It is likely to be fixed in time since we have a few years warning.

Problematic Historical Dates

The following historical dates all had problems or are important for other reasons:

Table 9-2 Historical anomalies

Date	Problem
January 1, 1900	Day zero for the UTC system. If your assets are marked with this date, one of your systems has a bad clock setting.
January 1, 1904	Day zero on Mac OS Classic systems. Another bad clock setting indicator.
January 1, 1970	Day zero on UNIX systems. Test this as well for systems requiring clock settings.
January 4, 1980	Day 0 for the DOS operating system. The clocks on Windows personal computers will reset to this if they lose their proper setting. It is not a likely date for an asset to have.
December 31, any year	Often used to mean "forever." The next day, on January 1, some things that are supposed to be retained forever might expire and be deleted.
July 1, 1999	The first day of fiscal year 2000 in the U.S. for a great many companies and governmental bodies.
April 6, 1999	The first day of financial year 2000 in the UK for a most companies and governmental bodies.
September 9, 1999	The date (9/9/99); another "99 Problem" date that is often used to test systems.
December 31, 1999	Millennium bug eve. Previously used to indicate a date infinitely in the future, this looked reasonable from a 1970 standpoint. Now it looks rather shortsighted. Not a likely modification date for an asset. People would have been partying and not editing media.
January 1, 2000	Millennium bug day. The two-digit year rolls over to "00".
February 29, 2000	The year 2000 is a leap year, a once-in-400-years occurrence. Leap years are every four years except for centuries, except for millennia, except for this millennia.
March 1, 2000	Check carefully that this is day number 60 within the year. All your programs and systems should indicate that it is Wednesday. Any system that lists March 1, 2000 as a Tuesday needs to be fixed.
December 31, 2000	This was the 366th day of the year 2000. Defective systems might flag this day as an error if leap year calculations are broken.

Table 9-2 Historical anomalies (continued)

January 2, 2001	This is the first day since 1932 on which you will be unable to deduce which element of a date is the year. During 2000, the year can always be identified as being "00". Month and day dates cannot be zero. January 1st, 2001 is unambiguous. On January 2nd, 2001, the date could be misinterpreted as February 1st. Use four-digit years! The opposite misinterpretation happens on February 1st, 2001.
September 9, 2001, 01:46:40 UTC	On some systems, the number of seconds since the UTC started requires 10 decimal digits after this time. UTC values printed out, as a numeric count of milliseconds will overflow a 9-character buffer.

Calendars

With the advent of groupware and more GUI-based applications, calendar exchange formats have become standardized. This is a second level of standardization over and above the time and date library calls that we can use inside our applications.

vCalendars

The vCalendar format is fast becoming one of the standard ways to exchange dates. If everyone agrees on a common interchange format, it doesn't matter what they do inside their application. Any fix of the values to comply with an internal format become part of the closed-box solution.

Look for these common interchange formats when you select software applications. I would certainly consider vCalendar objects as a useful way to move date and time information around a system.

By using the vCalendar (**.vcs** file) format, you can attach objects to mail messages and integrate them with your office systems. This might be quite useful when building applications that need to mesh with production admin departments.

Here is a version 1.0 vCalendar file:

```
BEGIN:VCALENDAR
VERSION:1.0
BEGIN:VEVENT
CATEGORIES:MEETING
STATUS:TENTATIVE
DTSTART:19960401T033000Z
DTEND:19960401T043000Z
SUMMARY:Annual Salary Raise
DESCRIPTION:Time to go and beg your boss for that raise.
CLASS:PRIVATE
END:VEVENT
END:VCALENDAR
```

iCalendar

The vCalendar design is an older standard exchange format for calendar data sponsored by the Internet Mail Consortium (IMC). The iCalendar format is a newer standard for calendar data and is described by RFC 2445. It is based on vCalendar and preserves the signature heading to maintain backwards compatibility.

Like the vCalendar format, this is a name-value pair file and unusually for an emerging standard isn't stored as XML. There is another variant called the *hCalendar* format, which provides a semantic XHTML version if you need it.

```
BEGIN:VCALENDAR
PRODID:-//Ximian//NONSGML Evolution Calendar//EN
VERSION:2.0
METHOD:PUBLISH
BEGIN:VTIMEZONE
TZID:/calendar.org/Europe/Helsinki
X-LIC-LOCATION:Europe/Helsinki
BEGIN:DAYLIGHT
TZOFFSETFROM:+0200
TZOFFSETTO:+0300
TZNAME:EEST
DTSTART:19700329T030000
RRULE:FREQ=YEARLY;INTERVAL=1;BYDAY=-1SU;BYMONTH=3
END:DAYLIGHT
BEGIN:STANDARD
TZOFFSETFROM:+0300
TZOFFSETTO:+0200
TZNAME:EET
DTSTART:19701025T040000
RRULE:FREQ=YEARLY;INTERVAL=1;BYDAY=-1SU;BYMONTH=10
END:STANDARD
END:VTIMEZONE
BEGIN:VEVENT
UID:20030821T212557Z-2393-500-1-2@somehost.example.com
DTSTAMP:20030821T212557Z
DTSTART;TZID=/ calendar.org/Europe/Helsinki: 20030818T100000
DTEND;TZID=/calendar.org/Europe/Helsinki: 20030818T113000
SUMMARY:foo
SEQUENCE:1
LAST-MODIFIED:20030821T212558Z
END:VEVENT
END:VCALENDAR
```

Because these are plain text files, they are easy to template and create with our content management systems. If we can reduce everything to a textual format of some kind, then it is easy to publish with existing web HTML and XML publishing technologies. That textual format might be a low level description like a vCalendar or it could be a high-level description, such as in a business graphics application that needs to be processed through a render server.

---

hCalendar: http://microformats.org/wiki/hcalendar

Sharing Calendars

The vCalendar and iCalendar standards are useful for exchanging time and date event information between systems. They are portable and cross-platform. The last piece of the puzzle is a calendar server where the calendars can be stored and synchronized.

The Darwin Calendar Server is a standards-compliant server that allows multiple users to collaboratively share calendaring information. It provides a shared location on the network to store schedules, and allows users to send calendars to each other and manage invitations.

In order to provide interoperability among multiple calendaring clients, the server implements the CalDAV protocol, which is an extension of WebDAV, which is in turn an extension of HTTP.

This used to be a proprietary solution but now Apple has released the source code to its calendar server implementation under an Apache 2.0 License.

Managing Time

Time values are sourced from the same UTC value as a date. We use time values quite differently though.

UTC

Coordinated Universal Time (UTC) is the new name for what we used to call Greenwich Mean Time (GMT). The name change avoids the confusion that arises when daylight savings time is in force at the Greenwich Meridian.

Resolution and Granularity

Time measurement is usually available to within a millisecond's accuracy within a computer system. This is certainly the case with JavaScript event scheduling within a web browser.

Portability Issues

There is a potential problem with storing binary time values. They can't be transported with any guarantee that the receiving system stores its time in the same format. It is recommended that time values are encoded into a textual format and then converted back again if you need a binary value at the receiving end.

Darwin Calendar server: http://trac.macosforge.org/projects/collaboration

Time Zones

If you work across international boundaries, then your systems will need to take account of time zones.

Most of the world is synchronized to the same minute settings and offset by an integer number of hours. There are some exceptions. India is offset by an additional 30 minutes (UTC + either 5:30 or 6:30), which means the minute values are wrong if you only add in an integer number of hours. Chatham Island, off the northern tip of New Zealand is adjusted to UTC+12:45.

Many different time zone maps are available online. Refer to the list of URLs for details or search Google and Wikipedia for "time zones."

Time zones appear to be allocated for purely political reasons. Geography seems to have little to do with it. India spans two physical time zones but has only one time zone value. China spans five physical time zones but has one unified time setting. This must be incredibly inconvenient for some people in China who are living 5 hours displaced from people at the other end of the country. The former USSR spans an even larger distance but has divided its population into areas that share one of eleven time zones.

Daylight Saving Time

Our efforts are complicated by having to include daylight saving time (DST), which is not always changed on the same date in different geographical regions. You need to know when those clocks go forward or back, and by how much. In most situations, an hour's difference is sufficient.

Changes due to DST are quite tricky to manage. The millisecond-accurate clock in the computer continues unabated and nothing disturbs its cadence. It just ticks those milliseconds away. It doesn't care what day it is or how you want to interpret the time. Daylight saving time is, after all, just a formatted version of the time.

You could work in a nonadjusted time frame. You would have to continuously add or subtract an hour as dictated by DST.

World clock: http://www.timeanddate.com/worldclock/
Time and date information: http://www.timeanddate.com/
World time zones: http://www.worldtimezone.com/
Time zones FAQ: http://www.worldtimezone.com/faq.html
Search Wikipedia for: "Time zone"

Twelve Hours or Twenty-Four?

From a computational point of view, the 24-hour system is easier to use than the 12-hour model. Although the a.m./p.m. suffix makes things clear, there could be some ambiguity if that is truncated accidentally. The 24-hour system is the most commonly used time notation worldwide although many people in the U.S. still use the 12-hour system.

The 24-hour notation is sometimes referred to as military time, and was referred to in the UK as continental time. In the U.S., 24-hour military time is presented without a colon. The 24-hour representation of 6 p.m. is '1800' instead of '18:00'.

The 24-hour system is standardized with ISO 8601.

Date and Time Arithmetic

When date and time values are stored in a binary form, usually in milliseconds, the numeric value is sometimes represented with date values in the integer and time values in the fractional part of a floating-point number.

If you use date and time values in Excel, note that Microsoft made a smart decision to put time values to the right of the decimal place and date values on the left. This is extremely useful when using time values in calculations.

Where the time is stored as an integer number of milliseconds, time values can be extracted using a modulo calculation or an `int()` function that eliminates the day offset value to leave the time of day as a remainder. Dividing by the length of a day in milliseconds yields day numbers, which can then be manipulated into a calendar date. You need to take care that you don't round down when you should round up or you will get an "off-by-one" error (actually that example would be an "off-by-two" error).

Usually the operating system or development library will provide all the time manipulation functions you need but occasionally you have to do it the hard way.

Standardizing Date and Time Formats

It seems that every country in the world has its own preferred date-formatting method. The most ambiguous combination is using UK and U.S. date formats in systems that need to exchange data. Because **DD-MM-YYYY** and **MM-DD-YYYY** look identical for a significant number of dates, you often have to think quite hard when you see a date and look at its context to work out which is which.

This is another situation where the best solution is to store a date/time value as a numeric count of milliseconds and use a date formatter only when it needs to be displayed in a human-readable context. Then the date formatter can be selected according to locale and user preferences, eliminating ambiguity. If you do need to display a date string, then a standardized format should be used.

ISO Standard 8601

The best general-purpose format to use for dates is ISO 8601. It is ideal for representing Gregorian calendar dates and times in the 24-hour system. The ISO 8601 standard includes these features:

- Calendar dates comprising year, month and day of the month.
- Ordinal dates comprising year and day of the year.
- Week dates comprising year, week number, and day of the week.
- Local 24-hour time of day values.
- Coordinated UTC.
- Time of day.
- Local time with offset to UTC.
- Combination of date and time of day.
- Time intervals.
- Recurring time intervals.
- Alternative formats.

When organizing documents in a file system, suffixing log file names with an appropriate date format has the benefit of sorting things chronologically when the files are listed in alphabetical order. However, for this to work, the date components must be organized so that they are in YMD order.

ISO 8601 Date Formats

The ISO organization standardized a useful date format in 1988 as being the most portable and least ambiguous way to represent dates as a string of numeric digits like this:

```
YYYY-MM-DD
```

The four-digit year value (**YYYY**) is assumed to be in the Gregorian calendar and the months (**MM**) and days (**DD**) are expressed as two-digit values.

An alternative format using the week and day number can be expressed as:

```
YYYY-Www-D
```

The year is again Gregorian, and the two-digit week number is prefaced with a letter **W**. The day of week can be expressed with a single digit. Monday is one and Sunday is seven.

ISO 8601 Time Values

ISO 8601 represents time with the 24-hour system like this:

```
hh:mm:ss
```

Date and time can be combined with a letter **T** as a delimiter for the time value:

```
YYYY-MM-DDThh:mm:ss
```

Less significant component parts of the date can be omitted to reduce the precision. The seconds count may not be necessary. Alternatively, a decimal fraction can be added to increase accuracy. ISO 8601 has these advantages:

- It is easily read and written.
- Multiple values can be directly compared with one another.
- Collation for sorting is straightforward.
- It works independently of the language being used.
- Units that are more significant are written to the left of smaller units.
- The notation is usually short.
- The notation has constant length.

Refer to Tutorial 34 for examples of how to output ISO 8601 date and time values.

The ISO 8601 standard recommends all-numeric date values and is isolated from locale problems where the names of days and months need to be translated. The standard leaves that up to the application or context in which it is being applied. Note that the standard expressly forbids any change to the ordering of day and month values. That eliminates the major source of ambiguity when scanning dates.

W3C-Standardized Dates and Times

The W3C organization has developed a profile of the ISO 8601 standard for date and time values. It reduces the number of formats supported to a much smaller set of alternatives in the interest of avoiding complexity and confusion. The ISO standard optionally allows the century to be omitted. The W3C organization thinks this might cause problems and disallows it.

These sub-sets of the ISO formats are recommended by W3C:

- Year.
- Year and month.
- Complete date.
- Complete date plus hours and minutes.
- Complete date plus hours, minutes, and seconds.
- Complete date plus hours, minutes, seconds, and a decimal fraction of a second.

Because the world is divided into roughly 24 different time zones, each zone is assigned a different letter. Greenwich Mean Time (GMT) is assigned with a special UTC designator ("**z**" for Zulu time). GMT is most often used as the basis for time values that involve crossing different time zones. Z indicates a zero time zone offset and is referred to using its phonetic name. GMT can advance or retard by up a second with respect to UTC.

 The UTC and GMT reference times are measured differently. GMT is based on the Earth's celestial position. UTC is calculated from a very accurate atomic clock. The UTC time occasionally has leap seconds added to adjust it back into synchronization (more or less) with GMT.

Alternatively, times are expressed in local time, together with a time zone offset in hours and minutes. A time zone offset of "**+hh:mm**" indicates that the date/time uses a local time zone, which is "**hh**" hours and "**mm**" minutes ahead of UTC. A time zone offset of "**–hh:mm**" indicates that the date/time uses a local time zone, which is "**hh**" hours and "**mm**" minutes behind UTC.

Both of these example dates represent November 5, 1994, 8:15:30 a.m., U.S. Eastern Standard Time:

```
1994-11-05T08:15:30-05:00
1994-11-05T13:15:30Z
```

Broadcasting Schedules

In many TV companies, broadcasting schedules are still constructed using 12-hour models. This might be how they are viewed by the audience, but internally the best practice is to maintain a 24-hour model or use a UTC value with an appropriate formatter for the output.

Milliseconds or Frames?

For television work, you could argue that the smallest time division should be measured in frames rather than seconds. This is fine within a single facility or even one national network, but it's no good if you are taking live video feeds from abroad and having to convert the time base from 29.97 to 25 fps.

Day and Date Issues

Note also that some data being broadcast may use different calendar schemes. The Program Delivery Control (PDC) codes used in the UK are based on a Modified Julian calendar and encode the date as a count of days since the reference date 16 November 1858. Time zone offsets are also only accurate to half-hour increments. The equivalent concept in the digital TV environment would be a trigger but we have a variety of different opportunities to synchronize digital triggers. We might want to synchronize to a transport stream, an element stream or the start of a program as it is broadcast.

The time formats for Teletext data are supposed to conform to UTC, but not all broadcasters do this correctly. Usually the problems are in the time zone and daylight saving time corrections.

Time Synchronization

If we are storing metadata, then we should synchronize the metadata item to within a frame number. Bear in mind that if you convert the footage from PAL to NTSC, the metadata needs to have its time code corrected, unless you are satisfied with metadata that is now only accurate to within a second. There are fewer frames (only 25) in PAL so your time code won't overflow. It might overflow if you convert in the other direction. The PAL system doesn't have any concept of frame numbers 26 to 30. It is possible that metadata will be discarded or associated with the wrong frame.

There are two simple ways to fix this:

1. Take the frame number and apply a multiple to it to map the frame numbering from 25 fps to 29.97 fps or vice versa.
2. Convert the time code to a millisecond-accurate value and then convert it back.

It might be worth engineering your system so that the metadata can be stored to a millisecond-accurate value. Then, use a time formatter to display a time code with the correct fps count.

If you are in the business of developing a media asset management system, you want to do the least amount of data correction and deliver a system that is as generic as possible.

Time Windows

Time windows have a beginning and end time (and possibly date). You need to be especially careful with time windows that last a whole day or more than a day because the time will wrap around from one day to the next. It is easy to get confused, especially if you have some "helpful" logic that allows users to select two times arbitrarily and orders them so that the earliest is first. Time windows that span midnight are extremely inconvenient if you don't consider the date too.

If you are designing software to drive a personal video recorder, you might want to ensure that any schedule slippage is taken care of by making the time window a little bigger. Allowing the time window to open one minute early and close 5 minutes late is probably sufficient. Sometimes, broadcast schedules will slip by 15 minutes or more in the small hours of the morning or if an important program has overrun earlier in the day.

The ideal solution is to use a trigger to start the recording. Even though this is technically possible, many broadcasters cannot be bothered to spend a few hundreds of dollars on the insertion hardware.

Dealing with Broadcasting Schedules

TV and radio schedules follow somewhat rigid patterns. They have minor variations to these patterns, but you might be able to simplify the user interface you present to your users and give them less work to do, if you can manage these regularly occurring events.

A season might last 13 or 26 weeks. There's a major cyclic pattern going on there.

Programs tend to be organized around a 7-day cycle, with weekdays being similar and weekends being somewhat different. Indeed, Saturday and Sunday may not be the same as weekdays—or each other—at all. Within our weekday schedule, we might repeat almost the same pattern of programs 5 times over.

Some programs could span midnight. Their start time is later than their end time, unless you consider the date value too. Be careful when creating the repeating pattern, as you need to remove the date part. This also causes issues because the program should appear in searches for either of the two days. Daylight Savings time makes it all horribly confusing for a couple of days that might be 23 or 25 hours long.

If you find yourself implementing something nasty, such as splitting a program that spans midnight into two parts so that the end time falls within the same day as the start time, beware! That is an unsatisfactory approach and it is going to lead to problems later.

Instead, make sure that you build your repeating cycle in a symbolic fashion and lay it down onto an absolute time foundation. Events are correctly placed into the time continuum and programs stay in one piece. It probably only requires a few small compensatory calculations and a few auxiliary objects.

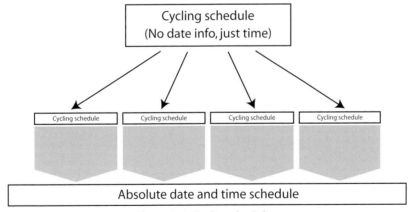

Figure 9-1 Cyclic scheduling

Merging Simultaneous Schedules

You may need to consider merging simultaneous schedules when developing electronic program guide (EPG) solutions. Merging schedules together to aggregate dates and times from several sources can be quite challenging. Take a TV or radio network that has a national service with regional opt-outs. You would want to start with the national schedule and add in the regional items to produce EPG or control information for the individual regions to use.

When working in a radio broadcaster's schedule administration office, I needed to build an application to manage the schedule for a day's worth of broadcasting. The editors in the regions needed to see their part of the entire broadcast in context. They wanted to edit their schedule for the opt-out times but they needed to share some data with other regions for the rest of the schedule.

I provided the users with a view that showed an entire day's schedule. This would be how their listeners would perceive the station's output for the day. Only those sections that they owned were editable (from their point of view) and marked as such to distinguish them from the parts they couldn't alter.

This turned out to be quite easy to build, once the object model was organized sensibly (see Figure 9-2).

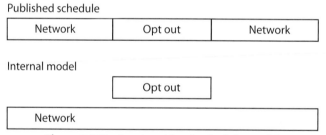

Figure 9-2 Regional and local schedule model

The underlying network schedule was used to construct a base schedule. Then the regional changes were applied to a copy to make a complete regional schedule. Because each program in the schedule is represented by an object, the ownership and hence editability can be detected and controlled at the individual program level.

On the BBC early evening news, this opt-in and opt-out happens at the scene level within a program. In fact, the continuity announcement before the broadcast is also a regional opt-out. This all works smoothly and has been happening regularly every evening for years. All of the presenters in the different regions are speaking to their own cameras simultaneously and all of them finish at precisely the right moment for their local services to switch back to the national news.

When merging schedule data together, you need to be aware of the overlap. If you only look at the beginning and end times, you might easily miss a clash.

Overlapping Time Frames

Coping properly with overlapping time frames requires special care and attention. Consider the schedule shown in Figure 9-3:

Figure 9-3 Overlapping programs

Note that there are two programs of the same genre on different channels.

Our single-tuner PVR is not going to record them without truncating one or the other. It will need to do a channel switch, which is why triggering is so important. Knowing that a program has finished allows us to switch channels to grab the other one as soon as we know the tuner is free. A fallback scenario would be to record as much of both programs as possible. The simple PVR devices decide not to record one or other of the programs, even though schedule slippage might allow both to be accessed.

Now consider the possibility shown in Figure 9-4:

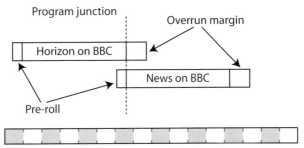

Figure 9-4 Overlapping programs on the same channel

This is an interesting scenario, because it illustrates another significant flaw in PVR programming. These programs overlap because of the one-minute extension at the start and the five-minute extension at the end to cope with overruns. One would be rejected by the UI design. The overlap does not consider the channel value. Because it is the same channel for both programs, they cannot possibly overlap. We could record the two as a segue. That is obvious to us as human beings, but computers with their deterministic intelligence won't make these decisions unless we build in some more "smarts".

If you think this won't affect you in media asset management implementations, think again. If you take incoming feeds and need to manage them within limited ingest server resources, exactly the same thing can happen even if you have a large routing matrix to switch things to alternative destinations. Although the problem looks different, the same resource-allocation scenario occurs.

PVR and EPG Related Problems

It has certainly been the case that some EPG and PVR data has not met the level of quality we would expect. Several notable examples have cropped up on screen. Table 9-3 lists the most egregious and all of them were probably caused by human error:

Table 9-3 PVR madness	
Error	*Description*
Classification	John Simpson is one of our most revered and senior foreign correspondents in the UK. He works most of his time embedded with troops in war zones and mainly presents very serious newsworthy programs.
	His program "Simpson's World" is not a comedy, nor does it feature Bart and Homer.
	Oops. My PVR listed it as related to the Simpsons cartoon series.
Start time	If you want viewers to record a program on a PVR or any other device, it is a good idea to broadcast it on time. Broadcasting a minute or two late is something we can cope with. Broadcasting 5 minutes early is not a good idea.
	Triggers would be better. PDC works sometimes on analogue. It is a little more tricky to do on DTV but technically possible.
Finish time	We need to be much smarter with the design of our systems in case programs overrun. A daily update into a PVR may not be optimal. A soccer match that overruns with extra time tends to push out the rest of the evening's viewing by 10 to 15 minutes.
	Triggers would help this too.
Overlaps	Overlapping programs need to be handled more gracefully. Especially when they are on the same channel.
Control	In the UK, a well-known PVR service once recorded a program autonomously. It was a complete disaster. This wasn't your usual automatic recording of programs that you might like, based on your usual diet. The program was scheduled for record by force-majeur and could not be deactivated, or deleted afterwards.
	It was the first program of a new comedy series broadcast for adults late at night. It was placed on the front page where young children could access it without any parental control. Unfortunately, the program didn't even air in the right slot and was truncated, losing the last 5 minutes.
	The viewing figures for that series tanked. It was a complete washout and a very interesting lesson in what people most emphatically didn't want to see happen with their PVR. Some correspondents were outraged and very few if any at all were pleased. Viewers remember things like that for a long time.

Recommendations

Almost every problem associated with date and time handling can be easily solved if we make good strategic decisions at the outset of our systems design.

The conclusion I came to while writing this chapter was that for all systems I design in the future, I'm going to rigidly apply Model View Controller principles to time values when possible. These principles would be defined as a starting point and modified only when necessary for functional reasons.

- My model is going to always store physical time values to millisecond accuracy instead of frames.
- My controller is going to map those time values and impose any necessary granularity for fps if required.
- My view will be according to the fps and the locale of the operating system.
- I will use 64-bit time values to avoid rollover and truncation.
- I will employ ISO 8601 standard-compliant output date formats, probably based on a W3C profile.
- Event data will be exported using iCalendar-formatted data files.

That way, all my dates and times will be stored internally to exactly the same format regardless of where the system is being operated.

Summary

Broadcasting systems could not function without accurate and complex time management systems. Dates and times show up throughout the entire life cycle of assets and metadata that controls them. Workflows rely on date and time calculations to ensure things arrive in a timely manner.

If you can standardize your time-management software and construct libraries of shared code that you can invoke in all your workflow tools, you will have fewer time-related problems in your metadata workflow.

Time and date values offer a fascinating topic to study. There is plenty of room for experimentation and further exploration. The resources are not hard to find, and a web search yields some useful starting points.

Now that we know about times, dates, schedules, and calendars, the next chapter will examine how we represent people and contact information. That information is often used with date and time software to arrange meetings, appointments, asset delivery deadlines and project management. These are all things that you might want to factor into a workflow.

Names, Addresses, and Contacts

People, Places, and Things

Quite a few years ago, IBM and Apple were working together with Motorola to develop the PowerPC chip. IBM and Apple also had two interesting software collaborations running at the same time. Kaleida Labs was developing some interactive multimedia players (ScriptX) while Taligent concentrated on object oriented operating systems design. Ultimately both companies were absorbed back into their parent companies or disappeared into obscurity but parts of their work live on in modern systems.

Taligent proposed an important concept called "People, Places and Things." Every object being used to construct your business logic was classified as one of these three types. It is an interesting abstraction, because it helps us understand and organize objects and content in a semantic way. This is better than the purely functional approach that had been used previously. We might argue that "things" is a too generic category and might need to be further broken down in more types, such as "times," "dates," etc.

Planning a new system by organizing the content in this way helps us factor the system design and group similar processes and code together. Then we achieve better reuse and sharing of resources and a system that is much simpler and more reliable.

The concept is similar to using normalization on a relational database. It is operated here at the semantic level instead of describing joins between data items. It facilitates a thoughtful approach to designing workflows and content systems.

Using the people, places, and things concept, this chapter deals with data related to *people*. There are some elements of place involved, because people have addresses, but the relationship is natural and the address-related information could be managed under the places heading.

vCards

The vCard is a file-format standard for exchanging personal data. They are an electronic business card; you will most often see vCards attached to e-mail messages. A vCard can be placed into a web page ready for customers to download. Online contact manager systems such as LinkedIn use them extensively. vCards are convenient containers and are supported so widely that they are a useful interchange mechanism.

The Versiticard idea was originally proposed in 1995 by the Versit Consortium. This was a collaborative project between several companies, including Apple Computer, AT&T (AKA Lucent), IBM, and Siemens. In due course, the administration of the standard was taken over by the Internet Mail Consortium (IMC).

The vCard standard is similar to the vCalendar/iCalendar standards that are also administered by IMC and referred to in Chapter 9. vCard standard version 2.1 is already widely supported. An update to version 3.0 is described in RFCs 2425 and 2426. The usual file name extension is `.vcf`.

An XHTML version of vCard is also being developed and is referred to as *hCard*. It is already being popularized by the Flickr and Yahoo! websites. If you need to convert between the two formats, check out X2V. There are some useful links at the Microformats web site. In addition, an XML vCard format has been developed by the Jabber Software Foundation and W3C has another. The W3C standard is entitled "Representing vCard Objects in RDF/XML." You could use XSLT to convert XML formatted vCards to other formats.

Here is an example of a version 2.1 vCard.

```
BEGIN:VCARD
VERSION:2.1
FN:Firstname Lastname
N:Lastname;Firstname
ADR;WORK;PREF;QUOTED-PRINTABLE:;Mytown 12345=0AMyCounty;My Street 99
LABEL;QUOTED-PRINTABLE;WORK;PREF:My Street 99=0AMytown 12345=0AMyCounty
TEL;CELL:+555-10-333456
EMAIL;INTERNET:me@ mycompany.ltd.uk
UID:
END:VCARD
```

This is a version 3.0 vCard extracted directly from the Mac OS X address book application.

```
BEGIN:VCARD
VERSION:3.0
N:Lastname;Firstname;;;
FN:Firstname Lastname
ORG:My Company Ltd;
TITLE:Technical Systems Architect
EMAIL;type=INTERNET;type=WORK;type=pref:me@mycompany.ltd.uk
item1.EMAIL;type=INTERNET:me2@myco.demon.co.uk
item1.X-ABLabel:_$!<Other>!$_
item2.EMAIL;type=INTERNET:firstname.lastname@mac.com
item2.X-ABLabel:_$!<Other>!$_
item3.EMAIL;type=INTERNET:me3@mycompany.ltd.uk
item3.X-ABLabel:_$!<Other>!$_
TEL;type=WORK;type=pref:555-413-998
TEL;type=CELL:555-413-938
TEL;type=HOME: 555-423-998
item4.ADR;type=HOME;type=pref:;;6 My Street;Mytown;Sussex;TN2 4TU;United Kingdom
item4.X-ABADR:us
NOTE:[Birthday] Jan 19\nLastname'\n'Firstname
PHOTO;BASE64:
  TU0AKgAAGwj...
Large block of base 64 picture data deleted
...Q29tcHV0ZXIsIELuYy4sIDIwMDUAAAAA
CATEGORIES:Band - B-Band, zPalmM515, Family
X-ABUID:91FB0E2E-36C6-11DA-BC2D-0003934CA32C\:ABPerson
END:VCARD
```

Multiple vCards can be stored in a single file by concatenating them together. Make sure you don't accidentally nest any of them. This makes the management and distribution of group e-mail lists very easy to accomplish.

Merging Address Books

Considering carefully how to merge several address books from different sources is important whether you use vCards or not. You need to find a field that you can genuinely rely on to match one card with another in order to identify duplicate cards. E-mail address is probably an attribute that is unique to a person. Telephone numbers won't do, because many people could share the same phone number when they work at a company or live together in a family or community. A person's e-mail address is supposed to be very personal. Mobile phone numbers are also very personal. You may check several fields for similarity. If you find no match, then you can add the card immediately. Duplicate cards need to be merged one field at a time, usually with some manual intervention to make a choice.

The Apple Address Book application presents any duplicate entries in a dialog that the user can respond to in order to merge the cards or keep them separate. This is fine if you are adding a few dozen cards, but the task is much more onerous if you are aggregating two databases with several hundred thousand names and addresses.

Sharing Address Books

Sharing address data is best accomplished with a database and some web wrapping. It is done in intranets all the time. You need names and addresses to be accessible to all your desktop applications, and that generally means that they must live in your local address book or be accessible to it.

If you are sharing contact details widely with a large community then they could be maintained centrally with a directory service of some kind. RFC 4519 describes the properties stored by Lightweight Directory Access Protocol (LDAP). You must subscribe to the LDAP service online to make the enquiry.

Address Formats

Addresses need to be formatted correctly according to local custom. Often, software designed in one country will be infuriating to use in another because the local customs dictate unfamiliar behavior. Many web sites still insist on address details specifying one of the two-letter codes for a state name in the U.S. Particularly egregious examples refuse to allow users to complete a registration process without selecting a state name, even if

---

Microformats: http://microformats.org/wiki/implementations

hCard: http://microformats.org/wiki/hcard

X2V tool: http://calendarswamp.blogspot.com/2005/08/x2v-xhtml-to-ical-tool.html

W3C vCard RDF: http://www.w3.org/TR/vcard-rdf

the user has already indicated that the address is outside of the U.S. This is unacceptable and due to sheer laziness on the part of the people building the system. You cannot expect customers to do business with your organization if you cannot show them enough respect to allow them to enter their address details conveniently.

When you implement the name and address support in the metadata input and editing system, do a little bit of extra research to find out what the local addressing formats are for the target user base. It doesn't require much effort to design a superset of fields and then display the ones that are needed based on a country selection at the start of the process.

Postal Codes

Almost every country has a system of postal codes. Most of them are numeric, but a few require letters and numbers to be arranged in a strictly formatted order.

The ZIP codes in the U.S. are five digits long but also feature an optional 4-digit zone code for use within the ZIP code area. Allow space for a dash between them. In the UK, the postcodes are divided into two parts. They are referred to as the out code and the in code. The first one always has two letters and a one- or two-digit value. The second, which is separated by a space character, has one digit followed by two letters. Refer to Tutorial 25 for a regular expression that will match the UK post codes and Tutorial 24 for another that will match the U.S. ZIP codes.

 Refer to Wikipedia for some informative articles on postal codes worldwide. Although we have only focused on the U.S. and UK here, there are more than a hundred other alternatives.

Country Codes

Country codes are short alphabetic or numeric codes that refer to single countries, and are sometimes called geocodes. By using consistent values to represent countries, all of your systems will integrate together more effectively when they share geographic data.

The most widely used scheme is ISO 3166-1. This should not be confused with the telephone dialing codes, which are defined in a standard called "E.164 country calling codes." The ISO 3166-1 standard defines the following:

- Two-letter (ISO 3166-1 alpha-2).
- Three-letter (ISO 3166-1 alpha-3).
- Three-digit numeric (ISO 3166-1 numeric) code.

The two-letter codes are used as a starting point to derive other geographic identification schemes, such as ISO 4217 currency codes and top-level domain names on the Internet, although the TLDs are not fully conformant to ISO 3166.

Search Wikipedia for: "Postal codes"

The ISO standard is not the only method used to identify countries. You should consider aggregating any different schemes you are likely to encounter in your metadata in a single table. Add more columns as necessary to contain each different code. That way, you can map more conveniently from one to another.

Country Names

There are many alternative naming systems for countries, including the following:

- The International Olympic Committee (IOC) 3-letter codes used in sporting events.
- The Fédération Internationale de Football Association (FIFA) three-letter trigrammes.
- The North Atlantic Treaty Organization (NATO) specific two-letter codes.
- Federal Information Processing Standards (FIPS) two-letter country codes.
- FIPS four character region codes.
- United Nations Road Traffic Convention international license plate codes.
- United Nations Development Program (UNDP) trigram country codes.
- U.S. State department diplomatic license plate codes.
- International Telecommunication Union (ITU-T) E.164 international dialing codes.
- ITU-T E.212 mobile/wireless phone country codes (MCC).
- ITU prefix for radio station call signs.
- ITU letter codes for member-countries.
- Maritime identification three-digit codes.
- European Union variations to UN-specified and ISO 3166 schemes.
- International Civil Aviation Organization (ICAO) aircraft registration numbers.
- The leading digits of International Standard Book Numbers (ISBN), which identify countries or language regions.
- The first three digits of GS1 Company Prefixes in barcode product numbers.
- ISO 639 language codes.

Your metadata system might have to cope with some of these. If you handle sports results for broadcasting, you should be aware of the FIFA codes for soccer teams, for example.

Currency

Although currency isn't strictly a location, it is a location-based value. International currency values are coded using a three-letter scheme that is described in ISO 4217, which also defines numeric codes for the currencies. This standard is designed to be resilient to changes that occur when governments or regimes are replaced.

Phone Numbers

When storing phone numbers, three component parts of the number should be put into separate fields:

- Country code.
- Area code.
- Subscriber phone number.

A significant proportion of the phone numbers in your system will be local to the country in which you are residing, and the country code for international dialing is not needed for calling within a country. For multinational companies that are centralizing their metadata storage on a global basis, the country code should still be stored but prevented from being displayed on screen when the user resides within the country to which it applies.

The area code is necessary for calling long-distance but within the same country. You may need to qualify this code so that a leading zero digit (trunk prefix) is removed when the international code is prefixed. Storing this in an additional column seems like a more complex solution than might be required. It is quite simple to organize. Then, for all phone numbers, either the international code or the leading digit is prefixed.

The subscriber number is unique within the local area code but may occur many times within an entire country.

In the U.S., phone numbers are 10 digits long, usually formatted as 3+3+4 digits. The international dialing code to dial from another country is another three digits (001). Allow four digits because some codes are longer. Dash or space characters are added for formatting purposes but need not be stored in the database. In fact, it is better if they aren't because it makes the database easier to search if you need to reverse lookup a phone number.

UK phone numbers are usually a five-digit local area dial code with a 6-digit number. The UK international code is four digits long (0044).

Phone numbers in the UK might be as many as 15 digits long while U.S. numbers might be as many as 13. There are exceptions to these rules. When you add formatting characters and an internal extension number, a UK number might look like this 27-character sequence:

```
+0044 (0)1214 661 777 x4545
```

UK numbers are moving towards a 10 digit standardized format.

Table 10-1 UK telephone number formats for the future

Fragment	Format
Area Code	2–6 digits
Subscriber Number	3–8 digits
Trunk Prefix	0
International Prefix	00

A formatted U.S. number might look like this 23-character sequence:

```
+001 555-413-7878 x4545
```

The ITU-T E.164 recommendation indicates that without formatting characters, all numbers should be 15 digits or fewer, even when including the international dialing code. Recommendation ITU-T E.123 describes how the international dialing codes should be presented.

If we want to allocate a single database field for a phone number, we should make it 32 characters long to be on the safe side. Dividing it into smaller fields gives us some organizational benefits. Table 10-2 lists the database table columns you could set up for a phone number:

Table 10-2 Structured telephone number storage

Component	Description
International code	At least 4 and possibly more numeric digits.
Optional local area code prefix	One digit, normally zero is probably sufficient.
Local area code	A 3 or 4 digit area code depending on local custom. Research this for territories other UK and USA.
Subscriber phone number	UK requires 6 digits, USA would be 7.
Extension phone number	Four or 5 digits should be enough for very large organizations.
Number type	It is useful to know whether the number is for a desk phone, fax or mobile.
Flag character	Is this a work or home number.

World telephone numbering guide: http://www.wtng.info/
Ofcom (UK phone registry): http://www.ofcom.org.uk/
UK country code prefix: http://www.wtng.info/ccod-44.html

Changing Phone Numbers

Take into account that telephone numbers change. They need to be updated individually when someone moves to a new house or job. Bulk changes are necessary when the telephone company changes the format. In the UK, the dialing codes for London have changed several times in a short time. Although the changes for London are described here, the changes across the whole company are even more wide-ranging and complex. The pace of change is increasing.

1. In 1922 an automated dialing system was introduced for London. It was called the Director system.
2. Sometime in the late middle of the 20th century (1966), London phone numbers are prefixed with the dial code 01 covering the entire Greater London region.
3. In 1989, the 01 code ran out of numbers and was split into 071 and 081 while the 01 code was banished. These codes were assigned to Inner and Outer London. People moved house or complained to the regulator so they could have the cachet of putting an Inner London number on their business cards—yes, it is sad but true.
4. In 1994/5, all UK codes acquired an extra '1' digit following the leading zero. London codes became 0171 and 0181 respectively.
5. In 2000, the London codes were changed again to become 0207 and 0208 for Inner and Outer London.
6. Recently the 0203 code was added to London and there are proposals to add others.

A little more long-term thinking might have avoided so many changes. Think of the consequences of this. Every company needs to have its stationery reprinted, its internal processes modified, its buildings and vehicles re-branded/labeled and also needs to update all its databases of phone numbers to refer to new values for all its contacts. Individuals need to do a lot of work to cope too.

Changing things like this once is excusable. Changing it every five years is unreasonable.

Phones Are Not Just for People

Phone numbers are being attached to objects and not just people. The increasing demand for telephone numbers to be assigned to vending machines so they can call for replenishment automatically will only make this situation worse. Mobile phone numbers are being used to update status information remotely and can be used to advise travelers when the next bus is due by fitting a black box with a display to the bus shelter in a rural location.

UK numbering changes: http://www.wtng.info/wtng-44-uk.html

Hierarchical Organization: Building a Model

When constructing a model of a user and location, the people, places, and things concept suggests that we should separate the name of the person from the address. This makes some sense. Many people could share the same address. When they share a domestic address, there need not be any further qualification.

In an office environment, the floor number of an address might be shared by several hundred people who each have a unique desk number or location. Carefully partitioning these values using a process of normalization will reveal how these should be allocated.

Phone numbers might also be shared across an entire organization, but extension numbers would be unique to individuals. Large organizations usually provide direct lines to individual staff members. A phone number might be attached uniquely to an individual.

Given the variations in phone number formats, it is better to keep those in a table of their own and then associate them through a primary/foreign key join. People would then map to phone numbers on a one-to-one basis (although many-to-one might work in some cases). People would also map many-to-one to an address. The object model in Figure 10-1 is constructed with one to one mappings.

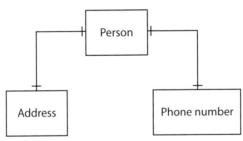

Figure 10-1 A simple person object model

Role-Based User Database Designs

When you build a user database (and this applies to other similar structures as well), you occasionally need to extend it with new properties. Provided the properties being added are simple, they might only require the addition of a single column. You might elect to add that column to the person table. You should ensure that normalization is still intact and that the table is still in its correct 3NF form.

Sometimes you want to add properties to the person table, but you know that an entire column isn't really justified because only a few (but an important few) user records need these extra properties. You may have a contacts database of crew for film productions. About 100 out of the 3,000 or so persons in your address book would be camera operators. You would like to store details of the camera that they use. In some cases, the operator has several cameras. Some of your 3,000 contacts work on a freelance basis and that is not exactly the same subset as the camera operators. A few others work in specific genres, and some have a driver's license and can provide their own transport. In total, that is about four different roles being described, and they don't neatly apply to the same subset of the database.

If we think of groups of properties as roles, we can attach them to the person table using a foreign key. That foreign key is the person ID. We can create a table of camera models and put the person ID that represents the specific camera operator in the foreign key column. This is neat, because we accomplish the many-to-one mapping that we need.

Now we can extend the object model. In fact, we can add as many new roles as we like, whenever we like without affecting any of the others.

This system has an additional side benefit. If we make the joins during the query process, we can find all camera operators that have a particular model of camera, and who can drive and who work freelance. The more sets you have intersecting the lower the chances of a match but some obvious combinations like that would be commonplace.

Figure 10-2 shows the revised object model.

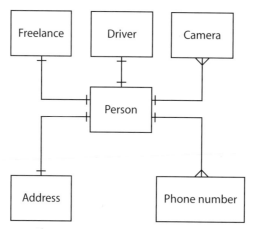

Figure 10-2 Role-based object model

In this object model, the telephone number is treated as a role as well. This allows the person to have more than one phone number. They only have one status as a freelancer and car driver, so a one-to-one mapping is fine for that. The camera is one-to-many, as previously discussed.

Recommendations

Here are some suggestions that will make your metadata systems deliver better quality results. This has a direct and probably measurable benefit of lowering your support and maintenance cost overhead.

- Wherever possible, use the available standards.
- For name and address data exports and synchronizing, vCards of version 3.0 or higher are useful.
- Use ISO 3166 country code values in your master database.
- Add mapping to other country code schemes in a centralized table.
- Set up input screens for names and addresses that are sympathetic to local customs.
- Build-in regular expressions to test the format of postal codes.
- Use ISO 4217 currency codes when necessary.
- Keep your currency and country codes up to date.
- Build your user registry database around a role-based model.
- Plan to cope with irregular but frequent changes to phone numbers at the individual and bulk level.

Summary

Maintaining lists of people and places, and their associated contact details and roles, is not particularly complex provided you normalize things correctly and place things into an appropriate table.

For simple applications, that level of complexity in the modeling is perhaps not required. For a few hundred names and addresses, you could use a single table with many columns. It isn't as flexible and extensible, but it is fine for small and limited projects.

Although we have covered addresses and country codes, we haven't dealt with spatial organization. Addresses and country codes are abstract, while spatial organization is all about physical location. We will look at that in the next chapter.

Spatial Data and Maps

Lost in Space

We often use spatial data without realizing it. When we use spatial data within metadata applications, there are a few important considerations. In order for search mechanisms to function effectively, we need to take into account a variety of subtle issues.

This topic is sometimes referred to as GIS, and you will find the terms listed in Table 11-1 cropping up in conversations about it. If you spare a little time to understand map-making theory better, you will be able to exploit that knowledge as you build your spatial metadata handling workflow.

Table 11-1 Geographic terminology	
Term	*General meaning*
GIS	Geographic Information System. A database of map data, often with overlays showing civil engineering, oil exploration pipelines, etc.
Geo-location	Locating a point within the geography.
GPS	Geographic Positioning System. An array of satellites that communicate with mobile devices to indicate the position.
Geo-Ref	A military standard for locating points for battle planning.
Geo-IP	The process of mapping an IP address to a geographic point.
Remote Sensing	Using satellite or aerial photography to map surface attributes and correlate them with a projected map.
Geo-codes	Standardized country codes.

Spatial Data Structures

There are varieties of different data structures that you may find useful when managing spatial data:

- Grids.
- Meshes.
- Nodes.
- Networks of nodes.
- Trees.
- Projections.
- Digital Elevation Models.
- Multilayered mapping data.

These are all well documented online and in textbooks. The United States Geological Survey (USGS) is a rich source of mapping related data. The Ordnance Survey provides the same service in the United Kingdom. Many other national mapping bodies will have useful information about localized mapping policies and projections.

Grids

A grid helps to organize a collection of points. Think of a grid as having a set of X-Y points measured in a Cartesian space. Grids are a useful way of mapping terrain so that a texture mapped image or informational detail can be located on that surface.

In a broadcast context, we might want to accurately locate the corners of a sports field so that we can develop a graphical overlay and superimpose some advertising or results. Our source image will likely be a rectangular picture from an image created in Photoshop. Mapping that to a soccer pitch is easy, if we can see the four corners and if the sports ground is genuinely rectangular.

This is similar to locating longitude and latitude points on an earth map. Many of the same algorithmic techniques can be applied.

The meteorological weather forecasters share data with one another using a gridded data set, which is stored in a standardized container. These GRIded Binary files are more often known as GRIB files. Several hundred values are stored for each grid point on the matrix. You can receive GRIB files from NOAA to experiment with yourself. The data is organized by different geographic regions. The details are available at the Global Marine Net web site. The files are generated every 6 hours.

Values on the grid are either averaged across the whole cell or measured as a point value where the grid points cross or at the centre of the grid cell depending on the kind of grid computation being used and the value being modeled.

GRIdded Binary data (GRIB): http://www.wmo.ch/web/www/WDM/Guides/Guide-binary-2.html

Global Marine Net: http://www.globalmarinenet.net/publications/grib.txt

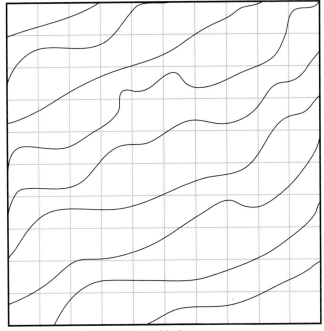

Figure 11-1 Gridded contour map

Meshes

Four-point grid squares map conveniently to textures but they don't always fit a complex shape. Triangular facets are better for covering difficult contours. These are used frequently in computer graphics. Understanding surface mapping is vital to using spatial information.

Sometimes the graphics system will build a triangular grid or mesh of points and texture map an image onto them.

A mesh is a way of connecting points together like a grid but it is more flexible. Where a grid is usually built with points that are spaced regularly and normally in two dimensions, a mesh can have different sized cells and they can be any shape. They will most likely have three or four vertexes (vertices/edges). Three or four points will determine the endpoints of those vertices.

Triangular meshes are used to generate 3D images. In areas of fine detail, the resolution of the mesh is increased. A grid is sampled regularly at the same resolution. A mesh can have different sampling characteristics in one part of the mesh compared with another.

Meshes are used in virtual studio production and are an integral part of the MPEG-4 standard where they are used to massively reduce the bandwidth need to deliver video conferencing by building a realistic looking avatar from a still photograph and draping that over a mesh of points which are then animated to create a talking head. At the resolutions available in mobile devices, this is good enough.

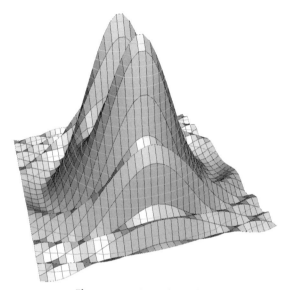

Figure 11-2 A mesh surface

Nodes

We use nodes in a different way to regularly gridded points. They may exist within a coordinate scheme on a grid or a mesh, but are used in situations where we want to locate features such as towns, special buildings of interest, or waypoints on a journey.

A node represents a location where a camera was set down and its GPS record imprinted on the video recording. Plotting those nodes on a map using a coordinate scheme that is appropriate and consistent with our metadata storage lets us find any video recordings that were shot near a certain point.

Networks of Nodes (Points)

Collecting nodes together and joining them into a network makes them even more useful. Two nodes may be quite close together but are not connected by a network line. To travel between them, we may need to move through other nodes instead of going directly.

By organizing a connected set of nodes, we can build software that calculates journeys. This how automated travel maps are produced. By attaching metadata to the nodes, we can traverse the network and accumulate data as we pass through each node.

We can add metadata to the connecting network lines and accumulate that at the same time. A network that describes roads might have the distance between the two nodes associated with the line. For a sophisticated journey planner, the mapping production company may have added some observations about journey time. The quality of the roads that the network line represents means that traversing the nodes can yield sufficient data to calculate a journey time estimate.

Creating large networks of connected nodes is no simple exercise. In information and archiving situations where we manage large collections of metadata and essence data, network node diagrams might be used to represent related topic themes. This gets deeply into semantic and thematic analysis of text, but you could locate documents or videos onto a coordinate space that represents ideas and concepts. Then, by measuring the distance between the nodes in that content space, you can find documents that cover related topics because they should be "nearby." The key to searching a system like this is to use a candidate document and compute its location within that coordinate space and then find its nearest neighbors. See Tutorial 36 for more detail.

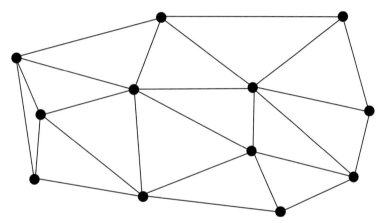

Figure 11-3 A network of connected nodes

Note how the nodes are connected but none of the connection lines are allowed to cross each other. Journeys from node to node can be connected together to form a route from any node in the network to any other. Usually, we are interested in the shortest route but sometimes we need to specifically block a connection to deal with a river crossing.

Trees

Another way of organizing nodes is by using trees, which implies that there is a hierarchical relationship. When calculating a journey through a series of connected network nodes, trees help to organize the points so the shortest route can be chosen.

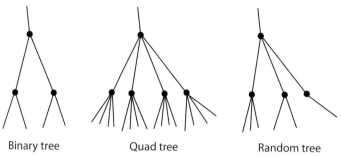

Binary tree   Quad tree   Random tree

Figure 11-4 Different kinds of tree structures

Trees come in a variety of types. Binary trees with only two branches at each node are used when rapidly searching a linear set of values in a database via an index. Quadtrees have up to four branches and are used in 2D graphics to recursively sub-divide the view space. By extending the concept, Octrees have eight branches per node and are useful for subdividing 3D volume; hence, they show up frequently in animation systems. Quad trees and Octrees can help speed up searches for intersections of 2D and 3D objects.

Understanding how tree structures work, helps to build a mental picture of the data you are working on. Trees are useful when tracking user journeys in an interactive system, such as when building a DVD menu structure. You might build a tree as a template in your authoring system and populate the nodes when you produce a new DVD.

Every tree has a master node that is the ancestor of all the nodes in the tree, which are called children. Each of the children that share a common parent are siblings of one another, but often those siblings will be ordered in a sequence based on an external context from which they are mapped.

A Document Object Model (DOM) in a web page is composed of nested HTML tags. Each tag is represented by an object in the DOM, and the containing tag corresponds to the parent object (or node) for any tags contained within it. Between every tag object is a text object, which in many cases is null (empty) but still present in the nodal scheme. The ordering of the child nodes in the DOM tree is based on their sequence in the HTML source text. Earlier content is represented by nodes to the left, while later tags and text are placed to the right. Previous-child and next-child properties yield the corresponding objects from their nodal locations in the tree structure.

Child nodes have children of their own, and so on down the tree. If we build these parent-child trees and maintain some metadata properties for each node or join, we can analyze the tree structure.

Search Wikipedia for: "Quadtree"

The Shortest Distance Between Two Points

Going back to our mapping example, our journey from networked node to networked node builds a tree. We construct a tree with all possible routes from our starting node to our finishing node and store a mileage figure at each node in the tree. The destination may be represented by several end-points or leaves on our tree. By aggregating the mileage figures as we walk down to each of those leaves, the one with smallest total is the shortest route. Wikipedia describes how R-Trees can facilitate this kind of searching.

Refer to Tutorial 37 for more discussion on this topic.

The tree walk is necessary to accumulate the node distances and to determine whether we should pass through points A and B or X and Y.

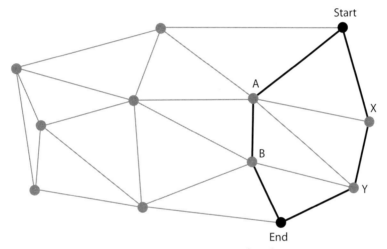

Figure 11-5 Two connected nodes

Projections

We measure map positions using longitude and latitude coordinates, which are points on a grid. These are generally accurate enough for most purposes, although some problems will occur at the poles where longitudes converge, as shown in Figure 11-6. That's what happens when you try to turn the surface of a sphere into a neat and tidy X-Y coordinate scheme.

Locating positions on a fine grid is often done according to a coordinate scheme laid down by a national body such as the USGS or the Ordnance Survey. Other countries have similar organizations.

Search Wikipedia for: "R-tree"

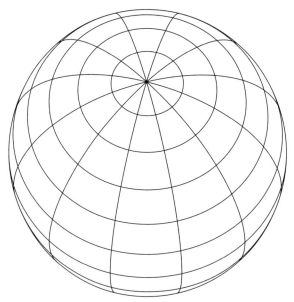

Figure 11-6 Projected distortion

Why We Need Projections

Projections are necessary because we are trying to map a Cartesian grid of X and Y coordinates onto the surface of a sphere. If we use purely longitude and latitude values, the distance between each coordinate point changes as you move up or down towards either of the poles. At any latitude, the horizontal distances are approximately the same.

We assume that the planet we live on is totally round and spheroid. In fact, it isn't. It is an oblate spheroid, which means it is a little bit flattened. The circumference is not perfectly round, either, and isn't even constant. For most users, this won't matter. The earth's orbit around the sun and the moon's orbit around the earth pull the continents around a bit throughout the year. These changes introduce small but important errors if we use purely spherical formulae to map a point on the surface.

Now, this might not matter to us in our lifespan, but if we are creating metadata with positional information that is important and that might be used for hundreds or even thousands of years, the accuracy of that metadata may change.

Selecting a Projection

The projection chosen by the surveying organization will be optimal for the area covering the national boundary and areas just beyond it. Coordinates from a country's surveying organization may not be useful outside that area.

Within an area of interest, mapping experts will choose one of many dozens of different projections to optimize the map in one way or another; Figure 11-7 shows one such projection, an Eckert-VI projection which severely distorts at the edges.

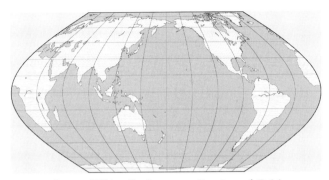

Source: Wikimedia Commons. Courtesy of: Reisio
Figure 11-7 Eckert-VI projection

For some applications, it is important to preserve the linear distance between two points. This will often cause the area to be modified in a nonlinear way. Other projections preserve the area at the expense of linear measure.

Projections tend to have a point in the center where the map is most accurate, with errors accumulating towards the boundary. Choosing the projection whose center is located over your area of interest is important.

One of the most useful books on mapping projects is *Map Projections—A Working Manual*, which is written by J.P. Snyder. Although it was published in 1987, it is still a remarkably useful book.

Rounding Errors

Whenever you manipulate spatial data, you need to be especially aware of rounding problems. When objects are located in space, they require a reference point. If you round off the result of a calculation and then use that as the reference point for a subsequent calculation, a cascading error soon begins to accumulate. Quite soon, you will find it difficult to close polygons, because the accumulated error has offset the end-point with respect to the beginning.

The correct technique is to store everything in an absolute coordinate space and transform it to the view space as it is drawn. Often you will find the operating system provides a drawing kit that solves this for you.

Digital Elevation Models

News programs are increasingly showing more complex terrain images, such as war zones, using Digital Elevation Models (DEM). The image you see combines the DEM data with satellite imagery that has been warped to fit the coordinate grid of the DEM. The two are combined in a graphics system, with the DEM forming a 3D surface onto which the satellite image is projected or draped. Using Digital Elevation Models and textured satellite image is also becoming popular with daily weather and traffic broadcasts.

Tracking

Making sure the coordinates are accurately tracked together is important. When you develop the fly-through for the news program, you use the coordinate scheme of the 3D model. At the most extreme level of complexity, we combine these 3D terrain models with real-world camera views and additional graphics overlays, an approach that has become popular for historical and archeological programs. Showing what Solomon's temple might have looked like, but superimposing it onto a picture of the scenery shot in the present day, requires careful mapping and tracking of coordinate reference points.

This uses grids based on different coordinate spaces and algorithms that map one grid to another on a point-by-point basis. If you don't get those algorithms right, the image will be distorted or the object you place into the scene will appear in the wrong place or have the wrong perspective transformation applied.

Artificial Reality Scenes

NASA has advanced the art of modeling and fly-through journeys as they have explored other planets. The Jet Propulsion Laboratory and its collaborators in industry and education have significantly advanced the art. A visually appealing and technically very impressive example is the NASA film *Flight Through Mariner Valley*. Viewers fly through a winding tributary valley that feeds into Valles Marineris, the "Grand Canyon of Mars."

The video was produced for NASA by the Jet Propulsion Laboratory and features high-resolution images from Arizona State University's Thermal Emission Imaging System multiband camera on NASA's Mars Odyssey. The images show details as small as 300 meters (1,000 feet) across. Many hundreds of individual frames were combined into a giant mosaic that was then colored to resemble the Martian landscape.

The mosaic was then draped over a computerized topographic model (DEM) for Valles Marineris. This was constructed by analyzing altitude measurements taken from NASA's Mars Global Surveyor spacecraft. Figure 11-8 is a still frame from the video, produced by: NASA/JPL/Arizona State University.

You can download the video from the NASA web site and view it for yourself.

Courtesy: NASA/JPL-Caltech.
Figure 11-8 Winding Side Canyon (Louros Valles)

Winding Canyon video download: http://mars.jpl.nasa.gov/odyssey/gallery/video/video.html

Multilayered Mapping Data

Maps can tell you many interesting things. Here is a list of the typical information you will find on a map:

- Coastlines.
- Roads.
- Rivers.
- Contours of height information.
- Bathymetry (contours of water depth in the ocean).
- Terrain and forestation.
- Power lines.
- Sewers and other utilities.
- Railway lines.
- Political boundaries.
- Property ownership boundaries.
- Industry and agriculture.
- Pollution deposits.
- Natural resources.
- Sub-surface geology.
- Points of historical interest.
- Special buildings (churches, post offices, police stations, etc.).
- Remote sensed aerial or satellite photography overlay.
- User defined annotation.

 You can simplify your maps by organizing your metadata into layers. Building layers whose visibility is dependent upon scale is also sometimes useful.

By the time all this information has been added to your map, it is going to look very messy. Mapmakers organize each kind of information into a separate layer so they can turn it on and off. This is called de-cluttering. The information is all still there but you only make visible what you need.

From ZIP Code to Geo-Ref

Mapping ZIP codes to geographic coordinates can be done in a variety of ways.

- Extent rectangle center.
- Centroid of area.
- Dead reckoning.

These are described briefly here, refer to Tutorial 36 to see why extent rectangles, polygons and hulls are important. For now, let's satisfy ourselves with a short explanation about each of them (see Table 11-2):

Table 11-2 Polygons and hulls

Item	Description
Extent rectangle	The smallest rectangle that just encloses an arbitrary shape.
Polygon	A connected set of points that draws the outline of a shape.
Regular polygon	All the sides are of equal length.
Hull	The polygon that fits best around an arbitrary collection of points.
Convex hull	This hull is drawn in like an elastic band. If there are any indents, they will not be found.
Concave hull	This hull pulls in tighter like a vacuum packed plastic bag. Any recesses will be located and the polygon pulled into those recesses and inlets.

Extent Rectangles

Sometimes you want to see whether things overlap or are in an adjacent region. A quick technique is to calculate the extent rectangle that boxes in the area of interest. This is sometimes called the Maximum Bounding Rectangle.

When you map an irregular shape, an extent rectangle is the smallest rectangle that fits round the set of points. It is computed by separating the X and Y coordinates into two sets and sorting them by value. The smallest and largest values are used to describe the corners of a rectangle that surrounds the shape (see Figure 11-9). For a series of nodes, this is quite straightforward. You need to find the smallest and largest X and Y values. They may not be associated with the same co-ordinate point which why you need to analyze each axis separately.

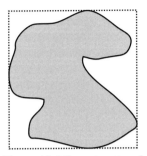

Figure 11-9 Extent rectangle

Extent rectangles may overlap, but the outline polygon hulls within them may not intersect with each other (see Figure 11-10). Using extent rectangles can speed up your location searching because you can eliminate many mismatches very quickly by testing to see if they are inside or outside the rectangle. Then only apply the polygon computation to those candidates that are likely to intersect.

Given two polygons whose extent rectangles have been worked out, if the right hand edge of the first polygon is to the left is less than the left hand edge of the second polygon, they cannot possibly intersect. That eliminates the polygons as far as overlapping is concerned in a single **if()** test.

Applying these techniques, massively speeds up the performance of your searching and matching tools.

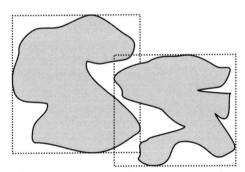

Figure 11-10 Intersecting extent rectangles.

For some applications, intersecting extent rectangles may be all you need to discover. If you want to match the coverage over a radius from a centre point, your polygon shape for the intersection is a circle. Drawing a rough approximation of a circle as a polygon lets you use the same generalized intersection algorithm and simplifies your application design.

Nonspatial Applications

You can apply this logic to nonspatial problems. It works with testing whether two lists might contain duplicate items. Sort both, test the last one of the first list against the first one of the second. We are looking for the same kind of extent-based overlap but instead of X-Y values, we are using code-points in character sets.

List A	List B	List C
Alvis	Opel	Ford
Aston Martin	Pontiac	GM
BMW	Porsche	Jaguar
Dodge	Renault	Jensen
Edsel	Skoda	Opel
Ford	Trabant	Pontiac
GM	Vauxhall	Porsche
Jaguar		Renault
Jensen		Skoda
		Trabant
		Vauxhall

Figure 11-11 Intersecting lists

List A and B do not intersect at all. The earliest item in B is 'Opel.' This comes after the last item in list A (Jensen). Because we know the lists are sorted, we can eliminate any possibility of duplicated items across both lists. When we compare list B and list C, the earliest item in B is between the first and last items in list C. We can see by closer inspection that list B is completely duplicated.

By testing the right items, we can infer whether a list is completely enclosed within the scope of another or only partially overlapping. This allows us to select the optimum processing strategy as each possible scenario arises.

Centroid of an Area

A centroid is the location of the center of gravity within a shape. The centroid of the area of the shape is a calculated balance point where the shape could be suspended in equilibrium and spin freely. It is not necessarily the center of the extent rectangle. For some shapes, it may not be where you expect. If the shape is reentrant and elongated, the centroid may be outside the polygon boundary.

Calculating centroids is straightforward, and there are many algorithms that you can download and test for yourself. Refer to Tutorial 39 for a numerical technique for dealing with irregular shapes. Engineering approaches where regular shapes are degenerated are well publicized in textbooks and online.

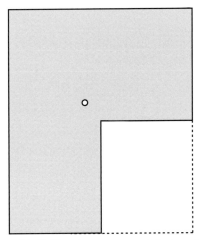

Figure 11-12 Simple nonsymmetrical centroid

Dead Reckoning

For some areas, we might want to make an editorial decision to choose a point that is neither the centroid nor the middle of the extent rectangle. Capital cities and county civic centers, will almost certainly not be at one of these easily calculated locations.

For broadcast metadata, we might want to tag our footage with the location of an organization that can give us rights to go and film again. That might be the governing body for the county, which will usually be in the county seat (called the county town or county headquarters in the UK).

Figure 11-13 East and West Sussex

The map in Figure 11-13 illustrates the complexity of choosing a city to serve as the "center" of a region. The area of East and West Sussex was once one single region called Sussex, with its county headquarters in Chichester. Now it is two regions, with two county HQ centers, one in Chichester and another in Lewes. Both are quite small towns. Neither is in the physical center of the regions they govern. The cross in the middle is the approximate center of the original region, but there is no major town near there at all.

Brighton is the largest urban area in the region. A city that manages itself and is politically and commercially separated from the rest of Sussex. Crawley is a major industrial and commercial area adjacent to an international airport (London – Gatwick), but there is no regional civil governing power centered there.

Historically, Hastings is the most important place, as it is the location of the last successful invasion of mainland Britain back in 1066. Hastings is controlled by Lewes as a county town, but its postal region is centered on Tunbridge Wells, which is part of the county of Kent. Tunbridge Wells is not the county HQ for Kent. Tunbridge Wells is a couple of miles outside the Sussex border.

Which of these half-dozen locations would you choose as the center of this region? It really depends on the context of your inquiry. Broadcasters would choose Tunbridge Wells, because that is where the regional BBC office is. Historians would choose Hastings. Government officials would choose Lewes and Chichester.

Context is everything in metadata and media asset management.

Implications for Broadcast Metadata

Territorial areas of responsibility or coverage may need to be described in your metadata system.

Consider a day in the life of a roving cameraman. On the map shown in Figure 11-13, they might be located in the Tunbridge Wells offices of the BBC. Their area of interest might cover a large part of East Sussex as well as Kent. Because Tunbridge Wells is near the Sussex/Kent border, we find that some commercial activity spans both counties. Yet, the officials in charge of the counties provide services that go up to the edge of their boundary and no further.

We can have situations where rights, location, taxation, and travel require the consideration of several overlapping areas with different metadata for each. You almost need to plot point-by-point to see whether your metadata location point falls within one or other area being considered.

Location Tagging

This is done with metadata, and it's why having some knowledge across a few disciplines other than broadcasting will help you to build better broadcasting metadata workflow systems.

Automated Tagging with GPS

Going out and shooting news footage on video and sending it back to the newsroom as a file with some associated metadata is becoming the de facto method by which newsgathering acquires its material.

Sometimes the camera is fitted with a GPS receiver and imprints the values on the tape automatically. That may or may not be a good thing; it really depends on what you are shooting and how you exploit that GPS data later on.

Object Location vs. Shooting Location

Suppose you send out a camera team to film the Straits of Gibraltar. Something might happen on the mainland of Spain, and the team grabs some great footage from Gibraltar. The GPS will say the footage is from Gibraltar, but the pictures are really recording something happening on the Spanish beach. You want that metadata to be modified to reflect what was shot, not where it was shot from.

This problem shows up again in the editing suite. See Tutorial 51 to see how this can be a problem during editing.

Network Domain Names

Being able to reverse lookup domain names based on an IP address or find an IP address given a domain name involves access to DNS. This is something you can do with a shell script wrapped round the **nslookup** command. Using a compiled language with access to a TCP/IP library is not much more difficult. In fact there ways to do this from any language.

Top-level domain names come in several types. The full list can be found at the IANA web site while a few examples are shown in Table 11-3:

- Country codes.
- Generic names.
- Infrastructure names.
- Top level special cases.
- Second level names.

Table 11-3 Example domain names and types

Domain name	Domain type
`.uk`	Country code
`.com`	Generic name
`.arpa`	Infrastructure name
`.test`	Top level special case
`.localhost`	Top level special case
`.invalid`	Top level special case
`.example`	Top level special case
`example.com`	Second-level
`example.net`	Second-level
`example.org`	Second-level

IANA web site: http://www.iana.org/domain-names.htm

Geo-IP Locations

Using the Internet to calculate a geo-location is becoming more reliable. Perhaps by mapping IP addresses to locations based on the registration database that the DNS is built around can give us some help. Certainly looking at router locations and working out where the jumps take you would give some indication of where a machine is physically located.

This might not always be reliable because this information is very hard to deduce accurately. Consider that a large corporate organization may register a single domain name where its headquarters are located and then route all its Internet traffic via its internal network. A multinational company might appear to have all its traffic being delivered to a U.S. location.

The same argument applies to router locations. We can't usually penetrate beyond the firewall. What we deduce is the location of the corporate or ISP gateway and may not necessarily be the real location of the user.

Since most individual users are on dial-up or broadband connections, they will most likely be connected via an ISP that is hosting their connection within that country, since it would likely be cost-prohibitive for them to connect via an ISP outside the country.

I am still a little suspicious of the ISP-based approach. I would be inclined to score the values accordingly in my database if they were derived from a source such as this.

Locations that were the result of a user Q & A session would score highest and are accurate unless they lie. ISP-based locations would be ranked next and Geo IP third.

Time will tell whether the Geo-IP services can achieve the complete accuracy that we need. This method is likely to be used for locating users within a national boundary. I wouldn't expect it to be more accurate than that. The user's post or ZIP code tells you exactly where they are.

Summary

We can start to build additional axes into our metadata searches. In addition to keywords and date/time values, we can also search spatially. This only works if we recorded the data in the first place and if we have correctly normalized all our coordinates to the same projection scheme.

It is not a case of putting in some figures that define a camera position. You must ensure that any coordinates recorded from cameras or entered by archive custodians manually are done in a consistent and compatible way.

I hope this chapter whetted your appetite to learn more about maps. Combining maps with modern file formats such as SVG for storing vector data is an area that needs to be further investigated. Mapping support facilitates sophisticated workflows to drive the information graphics in a news service for example.

Maps fit well with vector storage models. Satellite imagery, on the other hand, is purely pixel-based. We will look at pixel images briefly in the next chapter.

Paint Me a Picture

Graphics and Images

The national television networks' election coverage is filled with the latest and greatest 3D techniques, shown off in a glorious festival of colored pixels, driven by metadata received from outlying correspondents who are feeding the database with constant updates. 3D models are also frequently used to recreate news events where cameras weren't present, such as natural disasters and transportation accidents. Broadcasters and program makers can learn from some of the tools used in other industries, such as architecture, banking, energy exploration and medicine, and we'll examine some of those in this chapter.

 Graphics techniques are quite advanced but relatively easy to understand. As with the techniques in earlier chapters, you can find more information about them if you search online resources for scientific visualization topics.

There are opportunities to use advanced graphics rendering and modeling tools as part of the media asset management scenario, and metadata can enhance that 3D experience. Some of the techniques provide ways to manipulate metadata in three dimensions. This might sound a little strange until you think that those dimensions can also represent things like genres, topics, content owners, dates, and times. By organizing documents in a spatial framework, you can locate similar information easier than you might be able to within a one-dimensional chart or table.

Ingesting Photographs

Managing large collections of photographs is the sort of problem that has migrated down to the consumer's territory. During the 1990s, broadcasters assembled collections of digitized photographs that were served centrally to whole departments or divisions. In the BBC news department, a system called *Elvis* was used.

With the introduction of Apple's iPhoto application as a standard feature of the Macintosh operating system, this capability arrived at the right moment to help consumers manage the increasingly large collections of images they were amassing as they took to using digital cameras.

There are other third-party applications, such as iView Media Pro and with the latest version of Apple iPhoto (as of 2006), that allow you to manage image collections of as many as a quarter-million pictures.

To make the most use of such image collections, we want to examine the properties needed to be stored in the metadata repository. Table 12-1 lists some basic properties for still photographs. Many of these reflect the same issues as are raised by moving footage.

Table 12-1 Digital photograph properties

Field	Description
Picture ID	Uniquely identifies the copy of the image. As is the case with video, it is generated by your system, and you shouldn't have to enter it automatically.
Roll ID	Represents a roll of physical film. It can also be used to describe an import session to group digital images together.
Description	Describes what is in the picture. You can enhance this by adding particular keywords.
UMID	The same issues of uniqueness apply to still images as video images. Cropping, and color balancing an image or adding effects to it would merit a new unique identifier. We could argue that the a simple scaling of the image only creates a new variant and not a new unique image.
Size	For the practical purposes of searching for high and low quality images or images that have been produced for a specific purpose, we would want to know the image size. This is sometimes called resolution.
Photographer	Who shot the material. This is as relevant for still photography as it is for movies.
Date and time of shoot	When was it shot? This may be preserved by the camera and imprinted onto the file when it is stored in the camera's memory. A well-designed import mechanism would preserve this value. Using file modification dates alone is not 100% reliable. If you have a disk failure and recover the data, it will likely lose its time stamp.
Location of camera	Where the camera was when the image was shot.
Location of subject	Where the subject was when it was shot. Just as with video, this is not always the same location as the camera if you are shooting objects a long way away.
Camera type	Details such as the kind of camera, the film or video stock, the lens type, and any other useful settings such as aperture and film speed. Much of this information is stored in the headers of the image file. This is sometimes called EXIF data, and is important to the postproduction process.

Table 12-1 Digital photograph properties (continued)

Rights owner	Who owns the picture? This will determine how you can use it. The same caveats apply to still photography as to video regarding ownership and rights of use. While you might digitize someone else's pictures and store them in your system, if you have no rights to use them, then they are wasting space. You might still include such pictures in your system as reference comps but you should mark them accordingly.
Format	The format of the picture. This tells you whether the picture needs to be reprocessed for use. You may want to load RAW images from the camera rather than processed and enhanced images.

Generating images using scripts can be accomplished with Adobe Photoshop, which features as rich a scripting interface as that found in Illustrator. Adobe tools are well integrated with one another. It is feasible to perform script driven vector drawing in Illustrator and then transfer those images to Photoshop in order to operate on them as image pixel maps.

Publishing Images Via Templates

When we model things for illustrative purposes, such as financial data and statistical measurements, 2D diagrams are often sufficient. The resulting graphs and charts might look like 3D, but they haven't necessarily been 3D modeled. There is a sort of "2.5D" world that is flat and layered in the Z-axis and simulates 3D appearance with drop shadows, beveled edges, and pre-computed perspectives.

When building workflows, we might use tools like GD, Gimp, or even PV-Wave to construct images from script-driven systems. Desktop applications like Excel, Illustrator, and Photoshop might also come into play. SVG files are perfect for this kind of publishing. Refer to Chapter 17 for some information about the XML-based SVG files.

Nevertheless, it all starts with a design that is then made into a template. The same general approach of templating and introducing dynamic modification works effectively whether it is 2D, 2.5D or 3D graphics.

Building a Graphics Workflow

Some years ago, Adobe shipped a product called AlterCast, which was a server-based application that contained all the functionality of Illustrator, Photoshop, and some of the After Effects capabilities. Because it was server-based, you could deliver graphics rendering jobs to it and use it as a render server, much like the way that 3D animation work is carried out. The software is no longer available and, at the time, it was a quite expensive solution. You could build something quite similar in your workflow pipeline by wrapping Illustrator, Photoshop, and After Effects in some script-driven containers. Then they can pick up a job from a queue and feed it through the application. This could run in a server environment and deliver you some useful capabilities.

On the other hand, you might approach the problem by deploying an open-source solution based around GD or Gimp. The attraction of an open-source solution is that you can customize it to suit your needs. Building a batch controlled front end to queue rendering jobs and adding new import export formats is a challenge, but certainly not impossible to engineer. When you have the open-source application as a starting point, many of these things become much easier to envision rolling out as part of your system.

All the usual caveats regarding best practices apply, and you should avoid modifying the internal API functionality. Provided you only add to the existing code base, you should be able to roll in updates to the underlying open-source application with no breakdown of your workflow.

3D Graphics

Some broadcasters may need to generate 3D graphics automatically as part of their workflow. Especially for those election night broadcasts. A variety of approaches would work. You could load a metadata driven 3D model into a graphics rendering application. These systems tend to be proprietary and you need to find one that can accept an open standard model format. That graphics application needs to be controlled by a script.

It may be possible to use an open-source rendering library and build an application around it. For high quality work, you could generate RenderMan RIB files from metadata and hand them to a Pixar RenderMan server where fully animated video clips can be generated. That would be a high-end solution and although it is a sophisticated rendering engine, the costs of technology like that are decreasing all the time.

Volumetrics

Volumetrics is an offshoot of the 3D Computer Aided Drawing industry, which began in the 1970s and evolved significantly in the 1980s. Geometric solid modeling is used to design all kinds of engineering systems and has evolved to include a variety of related volumetric analysis techniques. Volumetrics is used a great deal in oil exploration to model the behavior of reservoirs. Modeling fluid flow with Computational Fluid Dynamics is an example. Whilst these are all serious engineering systems, we can subvert them to our desire to create attractive motion graphics for our broadcasting services.

CAD systems use constructive solid geometry (CSG) to make complex shapes by adding and subtracting simpler primitives in order to build compound shapes.

Parametric CAD systems apply control parameters to this process. You can produce, for instance, a generic description of a screw thread and parameterize its diameter and length. The CAD system then draws a screw thread according the required specification without you needing to model the intricate fine detail yourself.

If you want to build complex illustrative business graphics models, this same constructive solid geometry approach might be useful. By connecting the parameters up to your workflow, you can generate some interesting results that are driven automatically from your metadata.

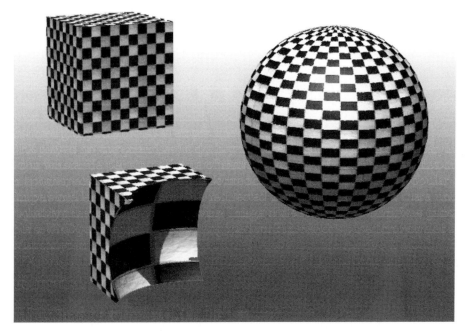

Figure 12-1 CSG model of sphere subtracted from a cube

Volumetrics is used in oil exploration to model the behavior of reservoirs. The reservoir simulators use iso-surfaces, which are made by locating points within a 3D lattice and then generating 3D polygonal meshes from them. These create onionskin models of underground reservoir structures. The values used and hence the shapes created might represent oil pressure or density.

This technique might help us visualize weather systems quite effectively, showing where the air pressure is high and humidity is changing across a landscape. This all contributes to making the display of complex data sets more intuitive to your viewers.

Voxel Processing

Recall the discussion on gridding in Chapter 11. Gridding is used to construct maps and study geological formations. Applying those principles in three dimensions is called voxel processing.

Voxels are cells on a 3D lattice that can contain values. We might attach metadata to a single voxel. A voxel cube can be represented as set of pixmaps in layers. A 2D representation would use pixels and a 3D version would use voxels; the word "voxel" is a combination of "volumetrics" and "pixels."

Consider mapping textual documents into semantic spaces. This could be done with a voxel system too. They are organized containers for data, constructed in a 3D space. By attaching more meaning to the voxel cube, we can run simulations. They become more interesting when we start to visualize them according to the metadata properties.

Figure 12-2 A voxel space

In a 3D graphics system, voxels could be implemented using particle mechanics, but in this case, we lock down and distribute the particles on a grid and the particles don't move. Then we can apply particle-rendering process to visualize the underlying data. When you start to examine data in this way, interesting trends and patterns emerge.

Gridding and voxel processing is used extensively in meteorological prediction, which is built around a volumetric grid that models the atmosphere. Each cell in the volume has properties such as temperature, humidity and barometric pressure. The software that brings the prediction model to life moves data from one cell to an adjacent cell according to wind vectors. Working at high resolution, the resulting values are plotted to create the weather forecasts that are broadcast on TV.

Extending to More Dimensions

Depending on the complexity of your data structures, you might extend to more than three dimensions. Document semantic mapping would certainly benefit from being mapped into more dimensions.

Adding a fourth dimension can be visualized with motion over time. A fifth dimension could be coded as color while a sixth could be modeled as brightness of an object. Seventh, and higher-order dimensions are harder to observe unless some dimensions are discarded. For selection purposes, data needs to be positionally and temporally mapped to X, Y, Z, and T.

In Figure 12-3, the search results are presented graphically. This is easier to understand than a textual listing. Document publication date is mapped to the X-axis and the search relevance (or ranking) is mapped to the Y-axis. Each dot represents a document that was yielded by the search.

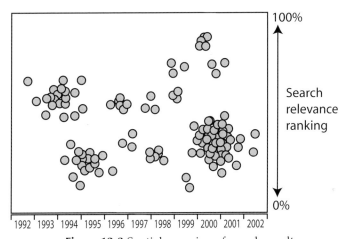

Figure 12-3 Spatial mapping of search results

Freeing your mind of a strictly real world spatial organization based on how things are viewed in their native dimensions allows you to explore new approaches to visualizing complex data.

Summary

This chapter was a brief look at some graphics related issues in the larger context of building a workflow. It is a large topic on its own. For most broadcasters, ingesting photographs is something that they can accommodate within an existing news organization without needing to re-engineer their business processes. Going beyond that into automated graphics production is too challenging for most. Those few that have made some progress have found the productivity gains to be profound. Reducing 30 days of day-to-day graphic production work to 3 days of automated effort gives your graphic designers back 27 more days of creative design time available instead of spending their lives churning out mundane production work like a sausage factory.

Graphics represent a largely untapped potential within workflow systems. Many people are manipulating digital photographs, but we haven't yet seen the breakthroughs we could accomplish with dynamically generated illustrations.

There is no reason why SVG files could not be created with the same ease as dynamically publishing a web page from a template. The publishing pipeline software would be almost identical. The difficulty seems to be in designing an object model and an authoring environment that drives it effectively.

The next step beyond imagery is video and moving images. It is just as ready to exploit automation to reduce our effort level. We will look at that in the next chapter.

Roll Tape!

Video and Audio

We often need to create metadata that describes video sequences. In fact, this is probably the area where our metadata can add the greatest value.

Content and asset management systems are available for storing video economically, typically costing between fifty and seventy thousand dollars and these numbers are decreasing as the systems manufacturers become more competitive. It is highly likely that you will have to modify or configure any system to work most effectively within your particular environment. Buying a solution is easier than building it but integrating it into your larger workflow context is going to take a little bit of work.

Ingest and Transcoding

Getting your media assets into your asset management system in a controlled and structured way is important. You need to extract the maximum amount of useful metadata from them automatically.

Your ingest point should do some work to analyze the content to find out if there is any embedded metadata that it can extract. Chapter 2 discussed the metadata attributes that might be collated at different phases of the production process.

Running a secondary pass over the content can exploit built in Artificial Intelligence (AI) to extract facial recognition data from visual content. Audio can be processed to recognize speakers and what they are saying although there are limits to how good the transcripts will be.

Some ingest software can 'read' the text that appears in the picture.

As the content is ingested, you might apply a trancoding process to it. Be careful not to transcode the content to an inferior quality format and use that as the archived master. You should store the master in the form it arrives. That is the highest quality it is ever going to be. If you cannot avoid transcoding the master, select a format that is at least as good or higher in quality and then use something like FlipFactory to convert it.

At the same time, you can create lower quality proxy copies for preview and desktop-based rough edits. This would be most useful in a large organization with a widely distributed workforce.

Dealing with Audio

The audio ingest point is where we apply any speech recognition and metadata extraction. Table 13-1 describes some useful properties you could extract:

Table 13-1 Feature extraction from audio

Property	Description
Track length	For finding tracks by length and allocating storage.
Dynamic range of the track	For automatic level correction.
Location of quietest passage	For calibrating pre-amplifiers.
Location of loudest passage	For calibrating compressor-limiters.
Potentially interesting locations	Timeline positions of passages that are in the top 10% of the loudness. You may want to define the threshold to be other than 10%.
Dividing long recordings into tracks	Timeline positions of passages that are in the bottom 5% of the loudness range. You may want to define the threshold to be other than 5%.
Music or speech	Analyze the frequency spectrum. Speech and music look quite different when analyzed as a frequency plot rather than an amplitude plot.
Phonetic track	Convert fragments of audio into phonetic tokens for searching.
Transcript	Given that there may be some errors, converting the phonetic data to a transcript might be useful.
Speaker	Sophisticated systems can recognize who is speaking.
Pitch extraction	Recognize musical notes in the recording.
Embedded control tones	Recordings used to drive multimedia projector systems would embed inaudible tones into the recording, which could then trigger slide changes.
Telephone dialing tones	If the recording includes a telephone recording, the Dialing Tone Multi-Frequency (DTMF) can be detected and numbers extracted.

Ingesting audio and transcoding between one format and another is straightforward, provided you guarantee to preserve the existing number of tracks. Each track can be treated as a monophonic conversion. Synchronization should be preserved because the timeline is shared and you shouldn't be performing any edits on individual tracks unless you are extracting them to use elsewhere in which case they will be creating new assets.

Editing operations must be applied uniformly to all tracks. Building a framework in which the edit actions can be maintained as a series of instructions that is then applied multiple times seems a logical way to go. We need tools built on platforms like QuickTime, which are able to manage, the multiple tracks but present us with an API that we only need to operate on as a single timeline.

Working with multiple audio tracks becomes a little bit more difficult if we need to change the number of tracks. Mixing down to a mono recording from a stereo recording is not always a simple case of summing and halving the resulting sample values. Purely mixing the two channels might introduce phase distortion effects, because the stereo image is not always just a pair of mono signals. Our ears perceive the direction of a sound by sensing subtle phase differences in the signals. Thankfully, we can delegate this sort of processing to libraries of code or tools that are already available. Working within a QuickTime-based application solves many of these issues.

Dealing with multichannel audio (e.g., movie soundtracks and DVD source material) may require us to mix down from seven channels to five or three or two depending on our target platform. The same phase-related concerns apply. Spatial considerations are important, too. The seven-channel mix was designed with a particular speaker placement in mind, and sounds are assigned and panned across tracks according to the spatial movement of objects seen in the video. The ambient effect is spoiled if a helicopter flies overhead and the sound that should have been in the rear speakers comes out on a center front speaker. It would ruin the immersive experience.

Editors understand this intuitively, and we need to distill that knowledge into our workflow if this is the kind of automation we are trying to accomplish.

Dealing with Video

The video ingest point is where we apply all the metadata extraction techniques we used for audio plus some additional techniques designed specially for video. Table 13-2 describes some useful properties you could extract. These are only the video specific items. All of the properties from the audio metadata table would apply to the soundtrack:

Table 13-2 Feature extract from video

Property	Description
Dynamic range of the video	For automatic level correction.
Location of darkest passage	For calibrating color correction.
Location of brightest passage	For calibrating limiters.
Potentially interesting locations	Timeline positions of passages that have a large amount of motion. If this coincides with a loud passage and you are watching a soccer match, it is probably a goal.
Dividing long recordings into tracks	Timeline positions of passages that have relatively little motion. The frame rate can be reduced in the proxy copies or these can be removed to shorten the track.

Table 13-2 Feature extract from video (continued)

Average color	Average the color for each frame and store the values in a separate track. It is useful for searching for similar scenes.
Cellular degeneration	While you are creating the average, also make a 2x2, 3x3, 4x4 and other very low resolution samples. Reduce the color values to 8 bits via an indexing palette and serialize the cell colors. These become search keys for finding images using a spatial search.
Speaker	Sophisticated systems can recognize the face of who is in the scene.
Feature extraction	Things like cars, buildings, flesh tones, sky, landscape all have characteristic properties. Perhaps it is a combination of colors or distribution of shapes or even frequencies of color changes. Profiling these properties through a neural network means you can feature extract some visual information. Even if it is not always correct, it might reduce the number of potential matches from a million-item collection to a few dozen candidates.
Embedded control signals	Sometimes, in-picture signaling is used to indicate the impending end of a clip when it is arriving via a video feed.
DOGs	Detecting when Digital Onscreen Graphics are present may be useful. Extracting their location and color by averaging over many frames might offer a possibility for reducing their visual impact through some further processing.
Channel identification	Certain footage will appear frequently during advertising breaks and as an interstitial between programs. Detect the channel idents to delimit the start and end of a recording.
Zero motion	Locations of footage with zero motion happening indicate that we can switch to a better still image compressor or that the feed is quiescent and it is not worth retaining the footage. This may be another way to detect program breaks.
Dead air	Total silence or black image means nothing is being broadcast. There is no need to store this in your asset management system. It also indicates a break in the program. Single frames of black might be used to mark something in a transfer. Usually more than a single frame would be used to ensure the break persists after compression takes place.

New video material first shows up at the ingest point and may be presented in a variety of different formats. DV is the most likely for newsgathering while higher-quality formats such as HDCAM or HDV might be used for dramas and movies.

The ingest workstation will process the video and extract a set of metadata that describes it. That system might be proprietary and bundled with the asset manager, or it may be purchased separately and integrated as part of the deployment of the asset management and workflow. Quite a few asset management systems have recognized that ingest is a specialized process. They defer to companies like Virage, which produces the VideoLogger, or Telestream who make the FlipFactory software. VideoLogger is probably the most sophisticated video ingest software available. It will perform facial recognition, voice recognition, and also extract any textual content that it can recognize using an OCR-like technique.

The output of your ingest system is a video file plus a metadata file with frame-accurate, time coded metadata values that you can import straight into your metadata schema. This is an opportunity to augment that metadata with additional production information that you might have available and which isn't automatically extracted from the video by the ingest tools. You can buy or build additional workflow tools to add that metadata and integrate them into the workflow.

If the asset management system is sufficiently open, you can ingest via your own systems or from a range of different ingest gateways. You can build e-mail gateways and mobile phone receivers. Then video can be delivered from field operatives or the public. Whatever the gateway, the process comes down to a file-transfer and scan operation.

Low-Cost Video Ingest Tools

Large news organizations have significant workloads as they deal with the incoming video material. Thankfully, almost all of it is shot on digital cameras, and the transfer from the camera into a workstation and storage into a file is straightforward. DV cameras, usually use a FireWire (sometimes called iLink) interface to import the video onto the workstation's hard disk. Applications that do this importing, often called capture, for a modest price (or even free) include iMovie (Macintosh), Kino (Linux), and Movie Maker (Windows), to name a few. Wrapping these tools in desktop automation script such as PowerShell or AppleScript, and possibly even UNIX shell scripts, might facilitate a low-cost ingest solution where the enterprise-scale ingest tools are not cost-effective.

Most DV cameras have a FireWire connection, and thus will load directly into the computer under control of a tool like iMovie. Professional DVCAM devices will also support FireWire of input, while higher-end systems such as DVCPRO will likely have a Serial Digital Interface(SDI) socket, which can be connected directly to the input of your broadcast-quality video card, such as a Black Magic Designs DeckLink.

Dealing with Analog Video

Processing old analog material is likely to cause the most difficulty, and a video digitizer with a built-in time-base converter—such as those from Canopus, Data Video, and Miranda—are ideal for ingesting material from VHS, Betamax, and 8mm Video analog players.

If you don't have a converter and your DV camera has analog video and audio inputs, you can dub to a digital format by connecting your analog machine to the camera. This produces reasonable results, provided you don't use tapes that have been mistreated and you can access the first-generation recording. It isn't production quality for TV, but it is good enough for semi-professional or possibly newsgathering solutions that often have to compromise on quality in order to access the footage.

Video Feeds

As new technologies emerge and are deployed into the broadcast industry, we find new ways to distribute and transport content. This is a constantly evolving process, which gradually trickles down to the consumer. Technologies that we might have used in the broadcast center eventually become useful in the household as well.

So it is with the technologies used for distributing video. In particular, consider the video feeds that arrive from news bureaus and provide a constant supply of packaged news items. In times past, these would have been delivered as a video signal that would have to be recorded at the receiving end. The industry is moving towards a file-based delivery via an IP network.

Likewise, consumers would have received their TV service as a video signal that they would have to record if they wanted to time-shift or archive the content. With the advent of broadband connections, that same video service might be streamed or delivered as packaged files.

This serves to illustrate that the problems of managing collections of video clips—which used to be an issue only at the broadcaster's headquarters—are now migrating down to the consumer household where tens, hundreds, and potentially thousands of hours of video will need to be "content-managed." The content rights owners demand this so that they can control the consumption. The end users will need this because they will not be able to find something to watch without it.

Metadata surrounding a video feed, whether it is streamed or packaged into files, is now of vital importance to everyone in the delivery chain. Whether you are a broadcaster taking a feed from a news service or a consumer time shifting some video, you need to know some things about that content. Some of the basic properties we need to know about are enumerated in Table 13-3.

Table 13-3 Video feed metadata properties

Field	Description
Channel	Where the recorder needs to acquire the content.
Date	The day on which your recorder needs to look.
Start time	The time the broadcast begins. This should always be assumed to be an approximate time. Even the most diligent broadcasters still slip their schedules by minutes and some programs run late by as much 15 or 20 minutes in the small hours of the night. Date and time might be combined into some universal time coded value based on an agreed reference point.
Duration	How long the program will run or the end time of the program. A duration value might be more reliable, but commercial breaks will need to be taken into account if the information source is other than the broadcaster.
Format	We may see a mix of high-definition and standard-definition material being broadcast, and the device will need to differentiate between the two.
Unique ID	Some kind of unique identifier for the program, for the same reasons noted in Table 13-1. This also allows a trigger signal to be broadcast to initiate the recording and indicate the in and out points within the broadcast.
Series container	Often, a program will form part of a series, and this needs to be indicated in the header for that program.
URL	As an alternative to recording the program, the content might be available via a download.

If the program is to be recorded directly 'off-air' from a broadcast with any degree of reliability, the broadcast transport stream should also transmit a trigger signal. This was proposed and implemented for analog TV and not all broadcasters implemented the service. For those that did, programs could defer their broadcast time by a considerable margin and still be recorded. The system was called Program Delivery Control (PDC) in the UK. The details are described in ETSI EN 300 231 V1.3.1 (2003–04) which is available from the ETSI web site. More information is also available at the 625 UK web site:

Introducing these signals into the digital streams being broadcast on digital satellite, cable or terrestrial, broadcasts would not be particularly difficult from a technical point of view. Likewise, any streams being delivered through an IPTV system. It requires that the

ETSI: *http://www.etsi.org*
625 UK: *http://625.uk.com/pdc/*

Given the so-called fire hose of information being thrust at us every day, we need to build ourselves a metadata-controlled repository of our own to manage our library of technical data. The anecdote of the cobbler's children always having holes in the soles of their shoes comes to mind. We are usually too busy solving other people's metadata problems to find the time to organize our own private archives.

play-out system generate a trigger of some kind. The solution needs to be open standards-based and interoperable, which causes some difficulty when proprietary platforms are used. Whatever trigger you use must be supported transparently by the MPEG-2 transport stream. Similar triggers are used to turn interactive components on and off.

The PDC standard also describes a useful set of genre tags. This kind of metadata information is incredibly difficult to research because it is buried deep in standards documents where you least expect to find it. As an engineer working on metadata systems, you need to constantly watch out for useful fragments of reference information and collect them together into a knowledge base so you can refer to them later.

Automated Ingest Techniques

Larger-scale systems can be engineered to automate many of the ingest processes. You could get a robotic tape loader and ingest the tapes one at a time without any human intervention. At the same time, you could scan an image of any tape labels that might be present. Often, tapes have bar-coded labels that uniquely identify a specific tape cartridge. This allows them to be taken offline or stored in a huge archive repository system. This is important because you must always be able to trace the provenance back to the original source copy of your material. It is likely to be the best quality version there is, and won't suffer any generational losses. If you have the money to spend (and you probably do if you are considering systems like this), the bar-coded labels can be affixed or printed directly onto the tapes as they are processed.

Building an automated system on this scale might be justified when processing huge archives of material. There are relatively few organizations with enough material or with sufficient throughput to justify a system like this. The solutions are likely to be a specially designed and require a bespoke development project and will be expensive. The component parts of those systems are readily available and need to be integrated with a sufficiently smart workflow control system.

Storage

Video content is stored in a bulk storage silo. This silo might have the following capabilities built in and managed internally:

- Hierarchical storage management.
- Automatic replication to a secondary server.
- Regular backup strategies.
- RAID organization with parity support for failed drives.
- Shared access via a storage area network (SAN).
- Shared access via network attached storage (NAS) support.

Some of these capabilities will themselves create new metadata. Backup strategies require the logging of what is backed up to which media so you can recover the exact item that you are looking for.

Our media asset management database knows what video was ingested, how it was stored in the silo and what its file system path is. You should never manually move an item in the storage silo. The MAM may never find it again.

Codecs and File Types

We talk about digital formats being lossless compared to analogue techniques. This is true but it needs to be qualified somewhat. It is lossless if no lossy compression is applied. Audio taken off a CD and stored in AIFF files is lossless but MP3 is not. MP3 is low quality when compared with AIFF. The AIFF standard is a distribution format and it is inferior to the studio recordings and masters. Studio recordings are sampled at twice or even four times the sample rate of a CD and with more bits. A studio recording is really the master. The same applies to video. Even the formats such as DV are a bit lossy. If you want to store genuinely uncompressed production quality content you will need huge amounts of storage.

Browse Quality Video Codecs

It is useful to create an additional browse quality proxy copy of any audio and video you are ingesting. The format you choose depends on whether this is an edit proxy or intended only for previewing. Edit proxies for video need to retain all the frames so an Edit Decision List (EDL) can be made frame accurate. Preview copies can be much lower resolution and a reduced frame rate. Editing proxy copies don't have to be full sized. It is the frames that are important.

For your proxy video—the video that you'll share with clients as a reference, as opposed the video that you'll use for broadcast—you'll want to use a modern codec like H.264 that allows for relatively high quality, even at lower bit rates. You should be aiming to achieve quarter-frame pictures at full frame rate but for lower-bandwidth connections, you may have to reduce the frame rate and/or picture size.

Consider the possibility of having two browse-quality proxies, one high bit rate and another very low bit rate. The client should negotiate the right one according to its connection bandwidth, and this should happen automatically. After all, that is done on the web for streaming every day. Why not in a media asset management (MAM) system?

Some quite high-performance systems are built with MPEG-1 browse video running at 1.5 Mbps. This would deliver SD quality at full frame with H.264 codecs. A bit rate setting of 250 Kbps and H.264 encoding is an optimum approach for browse-quality proxy video. You will need a compliant player, but H.264 is well supported. This shouldn't be a serious problem, even though the codec is still comparatively new.

Using Proprietary Codecs

It is vitally important to preserve the master DV (or other original) files unchanged and to use open-standards codecs for the proxy viewing. MAM supplier companies generally agree with this approach and indicate that preservation of RAW footage is desirable. They are less forthcoming on the technical details of the codecs used for proxy viewing, or perhaps the sales people simply do not know the answer (let alone understand the question). This requires a little digging as you talk to the suppliers.

Proxy video is often stored in a MAM using Real or Windows Media compression and occasionally one of the lower quality compressed formats that can be embedded in a QuickTime container. These are not archival quality although QuickTime supports a range of higher quality codecs all the way up to production standard formats. Choosing QuickTime as your storage container facilitates many subtle benefits because everything is unified and has a consistent format for playback and access. Hi-end professional users may want to consider MXF, which can do the same kind of thing and is being widely adopted as a portable container in the broadcast and production industry.

Unique Video File Types

For video, some file formats preserve the moving image sequence as a series of still frames that are encoded on a standalone basis. These formats are particularly useful, because every frame is a key frame. They can be edited if necessary. Several formats fall into this category:

- Motion JPEG.
- Motion JPEG 2000.
- Pixlet.
- Digital Picture Exchange (DPX).

Most of these retain all the images inside a single moving image file. DPX is different because the images are maintained as a set of sequentially named files, one file per frame. This is an image sequence. In fact, you can create these image sequences using any format you like. Alias Maya creates sequences of images like this when it renders an animation.

If you have QuickTime installed, you can assemble an image sequence into a movie or disassemble a movie into an image sequence. Other tools are also capable of this.

Dealing With Metadata in Video

Metadata is embedded directly into the video when it is shot on modern cameras. You may not be aware that your edit software is also putting metadata into the video as you edit it. You should check for the presence of metadata and ensure its quality is as good as possible before it leaves your hands.

Embedding Metadata

Sometimes, the only metadata that is available for the clip is that which the cameraman wrote on the box or on a label on the tape. Maybe you can decipher the writing, and maybe not. A quick fix is to scan the tape label as an image and make it into a poster frame at the front of the clip. Adding a frame is easy, and you haven't needed to create any special metadata tracks or use any special software. The nonlinear editor (NLE) you use to trim the track will provide the capability to drag a single image into the first frame of the clip and remove it when using the footage in a program.

Now that iTunes is being used for video delivery as well as audio, it is becoming relevant as a video librarian application for small-scale semiprofessional projects. The iTunes application embeds metadata into the QuickTime files it manages by adding annotations to the files in its library whenever you edit a property in the user interface. It does this for audio and video clips. This is useful, because you can copy the files to another iTunes system (provided you have the permission) and when they are imported, the iTunes information is used to populate the destination library.

Embedding metadata is a good thing to do as you edit and process your essence data. It doesn't bulk up the files much, and if the facilities are there, then why not use them?

Embedding TV Subtitles in MXF Files

The EBU subtitling group is working on a mechanism to embed subtitles as metadata inside an MXF container. Taking the details from their announcement document, a fragment of XML is coded using a schema referred to as DFXP.

The DFXP format uses namespaces to partition the attributes. Most of them are in the `tts:` name space (Timed Text Subtitles) but a few (that relate to unique identity values) are in the `xml:` name space. Local attributes are not in any name space.

To embed a subtitle into a MXF file, three component container XML tags are created:

- `<styling>`
- `<layout>`
- `<p>`

The `<styling>` tag is a container for `<style>` appearance definitions. Each `<style>` definition describes the appearance of some subtitle text.

The example **<style>** tag contains these attributes:

- **xml:id="uniqueStyleValue"**
- **tts:color="colorName"**
- **tts:backgroundColor="colorName"**
- **tts:fontFamily="fontDescription"**
- **tts:fontsSize="sizeInPixels"**
- **tts:textAlign="horizontalAlignmentValue"**

The **<layout>** tag manages a collection of region tags that control the positioning of the subtitle text on the screen. The **<region>** tags have these attributes:

- **xml:id="uniqueRegionValue"**
- **tts:origin="X-Y pair"**
- **tts:extent="X-Y pair"**
- **tts:displayAlign="alignmentType"**
- **tts:zIndex="displayPriority"**
- **style="uniqueStyleValue"**

The **style=""** attribute value points to the **id=""** value in the required **<style>** tag.

The **<p>** tag is a container for the subtitle text. It positions itself on the screen by pointing at the named **<region>** tag and has attributes that define when it will appear. these are its attributes:

- **xml:id="uniqueValue"**
- **region="uniqueRegionValue"**
- **begin="inTime"**
- **end="outTime"**

The **<p>** tag can accommodate **<span>** tags that alter the styling attributes to override the settings defined by the **style=""** attribute referenced by the paragraph's **<region>** tag.

Here is the XML code for a subtitle containing the following text:

```
"TV is composed of RED, GREEN and BLUE colors."
```

The three colors will be colored accordingly. First, we create the style tag:

```
<styling>
    <style xml:id="myStyle"
            tts:color="white"
            tts:backgroundColor="black"
            tts:fontFamily="proportional-sans-serif"
            tts:fontSize="24px"
            tts:textAlign="center" />
</styling>
```

Our default text is white on black. Now we need to define the area on the screen where the subtitle will appear in a **<region>** tag:

```
<layout>
    <region xml:id=myRegion"
            tts:origin="40px 40px"
            tts:extent="380px 32px"
            tts:displayAlign="after"
            tts:zIndex="0"
            style="myStyle"
</layout>
```

Now we need to create the **<p>** tag with its text content:

```
<p xml:id="01000314"
    region="myRegion"
    begin="01:00:03:14"
    end="01:00:07:16">
TV is composed of <span tts:color="red">RED</span>,
<span tts:color="green">GREEN</span> and
<span tts:color="blue">BLUE</span> colors.
</p>
```

This fragment of DFXP data can be embedded into the MXF file in a data partition placed immediately after the header metadata and before the essence to which it applies. This ensures that it is loaded before the essence is acquired and played back. It is up to the player to ensure the subtitles are presented when required.

This immediately suggests some possibilities for delivering news feeds and interactivity. Right now the standard defines just enough for subtitles but the mechanism does look as if it could be extended very easily to accommodate a much richer form of interactive and overlaid graphics.

Capture Everything Possible

Making sure sufficient information is captured at the time of ingest is important. If you have engineered a large system, then there is probably a relational database built into it to store the metadata. For a smaller outfit or the semi-professional video producer, an Excel spreadsheet may be sufficient.

With a little ingenuity, you could build a web-based interface with PHP that loads a MySQL database to log the data.

You should capture the information listed in Table 13-4 as a minimum. You will probably want to capture other information too. Note that information should be logged clip-by-clip, and you might have multiple clips noted for each tape.

Table 13-4 What to capture

Field	Description
Clip ID	This uniquely identifies the physical clip. It should be generated by your system automatically. It might include a description of where on the tape it is stored. You might maintain Clip ID and Tape ID values in different tables and relate them through a join in the database schema.
Tape ID	This is how you find this specific tape in your library. A separate database links these ID values to physical bin or box locations on a shelf, in a rack, in a building at a specific address. This value should correspond with some physical identifier on the tape case and be consistent with the one on the containing box.
Description	A short or long description of what's in the clip. You can enhance this by adding keywords, etc.
Unique ID	Unique identifiers are used to track a piece of content as it moves through your workflow and (perhaps) changes format. The ID should relate to what is in the clip. Arguably, cropping down creates new unique items, but there is really some kind of a tree-structured, parent-child relationship going on. Appending two clips also creates a new unique item whose parentage connects two trees together. Tracing this relationship can be complex, but it is vital to the process of managing rights identifiers and tracing the provenance of some material.
Duration	How long the clip is.
Camera operator	Who shot the clip.
Date and time of shoot	When it was shot.
Location of camera	Where the camera was when the clip was shot.
Location of subject	Where the subject was when the clip was shot This is not always the same location as the camera.
Camera type	Details such as of the kind of camera, the film or video stock, the lens type, and any other useful information such as aperture and film speed (if relevant). This data is important for postproduction.
Rights owner	Who owns this clip? This will determine what you can do with it. While you might digitize someone else's material and store it in your system, if you have no rights to use it, then it is just wasting disk space. You might still include such video in your system as reference clips but you should mark them accordingly.
Format	What is the format of the clip? This tells you whether the clips need to be reprocessed for use. Clips shot in the U.S. need to be converted if they are being edited into a UK PAL broadcast. The size and frame rate is different. Sometimes the NLE will fix this automatically, but it is good to know about it beforehand.

You can add many other properties to this table of metadata. As you process the clip, you may add image enhancement, color correction, and white balance, and you should record all of these changes in the media database. You should save the modified footage back as a new copy. All your work should be nondestructive in that way. It is highly likely that any operation you do will add another entry to the metadata table, even if it is just a version increment.

Whether you capture to an Excel spreadsheet, a MySQL database, or a larger system, information becomes far more useful once it is in an electronic form. The more structured that data, the more things are possible. It is easier to search a collection of Excel documents or a SQL database than it is to inspect a large collection of image scans of tape labels.

Dealing with Difficult File Types

It may be possible to extract more metadata from some file types than others. By metadata, we mean the image size, exposure settings in the camera, bit-depth, etc. You should not be discouraged because the image file format you are presented with is opaque and hard to decode. GIF files are relatively easy to unwrap as are BMP files. JPEG files are more difficult and some of the formats used for storing scientific visualization may be hard to understand because there is little documentation available about them. It may be possible to automatically convert that file to a format you can more easily decode with another tool. Provided the conversion itself preserves the image quality, you shouldn't have any problems. You can convert to a temporary file, which can be discarded after you have determined the parameters you need.

Forensic Analysis

Sometimes you are presented with a repository of content for which the metadata collection was nonexistent or very sparse. Typical scenarios involve rapid and premature launch of web-based video services that encoded content in a somewhat haphazard fashion and manually linked it to the web pages.

If you later add an asset manager to keep track of the clips, you might assume that all you know about them is their file names. This is still useful even if it is a bit sparse from a metadata point of view. For your first pass at creating a metadata wrapper, you'll need to collect their physical locations and create a record for each one in the asset management database. Then you need to go on a forensic data-gathering operation. You might have some external sources of information. You can inspect the file headers and deduce some useful information about the clips from those. What you can potentially discover depends largely on the file format being used.

Whatever else you can deduce may depend on whether there are text tracks or an object-structured file format with some embedded comments. Anything you extract needs to be put into the asset management database. This means that you need to ensure your asset management database is open structured enough for you to insert additional data. The manufacturer of the asset management system should provide you with some API hooks that will help you add new metadata entity fields.

Recovering Legacy Metadata

Sometimes you inherit a system that contains some essence data, but the metadata was not properly extracted during the ingest phase. Perhaps not even having a list of what is there. This is challenging, but possible to solve.

You should survey the repository first to assess the size of your problem. You will need to know roughly how many clips you need to process and what their file types and any other properties are. Some of the UNIX command line tools make this easy to ascertain. This script assumes that the repository is mounted in your local file system at a known mount point. The "find" command will generate a list of files in the file system; the resulting list is sliced in two where the filename and extension are separated by a full stop. The resulting column of file name extensions is passed through a **sort** and **uniq** filter so that the output is a list of file types in the repository.

```
find ./videos -name '*' -print | cut -d'.' -f3 | sort | uniq
```

We might extend this with some UNIX command line **grep -v** instructions to discard spurious file types that we know are not genuine essence data. The tutorials illustrate how useful this kind of command line tool can be. Once we have a list of file types, we can formulate a strategy for extracting header data from them and processing all of the files one at a time to generate a new metadata ingest.

We can usually deduce things like the frame size, frame rate, video format and codec with a cursory inspection of the file. Analyzing for genre, good and bad shots, and facial recognition is best left to specialist tools like VideoLogger.

On some systems, we may be able to drive a GUI application to extract that metadata in a more structured manner, such as AppleScript driving QuickTime Movie player or Windows PowerShell accessing the video through a specialized cmdlet.

Refer to Tutorial 40 and Tutorial 43 to see how to extract metadata from image files and Tutorial 44 for video metadata extraction.

Processing Your Content

Nonlinear editors embed useful hints into your video. Later on, downstream processes can exploit it. Final Cut and iMovie embed chapter marks so that DVD authoring tools can automatically build menus. Final Cut also embeds details of cuts and transitions so that compression software can organize the bit rate buffering to allow additional capacity to handle a transition that would otherwise increase the bandwidth demands momentarily.

Editing Video

Editing video with a soundtrack is not unlike editing multitrack audio inasmuch as you must apply the same operation to multiple tracks in a consistent manner.

Edit decision lists (EDLs) use a proxy copy to rehearse the edit, which is then conformed on the full resolution master copy by a craft editor. This technique is beginning to fall into disuse now with the increasing popularity of products like Apple Final Cut Pro, Adobe Premiere Pro, and various Avid NLEs, which edit at full resolution and quality directly.

Cutting news content is quite different to cutting natural history or sports. Drama and narrative are different again. You can't simply grab a sequence from one place and cut it in without considering the "grammar of the edit." A grammar applies to the audio editing as much as it does to the video. The grammar of the edit is a rational way of describing how and why a cut is necessary:

- Is there a motive? Perhaps to look at a close-up of some detail.
- Do we want to convey some information by editing?
- Improving the composition.
- Enhancing the sound (audio only edits).
- Choosing an alternative camera angle.
- Maintaining continuity.

For more advice, see Roy Thompson's Focal Press book entitled *Grammar of the Edit*.

Integrating Your MAM with Edit Tools

Most MAM suppliers profess to deliver content into an editing system. Often the process of editing will create a new clip that needs to be ingested as a distinctly new asset and not replace the clip(s) from which it was edited. You might want to find out if simple topping and tailing of a clip to remove dead footage at each end means that the new edited content replaces the old. This might be reasonable if only a single clip is passed to the NLE, whereas a collection of clips indicates that a new sequence is being created. You may prefer a completely nondestructive approach. The process of sending a clip to the NLE and coming back to where you were originally in the MAM is called *round tripping*. It is used in DVD authoring environments where an NLE and an FX package are integrated into the workflow. Prepress does the same thing with embedded Illustrator and Photoshop images for print publications. Ask to see a demo and have an explanation of the MAM product's round-tripping support.

Automation and Scripting

QuickTime 7 provides powerful automation capabilities that streamline your digital media production workflow. On Mac OS X, video tools can be scripted with AppleScript or the GUI workflow builder, Automator. If you install QuickTime onto a Windows operating system you get the same kind of full-featured workflow control, but instead of AppleScript, you can used any COM hosting tools such as Visual Basic C#, JScript (JavaScript), VBScript, C, or C++. Windows Vista users can expect to combine PowerShell scripting with the QuickTime tools.

This kind of scripting organizes multiple applications as building blocks in a processing workflow. You can use them in ways the developers never anticipated.

The Automator workflow provides similar solutions already built as components that can be slotted together:

- Add a URL to a movie. When a viewer clicks in the movie, the web page opens in a web browser.
- Automatically capture video using the new AV Capture feature in QuickTime 7 Pro for Mac OS X.
- Drive workflows with an iCal alarm.
- Add your own actions to extend Automator using your favorite scripting language and Xcode.

Mac OS X AppleScript support provides additional features, which can also be turned into Automator workflow items:

- Archive video in FileMaker Pro.
- Create titles in one program and automatically add them to an existing QuickTime movie.
- Replace the audio track.
- Add text tracks.

Windows software developers can build standalone Windows applications that use QuickTime without needing to master QuickTime's C/C++ API. Write your workflow scripts using one of the available scripting languages on your Windows platform and drive QuickTime through an Active-X control.

If your Windows server can run a Visual Basic, C#, or JavaScript application that uses QuickTime, you can create custom QuickTime content dynamically for delivery via the Internet. This provides a portable video playback solution for Internet users regardless of whether they are using Windows or Mac OS X clients. It also works in any browser that can host the QuickTime plug-in.

A large collection of useful scripts is available on the Apple web site.

Output

The output process is similar to that for any other type of content, but video requires some different output formats and timing may be more critical than when you publish web pages. Your organization may be part of a broadcasting network, in which case the play-out and master control systems are of some interest. They will need to be carefully integrated with your media asset manager.

Perhaps you sell your content to third parties for them to repurpose as they see fit. This will require connection to e-commerce or business-to-business (B2B) systems for billing purposes,

---

Apple QuickTime: http://www.apple.com/applescript/quicktime/

Other Content types

Metadata applies to all kinds of time-based content as well as video. Embedding the metadata into the files, ensures it is carried to where it is needed for editing and playback.

Animation

Moving beyond simple still images to manipulating moving images is the territory occupied by Adobe After Effects and other special effects and animation software. Inside After Effects, you can create expressions that can be key-framed and many plug in effects tools have their own internal scripting capabilities. This can get quite sophisticated.

Metadata can provide some useful savings here because you can maintain the content in an unrendered form. Simply store the component assets and the necessary key frame animation instructions. Then later you can render the compositions when they are required. If you render the compositions directly, you not only save space but they get scan converted just once to the target size they are required. The alternative is to render earlier and resize which can sometimes add unwanted artefacts.

By slightly modifying the control parameters and creating a collection of still images with a graphics utility, you can create animated sequences. You can then turn these into a playable form by loading them into the QuickTime movie player and exporting the result as a compressed video. This is applicable to web content creators, software developers, broadcasters, and DVD/CD-ROM producers.

Presentations

The concept of having a grammar of the edit translates to multimedia presentations and interactivity too. The grammar of the presentation has to do with the visual metaphors. If you are putting Karaoke-style lyrics on the screen, you need a visual cue to indicate that a lyric is being repeated.

This may be much more commonplace than you imagine: audio-visual systems are used in a significant number of churches. There is sufficient use of this presentation format that the National Association of Broadcasters hosts an entire separate Worship Technology conference track that grows significantly larger each year. In a worship presentation scenario, a grammar of the presentation for repeated chorus lyrics might be to use a simple flip transition to go to a duplicate of the same slide.

For teaching sessions and conference presentations, you might use a different (major) transition to signify that you are changing to a new topic thread. The transition between slides within a topic thread should be a much less visually extreme. Use a cube rotate transition for topic changes and a simple dissolve for slides within that topic. Other transitions, such as a slide to the left, might indicate an excursion into a side issue with a corresponding reverse slide back to resume the original thread. This is analogous to a box out in a book or technical manual.

All of these transitions must have metadata associated with them.

Interactivity

We have similar issues with introducing a grammar into our interactive content. Developing consistent models for our navigation helps the viewer feel comfortable with where they are in a user journey. Navigation should be simple and unambiguous. Sometimes, we see interactive DVD menus that are triumphs of design over ease of use.

For automated systems to produce this material in wholesale industrial quantities, we need a well-designed grammar that is easy to understand. Once this is templated, we need only consider additions or extensions to it when we are trying to assimilate some content with a new visual or structural form.

Getting the grammar right in the first place is key. If we get it wrong, then we end up creating a huge body of content that is difficult to use. We might as well have not bothered.

Even that might not be the disaster that it appears to be. In the same way that we can abstract the style and content in a web page container, we should be able to apply the same strategy to our interactive content. By separating what we have to say from how we say it using a consistent content model and a collection of templates to describe the interactivity, we can republish the same content with a different interactive grammar.

We would want to design our system to do that anyway for technical and architectural reasons. The optimal way to achieve repurposing is by having a publishing pipeline that is template-driven.

Summary

We have looked at some of the issues relating to metadata extraction from video and audio as we ingest them into our storage and workflow system. This is part of the process that can greatly benefit from automation. Delivering feeds and files to an ingest system and then steering that ingest process is not something that human beings find stimulating to do. Automation will improve the quality by eliminating the errors that happen when operators get bored.

Dealing with video completes the survey of the different kinds of media we might want to build a broadcast or Internet publishing workflow to manage. In the next chapter, we will look briefly at rights issues and how they might impact our metadata workflow process.

Rights Issues

Protecting Your Data

Anyone who works in the broadcast field is well aware of the central dilemma facing content owners. How do we protect our intellectual property on the one hand but still make our assets available for use by our legitimate customers? It's a tricky proposition, but there are a few interesting safeguards you can use, even though no content-protection method is foolproof.

The protection scheme is added as kind of wrapper around the content. Our metadata can describe the range and scope of the usage rights to avoid accidentally using the assets in a context that breaks the license conditions. We should be able to 'red-light' the item in a content search if necessary.

There are guaranteed protection mechanisms we can implement to stop unauthorized use of our material. The workflow/content management system can be used to track and monitor such mechanisms as we might deploy in addition to keeping track of the content itself.

 Rights management needs to be applied from the camera to the consumer. there's no point protecting against consumers copying content if the assets are stolen during the production process. Content must be protected from the point of acquisition.

Ensuring that you can trace the provenance of a pirated copy of a movie, CD, or image is probably the most effective approach towards preventing widespread piracy. Given the ingenuity of copyists and the fact that it is arguably quite reasonable for someone to purchase something on one media and play it on another device, it is a vain hope to believe that it is possible to prevent duplication entirely. The best technique for tracing provenance is the use of unique user specific watermarks.

Watermarking and Steganography

Watermarking has been used to protect currency and other important documents for hundreds of years. The technique is based on indelibly marking the substrate of the paper. As the paper is manufactured, the process involves the drying of wood or cotton pulp into sheets. By pouring the pulp over a raised impression before draining off the liquor, certain areas are made slightly thinner and hence transmit light. Almost photographic image quality can be produced by skilled paper manufacturers.

Unlike the watermarks on currency, which can be seen by the naked eye, most effective digital watermarks are examples of applying steganography techniques. Steganography is the art of hiding or encoding information in a way that doesn't disturb the underlying data. The untrained user will not be able to read the information and will be completely unaware of its presence. It is a form of hiding information in plain sight. Well-implemented steganography schemes will survive the transformation of the data. Scanning an image and scaling it would normally remove simple steganography, but some advanced schemes will survive even this.

To encode hidden identifying marks, you need to look at the data that is being protected and apply a technique that fits with that data and leaves its structural form unchanged. The encoding is bound to alter the underlying data slightly, but in a way that cannot be detected when viewed.

Although the watermark is embedded in the essence data, we might record the key values in the metadata for that essence data. In fact, that gives us a useful hard link between the metadata and the physical asset at the primary key level.

The hidden coded data needs to be extracted and decoded by the data owners but must not be so easily detected that it can be removed by someone intent on copyright infringement. The only weapon you have available is to make the removal prohibitively complicated. This means multiple encodings in different places with different techniques. If the obvious marks are removed, some vestigial markings that were not spotted by the perpetrator will remain intact.

Detecting Data Theft

Ideally we want our metadata and essence data to be accurate, detailed, complete and not have any erroneous content. How can you tell the difference between a database listing some information that you created and are selling and one that I own and market?

Perhaps we both did our due diligence and created an exactly similar data set. Or perhaps I made a copy of your product and put my name on it. How would you know I did that?

There is a technique called peppering which seeds a database with intentional changes to the data which whilst they are technically errors, they don't materially affect the accuracy of the database as a whole. Peppering your database to identify unauthorized copies is discrete and doesn't cause any difficulty to your end user. It is a kind of watermarking that you can use on structured and unstructured data.

Peppering maps is accomplished by introducing nonexistent features. A nonexistent road is a technique used by street mapping providers. If a competitor publishes a similar work, locating any streets that don't genuinely exist but are present in the competing publication is a clear indication of theft.

There is no substitute for doing your own survey and data gathering. Whatever means you use to incorporate someone else's data set into your own, unless you know where the peppered data is, it will get included in your data and evidence will be there to prove you copied someone else's work. Unless you do your own data gathering honestly you can be traced.

Likewise, directories of companies and anything that has lists or tables can add fictitious items in a way that causes minimal annoyance to the customer.

This won't prevent people stealing your intellectual property but you can trace the provenance of the original that they copied and take that person to task for allowing their copy to be duplicated and distributed. Knowing that is possible should be sufficient as a deterrent.

Protecting Text

Protecting text against theft or ensuring that its provenance can be traced is accomplished by placing additional punctuation or white space into the text. If this is done in an electronic copy, encoding all manner of secret messages becomes possible.

If you think about the way that text can be manipulated, you can trace individual copies of confidential documents without them being obviously numbered or named. In fact, you probably would place the recipient's name on the cover and indicate that the document is a numbered copy. The label is a deterrent but won't stop someone from duplicating your document. Placing paragraph and line breaks in particular places, or adding or removing a word here and there are all useful indicators when it comes time to confront the person who leaked your document to the wrong people.

Companies routinely give projects code names and use different code names for different groups to whom they divulge the information. When rumors of a new product surface on discussion boards in the Internet, the group who compromised the product launch can be identified. By the use of intersecting sets, you can narrow this down over several incidents to identify the person responsible.

Protecting Images

Protecting images is a little more difficult than protecting text, because there are spatial relationships that must be preserved. If we alter the value of a pixel, then it shows up clearly against its adjacent similar colored siblings. By applying what looks like noise to the image, we might disguise an encoding as a dithering effect. Areas of solid color might have subtle changes instead of having the same color all over.

A differential coding technique could be used where a reference image is retained in the content system and a differentiating algorithm is applied to a suspected copy. The differences can be exaggerated to expose the hidden coded watermark.

Coding is less likely to be visible in the color information than in the luminance. Schemes that take account of how human vision and perception work are likely to offer more scope for encoding larger amounts of data. In the same way that we can encode by hiding punctuation in the text, we can encode by cropping or subtly scaling an image. This would be impossible to detect without collecting many copies of the image and aggregating them together and comparing them.

Protecting Film and Video

Hiding watermarks in moving video is quite challenging. It is particularly difficult to hide them in video scenes that include a camera pan. This is because as the camera pans, the watermarking reference points remain stationary. It creates an effect as if the image was projected into textured wallpaper. Suddenly you have a textured pattern that is moving against the natural motion of the pan.

While the camera was stationary, the human eye forgave the imperfections introduced by the watermark. Once the camera moves, the only stationary reference in the image is the watermark and our eyes pick this up immediately.

The solution is to deduce the motion in the scene and work out a tracking vector, which can be applied to the watermark as well. This requires significant computing capacity. You may elect to introduce the watermark only on certain scenes rather than encode the whole movie. This is a lot easier if the panning head on the camera tripod had a motion sensor and embedded the values in the video as metadata. Then a tracking vector can be used that exactly matches the video motion.

Movie distribution companies have introduced blatant watermarks into the prints they send out to movie theaters. When watching a movie, you will occasionally see a subliminal flash on the screen that many viewers mistake for a large speck of dirt on the film. If you look closely, it is a carefully structured symbol that is unique for each print and will show up in a pirated copy distributed on DVD. This allows the provenance to be traced back to the exact print that was compromised.

Cutting a scene longer or shorter by a frame for each copy you distribute is easy to do but hard to detect unless you have access to more than one copy and the master. With automated production systems, especially the kind we might build with a workflow system, this becomes easy to do. The length of a specific scene in the movie can then encode your key information in the frame count. Hiding values invisibly in videos like this leaves no visible artefacts. Other schemes imprint flashes and what looks like film grain noise on the print, which detract from the viewer's enjoyment. With footage being delivered via IPTV systems, cutting a specific instance of the file on a per customer basis is not technically challenging. If that film ever made it onto a pirated DVD you could trace it back to the specific customer account.

This allows people to have the fair use they require in the knowledge that they will be traced if they engage in commercial piracy.

Advanced Techniques

Watermarking and steganography is an area where engineers are constantly searching for new approaches. It is somewhat related to cryptography in that whatever can be encoded can be decoded, given sufficient computing capacity and time.

We might begin to exploit the data structures inherent in video compression as a more sophisticated way of encoding a hidden marker. When compressing video, a macroblock is tested for similarity to other already-encoded blocks. If it is similar, it can be discarded and one of the existing blocks substituted in its place. At the expense of wasting a few bytes an identical macroblock can be coded in or not. Whenever you have a decision point like that, you create an opportunity to encode some hidden information. The presence or absence of a macroblock in an encoded and compressed video can indicate one binary digit of value, which contributes to an encrypted serial number. You just need to detect it by comparison against a database or reference copy.

From the Broadcasters' Point of View

The rights issues affect the broadcaster by determining when, where and how content can be broadcast to their viewing public. This is important and broadcasters need to comply strictly with the requirements laid down by the asset suppliers or they risk being fined or having to pay additional license fees. These can sometimes be far more expensive than the original terms.

Content systems typically indicate whether footage can be used with a traffic light system that uses Red, Amber and green to indicate the rights of use. This applies to video, audio and still images. It also applies to stock backgrounds, sound effects and ambient music that might have been captured in the background as well. We haven't yet explored how this affects interactivity as that aspect of the industry is still evolving but it is likely it will be affected in the same way in principle.

From the Consumers' Point of View

Consumers want to enjoy the media assets they have purchased. A de-facto state of fair use has been established by precedent over the years where consumers feel comfortable with moving content from one medium to another. Perhaps listening to music from a CD by duplicating it onto a tape cassette so they can enjoy it on the move. Likewise, storing recordings on their iPods.

In trying to solve the issues of piracy, these fair use rights are being eroded by the asset owners. Nobody can excuse the actions of commercial pirates who steal content and redistribute it thereby depriving the original artist of their rightful earnings. On the other hand, it doesn't seem right that storing that asset in another form, merits a further charge. We paid to enjoy the content not the medium.

This is bound to continue to be debated at length for some time yet. Over the next few years we may reach a workable compromise that allows sufficient fair use to a genuine consumer and gives the authorities the necessary tools to trace pirates and the few consumers or industry operatives who supply them with master copies of the assets.

Summary

Rights protection is not only about content. It may affect the software you use and the products you make. Being a noncommercial organization does not excuse you of the responsibilities to follow copyright and intellectual property laws. You still cannot use content from other sources unless you have the rights to do it.

Having sorted out those issues regarding the content and software you want to use, you now need to integrate your workflow with the rest of the enterprise. That is where we shall go with the next chapter.

15

Integrating with Enterprise Systems

Working on a Large Scale

Whenever you build a workflow, you need to understand how it fits into the context of the wider world. Your input most likely is coming from somewhere—another person's system probably—and your output is going somewhere, too—also another person's system as well.

Larger enterprises may need to integrate several large systems. Each one of them will have a workflow process within it but the end-points of those processes need to be joined up.

Understanding metadata is important when designing or selecting a Media Asset Management (MAM) system.

DAM vs. MAM

The differences between Media Asset Management and Digital Asset Management are somewhat blurred. Describing those differences between DAM and MAM can involve some subtle distinctions. As the two kinds of system are evolving, they solve much the same problems. Architecturally they are converging.

Media Asset Management is largely concerned with collating audio and video assets and managing their storage and production. Digital Asset Management throws its net much wider and includes documents illustrations and databases.

In the wider world, the usage of the word 'media' includes non audio-visual forms such as print, text and data that is supplied as a feed or service.

I would suggest the term media allows us a slightly wider remit since we can also describe analogue media forms which have not themselves been digitized but may have a digital metadata wrapper that describes them.

We might apply a strictly MAM approach inside a broadcaster but use a DAM approach to distribute the content being produced along with assets from other kinds of providers.

On the whole, since the book is aimed somewhat at the broadcasting industry, we will be concerned with Media Asset Management systems. You'll see the abbreviation MAM used to describe them. Many of the issues also affect the wider Digital Asset Management community. Where you see MAM, the term DAM often applies equally well.

Product Banding

The various MAM products seem to organize themselves into discrete strata or bands of functionality:

- Single-user nonshared storage management.
- Multiple single users collaborating with distributed and shared media.
- Small-scale workgroup on shared repository.
- Large workgroup on enterprise repository.
- Broadcast or IPTV play-out automation driven systems.
- Multimedia authoring resource librarians.

Implications for Asset Management

Many of the issues that we might have had to solve with a workflow-engineering project relate to storage. In the past, we would have had to devote considerable time to engineering a unique solution, but now we can buy solutions off the shelf. Our unique workflow framework becomes much easier to build, because we are gluing it around an already implemented and working infrastructure.

Of course you still need to exercise due diligence when selecting your media asset management system in order to attach your workflow to it. Look for systems that are designed to be both open and extendable. The more opportunities they give you to attach input processors, the more likely you can build a workflow to feed the MAM system. This is quite important, because this is where you introduce the metadata to the system.

The output end of the MAM is concerned with user queries and selecting material. This may allow you to sell the assets on a licensed basis or perhaps route them to a play-out architecture. Either of those mechanisms may be part of the workflow engineering you do to attach the MAM output to a useful destination.

Media Asset Management System Issues

If we are integrating a media asset management system with a workflow, we need to consider some implications before we select the MAM system we intend to purchase or design. The following points are important and need to be considered as you plan the design, purchase and deployment of a MAM.

Ingest is Well-Integrated with the Database

All of the major MAM systems, and most of the minor ones, are strong on this point. Remote ingest is normally handled through a receiving system with a staged repository that then loads the database, a process often based on watch folders.

Some systems have robust storage management and but are not as strong on ingest. Many MAM systems use Virage VideoLogger and Telestream FlipFactory as OEM solutions to handle ingest. VideoLogger generates extremely rich metadata, including some generated by facial and speech recognition. You may pay a premium for this level of metadata extraction but if it increases the revenues from your material being sold more frequently it is worth paying. But ingest can be done by any application that can create a DV file and generate an XML file for loading the metadata.

Web User Interface for Portability

Adding a web browser-based user interface for ingest has become the preferred approach. Systems that don't already support it are adding it for the next release, some as an add-on module, others as a core feature.

A Web User Interface (WUI—pronounced Wooey?) is valuable because it doesn't require a client application to be installed. It might require browser plug-ins to support proxy viewing if the proxy video format is not natively supported. This is a trivial installation and the plug-in can be hosted for delivery on request. As a rule, web access also goes hand-in-hand with Internet-compatible access, meaning your customers will be able to access the system remotely.

Most MAM suppliers are also developing or have created a native client, an application that talks directly to the database and allows for a much richer UI than can be accomplished with a WUI. Web-based UI design is constrained by what is possible with DHTML and JavaScript. Java applets introduce more features, but a stand-alone client application will always out perform a web interface. Generally, native clients can only be used in-house.

Deploying Servers Outside of Firewalls

To avoid giving access through the corporate firewall, some companies deploy asset management servers outside the firewall. This can be a bit troublesome. You should examine the possibility of installing a proxy server and bringing the asset management system back inside your boundary firewall, even if it is on its own sub-network for performance reasons.

Some product providers may be able to help with this issue. Advanced Digital Asset Management Systems is one example, although its solutions are possibly more powerful than you will require. Focus Enhancements' ProxSys is another, and Focus claims that the system is used by the German Air Force outside of a firewall. Because it is a UNIX-based solution and all the communications ports are closed by default, perhaps this is safe enough.

If you choose a UNIX solution, then placing it outside the firewall may well be fine. It is a very high-risk scenario to place a Windows-based server out in the open like that without the expert systems administration skills required to configure its security settings. Whilst those skills are still required for UNIX systems, the defaults are more likely to be benign. On UNIX systems, the default is for services to be deactivated and closed whilst the default on some versions of Windows is for them to be enabled and open. Beware!

Client Access

Controlling access by clients will most likely come down to group access control protocols. Careful use of projects for each client may also help you manage and limit access. Each turnkey system has subtly different rules mechanisms, and it might be a good idea to prepare some sample use-case scenarios that you can walk through with the suppliers product specialists when you have a meeting with them.

When questioned about the number of possible concurrent users, the bigger systems providers said that many multiple users proposed no problem. It depends on the scalability of the design. This area needs to be discussed in detail with each provider. Some will connect into your existing Lightweight Directory Access Protocol (LDAP) system (if you have one), which provides a degree of single-sign-on control.

Duplication and Redundancy

Some MAM system suppliers state that their systems are fault-tolerant and do not require a secondary backup system. Some products don't have this fault-tolerant design. This needs to be explored carefully during the evaluation and architectural planning process.

A fault-tolerant system doesn't remove the need for a secondary server. It requires a structured approach to backing things up though. A popular approach is to distribute the essence data servers and use a high availability cluster for the metadata database. Architecturally, this is like building a SAN but with much more metadata organization placed around it.

Backing Up the System

Note that when you run a backup of the content of a MAM, it is likely that the essence data and metadata will be backed up independently of each other, because the essence data is in a file store and the metadata is in a database. Making sure those backups are synchronized if they are ever restored might cause some headaches if you don't plan and test it properly.

Systems implementers put together a robust backup solution and check that there are things on the backup media (usually tape). Occasionally they will bring back a single file. I have rarely seen anyone test the full restore capabilities until they are in extremis with a dead system. That is not the ideal time to discover your backup is incomplete or lacks referential integrity. Implementing a backup strategy and disaster recovery plan is not enough. You need to test it thoroughly and periodically to see if it works well before you need it to recover from a disaster.

No Formal Metadata System in Use?

The formal metadata scheme and the sub-set of properties from it that the media asset management system supports doesn't seem to be mentioned in many of the product data sheets that describe MAM systems.

A few suppliers mention things like the Dublin Core Metadata Initiative (DCMI). For most systems, you will find that their metadata schema is flexible enough to define any field you need. Additionally, they will likely have scripts or templates that can be applied to configure it to match popular or open standard schema.

It is debatable whether you would want an entire schema to be implemented. Storing the minimum required amount of metadata to get the job done is a good thing. Just enough and not too much seems to be the right philosophy. There is nothing to prevent you going the whole way with a complete metadata scheme, but it is unlikely your users will bother to fill in all the fields.

Size of Storage Silo

You're not likely to encounter problems with building a big enough storage silo. The storage array is something that could be sub-contracted to a company that specializes in storage, but that may already have been done on an OEM basis by the MAM product developer.

Check to see whether the storage system you are selecting supports virtual disks or meta-disks, which can be grown by adding extra platters. A better approach might be to use Network Attached Storage (NAS) and add new NAS servers as needed. Since the metadata database describes which NAS volume a file might be on, you get the effect of a meta-disk by using the database as a virtual directory structure.

Consider SAN architectures too. An Apple XServe with the XSAN and X-RAID makes a cost effective silo.

Summary

If you need a media or digital asset management system, the chances are you will buy it in and then "glue" it to your existing workflow. Concentrate on asking probing questions about this integration when you talk to the suppliers.

Unless you particularly want to build a system, buying the solution is almost certainly cheaper. You may need to make some (hopefully small) compromises.

Asset management systems facilitate data exchange, and so we will examine data exchange formats in the next chapter.

16

Data Exchange Formats

Document Conversion

We often think of converting image and video files from one format to another. It is such a commonplace operation that we don't think about it at all, it just happens routinely. Oddly, we don't think of converting other kinds of data quite so readily.

As a rule, spreadsheet data and word processor documents seem to be entered as Microsoft Office or Open Office content and that's where they usually stay.

If we can free ourselves a little from that straitjacket, we can perform some remarkable things with that textual data. It is quite amazing how easy it is to process the contents of those document formats if we are prepared to export them to another form.

If you use Java, there are new libraries and tools for interchange that let you operate at a higher level directly with the Excel and Word document formats. We'll talk about those shortly. First, we'll look at how to publish to a variety of formats with a text-based publisher.

File Conversion Issues

To convert a source file to the target format, sometimes it is necessary to translate using intermediate formats along the way. This is not ideal as generational losses might happen at each stage. The shortest route with the fewest hops is the best. Although we are working in digital all the time, losses are not supposed to happen, but some formats compress the data using a lossy conversion. See the discussion on information float in Chapter 4. The same 'frictional' losses can happen with sound, still pictures and video when we convert them.

Apache Jakarta POI

An interesting open source project is beginning to gain some traction where you want to interface your Java-based tools with Microsoft Office. The POI project includes APIs for manipulating Microsoft OLE 2 Compound Document format files using pure Java.

This interface can read and write MS Office (Excel, Word, etc.) files without having to resort to file exporting and script wrapping. You don't even need the Microsoft applications to be installed at all and because it is Java-based it works on platforms where Microsoft Office has never been and will never likely be released.

This project is being enthusiastically supported by developers. At the moment, it is only a Java-based solution. These projects have a habit of migrating to other languages quite quickly so we may yet see ports that let us use it from C language directly without having to bridge to Java.

OLE 2 Compound Document Format-based files include most Microsoft Office files such as XLS and DOC as well as MFC serialization API-based file formats.

The open source community tends to collaborate well across project boundaries. Other projects such as Cocoon, Open Office Org, and Lucene are actively supporting and collaborating with POI. This helps to create a critical mass of developers and tends to lead to high quality solutions because of the large community of developers who are testing, bug fixing and adding new features.

The components available are:

- POIFS for OLE 2 Documents.
- HSSF for Excel Documents.
- HWPF for Word Documents.
- HPSF for Document Properties.

Spreadsheet Interchange Formats

Spreadsheet applications can save files in SYLK and DIF formats. These are quite different formats that both contain a structured description of a spreadsheet.

The beauty of these formats is that they unroll a binary file and express it with purely printable characters within the ASCII code set. This means that we have converted the document into a form that can be operated on by already existing web-publishing tools.

If we can dynamically publish a web page because HTML is a text-based format, we could dynamically publish an RTF or SYLK file. Then, we can target Microsoft Word and Excel as potential readers for our dynamically generated content.

Spreadsheet SYLK Files

It is useful to measure the performance of a media asset management workflow. It might be one of the core requirements as a business information deliverable. Consider the principle of going the extra mile so that your customers don't have to. Populating a Spreadsheet with data from your workflow instead of outputting a plain text file is one of those time saving things that your users will be pleased to receive. They will be delighted that you took the trouble.

If you examine the export capabilities of Excel, you will discover the SYLK file format. It is exactly what we are looking for.

The tag replacement mechanism in the publishing system needs to ignore the actual file type and replace the markup it understands. It does not care about the rest of the file. It locates its own tags and replaces them with the new text that it has created. If we build a content publishing workflow that is too highly structured and which insists that its is given a well formed XML file to work on, then we are closing doors and constraining what we can publish.

Jakarta POI: http://jakarta.apache.org/poi/index.html

Lucene text searching library: http://lucene.apache.org/java/docs/index.html

Cocoon web development framework: http://cocoon.apache.org/

To work on arbitrary raw text content such as spreadsheets, we need to work in the raw text domain. Working in well-structured XML tags means we are operating in an information domain. This might seem to be a subtle distinction but it is important. The raw text access underlies the structured form of access.

Refer to Tutorial 52 which describes how to dynamically publish a SYLK file through a web driven PHP mechanism.

Spreadsheet DIF Files

If for some reason, you can't use SYLK files, then DIF files may do an adequate job instead. They are less sophisticated because they were developed much earlier. In fact, these files go all the way back to VisiCalc which was the progenitor of all the modern spreadsheets. Modern spreadsheet applications like Excel will import them quite happily.

Word Processor Exchange Files

The bulk of the content being produced for Online and Interactive TV use is textual. This is probably going to be edited in a word processor such as Microsoft Word. Integrating Office tools that process text is an important strategic goal. Identifying the optimal format for exchange is quite straightforward. The best choice depends on what you intend doing with the content.

RTF Document Files

The most likely exchange format for textual documents that we can exploit in a workflow is the RTF document format. This was developed by Microsoft and has been adopted as a useful interchange format by many other systems.

When a document is saved using RTF, images that are embedded within the document are encoded and included in the document. By way of a future-proofing caveat, we should bear in mind that this may not always be true if smart image links are used by the application that creates the RTF file. We would expect those images to be represented by a file name that can be located within our local storage. Perhaps that is a more useful approach anyway.

If we can develop a suite of tools to process RTF files, we might be able to extract images and identify where text styles are used. If those styles are named consistently and intelligently, we should be able to infer some structure, ignore the stylistic markup, and retain the structural markup.

We shouldn't pretend that this is going to be easy but it should be possible. Understanding the rules of RTF formatting and structure requires that we obtain a copy of the RTF standard. This is evolving and is re-issued from time to time. Make sure that the version being used in the file you are working on is one that your tools have been designed to access.

RTF 1.5 standards documents: http://www.biblioscape.com/rtf15_spec.htm

Microsoft Office XML

Recent versions of Microsoft Office (for example, Office 2003 on Windows) can store their documents in an XML-based container. This is expected to improve significantly when Office version 12 ships in 2007. Support for XML will be available on the Mac OS X version of office at that time. Microsoft has considerable expertise with XML. Recall that Internet Explorer was a useful XML inspection tool even when other browsers could not access XML files properly.

XML import/export formats facilitate the integration of the office tools with a work-flow. XML is well understood, there are many tools, and libraries we can use to build our workflow components if our starting point is an XML file.

There is a note in the Microsoft online documentation about Office that the XML schemas are concerned with style and appearance and additional customer specified schemas may be necessary in order to add content semantics. It certainly is the case that the XML obtained by saving a Word document is not easy to work on. Nevertheless, this is a move in a more portable direction.

Refer to the Mactopia developer resources for more help with AppleScripting and interchange between Mac OS X and Windows-based Office installations.

The next major upgrade of Office for 2007 will introduce many more useful features that we can exploit in workflows. The Mactopia web site suggests that VBA will not be supported at all on the next version of Office for Mac OS X. You will need to write automation and scripts using AppleScript thereafter. This might cause us a few integration problems because some workflow scripts will need to be reworked. Whilst you might upgrade, to the new version, don't throw away your old one. It might be useful.

It isn't yet clear whether Office version 12 for Mac OS X and Windows will be the same thing. Certainly some features of Office 2003 for Windows are not present in Office 2004 for Mac OS X. The two product lines are separate applications that appear to be based on completely independent development processes, which might share some features that are implemented 'near-identically' by different teams. The expectation is that Office version 12 which we will probably know as Office 2007 will be more compatible across both platforms.

Open Office ODT files

Working on Microsoft Word files can sometimes be cumbersome. Imagine the scenario where you want to put many hyperlinks into a document or cross-link between sections of a document so that when you distill the file into a PDF, it becomes navigable. The UI for this involves far too many mouse clicks and unfolding of text document structures represented as nested menus.

MS Office for Windows: http://office.microsoft.com/

MS Office for Mac OS X: http://www.microsoft.com/mac/

MS Office tools and resources for Mac OS X: http://www.microsoft.com/mac/resources/resources.aspx?pid=fordevelopers

You may find it easier to load your document into Open Office and save it as an ODT file. Then you can open the ODT archive package (it is a standard zip file) and extract a clean and well-organized XML version of your Word document. This XML is of a much higher quality than the Microsoft XML produced directly by Word.

If you inspect the XML file (you may have to fix up the line breaks first), you will see the links and anchors are much easier to edit in this environment than they were in Word.

All of the images have also been conveniently stripped out and saved together in a folder. You can do a branding update to your document by swapping that folder of images for another one—provided the images correspond with one another as matching sets.

After editing in the XML domain, you can repackage the file, open it in Open Office and save it as a Word Document. This round tripping is quite robust but you may observe some minor text re-flowing that can put a page break in a different place.

This technique lets you do all kinds of other powerful tricks such as renaming all the text styles in a document. There are arcane find and replace techniques in Word that will do that but this is far more intuitive.

Adobe PDF Files

Adobe PDF is the most portable document format across the largest range of platforms. Indeed, PDF is now used as the imaging model for all onscreen presentation in the Apple Mac OS X environment. This replaced the display PostScript that was used in the NeXTSTEP operating system on which Mac OS X is based.

PDF is available everywhere. Adobe is rapidly evolving new flavors of PDF to support even more industries than they did before. Movie playback and storage of 3D models as well as the built in JavaScript and forms handling support move PDF more towards the kind of applications that we might have used Macromedia Flash for in past times. Some functionality is only supported on Windows platforms. You must check at the Adobe web site whether the platform you are using in your workflow has the features you need.

Now that Macromedia and Adobe are the same company, this convergence of Flash and PDF is likely to continue. The first fruits of that are already emerging with the integration of Macromedia's conferencing tools with Acrobat in the form of Adobe Connect. As Flash becomes more integrated, we then have a platform on which we can publish interactive content. That platform would be more widely available than any other target platform we could publish to.

I have some small worries that this evolution of PDF will break something or detract from its near perfect suitability for long term document storage but perhaps that fear is unfounded and best dealt with by careful use of profiles.

PDF files are a little more problematic to integrate into a workflow than plain text or RTF because the text is stored in an encoded form and is not necessarily stored continuously in a single block. It is also prefaced by a position on screen and this means that some files contain the text run in a sequence other than that which we would choose to read it.

Open Office Org: http://www.openoffice.org/
Adobe: http://www.adobe.com/

Extracting the text requires that the page be imaged and then 'read'. This is why an OCR approach is often the most effective way to extract text from a PDF file.

Provided you have rights to open and extract or edit a file, Acrobat 8 introduces some useful new exporting features that alleviate some of these issues. If they can be driven from a script within the workflow, we have a useful conversion tool at our disposal.

The printing industry has demonstrated that it is possible achieve portable documents by constraining the PDF files to only use a restricted set of functionality which is defined by a separate body. The PDF/X profiles and the other similar derivatives seem to work well when constructing pre-press workflows. The PDF/E and PDF/A profiles are also being developed for engineers and archivists respectively.

Adobe is aware of this and they have a good record of accomplishment at developing robust and well-conceived architectures. We shouldn't be overly concerned about the long-term direction that PDF is going in.

Although PDF is an optimal format for storage and duplication, using it as an interchange format is a little more complex. Adobe tools such as Illustrator and Acrobat are able to open and deal with PDF files. Most other tools that cite them as an input source can merely place them. It might be a smart placement, which allows a round trip to a PDF editor with an automatic update on the return. The application that is placing the PDF file into a canvas doesn't really understand the internal structure. It may be using an Adobe supplied rendering engine.

Some third-party solutions have found that imaging the PDF file and then accessing the pixel map as if it had just arrived from a scanner and pushing it through an OCR program can extract meaningful text from the PDF file.

Opening PDF files and scanning them is also possible and because they are a raw text format, we can apply the dynamic publishing techniques provided we are careful not to break the PDF syntax. Extracting the text is difficult because PDF distillers and output libraries do not insert a coherent run of text into the document in the order that it reads. A PDF file contains the text as a series of disconnected pen-position and text drawing commands. It is after all an imaging standard not a text interchange standard.

Given that extracting content from PDF files is sometimes difficult, we might prefer not to use it as an intermediate format in our workflows if we know that we want to extract the text later.

UNIX Roff and Friends

On the UNIX operating system, text processing is mature and well established. You can use many different text-processing tools. Originally, they were intended for hand editing the markup and then running them through a render process to create the output for a typesetter or hard copy device.

Just because they are old tools does not mean they can't be useful. A modern workflow system can still make use of these processors because the automation mechanisms are all well tested and reliable.

Conversion utilities will make short work of transforming these document formats into something else. That 'something else' might be more difficult to create directly from within your workflow. This is an easy way to solve the problem. The most popular implementation is called **groff**. Wikipedia has an interesting article on **troff**, which is its predecessor. The online man pages in your UNIX workstation will tell you more.

OK, it is not XML, or even SGML-based. However, if it works and solves a problem that's OK. These have been around for so long now that they are de-facto standards.

TeX

The TeX and MetaFont markup languages were developed by Donald Knuth in order to typeset some complex notation that he wanted to publish. This is still used for complex scientific and mathematical typesetting.

It is easy to produce with templates because it is textual in its source form and because it has been around for a long time there are a variety of tools and processors for it. Writing TeX code from scratch is a highly skilled activity although very popular in academic circles.

A macro layer called *LaTeX* augments it with a descriptive markup language, which makes TeX-based content much easier to deploy.

SGML

SGML inherited the abstraction concept we use today from earlier work by Dr Brian Reid on a project called *Scribe*. That abstraction is the separation of content from form and style. Many markup languages have evolved from that early work, including SGML, XML, HTML, LaTeX and PostScript as well.

SGML promoted the idea of a DTD, which enabled users to create their own markup languages. Like XML, SGML is a meta-language and is described in ISO 8879.

You probably won't need to use SGML unless you are developing markup languages of your own. For most users, XML and its derivatives or even plain HTML will meet their needs. There will be a select few who need the power of SGML to get their work done.

SGML is complex and hard to use and mastering it is a specialist skill. Once a template has been developed, it can be produced dynamically. The hard work of developing a workflow process only needs to be done once.

Runoff tools: http://www.netadmintools.com/html/7roff.man.html

Illustration Exchange

Exchanging pictures between systems or passing them through the workflow requires that you think about the relative merits of moving vector data vs. pixmap data. Draw or paint. Illustrator or Photoshop. CAD models or rendered images. It is analogous to delivering a table of numbers or an image of a pie or bar chart.

Vectors and raw data have some structure, which might be interrogated. By the time an image has been rendered, there is not much you can do with it apart from remap the colors and scale the picture to fit the target display rectangle.

A lot of useful work was done on pixel-based interchange mechanisms in the 1980s and 90s. The Portable Bit Map and Portable Pixel Map formats and interchange libraries were developed around that time. Some work has been done recently on interchanging vector data. This happens a lot in the 3D graphics and visual effects industry as models are exchanged between the different animation tools.

CAD systems are also good at exchanging drawing information with formats such as DXF and IGES. This throws up a problem with the overloading of jargon words. There are two kinds of DXF files. One used by AutoCAD systems to exchange CAD models and the other is used to exchange movie files in postproduction. The industries are sufficiently separated that problems don't often crop up.

EPSF

Encapsulated PostScript files may be another alternative, although constructing these files requires detailed knowledge of PostScript coding and that is a somewhat rare skill. Adobe Illustrator may also help you with this. It is a useful exchange format. The EPSF images can be nested (placed) inside other images and a component-based approach to constructing your pictures might be developed. PDF files can be created by re-wrapping EPSF content.

CAD Export Files

DXF files are one of the interchange formats used by Bentley, Intergraph, AutoCAD and other CAD software applications that are favored by engineering and architectural companies.

The oil industry makes great use of CGM Metafiles, which store visual information. The format is different but these are designed to address the same tasks as SVG files. CGM files have been around for about 20 years and evolved out of the GKS and CORE graphics standards from the 1980s.

You will encounter these formats if you need to import engineering, building or mapping resources from other organizations.

TIFF Byte Order Mark

The Big-Endian/Little-Endian data issue arose with TIFF files when they were first deployed. At the time, you could not tell whether a TIFF had been created on a PC or Macintosh system. This was important, because numeric values in the file needed to be interpreted with the endianness taken into account.

TIFF files are manufactured in Intel and Motorola compatible bit ordering. This big-endian—little-endian issue often crops up when moving binary data between systems.

The first two byes in the file indicate the byte order used within the file. The only two legal values are shown in Table 16-1:

Table 16-1 Tiff BOM values

Endian	Letter code	Hex code	Decimal value
Little	II	4949	18761
Big	MM	4D4D	19789

In the "II" (Intel) format, byte order is always from the least significant byte to the most significant byte, for both 16-bit and 32-bit integers. This format is called *little-endian* byte order. In the "MM" (Motorola) format, byte order is always from most significant to least significant, for both 16-bit and 32-bit integers. This is called *big-endian* byte order.

Now that Macintosh systems are based on Intel processors, the original reason for this seems to make little sense. The code written to handle TIFF files on Mac OS X will be designed to work with Big Endian data and is not likely to change and it can open and process the alternative format anyway.

You may decide to export one or other of these two formats but you should allow the import of either.

Multimedia Interchange

To be able to operate on a variety of media types we should develop a taxonomy to organize the media types first. These are the main kinds of content that we would want to operate on in our workflow:

Table 16-2 Multimedia interchange

Media	Content
Audio	Speech, music
Video	Programs, animation, live feeds
Graphics	Vector, raster
Interactivity	Navigation, input devices
Auxiliary	Alpha channels
Environment	Scenes, user journeys

Next, we have to come to terms with storing our multimedia. Storing the component media types is easy by comparison. Our multimedia presentation can be done in two ways. Either by containment or by reference.

Table 16-3 Containment vs. reference

Format	Containment	Reference
Windows Media	√	
Real	√	
QuickTime	√	√
SMIL		√
XML		√
MPEG-4	√	√
Flash	√	
Shockwave		√

The upside of containment is that all the assets are embedded within the file. If you have the file, you have all the assets. The downside is that you have a large file containing some assets that you may not use. The linkages are also hardwired. A dynamic presentation is much harder to manufacture.

Media content architectures that use an indirect reference to the assets have the advantage that components of the presentation can be exchanged without altering the controlling document. The downside is that if the network connection is lost, you may have the referencing container but be missing some of the assets. This degrades the user experience.

QuickTime and MPEG-4 are the only ones listed in the table, which can be both containment and reference architectures. This is a by-product of their object-based design. MPEG-4 inherited this capability when it adopted the QuickTime file format as the basis for its own file containers. This may change as platforms like Flash are evolving very rapidly and might adopt some of these attributes as well.

MPEG-4

The MPEG-4 standard is often thought of as a video codec. This standard describes much more than that. It looks like being an important container for multimedia content but it is experiencing a very difficult birth.

There are now 22 parts to this standard. It keeps getting bigger and bigger. It is probably now too large and complex to be adopted and implemented in its entirety as a single standard.

Two of its component parts are alternative video codecs. The collected standard is referred to as ISO/IEC 14496.

Table 16-4 Parts of the MPEG-4 standard

Part	Title	Description
1	Systems	Synchronization and multiplexing of video and audio.
2	Visual	A video compression codec for visual data. Superseded in efficiency by H.264.
3	Audio	Advanced Audio Coding (AAC) tools.
4	Conformance	Procedures for testing conformance to other parts of the standard.
5	Reference	Software for demonstrating other parts of the standard.
6	DMIF	Delivery Multimedia Integration Framework.
7	Optimized reference	Supplement to Part 5.
8	Carriage on IP	Specifies a method to carry MPEG-4 content on IP networks.
9	Reference hardware	Hardware designs showing how to implement other parts of the standard.
10	Advanced Video Coding	Identical to the ITU-T H.264 standard.
11	BIFS	Scene description and Application engine.
12	Base Media File Format	Generic file format for storing media.
13	IPMP	Intellectual Property Management and Protection Extensions.
14	MPEG-4 File Format	Container file format for MPEG-4 content based on Part 12.
15	AVC File Format	Storage of H.264 video based on Part 12.
16	AFX	Animation Framework eXtension.
17	Sub-titles	Timed Text subtitle format.
18	Fonts	Font Compression and Streaming.
19	Textures	Synthesized Texture Stream.
20	LASeR	Lightweight Scene Representation.
21	GFX	MPEG-J Graphical Framework eXtension.
22	OFFS	Open Font Format Specification.

If we can cope with the complexity of what is a large and comprehensive standard, this might be a way to develop the kind of multimedia interchange product that we need at the core of our content management system.

Because it is an MPEG standard, it is supposed to be open and integrates well with the other important standards that metadata engineers are interested in. namely MPEG-7 and MPEG-21.

For interactivity, we would be interested in the systems layer described in Part 1, the scene description (BIFS) in Part 11 and the alternate lightweight scene description (LASeR) in Part 20. Other parts of the standard also have some impact on the construction of metadata systems:

MPEG-4 Licensing

This standard has been under development for 8 years and aside from the AVC and AAC video and audio components, the rest appears to be as far from being widely adopted as it ever did.

The major downside to new and emerging open standards is the punishingly high license fees to use them. The use of proprietary technologies with strings attached significantly undermines the entire open standards ethos.

The whole edifice is likely to collapse under the licensing requirements. It is too hard and expensive to get a workable license and make a profit. It is a perfect example of how a combination of lawyers and accountants can completely kill a viable and highly useful technology before it even has a chance to establish itself.

The hundreds of people who devoted significant time and effort to developing MPEG-4 must be bitterly disappointed at the licensing mess that the standard has gotten into. This could all have been avoided by mandating that proprietary interests should be left out of the standards design process.

You would be wise to consider this carefully if you plan to use MPEG-4. Some due diligence is required to construct models that are genuinely rights free.

The best place to look for information about MPEG related matters is the MPEG Industry Forum. Refer to Appendix B for some information on MPEG-7 and 21.

Professional Exchange Formats

There are groups of file formats, which are used in film and TV production for moving very large or very high quality content around. They aren't all designed with the consumer in mind at all. Five principle formats are important.

- Digital Picture eXchange files (DPX).
- General purpose eXchange Files (GXF).
- Material eXchange Files (MXF).
- Advanced Authoring Format files (AAF).
- QuickTime.

The most complete coverage of these file formats can be found in the *File Interchange Handbook*, edited by Brad Gilmer and published by Focal Press in 2004 (ISBN 0-240-80605-0).

Digital Picture eXchange (DPX) Files

In a world where we try to compress film and video down to its smallest possible size and carry it around in a packaged format within a single file, DPX goes completely the other way. Because they are used in film production, they don't escape 'into-the-wild' and wouldn't be a great deal of use to a consumer if they did.

DPX makes no compromises in quality to store a film in a small container. Instead, it uses one whole file per single frame of moving picture information. The files can also contain a rich metadata payload in the form of extensible headers. Any popular aspect ratio can be stored in DPX files.

Probably the closest modern moving image codec is Pixlet, which was introduced by Apple several years ago. This was developed for Pixar and is based on Wavelet coding. The Pixlet codec stores individual single frames. Another close relative is motion JPEG.

DPX image files are based on TIFF images with SMPTE time code and film edge code added in addition to other metadata.

General eXchange Format (GXF) Files

The GXF format was standardized by SMPTE as standard 360M and is used for exchanging broadcast quality material between post-production facilities houses and broadcasters. It describes a file and a stream format. Content can be delivered on tape or via a serial interface.

The GXF standard defines a generic container. What you store in that container is up to you. It does not define any particular flavor of video. You might find any of the following in a GXF container:

- Motion JPEG.
- Uncompressed audio.
- Time codes.
- MPEG video.
- DVCPRO video.
- High definition MPEG-2.
- Dolby Digital audio.
- Dolby E audio.

GXF stores fragments of media in a packetized or chunked form where the fragments are organized by time. Several separate streams of media may be interleaved. No one packet is guaranteed to be followed by another that belongs to the same stream. In this respect, it is similar to QuickTime and AVI.

Material eXchange Format (MXF) Files

The MXF file format evolved out of the Pro-MPEG Forum and their integration projects that were driven by a group of manufacturers who collaborated with one another to achieve interoperability. The AAF Association were also involved in the process.

MXF and AAF are two different file formats but it is possible to convert back and forth between them. This is one of the fruits of having the AAF Association involved in the development of MXF.

The MXF containers like GXF do not mandate any particular essence format for carriage inside them. They can convey a variety of different kinds of media. Even if a system can unpack an MXF file, there is no guarantee that it can support what it finds inside.

MXF is a major contribution to the management of essence data with metadata descriptions. It can support the coding and embedding of metadata using KLV techniques. The files convey a rich set of descriptive material as well as the essence data.

Advanced Authoring Format (AAF) Files

The AAF file format was designed for exchanging content between content authoring tools. It evolved from contributions made by several companies as it was developed:

- ASCII-based Edit Decision Lists from CMX.
- Open Media Framework from AVID.
- Film Log EDL exchange from da Vinci Systems.
- Avid Log Exchange.
- AES-31 audio interchange.

MXF takes a subset of the AAF internal object storage model and rewraps it using KLV constructs. The files are physically different but logically similar.

QuickTime Files

QuickTime is a multimedia platform technology developed by Apple Computer. It is used by consumers but is also the foundation on which complex video tools such as the Final Cut Non-Linear-Editor is built. Tools such as iMovie could not exist without QuickTime.

 QuickTime is often thought of as a video codec but it is much more than that. It is a nexus for converting many different still image, audio and video files from one format to another.

You can take a video and break it into individual file per frame image sequences. This is like DPX. QuickTime can also convert graphics file formats from one to another and reconstruct that image sequence onto a timeline.

Take into account its audio conversion tools and its MIDI playback and rendering capabilities and you have a tool that sits at the foundation of CD and DVD authoring tools as well.

QuickTime is hugely powerful, although the emerging MPEG-4 standard comes close. Flash looks the same but the similarity is only skin-deep but it too is catching up very quickly.

Most people don't realize all this power is available at their fingertips even though they use it every day when they load an AAC compressed audio file or a pop music video into their video iPod.

Summary

These are a selected few of the interchange file formats we might use within the workflow. Any file format is a candidate for use. You know what your workflow is being designed to do and that could involve any data type you can imagine. Using file formats that are more popular means, you are more likely to find tools that operate on them. We would hope that open standards offer us the widest possible choice.

XML represents possibly the most popular file format for transporting any kind of data that there has ever been. Although we are looking at alternatives to XML, we should understand a little of what it could offer. Then we can incorporate it when appropriate. The next chapter will explore XML from an applied point of view.

XML-Based Tools and Processes

XML Rules—OK

XML is taking over the world.

Well not really, but eXtensible Markup Language (XML) is the native file format for Open Office Org, AbiWord, and the iWork applications from Apple (Keynote and Pages). Microsoft is moving towards a web-centered XML specification, which will allow XML files to be created and edited by any of the Office components. The current version for Windows supports some XML export but version 12 of Office (due in 2007) is expected to improve on this significantly. There are many other XML tools, filters, and editors available, some proprietary and some open-source.

In this chapter, we will briefly look at some XML technologies. There isn't room to delve in too deeply. If you intend to use XML, you should spend some time researching and testing the tools.

Don't Believe All of the Hype!

Historically we might have spent a great deal of time developing glue-ware for our work-flow systems. This glue would be necessary because of all the different kinds of data files being created in incompatible formats. Exchanging data between one system and another used to be difficult.

These days, most modern applications are able to exchange data with each other by sharing XML files. You need to take some of the marketing claims with a pinch of salt. Often an XML import/export is touted as solving all of the interchange problems. It is certainly true that an XML interchange can help but if the XML is poorly formed or constructed using an incorrect, outdated, or inappropriate DTD, then it still won't be compatible. If it is used correctly, XML can be a powerful tool for interchanging, transforming, and encapsulating a wide variety of data.

What is a Markup Language?

A markup language embellishes text with extra information about the text. The embellishment might add style and appearance control or define regions of the text as having some semantic meaning. This is expressed using markup. The best-known of all is HyperText Markup Language (HTML).

HTML is descended from a long tradition of markup languages that have been used in the publishing industry to create books and other printed matter. All of the participants from author to typesetter (via editors) make use of markup to convey information about the text. Therefore, all markup is metadata, since it describes, structures or formats the essence text and is not intended for view by the public, even though it may affect how the public perceives the essence text.

Markup languages can be classified in several categories:

- Structural.
- Formatting.
- Descriptive.

Structural Markup

Structural markup organizes the internal structure of the document and is quite separate from styling or semantic meaning. The tags in the encoding delimit structural parts of the document. Three that we are already familiar with from HTML are **`<head>`**, **`<title>`** and **`<body>`**.

In a nontagged document, we might determine the organization and hierarchy of text by other characteristics such as the placement of new line markers and tab characters.

In a mail message or HTTP server response, the presence of an empty line (two successive new line markers with nothing in between) indicates where the headers end and the body of the response starts (see RFC 2822).

Formatting Markup

Formatting markup is concerned with the presentation of the text by embedding style commands into the documents. Sometimes it is referred to as styling markup. That is an outdated approach now that we apply style sheets. In the HTML world, we are familiar with **`<em>`**, **`<strong>`** and **`<font>`** tags. Going forward, the abstraction of styling into separate and potentially shared style sheets means that much of the markup disappears and is now moved into style sheets that are connected to our document with **`<link>`** and **`<style>`** tags. This approach is built around the semantic markup where style is applied according to the meaning of a piece of text rather than its physical location.

Formatting text by embedding style directly into the text inhibits us from reusing it for other purposes. That styling needs to be removed, and that's not easy to do. A simple global search-and-replace is not reliable enough to exchange styling commands for structural markup. We need to transform using an object model. This is where the parsing approach used by an XML-based process like eXtensible Stylesheet Language Transformations (XSLT) comes into play.

Examples of formatting markup languages are the traditional UNIX-based text-processing tools: **`nroff`**, **`troff`**, TeX, and Adobe's page description language, PostScript. Formatting markup has been used for many years in publishing applications, which are operated by highly skilled typographers who have had to learn many fine points of the markup languages.

Semantic Markup

Semantic markup adds meaning to a document. The markup looks physically similar to structural markup. Instead of describing physical parts of the document, it applies meaning to the text contained inside the body it is tagging. It is completely abstract from the text and implies no styling whatsoever. Because we earlier moved all our styling into a separate stylesheet, we are now able to apply that styling in a more logical way.

Because a fragment of text can be labeled as a product name or price code, we can apply styles to objects of a similar semantic type. Sales price and discount amount, for instance, can be distinguished from each other now and styled accordingly.

This approach is used in syndication schemes like Atom, which marks a new item as having been updated. On its own, that means nothing and is invisible to the user. If the RSS browser chooses to, it can highlight any updated items by applying a style directly to those objects and only those objects.

If we can distinguish between semantics for applying style and appearance control, then we can leverage those semantics to pass meaningful documents from one application to another. This is the core of why XML is so powerful. If there were one single reason to use XML (and there are many others), this would be it.

A variant of semantic markup (called *generic markup*) seeks to describe document content in ways other than by a strictly hierarchical tree structure. Trees are useful, but they are not the best way to represent all content. Books can be organized into trees, but as we reach the more fine-grained organization of the text in manuscript, the nested structure begins to get in our way. A book is serial and linear in nature.

The important thing is to indicate the semantics. Possibly not maintaining a tree -like structure to the layout. Internally, even documents that don't look tree-structured really are for purposes of XSLT transforms. The tree still has a top node but builds a flatter structure with fewer levels underneath.

XML

XML is a metalanguage, a language that can be used to describe other languages. It covers a huge range of file-based storage structures. If an application is expecting to import a MathML file and you give it a NewsML file instead, the interchange won't work. The Document Type Declaration (DTD) differences might be handled quite gracefully and some systems may be able to import freeform XML data of any kind without being told what kind of data it is.

XML does provide supporting mechanisms that would allow you to embed a MathML formula inside a NewsML story, and the name-spacing mechanisms and DTD support would ensure that both could coexist and their intent and meaning could be understood unambiguously by the receiving application.

Table 17-1 lists some XML-based language schemas.

Table 17-1 Some XML schemas

Language	Purpose
ChemML	Chemical modeling.
MathML	Mathematical formulae.
NewsML	Syndicated news stories.
GML	Geography Markup Language.
RDF	Resource Description Framework.
RSS	Really Simple Syndication.
Atom	Atom Syndication Format.
XHTML	Web page content.
SVG	Vector graphic diagrams.
DocBook	Book manuscripts.
MusicXML	Music scores.
XBEL	Bookmark exchange.
XUL	XML User Interface Language.
XSPF	XML Shareable Playlist Formal.
Open eBook	An XML-based format for producing eBooks.
XBRL	eXtensible Business Reporting Language.

XML Features

XML describes a tree-based structure for organizing information storage. Information is represented as text, with markup describing a hierarchy of *character data*, container-like *elements*, and *attributes* of those elements.

The smallest unit of information is a single *character*. Any file containing valid XML is a *document*. The structure of the document is organized into a series of nested tag-delimited *entities*. The names of the entities, their permitted hierarchy, and the meanings of the elements and their attributes mean are defined by a *schema*. This schema is customizable by the end-user.

Because XML is a metalanguage, it defines a syntax, which can be used to define new languages. This syntax is rigid but powerful. The rigid structural rules allow all applications to parse an XML file even if they cannot fully understand the meaning of its entities. The schema description provides the semantic detail that the rigid structure lacks.

Because XML is based around Unicode, it is truly international in scope.

Basic Syntax Summary

XML is easy to understand. We won't go into it very deeply but a little basic knowledge is useful. Then we can apply XML files to our workflow. There are many books on XML, and there is no need to repeat them here. We will learn just enough XML to be dangerous.

We will also briefly look at the range of XML-related technologies. These are useful when we come to apply XML in a practical way. XML Namespaces allow us to embed data belonging to multiple DTDs in the same document.

XML Version Header

The first line of an XML file declares the XML version and the text encoding. It is optional, although it is good practice to include it. The character encoding is also optional but helps the parser make sense of the file.

```
<?xml version="1.0" encoding="UTF-8"?>
```

Document Type Declaration (DTD)

The next line could contain a Document Type Declaration (DTD). This is optional. It can be embedded in the document or included from an external source. That external source need not be on the local computer. It is like including a stylesheet in an HTML web page. The **<!DOCTYPE>** entity tag looks like this:

```
<!DOCTYPE mydoc [
        ... entity declaring stuff here ...
]>
```

You can define entities that represent characters, new element tags, or included files, which can contain standard sections of XML that are boiler-plated together.

The DTD is inherited from Standardized General Markup Language (SGML) and is the oldest schema format for XML. DTD support is always provided, since it is defined in the XML 1.0 standard. It is limited for several reasons:

- DTD does not support the more recent XML features.
- DTD cannot support namespaces.
- DTD is not flexible enough to fully represent some formal aspects of an XML document.
- DTD describes the schema in a non-XML syntax, inherited from SGML.

Because of these limitations, DTDs are gradually being superseded by XML schema language.

Element Tags

The basic unit of storage in an XML file is an element. An element has a name. It might have one or more optional attributes (like an HTML tag). The element name is used as a markup tag. It usually has an opening and closing variation. Between the matched pair of tags is the element body. Elements can be nested within each other. In fact they usually are.

```
<elementname attribute="value">content body</elementname>
```

Element tags must be correctly nested. An element whose open tag is not at the same nested hierarchical level is wrong, and the parser will reject the file.

There must be one single root element at the top of the file. This element is normally named after the schema if a DTD is specified. This element is called the document element and is the root of Document Object Model (DOM).

There is a special shorthand way to represent an element that has no other elements nested within it. These two lines are functionally identical.

```
<mytag></mytag>
<mytag />
```

Character Entities

If we need to use a character that cannot be typed on our keyboard, or one that XML deems to be a markup character, we must escape it so that the parser interprets it correctly. This was covered in some depth in Chapter 6. To recap, character entities can be described with an entity reference name or a numeric character reference to the code point within the character encoding for the document.

XML understands five named character entities, which are all prefixed with an ampersand (`&`) and terminated by a semi-colon (`;`). They are summarized in Table 17-2:

Table 17-2 Pre-defined XML character entities

Entity	Character represented
`&amp;`	&
`&lt;`	<
`&gt;`	>
`&apos;`	'
`&quot;`	"

More user defined character entities can be declared in the document's DTD.

Numeric character references contain the '**#**' character followed by a value instead of a name. The value can be a decimal value or a hexadecimal equivalent with a preceding '**x**' character. This value is the code point within the Unicode character set. This provides a way to describe characters that would be impossible to type. It gives access to the full range of international symbols that include Arabic, Chinese, and Japanese, etc. We can use this in place of names if we want to.

Here is a single line in the DTD that defines the copyright symbol using the hexadecimal numeric notation and maps it to a named character entity. We will use **copy** as a name since that is consistent with HTML. That copyright symbol can then be used in a subsequent declaration.

```
<?xml version="1.0" encoding="UTF-8"?>
<!DOCTYPE mydoc [
   <!ENTITY copy "&#xA9;">
   <!ENTITY message "Copyright &copy; 2007, Focal Press">
]>
<frontmatter>
   &message;
</ frontmatter >
```

Because XML only has the basic five entities defined, each of the set of rich character entities that HTML supports would need to be defined in the XHTML DTD.

CDATA and #PCDATA

A **CDATA** (character data) section is the mechanism for including text in an XML document but indicating that the parser should ignore it. It is raw character data, but the parser knows that there is nothing in it that it should examine further to extract document structure. It is bounded by the following markup:

```
<![CDATA[" content here "]]>
```

This is a neat way of embedding some XML code within a document but preventing it from being parsed. This could be useful in a workflow scenario where you are passing some instructions to a remote system. Bury them in a **CDATA** section and they should survive transformations and still be intact on arrival. You must not include the text "**]]>**" without escaping it, or the **CDATA** section will be prematurely terminated.

A **#PCDATA** (parsed Character Data) section indicates that the contents of an element can contain a mixture of character data and markup. It will be parsed and, if necessary, the parser will drill down to examine any lower level document hierarchy. Character entities will be expanded along the way.

The **CDATA** keyword is also used to define the string data type for an element attribute. This is not the same as a **CDATA** section, which is in the element body.

XML Document Structure

We only want to use correctly structured XML documents. If we interchange incorrectly structured documents, it causes problems further down the chain of processing when the file is encountered by a parser that rejects it. A correctly structured XML document must be well formed and valid. The parser is expected to refuse to process the file if it is not well formed.

Well formed documents conform to these XML syntax rules:

- Only one root element.
- Nonempty elements have a start and end tag.
- Empty elements have a self-closing single tag.
- All attribute values are quoted.
- Tags must not overlap but can be nested.
- All characters are correctly defined within the document's declared character set.
- Element names are case-sensitive and must match in opening and closing tags.

A valid document is well formed and complies with the rules described in a schema or DTD defined by a user.

XML Data Binding

If the document is well formed, then the parser can construct an object model when it processes the document. There are two principle alternatives: DOM and SAX. DOM stands for Document Object Model, and will be familiar to JavaScript programmers who have worked on the internals of a web page. SAX is a serial parser that works a little differently.

The DOM has bindings to all the popular programming languages. In a web browser, that binding happens automatically in other contexts, you may need to locate the root object and parse the document tree to create the object model which you can then access through your chosen language binding.

Document Object Model (DOM)

DOM is a hierarchically organized object tree that replicates the nested tag structure very closely.

The entire document can be navigated as if it were a tree of "node" objects. Each object corresponds to an element tag. A DOM is usually created by the parser as it scans the document for the first time.

The data types in the DOM nodes are abstract. The context of the implementations provides a specific binding. DOM structures are memory intensive, because the entire document needs to be loaded into memory for the tree to be constructed. That tree needs to be complete before any access to the DOM is allowed.

At least two copies of the document now reside in memory, the raw source version and the DOM.

The SAX Parser

An alternative to loading the entire document into memory and creating a DOM is to parse the document from beginning to end and deal with objects as they go past.

SAX is a lexical, event-driven parser that reads a document in serial fashion. When a tag is encountered, SAX calls a handler for that tag. Nesting is managed by incrementing counters when start tags are processed and decrementing the appropriate counter when a closure tag is encountered.

The callbacks mean that SAX is fast and easy to implement. The downside, as with any serial processor, is that random access is problematic.

Schema Design Choices

Schema design needs some care to achieve a design that is flexible but not too verbose. One particular point worth thinking about is whether to use a new element tag or add a property to an existing tag when creating a new structure value.

Both of these are legal XML and convey the same information. One is more compact than the other and needs to be accessed differently when you operate on it with scripts or filters.

```
<superhero>
  <name>Batman</name>
</superhero>

<superhero name="Batman" />
```

The first form creates a new child object in the DOM tree. The second does not add a new tree layer. Instead, it adds a property to the parent object in the layer above where it would have been created if it were implemented as a tag.

Navigationally this is different. The connections between nodes, and hence the parent-child object relationships in the DOM makes a different structure. Access to a property rather than an object's body content does not use quite the same syntax.

To decide which approach is best, apply the same kind of normalization principles that we discussed in Chapter 3, and then decide whether the new value merits a new object class or whether it is merely a property that belongs to an existing class.

One of the difficulties with XML is that relational joins that can be traversed in either direction are very difficult to express in XML. Which of these is the most appropriate way to nest a musician and band element?

```
<musician name="John Lennon">
<band>Beatles</band>
</musician>

<band name="Beatles">
<musician>John Lennon</musician>
</band>
```

XML Schema Language

DTD-based descriptions are now being replaced by the W3C-standardized XML Schema Definitions (XSD), which are much more powerful than DTDs ever were. W3C XML Schema (WXS) implementations have several advantages over the older format:

- A rich data-typing system.
- More detailed constraints on logical structure of a document.
- More robust validation.
- XML-based format.

Not everyone is happy with WXS, because it is a very large specification. The XML basis makes it verbose, whereas DTD was relatively compact. An XSD can be quite hard to write efficiently. The validation of the schema before we use it to validate the document that must conform to it is a large processing overhead. Even though it is more advanced, it still has some limitations to its modeling capabilities.

RELAX NG

An alternative to both DTD and XSD is the Regular Language for XML Next Generation (RELAX NG) schema language. This hybrid can be described in an XML form but is readily converted to a compact form for deployment. This gives us the advantage of using XML editors to compose it while removing the validation overhead of XSD.

There are other schema languages that you can use to describe your document structure. An ISO-standardized language, Document Schema Description Languages (DSDL), is emerging, as is Schematron Assertion Language. These are not yet widely used but may become more popular in due course.

XML Namespaces

XML namespaces let us embed element tags from multiple DTDs into the same document. These different vocabularies frequently contain the same element tag names but they mean something entirely different in each DTD. We must avoid those element name collisions.

XML namespaces does this by adding a prefix and a colon to the element tag name. That prefix is defined at the head of the document with the inclusion of the DTD.

This allows us to combine markup languages into hybrid standards such as XHTML+SMIL or XHTML+MathML+SVG.

W3C XML namespaces specification: http://www.w3.org/TR/REC-xml-names/

This fragment of XML shows how two namespaces can be combined in one document. It is quoted from the W3C standard "Namespaces in XML 1.0 (Second Edition)".

```
<?xml version="1.0"?>
<!-- both namespace prefixes are available throughout -->
<bk:book xmlns:bk='urn:loc.gov:books'
         xmlns:isbn='urn:ISBN:0-395-36341-6'>
    <bk:title>Cheaper by the Dozen</bk:title>
    <isbn:number>1568491379</isbn:number>
</bk:book>
```

The name space exists for the element that it is specified in and any elements contained within it. Closing the element also disposes of the namespace.

Controlling XML Appearance with CSS

XML can be styled for rendering in a browser with CSS style sheets. The XML document must include a reference to the style sheet in order to make the linkage. HTML uses the **<link>** tag. XML does it like this:

```
<?xml-stylesheet type="text/css" href="myStyles.css"?>
```

 Yes, that was an intentional different spelling and not a typographical error. XML likes its stylesheets to be all in one word while CSS prefers style sheets as two words.

You can use client-side XSL stylesheets if you prefer them to CSS style sheets.

eXtensible Stylesheet Language (XSL)

An eXtensible Stylesheet Language (XSL) filter can transform an XML document for display or printing. XSL can be used to convert XML data into HTML or other formats. These transformations can be applied at the server or client end of the transaction.

If your target browser supports it, then client-side XSL Transformation (XSLT) is specified like this:

```
<?xml-stylesheet type="text/xsl" href="myTransform.xslt"?>
```

It may be more convenient and predictable to perform the transformation at the server. This uses XSLT tools that take XSL stylesheets as an input to control the processing.

XSL Transformations (XSLT)

XSLT is useful for converting between different XML schemas or to turn XML data into web pages and PDF documents.

XSLT is an XML-based document transformation language. The XSLT processor uses an XSLT stylesheet to guide the conversion of the XML document object tree into another tree that is then serialized as XML, HTML, plain text, or another format supported by the XSLT processor.

A new document is created by applying a filter to the old document, leaving the original document unchanged. If required, the new document can be output as standard XML syntax or some other format. HTML or plain text files are often generated as output documents.

An XSLT process will begin at the start of a document and work towards the end. The processing is managed by matching tag nodes to rules in the stylesheet. When a match is made, a substitution happens and the output is constructed from stylesheet content rather than source document content. When no match takes place, original source document content is output.

XSLT processors are now a standard component within operating systems.

Refer to Tutorial 55 to see how to convert XML to HTML with XSLT.

Other Important XML Technologies

New component technologies are being developed for use in processing XML content. Some of them improve on existing techniques; others will replace the "old way." It is difficult to predict which will survive and when they will be ready for deployment. The W3C organization is the best place to check for status updates on a periodic basis.

Table 17-3 lists some interesting technologies that you should research further.

Table 17-3 Other XML technologies	
Technology	*Description*
XPath	Refers to individual fragments within an XML document. Used by other tools that need random access. XPath works like DOM and uses path expression language for selecting the required data within XML documents. It is a little bit like using UNIX directory paths.
XSL FO	eXtensible Stylesheet Language – Formatting Objects has been designed to describe the page layout using an object-oriented model. Where HTML describes a web page, XSL-FO describes a printed page. It can be processed to create RTF and PDF files with the XSL-FO tools.
XQuery	XML Query language is defined by W3C as a language for querying, constructing, and transforming XML data. It works like an SQL query on a relational database but searches an XML document instead. It may overlap with some tasks to which XSLT is better suited. It is currently read-access only.

Table 17-3 Other XML technologies (continued)

XUpdate	A lightweight query and update mechanism that has now apparently gone into hibernation.
XPointer	Describes a system for addressing components of XML-based internet media.
XML Signature	Defines the syntax and rules for creating and processing digital signatures on XML document content.
XML Encryption	If we need to encrypt a document for security or privacy, XML Encryption defines the syntax and rules for encrypting XML document content.

Binary XML Formats

XML documents are textual. They are not very compact, even though they are usually quite small. Once you insert any amount of content, they begin to bulk up. They compress well with gzip compression, because the text contains many similar characters that compression software can exploit to reduce the size. This requires that the document is decompressed first. A better solution would be one where the document was as compact but could still be parsed directly.

Binary XML, or Binary eXtensible Markup Language, describes any technique for encoding an XML document in a binary data format. A binary XML format reduces the verbosity and complexity of parsing but also gets in the way of casual text editing. The conversion between source and binary needs to be simple and lossless. On the plus side, a binary format can be accessed randomly and is easier to index.

No clear winner has yet emerged. ASN.1 coding is being used for some prototype projects under the name of Fast Infoset which is being developed by Sun Microsystems.

DocBook

DocBook is a markup language for describing technical documentation content in an XML container. It was designed by HAL Computer Systems and O'Reilly Media for authoring computer hardware and software manuals, but it is applicable to any kind of documentation. DocBook is now maintained and administered by the DocBook Technical Committee at the Organization for the Advancement of Structured Information Standards (OASIS).

The DocBook standard is a wholly XML-based description of an entire book. It embodies markup that describes sections, paragraphs, chapters, and all the other components that you need to create a book.

It is not particularly easy to work with directly. A few DocBook compatible tools are beginning to be made available. Typically, you would edit in a word processor and save as DocBook. If this is not possible, then converting to DocBook from a format you can export is the next best thing. You don't really have as much control as you might want over the DocBook content that is created in this fashion. A manual fix-up might be necessary. If you are publishing DocBook content from scratch then you have as much control as you need.

Once you have the valid DocBook content, you can use XSL stylesheets to convert it to any other format you need. The OASIS team manages a collection of definitive XSL stylesheets that convert DocBook XML into many other useful formats.

There are XSL stylesheets to create a web HTML version, PDF, and RTF for import back into Word. Because it is XML, you can transform it into any other format you need.

Developing large-scale reference books in a database and rendering them out as a DocBook structure is a particularly useful approach. The DocBook content can then be processed with XSLT into a variety of other formats such as HTML, PDF, and RTF for publishing in paper form, all without any further human intervention. This is a powerful magic indeed.

DocBook is available as a DTD in SGML- and XML-compatible formats, with the XML version being available as RELAX NG and W3C XML Schemas. The RELAX NG version is considered the "normative" or master parent form from which the other formats are generated as DocBook version 5.

DocBook is being widely adopted by the open source community and is growing from strength to strength.

Editing DocBook is like editing any other kind of XML. The documents can be manipulated with any text editor. the EMacs editor comes with a built-in DocBook schema to be used when you edit in XML and the XMLmind application allows you to view the DocBook document while writing. It isn't like writing a book in Word. We might have a love-hate-relationship with Word, but it does provide many useful word-processing tools. An XML editor is designed to be good at editing XML. It probably won't have a grammar and spell checker built-in which is one of the advantages with Word.

Open Office ODT Format

Open Office is an interesting application because it is an open source project. If you need to add features to your office applications you typically forward them as suggestions to the manufacturer and eventually if they deem them to be worthy, thy might introduce them. But that process takes years and you don't often get the feature implemented the way you would have liked. By the time you get it, your need for it has long gone.

With Open Office, download the source code and if you or someone you know has the necessary skill, your feature request can be added immediately. Simple things might only take a few minutes but if it takes a few days or a couple of weeks its is still a powerful alternative.

If your feature upgrades are useful, they can be returned to the pool for everyone to benefit from them.

Open Office stores its files in formats and containers that you can access with other software. This provides leverage when constructing workflows and can also help significantly when you are trying solve problems with proprietary formats.

Because the Microsoft Office support is also robust, you can operate on Word and Excel documents by converting them to their Open Office counterparts.

DocBook resources: http://www.docbook.org/

The ODT files are a robust way to represent word-processed content. This format is an optimal choice for long-term archival storage of document content. It is much better than the XML produced by Word.

Word Documents can be saved as an ODT file. An ODT file is a ZIP archive containing the DOC file content but converted to an XML form and having the illustrations stored in a separate folder. The styles are abstracted and stored separately and so is the document metadata.

Performing conversions on these XML files is easier than trying to do those changes inside Word. Extracting the metadata from an XML file is certainly easier than trying to parse it out of an RTF file.

Scalable Vector Graphics (SVG)

The Scalable Vector Graphic (SVG) schema is an increasingly popular format for delivering illustrations in a compact and XML workflow-friendly format. This is an XML-based description of a vector drawing, which can be rendered at the receiving end of the transport infrastructure. Because it is vector-based, it is useful for mobile applications.

If you are preparing illustrations for insertion into a DocBook project, you should consider using SVGs. Because they are XML-based, those illustrations can be inserted using a namespace that allows them to coexist with the DocBook schema. This allows you to publish the text and graphics from a single template.

You can use SVGs to create stationary images for print or as part of an animated sequence in a multimedia presentation. The standard is managed by W3C and is becoming more widely used. You can, export Illustrator drawings as an SVG image.

SVG supports three types of graphic objects:

- Vector shapes.
- Raster images.
- Text.

Objects can be grouped, styled, transformed, and composited onto rendered objects. Your text is flexible enough to remain searchable, even though it is part of a drawing.

Images can be transformed, with the transformations being cascaded or nested within each other. Images can be clipped, alpha masked, filtered, or used to create a template.

SVG images use DOM for interactive and dynamic control, and support the complete XML DOM. This provides a way to achieve animation by activating the images with ECMAScript controls. For ECMAScript read JavaScript. They are fundamentally the same provided you are only considering the core language.

If you have used JavaScript in a web page, you will be familiar with the event model and you can attach scripts to **onmouseover** and **onclick** events.

SVG images are saved in **.svg** files and can be gzip compressed and stored in **.svgz** files. The SVG files compress extremely well because they are fundamentally a text file format. SVG images are infinitely scalable with no pixelation artefacts and are much more compact than a raster file, even when uncompressed.

SVG represents a new way to add graphical elements to web pages, user interfaces, and editorial content. When combined with AJAX techniques, some compelling user interfaces can be constructed.

SVG comes in two main flavors. The full version is intended for use on desktop and large-screen computer systems. SVG Tiny was designed to be used on mobile devices such as phones and PDAs. There are three flavors in all:

- SVG Tiny – For use on cell phones.
- SVG Basic – For use on PDA devices.
- SVG Full   – For large-screen devices.

The DOM support is somewhat restricted in the Tiny and Basic variants of SVG, compared with the support available in the Full implementation.

SVG is becoming popular as part of the MPEG-4 LASeR specification, which mobile operators are using as a format for describing interactivity.

Because Flash is so dominant, SVG adoption is still lagging behind. Some browsers support SVG natively (Opera and Firefox) while others require a plug-in to be installed (Safari and Internet Explorer). Current practice is for SVG-enabled web servers to optionally rasterize the image in the server. The client can negotiate and elect to receive a vector or raster version of the image.

If you want to use SVG in your workflow applications and need to render them as a pixel image, you can use a library such as ImageMagick. It is basic but useful and written in Java. It will be portable to all the operating systems that have Java installed. Table 17-4 lists some SVG drawing tools.

Table 17-4 SVG tools

Name	Description
ImageMagick	Java-based rendering library
Inkscape	Open-source SVG drawing program.
Batik	An SVG Toolkit for use by Java applications
SVG Salamander	Open alternative to Batik for Java
GNOME project	Integrated SVG support via the **librsvg** open source library since 2000.
Adobe Illustrator	The industry-standard application for import and export of SVG images.
Adobe SVG Viewer	A web browser plug-in.
Corel SVG Viewer	An SVG browser developed by Corel.
SVG Perl module	Support for creating SVG files from within Perl.
QtSvg	Trolltech's QuickTime component module.

Because SVG is XML-based, we can operate on it with the same tools as we would use for web pages and develop some dynamic publishing pipelines to create SVG images. You might want to write this export format into your requirements when sourcing a new drawing application. CAD systems and 3D modeling software might be a helpful editing tool, but may not readily export to SVG without you buying or building some translation glue-ware.

Adobe Illustrator is a useful application to consider for creating SVG files. It can be controlled by AppleScript, and the same interfaces should be available when it is executed on other platforms, even though the scripting language will be different. Adobe provides several hundred pages of documentation covering the scriptable capabilities of Illustrator. It is available free to everyone running Illustrator on Mac OS X. However, not many users delve into this level of control.

Perhaps scripting an illustration application is too much to ask of people whose main expertise is in the area of creating beautiful images and graphic designs. We shouldn't expect them to understand scripting at that level, because software engineering skills are required. At this point in the multimedia industry, we should be putting together multi-skilled teams with designers and software developers placed in close proximity to one another in order to exploit these capabilities.

The scripting capabilities of Adobe Illustrator were demonstrated by the Showtime network some years ago on Mac OS Classic with Adobe Illustrator version 7.

MathML

Mathematical Markup Language (MathML) employs XML to represent mathematical symbols and formulae. This will facilitate using mathematical formulae in web pages and will fit into a publishing strategy built around DocBook.

MathML predates the work on XML namespaces. This has led to it being used in a non-namespaced fashion. Recommended practice is to migrate towards a namespacing policy to allow it to coexist with any content created with different DTD schemas.

An auxiliary standard called *OpenMath* has been designed for adding semantics to formulae. It is compatible with MathML.

MathML is supported OpenOffice.org and KOffice, as well as proprietary mathematical software products such as Mathematica.

NewsML

NewsML is a versatile XML-based standard for the tagging of news stories and associated documents (e.g., photos) for global exchange between multimedia news organizations. It was developed by the International Press Telecommunications Council (IPTC).

NewsML is useful when exchanging content between systems inside an organization and with other companies.

MathML namespace URI: http://www.w3.org/1998/Math/MathML.

NewsML: http://www.newsml.org

NewsML is designed for electronic news syndication and distribution and does not support all the capabilities required for paper-based news production. It is concerned more with managing the content of the news story than its actual appearance. The News Industry Text Format (NITF) can be used to augment it for traditional publishing uses.

The news story is the core object with reference to related media items and any meta-data required to manage them. The same story can be provided in multiple languages, or video clips in alternative formats. It also works as a container or a reference-based architecture. Using it as a reference-based architecture avoids transmitting content unless it is needed. This helps to conserve network bandwidth.

XML Strengths

XML has many significant strengths:

- The format can be read by humans and parsed by a computer application.
- Unicode is fundamental to XML, which allows it to contain anything that can be written.
- It can represent record-based structures.
- It can represent lists of data.
- It can describe trees and hierarchies.
- It is self-documenting. The tags describe the entities *in situ*.
- Strict format rules make for simple parsing software implementations.
- Large and small documents can be stored in XML containers.
- It is standards-based.
- Almost any type of document can be represented.
- Files are rendered as plain text and can be read anywhere.
- There are no license restrictions on its use.
- It is completely platform-independent.
- It is immune to technology changes.
- It has more than 20 years of use in large-scale projects.
- Many people have experience with XML.
- A wide range of software is available to process XML.

XML Weaknesses and Caveats

XML is great for connecting systems together, but we should not be too complacent. XML is not a universal cure for all the interchange problems that we might have had in the past. XML has many advantages, but bear these points in mind too:

- Older (legacy) software applications will not have an XML gateway. XML can't be used to integrate software that doesn't understand it.
- XML is a collection of technologies (XSL, XSLT, XMLNS, etc.), not just one.
- Some data types with ML in their name (such as SGML) are not XML.

- Some data types without ML in their name (such as DocBook) *are* XML.
- Some applications that export XML may only export styling descriptions and not semantic content structures (such as MS Office).
- XML syntax is verbose and somewhat redundant. The same thing is marked up more than once, where once would have been enough.
- XML is not the most compact textual format. It does waste storage space.
- XML is not well suited to low-bandwidth and limited amounts of memory, as is the case with cell phones and PDA devices.
- XML parsers need to cope with recursion. This causes performance problems and drains more CPU power than is required to deal with simpler text formats.
- Opinion is divided on whether XML can be slimmed down.
- Only a limited range of data types is supported. Numeric data is represented as text. XML has no knowledge that a number is a numeric value. This can be fixed by the schema design.
- Hierarchical models are not relational. Things can only be nested one way.

Recommendations

XML is an excellent choice for integrating modern workflow systems. Here are some suggestions to consider when building XML-based workflows:

- Select XML as a serious candidate for interchange, but don't believe the hype that suggests you can use it to solve every problem. It is good, but it isn't always appropriate.
- Examine the DTDs and schemas available and see whether there is already one you can use. This is better than developing your own.
- Make sure both ends understand the same version of the same DTD.
- If you use more than one schema, use namespaces to partition them.
- Find ways to convert non-XML formatted data to XML.
- Likewise, you may need tools such as XSLT to extract data from XML into other formats.
- Understand DOM hierarchies and experiment with them. You can develop many useful insights with JavaScript and a web browser.

If you do use XML, then you need to access it (or any other alternatives) via an API of some kind. This is how your workflow tools will connect to one another and exchange information. We'll examine API alternatives in the next chapter.

Interfaces and APIs

Matching Connections

A big problem with building effective and reliable workflows is the exchange of data between component applications. Finding a compatible format and workable transport mechanism is not always easy.

Integration

Several different techniques are candidates for connection between different applications:

- Exchanging data through direct import-export.
- Importing and export of data through glue-ware.
- Signaling via event scripting.
- Data exchange via clipboard.
- Data exchange via drag and drop.

Direct Import-Export

Exchanging files directly is possible where both applications support a common data exchange format. It is the ideal solution, even though you might wrap it with scripts to automate it, because it is bound to be the most reliable and readily automated. Be careful with profiles that dictate range limits on values defined by a standard. You need to use compatible versions of the profiles that constrain how a standard is applied. You also need to be careful with data sizes to avoid truncating any values.

Import Export Through Glue-Ware

This mechanism uses an intermediate application or some scripting logic that understands formats in common with either of the main participating applications. This is necessary where the two applications do not share a common data format but the translation is viable. You may have to write this exchanging application. For some solutions, a third-party application or plug-in extension module may solve your problem. Typical examples include media asset management systems and nonlinear editors. Both understand edit decision lists (EDLs) but not necessarily in the same format. A little massaging of the data with glue-ware cures all the ills.

Communication via Event Scripting

If your operating system framework supports the communication between applications with scriptable events, you may be able to write some scripts that can inquire of a source application and communicate to a target through its scripting interface. AppleScript on Mac OS X is a useful tool here, and PowerShell on Windows Vista might offer the same kind of help.

UNIX signals are a similar mechanism. Adding signal handlers to your applications is quite straightforward and well documented in C programming guidelines both online and in developer oriented books.

A signal handler does nothing until a signal arrives. The signal interrupts the normal process execution, and the handler then decides what to do about it. It might quit the program or it might read its initialization file again. It all depends on what you configured in the signal handler source code and which signal arrived.

Data Exchange via Clipboard

Using cut and paste to move content between applications is a useful technique. You need to be aware of how a clipboard works internally to avoid unexpected problems.

It appears that the clipboard is magically smart enough to format the content so that the receiving application gets precisely the right kind of data pasted in that it needs. The cut or copied selection is stored in the clipboard in several alternative formats. The receiving application can then select the one it can use most effectively.

Some subtle bugs arise when those formats contain different data. Switching on auto filters in some versions of Excel, choosing a subset in one column, and then copying that data to the clipboard results in odd behaviors in some target applications when you paste the data in. If the application chooses the raw unformatted text data from the clipboard, it gets a different set of lines than if it is able to understand the RTF formatted version.

It appears to be a bug in the application doing the pasting but it is really a bug in the application doing the cut/copy.

You can force the type conversion by pasting into an intermediate container with a limited data type. Pasting styled text into an application that only works with unstyled text and then copying the pasted data to the clipboard again effectively removes all the styling.

Some applications store the weirdest variations. A music application might store MIDI sequence data in the clipboard but also store a picture of the music score for portability. Pasting into an application that does not understand the MIDI data ends up with an image being inserted. Very odd indeed! Not at all what you might have expected.

Drag and Drop

Drag and drop is a special case of how the clipboard exchange mechanism works. It effectively does a cut and paste but does not destroy the current clipboard contents. Its effectively doing cut and paste with an ephemeral clip store but is subject to the same issues as clipboards. Making sure that the correct version is pasted or dropped is a critical point of potential failure. As with clipboards, you don't have a great deal of control over which version is pasted.

Application Programming Interfaces (API)

Application programming interfaces (APIs) are your opportunity to exploit the software you have available in ways that perhaps the software designers never imagined. This is where you gain the leverage to add value as a systems architect. Knowing a range of API structures and capabilities allows you to envision new connections when you conceive a new workflow. The Showtime movie channel trailer generation tools have a workflow that is based entirely around off-the-shelf products glued together with AppleScript.

If you know that Application A can output a textual data file, and that Application B can import and process a textual input file, then—provided the format of those files is compatible—you have a means of connection for transfer of data. Knowing that you have XML support in both apps indicates that a transfer connection is possible at the physical level provided both applications can operate on an XML file formatted according to the same DTD.

Software Development Skills

Having some software development skills available can help with a difficult integration. Being able to write a short piece of glue-ware can save the day.

If you know one computer language, then you can certainly cope with all the other contemporary languages. They have all stolen good ideas from each other and look amazingly similar. Whenever a new language innovates something, all the others assimilate the idea when the opportunity arises. Although languages appear to be functionally similar, they aren't all designed to do the same thing. They are all structurally different and work in different contexts. Table 18-1 lists the original purpose for various languages.

Table 18-1 Computing language specialties

Language	Core expertise
Fortran	Mathematics and graphics coding for science and engineering.
COBOL	Records and commercial coding for use in the business and finance sector.
Basic	General purpose and beginners.
Lisp	Lists of text.
Java	Portable Internet solutions.
JavaScript	WebPages and forms handlers in Flash and PDF.
C	Systems code.
Forth	Originally designed by astronomers but now used in Open Firmware and for embedded applications.
PostScript	Page description language.

Some languages are interpreted. An application reads the code and makes decisions about what to execute. Compiled applications run directly in the CPU and leverage the raw power of the computer.

PowerShell, AppleScript, and UNIX Command Line are all very similar. They do the same sort of things. Whichever one you have available on your platform, it is worthwhile learning about it.

The Importance of Wrapping with Scripts

When you build a workflow, it is important to take advantage of the capabilities offered by the applications you are employing. Human beings are not designed to do repetitive tasks. It is important that the applications are integrated smoothly and that the workflow eliminates any unnecessary user intervention. Boredom leads to stupid things like town names being stored in the county name field instead.

Encapsulate what you want to do in a script wrapper that talks to the application and instructs it what you want done. Then integrating all of those applications together is easy. Call those wrappers as if they were subroutines in a library.

If you can wrap all the apps you want to use, then building workflows is incredibly easy. By focusing on a single application at a time, we can solve the wrapping problems. Applications that are designed with this in mind will be easy to wrap with a script. Those applications that were not designed to allow this may need a little more work and the implementation of some script code to drive the graphical user interface (GUI) directly. Command line tools can be wrapped so they can be called from the GUI environment. Alternatively, you can enhance your wrapping so that the GUI layer can be driven from a command line. You decide how you want to approach it.

Running Scripts from within Apps

Sometimes, applications allow you to install scripts as plug-in extensions. The Visual Basic interpreter that Microsoft embeds in its office applications is an example of an internal proprietary scripting mechanism that is based on well-known open-standard language syntax.

Some applications are designed to host JavaScript with an embedded ECMA standard-compliant interpreter, which lets you leverage your web developer skills. Adobe PDF forms handlers and Flash ActionScript are examples of cunningly hidden JavaScript interpreters.

Applications running on the Mac OS X platform can take advantage of the built-in AppleScripting capabilities of the platform. This is exemplified by applications such as the default Mail client that can execute an AppleScript when triggered by a rule that matches certain criteria in a mail that has been received.

Let's think about that for a minute. You could set up a mail rule that matches a very specific e-mail format that you can predict. Whilst you are away from home, you can send e-mail to your home system from another desktop somewhere else. When your home system receives that e-mail, it can execute the AppleScript and carry out the task you deferred.

Always look for the script mechanisms within an application. They may give you an opportunity to drive your workflow in interesting and useful ways.

Windows users have similar capabilities offered by Windows Script Host, JScript, Visual Basic, and PowerShell depending on which operating system vintage they are using. Additional third-party solutions are available, too.

Running Apps from Scripts

Some applications lend themselves to being scripted. UNIX command line-executable applications have for a long time been designed by default to take command line parameters, and since they are called from the shell in the same way whether a human being or a script executes them, they are inherently scriptable.

Scripting a GUI interface is a little bit more tricky. AppleScript and PowerShell are the way to go here, but inevitably, the scriptability will depend on whether the application developer has connected it up in the first place.

Some developers implement the full functionality and allow you to record a series of actions to construct the starting point for your script automation. If an application is scriptable and recordable, then the next step is to examine just *how* scriptable it is.

Adobe provides approximately 750 pages of documentation each on Illustrator and Photoshop scripting. It is not obvious unless you go looking for the documentation, and you may need to install plug-ins to activate it on some versions, but it is there. Microsoft likewise provides extensive documentation of their scripting interfaces.

Microsoft Excel has been AppleScript-compatible for a long time, and Word has become increasingly useful in this area with more recent version upgrades.

Of the nonlinear editors, Video 100 has probably the most sophisticated script control. Oddly, Apple's Final Cut Pro still lacks support for AppleScript, although several other applications in the video-editing suite (as well as the Shake compositing tool) do let you write AppleScripts to control them.

You can tell an application to open a file if it is sufficiently scriptable. Alternatively, you can tell the desktop controller (Finder on Mac OS X and Explorer on Windows) to open the file either indicating a specific application or by using the default app that is associated with that file type and hoping it is the right one (never assume defaults are correct unless you test first).

File Interfaces

File systems provide several ways that you can use to connect components of your workflow together. There are good and bad ways to do this.

Think of a directory or folder as a container. Now you can use this as an exchange point between two stages of the workflow process. If there is anything difficult and complex about this, it has to do with signaling that a new item has been placed in the folder and alerting the next process in the workflow sequence that it can start processing.

Some applications can be set up to watch a folder. The specific mechanism they use to do this depends on the operating system. On Mac OS X, they would register as an observer and receive an event call when the folder contents change. This mechanism is used by most applications on Mac OS X and ensures that whenever a change happens, the screen display is updated almost instantly to reflect the change.

Other operating systems may use a different technique, but the effect is that adding an item to the folder will send a triggering event, message or signal to the observing application. How that application chooses to process that trigger is up to the developer. There may be some protocol that allows it to invoke a different script or function handler, depending on what exactly has happened.

Without this triggering mechanism, watch folders can be implemented by checking the folder for changes every minute. This might be set up as a regularly scheduled event that runs a shell script every minute to check for a new file and run a processing application only when needed. On UNIX, this uses the **cron** scheduling utility. This works well enough but it is quite an inefficient way to wait for a file to be delivered. This technique is called "busy waiting," because the computer can be quite busy when it is constantly checking for new files.

Deferring Watch Folder Actions

You may want the receiving workflow application to notice a new file coming in but only do some initial preparation and not process it until you have completely finished writing or copying the file. This is an issue if files are being copied across a network and the application that processes them can deal with the file contents faster than it can be delivered. If you can defer the processing until you know the file has completely finished being delivered then the processing can run more smoothly.

You can do this by setting the watch mechanism to look for files only of a specific file type. Let's assume we are forwarding an image file in a JPEG container. The file would normally have a file extension **.jpg** to indicate that it contains an image. If we copy that file to a remote destination but ensure that it is stored in a file with a **.jpg_** file extension, any logic that is looking for a **.jpg** file extension won't see it because of the trailing underscore on the file extension. At the very end, when the copy is complete, we do a remote rename to change the file extension from **.jpg_** back to **.jpg**. This is quite easy to do with FTP and in fact you can wrap FTP transfers in some script code that does all this sort of thing automatically without you having to implement it every time yourself.

Opening Processes as Files—popen()

Another way to exchange information between workflow components is to open a process on the same computer and read or write to it as if it were a file. Not all operating system versions support this. If the **popen()** call is provided in the API libraries for the C language compiler on your system, then you have a way to do this.

Whatever you write to the process is interpreted as if it were keystrokes. Any output that the process generates can be accessed by reading from the file buffer associated with it. This is useful because writing applications that put things into and read back from files is easy to do. The operating system does all the work to map the process to a file buffer. This is an under-appreciated and not often used capability.

System Calls

The **system()** API call is a similar concept that provides a way to run a shell command from inside a compiled application. This is part of the operating system's C language libraries and it is quite easy to access from other languages that are compiled and linked at the object code level.

Cross Language Bridging

Object code should not be confused with object-oriented programming. It is a means of compiling to an intermediate form that can be aggregated and turned into executable machine code. Any compiled language can produce object files, and provided you adhere to parameter passing conventions correctly, you can call functions in one language from the code written in another.

Be sure to call by selector, value or reference according to what parameters the receiving function expects to be passed. You may need to coerce the arguments to the correct type in the calling source code. This is often done by wrapping the argument in a glue function that converts the data type to one that is compatible with the interface. Table 18-2 lists some typical glue functions used in Objective-C and other languages.

Table 18-2 Wrapper functions

Wrapper	How it works
val()	Pass a parameter as a value. Only limited types of data can be passed like this. Characters, integers and Booleans are obvious. Short strings if they are 4 characters or less. Floating point values if they occupy 4 bytes. Longer strings and high precision numerics cannot usually be passed as values. This function is sometimes implemented as a way to fetch values from objects using key values as parameters that is subtly different to locating the value stored at a pointer location.
ref()	Passing values by reference forces them to be stored somewhere and a pointer to that location passed to the API instead.
sel()	Create an action selector that can be called by an OS function that is given the selector. It is used to build callback mechanisms for sort and search for example.

Here is an illustration of how these mechanisms work in general terms:

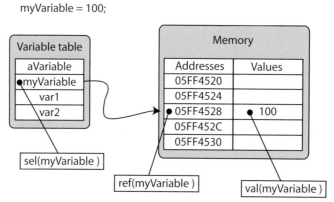

Figure 18-1 Accessing entity values

The selector uses an indirect reference to reach the value. This allows it to be loosely coupled. The reference can be resolved at run time and could be steered by a property value that is user defined at run time. The reference passes a memory storage location and the value function picks up the value from that location and passes what it retrieves.

Services, Ports, and Daemons

If you are building process components for your workflow and want to distribute them across several machines, check out the launch daemons and the services file. This sets up a listener on a specific port, and when an incoming connection arrives, your application is run and connected to the network traffic.

This is great for workflow processes that need to be fired up on demand at irregular times but they don't merit having a server process running continually. See the discussion earlier on about

From your point of view as the application writer, all you need to do is read some input and write some output in response. The operating system wraps your application in a network management container and does all of the complicated TCP socket code for you.

When your application quits, the process dies. This is an efficient way to implement services. It's how Telnet, FTP, and other services can be installed and available but without using any machine resources until a request for them arrives. At the networked node corresponding to the IP address for as remote machine, the launch daemon will map that port number to a service via the **/etc/services** configuration file. That service is described in a further configuration file whose name, location and format depends on which launch daemon is being used.

Windows has its own services architecture. There are three possible launch daemons on Mac OS X depending on the vintage of your system. Other UNIX systems may support only **inetd** or **xinetd**.

Table 18-3 Mac OS X launch daemons

Model	Availability
inetd	Early Mac OS X and classic UNIX systems.
xinetd	Later Mac OS X 10.3 (Panther) systems.
launchd	Recent Mac OS X 10.4 (Tiger) systems.

The launch daemon will consult an appropriate configuration file to map the service name to an executable image and some run time environment definitions. This includes security mechanisms to define the user under which the remote process will run. It runs the indicated executable and passes such parameters to it as it has been given. The process will accept the incoming port connection and communicate with the client.

The executable will communicate with the client through the port by using its standard input and standard output which will have been redirected by the operating system so they are connected to the incoming network packet stream.

Standard error continues to point to somewhere the errors can be logged on the local machine.

Internet Access Methods

Web servers communicate using port **80**, although they can be configured to communicate on any port. Sometimes port **8000** or **8080** will be used to avoid problems with using ports in the lower (and more secure) range below **1024**.

Within the physical port communication, the clients can use a variety of protocols to pass their message. The most familiar is **http:**. You will also have encountered **https:** and **ftp:** protocols. There are others. Even within these, there are variations. Within the **http:** protocol, you can **GET** or **POST** your request.

You can use these mechanisms to build workflow control and monitoring. The output of one process could write to a static file in the **HTDOCS** directory. You need to be careful to ensure the file cannot be requested when it is partially written.

Alternatively, you can add some CGI script-based handling, which provides access to dynamic content. Databases such as MySQL can be accessed with PHP code. All of these software tools are free, open-source, and very powerful.

Using PHP and MySQL, you could call a specific URL whenever a resource is used in your system. This could log usage of your resources. Perhaps some process is taking feeds from a news service and could package them and load them into the database. You could do that with SQL but there could be networking and firewall constraints that stop you doing it with a direct SQL connection to the database.

These are all tools to be added to your available range of choices. There is no single right or wrong way to solve these problems. If you have several viable alternatives, you can weigh them according to their merits and select the one that most closely fits your business needs.

Calling a web page with PHP code could be a means to generate a trigger that runs a script in the next stage of some workflow logic. There are many different ways to do this, not all of them obvious at first.

Remote Scripting with AJAX

Remote scripting allows scripts running inside a browser to exchange information with a server without refreshing the entire page again. By calling certain URLs, scripts can be executed in the server and return only the required data. This is not quite the same as dynamically generating a page. The techniques have evolved through several different approaches to the Asynchronous JavaScript And XML (AJAX) technique, which is rapidly gaining in popularity.

AJAX makes web pages work much more smoothly. It works well because only small fragments of data are being moved back and forth instead of whole pages. This helps to avoid network saturation and makes better use of the available bandwidth.

AJAX exploits all of these technologies:

- XHTML (or HTML).
- CSS.
- DOM.
- ECMAScript (JavaScript or JScript varieties).
- **XMLHttpRequest** objects.
- Sometimes an **<iframe>** object is used.
- PHP or CGI-based dynamics in the server.
- XML for transferring data between the server and client.

AJAX is a combination of technologies, rather than being a technology itself, so it should be classified as a technique or philosophy.

You can achieve very satisfactory performance with a well-designed AJAX implementation. The trick is to avoid calling the server unnecessarily. On the other hand, infrequent calls means more bulky downloads. Achieving the best possible balance is the trick.

The data being exchanged on AJAX implementations is often XML. It need not be. Plain text or coded binary are as effective. You need to work out how to decode it at the receiving end with some JavaScript code.

Some AJAX implementations use a hidden **<iframe>** to transact the messages between the client and server. On arrival, the message is extracted and the data parsed out of it. The **<iframe>** elements are not yet obsolete, but that could happen. The W3C organization recommends using an **<object>** element instead. These are both important tactical ideas, because they help to work around the changes to the browser history, which could cause problems if the user clicks on the [back] button. Careful use of the URL fragment identifier after the **#** symbol can alleviate these history problems and provide a book marking facility.

Simple Object Access Protocol (SOAP)

Remote Procedure Call (RPC) support has been in existence since the mid-1980s. It provides a way to execute some code remotely by means of a simple request. RPC evolved into XML RPC, and now it has become Simple Object Access Protocol (SOAP). SOAP is designed for exchanging XML-based messages across a network with HTTP. SOAP facilitates the construction of web services with a messaging framework upon which higher-level protocols can build.

SOAP messages (containing XML) can be passed via SMTP and HTTP. SMTP has not proven to be as popular as HTTP because HTTP works well with the existing web-based server infrastructure. SMTP can be transferred to a mail sender but connecting a mail client at the other end to read a mailbox means its isn't at all interactive. It has a major shortcoming in that it is asynchronous, and for RPC to be reliable, we would really like the communication to be synchronous. HTTP is about as synchronous as we could expect a general-purpose request-response interface to be. It isn't a real-time interface though, and some latency is present which may render it inappropriate for some applications.

SOAP can work within enterprises and through corporate firewalls, which immediately gives it some advantages over other messaging protocols.

The SOAP protocol works like this. First, a client contacts a known web service with a query message. In this case, the request passes an object ID value:

```
<soap:Envelope xmlns:soap="http://schemas.xmlsoap.org/soap/envelope/">
 <soap:Body>
  <getObjectDetails xmlns="http://objectstore.example.com/ws">
   <objectID>12234</productID>
  </getObjectDetails>
 </soap:Body>
</soap:Envelope>
```

You can see that the message makes use of XML namespaces to avoid collisions with any embedded data values.

The web service formats its reply message with the requested object information and returns something like this:

```
<soap:Envelope xmlns:soap="http://schemas.xmlsoap.org/soap/envelope/">
 <soap:Body>
  <getObjectDetailsResponse xmlns="http://objectstore.example.com/ws">
   <getObjectDetailsResult>
    <objectName>Top story today</objectName>
    <objectID>12234</objectID>
    <description>Video clip of news story</description>
    <timecode>00:10:23</timecode>
    <rightsToUse>green</rightsToUse>
   </getObjectDetailsResult>
  </getObjectDetailsResponse>
 </soap:Body>
</soap:Envelope>
```

Command Lines

You should learn about the command line environment on your system. On Windows, that means the entire set of legacy scripting tools such as WSH, JScript, VBScript, etc. Going forwards, you should be planning new engineering projects on Vista around the PowerShell scripting environment.

On Mac OS X, learning AppleScript and UNIX shell programming is a useful skill. In fact, I would classify UNIX scripting as a skill that is worth knowing regardless of the platform you work on, because your operating system will either be UNIX-based or capable of hosting a UNIX-like shell-scripting environment.

On all platforms, finding out about Perl and PHP and any other emerging technologies give you additional tools to get the job done.

Use **curl** for script driven access via **http:** and other protocols that it supports. But also refer to the **curl** web page for details of additional tools that you should use instead of **curl** for certain tasks and other tools which augment **curl** for certain applications:

Job Control

Shell-based command lines support the idea of spawning off a process but putting it into the background. This is useful for workflow processes that need to run synchronously and which don't require user input or constant monitoring. Rendering, rasterizing and conversion processes are candidates for this.

Putting things into the background can be done in several different ways.

Background Processing

You can tie background workflow jobs to your current process. When you log out, the background process stops too. That is not always a good idea. This is great for workflow tasks that need to run at low priority. They will tell you when they are done but you don't want to watch them do it.

Persistent Background Processing

Another approach is to throw the process into the background and detach it from your foreground command line shell. When you log out, it continues running. This is appropriate for workflow tasks that run at low priority where you don't really care when they are executed provided they are guaranteed to be executed. Don't shut own your computer in the meantime unless you know they are finished.

Curl related tools: http://curl.haxx.se/docs/relatedtools.html

Daemon Processes

A third possibility is to daemonize the process. That detaches it and gives up ownership of it to the operating system. The process continues running as a background daemon, possibly listening to network ports and servicing users that contact it from remote locations. This how you run Apache web servers. It is useful for continuously monitoring workflow processes and keeping a system tuned.

Regular Scheduled Processes

If the process needs to run regularly, it can be scheduled with the **cron** tool (or its equivalent.) You could use your desktop calendaring and event management tools in a similar way in the GUI context. Workflow tasks that need to be run overnight, every day, or once a week—such as log analysis, system management, backups, and reporting processes—will work well with this approach Housekeeping on a media asset management system is another possibility.

Queued Processes

If you have a queue manager running, then jobs can be dispatched to that and run when the resources are free. Workflow jobs that need to be processed at moderate to high priority as soon as possible would fit this model.

Summary

We have explored some of the simpler integration opportunities in this chapter. You can develop strategies of your own along these lines or invent something entirely new. The goal is to move some data from the output of one workflow step to the input of the next and to generate a trigger of some kind to kick the next phase into action. How you accomplish that is irrelevant. Sometimes you need to be devious. Lateral thinking and a slightly crazy mind helps. Asking yourself questions like "what if I do this?" or "why not do it that way?" is a good starting point.

Now we are getting to some higher-level ideas. In the next chapter, we start to look more deeply at scripting as a way to connect things together.

Scripting Layers

Joining Systems Together

Designing workflows is always going to involve connections between different operating systems, even if it only takes place at the boundaries of your domain.

If we can reduce the differences between the systems somehow and choose technologies that are common and supported across the target platforms, we will reduce our workload.

The world has become a somewhat simpler place for workflow engineers and software developers since Apple introduced the UNIX-based Mac OS X operating system. We now have to contend with only two systems architectures when we build applications: The UNIX world and the Windows world.

They are still very different places to work and don't willingly share resources or interchanges of data. Most of the important integration issues between them have been solved, and if you use open standards and open-source technologies, you won't have many show-stopping integration problems. You will face challenges, to be sure, but they won't be impossible to solve. Take comfort from the fact that it wasn't always that easy.

The approach you take to building applications will be different in each of the environments. Indeed, building a UNIX command line, X-Windows, Mac OS Classic or Mac OS X Native apps are four quite different scenarios, and that's just on one operating platform.

Technologies and Platforms

In the mainstream, there are two generic types of Operating Systems (Windows and UNIX) and the platforms fall into three fundamental flavors: Mac OS X, Linux and Windows. There are others of course but IBM is now Linux-based and Solaris looks like Linux because it shares a similar UI.

Linux and Mac OS X share some common technologies for programming, tool building, and data preparation, because they are both UNIX-based. It is very likely that many APIs you may already use on Linux are also present on Mac OS X. Windows has many similar capabilities but they are implemented differently and are not source code compatible.

Some open-source solutions allow a degree of enhanced portability because someone has worked hard to create the necessary joining code to connect to the correct API calls in Windows. Mac OS X also supports additional capabilities that are not available on any other platform, as does Windows. Adding POSIX and UNIX services for Windows to your Microsoft system gets it very close to having a feature set identical to Mac OS X or Linux, at least as far as writing workflow code is concerned.

Table 19-1 lists a nonexhaustive selection of candidate technologies for each of the three operating systems, and where they are available or what the substitutes might be. There is an amazing degree of commonality across all the platforms once you get away from OS-proprietary formats.

Table 19-1 Technologies and platforms

Theme	OS		
	Mac OS X	*Linux*	*Windows*
Command line	Bourne shell	Bourne shell	Bourne shell
Shell scripting	Bourne shell	Bourne shell	Bourne shell
Web CGI	Apache	Apache	Apache
Application control	Bourne Shell, AppleScript	Bourne shell	Bourne shell, PowerShell
Internal macros	JavaScript, Visual Basic, AppleScript	JavaScript	JScript, Visual Basic
Dynamic web content	JavaScript	JavaScript	JScript
Data storage	csv, tsv, XML	csv, tsv, XML	csv, tsv, XML
Data transformation	XSLT, CLI, Perl	XSLT, CLI, Perl	XSLT, Perl, SFU, CLI
Web browser	Safari, Firefox, Opera, Internet Explorer	Firefox, Opera	Internet Explorer, Firefox, Opera
Documentation	Pages, Word, Open Office	Open Office	Word, Open Office
Spreadsheet	Excel, Open Office	Open Office	Excel, Open Office
Presentation	Keynote, PowerPoint, IndeView, Open Office	Open Office, IndeView	PowerPoint, IndeView, Open Office
Audio and Video encoding	QuickTime, Real, Windows Media, DivX	Real, DivX, Ogg Vorbis, etc.	QuickTime, Windows Media, Real, DivX
Video tools	QuickTime, iMovie, Final Cut, LiveType, **ffmpeg**	Kino, **ffmpeg**, Open source tools	Premier, Avid, Windows Media, Ulead, Canopus, Optibase, **ffmpeg**
Audio tools	Logic, SoundTrack, GarageBand, Sibelius	Open source tools	Cubase, Cakewalk, Sibelius

Table 19-1 Technologies and platforms (continued)

Theme	*Mac OS X*	*Linux*	*Windows*
		OS	
Music language	MIDI	MIDI	MIDI
Other scripting	Perl, Python, Expect	Perl, Python, Expect	Perl, Python, Expect
Compiled programming languages	Objective C, ANSI C, Java, C++	Objective C, ANSI C, Java, C++	Objective C, ANSI C, Java, C#, C++
International typography	Unicode 4, Unicode 5 soon	Unicode 4, Unicode 5 soon	Unicode 4, Unicode 5 soon
Multimedia	Flash, Wired QuickTime	Open source, Flash tools	Flash, Wired QuickTime
Vector graphics	Illustrator, SVG	SVG	Illustrator, SVG
Raster graphics	PhotoShop, PBM, NIH, Gimp	PBM, Gimp	PhotoShop, PBM, NIH
Portable text documents	PDF, RTF, DocBook, ODT	PDF, RTF, DocBook, ODT	PDF, RTF, DocBook, ODT
Typesetting	LaTeX, PDF, PostScript, DocBook, ODT, `groff`	LaTeX, PDF, PostScript, DocBook, ODT, `groff`	LaTeX, PDF, PostScript, DocBook, ODT
Databases	OpenBase, PostGres, CoreData, MySQL	PostGres, MySQL	SqlServer, Access, MySQL
Scanners	TWAIN SANE	TWAIN SANE	TWAIN SANE

Notes:

- Many Windows plug-in libraries (DLLs) can be used on Linux platforms through compatibility wrapper environments.
- Many open-source projects have ported implementations for all three platforms.
- Anything we describe for Linux, much of what we describe for Mac OS X and some of what we describe for Windows will port to other UNIX platforms such as SGI, SUN, HP and IBM.
- Bourne shell is available on Windows as an add-on from open source or as part of Microsoft UNIX services for Windows.

You can see that all platforms share some software or technologies in common in most categories. Those are the ones to select for your workflow design.

A Taxonomy of Scripting Environments

Over the last few years of architecting content systems for multimedia production, I have developed a taxonomy of scripting that I use to describe how we construct these systems. Scripts fall into three categories:

- Outer scripting.
- Inner scripting.
- Plug-in scripting.

Now, when I am selecting tools for a workflow, I look for applications that have an AppleScript/PowerShell interface, plug-in support, and macro handling, because these are candidates for being linked together into larger and more complex workflows.

Finding the junctions between these and providing mechanisms for passing parameters between them or calling procedures (sending events) across them is key to unlocking the leverage of these control layers. They can be imagined as a series of onionskins enclosing the different layers of functionality in the static parts of the application and OS.

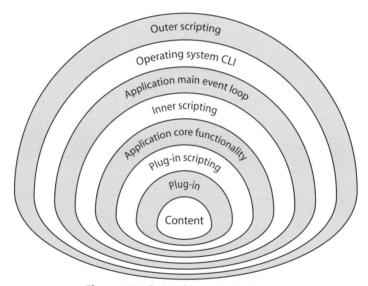

Figure 19.1 Onionskin scripting layers

Examples of these different scripting layers are summarized in Table 19-2.

Table 19.2 Scripting layer taxonomy

Layer	Example
Outer scripting	UNIX command line, Bourne shell, and AppleScript on Mac OS X; WSH/PowerShell on Windows. With outer scripting, we can accomplish job control and linkage of processing steps being handed from one application to another even when those apps are not designed to communicate directly with each other.
Inner scripting	Expressions in Adobe After Effects or FX-Script in Final Cut Pro; Word Macros, Excel Macros. This layer allows us to extend the tools available inside an application or to couple various functions. Outer scripts might call these inner scripts. That is an important junction point. Field codes in Word documents and conditional formatting in Excel operate at this level but they aren't so readily accessible to the scripts. They are more of a passive mechanism but useful all the same. The field codes in Word can accomplish some major things with dynamically generated content and hyperlinking to make documents navigable.
Plug-in scripting	The Python interpreter in the Profound Effects plug-in for Adobe After Effects. This is one specific example. Many plug-ins have scriptability. In this case, the Python interpreter is able to call out to an SQL database and load data that it uses to render video content dynamically and pass that back to After Effects as its output. This closes the loop and gives us a further level of call-out capability. Plug-ins can sometimes be driven by the inner scripting mechanisms bound into the application. This is another important junction.

UNIX Shell Script

UNIX shell scripting is a macro or captured series of commands, which are the same as if you had typed them at the keyboard. They are stored in a text file and interpreted line by line when they are executed.

There are varieties of different shells you can choose from. Some are upwards compatible while others have a completely different syntax and will throw an error if you use the wrong one to execute a script intended for a different shell. These are a few of the most common shells you will find:

- Bourne.
- Korn.
- C-Shell.
- Bourne Again.
- tcsh.

These shells are all available as open-source projects, and various enthusiasts have taken them and ported them to work properly on Mac OS X and Windows operating systems. Mac OS Classic, now deprecated, never had a command shell of its own, relying instead on an application like the Mac Programmers Workshop (MPW) to provide this. Windows has several scripting shells already. Mac OS X is UNIX-based anyway. These shells are provided by default, although you may need to add the free, downloadable Xcode developer IDE to ensure you have the complete toolkit.

Bourne shell is important because it is guaranteed to be available on all UNIX systems without installing any additional software. The others may be present, and can be added if they aren't. In a few cases Bourne shell isn't installed, but the compatible Bourne-Again shell (bash) is. Learning Bourne shell syntax is still worthwhile. It is also worthwhile learning the **vi** text editor for the same reason. In extremis, it may be all you have to work with to avoid a major disaster in the making.

 Perl has much in common with command line shells but it isn't a shell.

AppleScript

AppleScript isn't a shell, but it can run applications. It is to a GUI environment what shell scripts are to a command line environment. It is able to string multiple GUI applications together and build workflows from them. It doesn't do input/output redirection, but it can take a file saved by one application and open it in another.

The Automator workflow tools in Mac OS X are built in the spirit of a shell-like workflow, and you can create new plug-in Automator items of your own if you need to extend it.

AppleScript relies on applications having been factored correctly when they were designed. Factoring is the separation of menus and handlers. This follows from the Model-View-Controller concept. AppleScript becomes the controller and interacts with the model. Once the functional code is separated, an AppleScript API is wrapped around it and described in a dictionary object.

This dictionary can be loaded by the AppleScript executive and used to extend the capabilities of the scripting language. A **tell "application"** ... **end tell** construct in the script source creates a namespace within which the script can execute commands that are defined by the application cited in the opening **tell** command.

Windows Scripting

Windows operating systems have supported a variety of different scripting interfaces ever since Windows was first released. In the early versions, the MS-DOS batch files allowed some limited scripting capabilities. Later, we had JavaScript-based scripting (JScript) added as a by-product of the Internet Explorer evolution. This, coupled with Visual Basic and Windows Script Host, allows much of the operating system to be controlled by scripts.

Windows Vista will introduce PowerShell, a new and extensible scripting environment that is the most powerful that Microsoft has yet produced, to many enthusiastic new users. It has some nice capabilities, such as piped I/O redirection, that are clearly influenced by UNIX shell designs. You can create and add your own components, called *cmdlets*, to extend the language if you need extra functionality.

Even with the information available at this early stage in its lifecycle, PowerShell looks like it is going to become the scripting language of choice for many Windows developers. Major workflows will certainly be implemented in PowerShell. None of the other scripting languages on Windows approach its capabilities. Bridging to those other scripting environments to run legacy scripts and access to any user installed power tools like Perl will be important.

Microsoft designs its applications to support add-ins. Office applications like Word can benefit from this. You can add file exporters that solve an integration problem if you need to export to file format that isn't already natively supported. PowerShell will be extensible in the same way.

Microsoft Services for UNIX

In order to add some UNIX-like capabilities to Windows, you can either download and build open-source tools yourself or install the Microsoft Services for UNIX (SFU). This provides a UNIX user environment running on top of a Professional or Server-oriented Windows operating system foundation. It is expected to be built in to Vista and available as a standard option.

Aside from POSIX-compatible support, you get access to all the command line tools that you would expect and command line wrappers for things like Visual Studio. X-Windows is supported too. Anything that isn't already provided is available as a download, usually in a binary and ready to run form.

When you use UNIX to build tools for a distributed workflow, the **uname** command yields the name of the operating system. In the context of the SFU environment, the UNIX operating system name is **Interix**. You need to know the operating system name in order to build portable solutions. Sometimes the code needs minor tweaks for different versions of UNIX. Use this as a key to select the appropriate functionality.

Attachable Applications

An attachable application is one that you can attach scripts to so that they can be called from inside the application. These applications typically have a Scripts menu or some other means of calling a script, perhaps as an extension to an internal actions processor or as the result of matching a mail rule.

Scriptable Plug-ins

Plug-in modules inside other applications may add some scripting support. Profound Effects adds a Python interpreter to a plug-in module inside Adobe After Effects. At this

---

Search Wikipedia for: "Microsoft services for UNIX"

level we are working on rendering processes that are applied to an individual frame within a movie sequence, possibly even working on a single layer within a multiplane composition. We could still access a database and pull down some records to control what we want to draw into that rendering layer. This is powerful stuff indeed.

Remote Scripts

Running scripts remotely usually involves two or more computers. Perhaps one is running a script that is controlling processes on another machine, subject to having adequate security permission. Alternatively, perhaps a single instruction from a master machine is causing several scripts to execute asynchronously on a remote slave machine. There are many different ways to configure remote scripts.

You might be using the remote machine as a service of some kind, perhaps dispatching some assets to it, performing a task that might be licensed only to that machine and then retrieving the output result. A little bit of network-based workflow could easily save its development costs in reduced license fees.

POSIX

The POSIX standard describes the user interface and required software support to create a standardized API upon which applications can be built. By using a POSIX API, you can be reasonably sure that your application will compile and run on the target operating system. If it doesn't solve all of your porting woes, it will reduce them to a manageable size.

The POSIX standard decrees that Korn shell and a basic set of command line tools is available. It also mandates what libraries and what functions they support will be available for compiled language software. The standards document also describes how process threads should be implemented.

Most operating system variants now conform to POSIX. This isn't a UNIX-specific standardization activity. Windows supports POSIX, too. More recently, standardization work has resulted in the Single UNIX Specification, which is administered by the Austin Group, and the Linux Standard Base specification. Both of these are meaningful attempts to unify all the different versions of operating systems so that vendor applications can be recompiled across a wider range of target operating systems with the minimum of OS-specific code being required.

This is all good news for us if we need to build workflows across multiple architectures. We should be able to recycle library code wherever it is needed.

Summary

Now we have an idea of the structures that we can use to build our workflow. In the next few chapters, we will look at some of the technologies we can use to construct it.

Search Wikipedia for: "POSIX"

UNIX Command Line Tools

The Power of the Shell

On UNIX operating systems, the command line interface is tremendously powerful and useful. It is great for building processes that "do stuff" with text. Since most of the workflow data structures we want to create are based around creating or manipulating a textual file, this makes UNIX an excellent choice for building processors for XML and other text files.

UNIX systems include desktop systems from Apple up to large mid-range computers from IBM, HP and Sun Microsystems. There are servers to suit any performance need or financial limitation. From the programmer's point of view, they all look amazingly similar.

 The UNIX style of scripting is available on Windows if you install the Microsoft UNIX services add-on.

There are fine points of difference in their libraries but these really are quite trivial.

What Is a Command Line?

In UNIX, we have the concept of a Command Line Interface, which is an executive environment. In an environment like that, you type a command and press return. The shell processes it and returns control to you. It provides a framework within which commands and scripts can be executed and it maintains some state that describes your session.

In a GUI environment, the shell is implemented as a desktop management application. KDE on Linux, Mac OS X Finder, and Windows Explorer. They do a similar job but don't have a command line interface; instead, they use a mouse pointer and a button.

What Is a Shell?

Shell scripts evolved from the original UNIX command line implementations. The original Bourne command shell was designed to accept keyboard commands, locate an executable application that corresponded, and then run it.

A shell executes commands and spawns them off into their own separate process space that has its own memory and resources. A simple command line interpreter need not do that. It might parse the commands and execute them within its own process space, memory and resources. Command line interpreters which are added to GUI operating systems that don't have the underlying multiple process support that modern operating systems enjoy have to be implemented as an application. The disadvantage is that if the command crashes, the computer often does too. Older versions of Windows and the Mac OS Classic operating systems are typical examples. A shell executive that spawns sub-processes protects you from that

Some commands look like a shell but aren't. Python and Perl behave in many ways like a shell environment but they aren't really designed to replace the command line interface of a Bourne shell.

Keeping an open mind and being prepared to try new things is a route to becoming a better workflow engineer. Don't get too comfortable with any particular toolset. Experiment. Lots!

You have a range of shell environments to choose from, all of which do broadly the same job. Each environment offers a few uniquely useful features that the others don't. Since this is where you will spend most of your time in a command line environment, people naturally become attached to one shell or another and it is hard to get them to change once they have got used to one.

Standard I/O

If you add features to the shell, those features wrap around all of the commands you execute there. Any environment variables you create in the shell environment will be inherited by the sub-processes (commands) it spawns. If it modifies the way that keystrokes are passed or output is printed the sub-process won't know but the shell can wield some impressive leverage because it knows that the sub-processes don't know or care what it does with their input and output.

UNIX is built around the concept of standard input/output channels. These are implemented to look like files from the point of view of the software running in a UNIX process.

There are three main I/O channels set up by default on every process:

- Standard input where keystrokes go.
- Standard output where you print things to—usually the screen.
- Standard error where warnings go; this is usually redirected to standard output.

You can run the UNIX commands in process contexts that attach those standard input and output channels to other things. Your shell command line environment can instruct the process to redirect its input and output elsewhere. The shell exploits these capabilities to provide some powerful redirection mechanisms.

Shell Input Redirection

UNIX processes are designed to accept their input from a predictable and consistent file-structured input stream. This is called *standard input*. Keystrokes will be routed to this file buffer unless you redirect the input to take its stream from a different place.

Input to a command can come from the keyboard, but it could be redirected and come from a file instead. The keystrokes are effectively stored in a macro that is played out to the input stream. That input stream can be a file on disk or elsewhere. A set of commands can be stored and repeated as often as needed. That file could be created dynamically, perhaps by some part of your workflow or publishing system. Another possibility is that the shell can redirect a stream of input, that it is creating itself. It will continue until it encounters an end-of-file indicator and then reconnect the standard input back to its default condition.

Shell Output Redirection

Anything that you output or print (as a result of some operation in your application) goes to the screen display, which is really an emulation of a character-based terminal and is implemented as another file. This file is called *standard output* and all output goes here unless you redirect it to another file.

If something you do causes an error, a warning or informational text is presented. This is displayed on the screen but only because the standard error stream is by default directed to the standard output. You can direct the standard error and standard output to different places, neither of which has to be the screen.

Output and error streams can be redirected into a file and stored there until you want to process them with something else. This could be how your workflow gathers the output of a UNIX command. If everything has worked correctly, the error output should not contain anything.

Redirecting Output to /dev/null

You can redirect to a null device if you want to discard the output.

If the process output is of no consequence, you can use the redirection mechanisms to write it into a garbage can. This is called **/dev/null** or sometimes referred to as the "bit-bucket" or "the round file," so-called probably because a wastepaper basket was circular. This is a useful device, because any file-based operation can use it as a valid file for test purposes but you know that anything that is written to it vanishes. Don't store anything there that you want back again. It is not like the trash folder on your desktop. It works like a *Star Trek* trash disintegrator. Write something to it. Poof! It's gone—instantly.

Pipes

Adding a pipe after a command with the vertical bar (|) redirects the output of one command to the input of another. This uses the redirection of standard output and standard input as described above. The tutorials in Part 2 of this book use this capability a lot. Piped commands make it easy to filter text through a series of processes. Each process is quite small and simple, but together they are incredibly powerful. You need to conceive your workflow as a collection of simple tasks.

Under normal circumstances, if you execute a command on the UNIX command line, its output will be sent straight to the screen. The **ls** command will list the files in a directory. If you follow the **ls** command with a vertical bar character (|) and then add another UNIX command, the output of the first will be redirected to the input of the second.

Therefore, the **ls** command on its own will list our directory but the **ls | wc -l** command will count the files in that directory and display the result of the **wc -l** command. We won't see the list of files because the **wc -l** command ate that as its input.

This is very very useful. You can build extremely intricate filter chains with these pipes. You can also edit text and sort, merge, slice, extract, and combine things in all kinds of ways. Because each tool on its own does something basic and simple, they are fast, robust and very quick and slick to run.

Check out the tutorials in Part 2 of the book to see how you can exploit this capability.

Bourne Shell Redirection

If necessary, standard input, output, and error streams can be redirected to new destinations. The details are enumerated in Table 20-1 for the Bourne shell. The other shells do the same thing but their syntax may be slightly different.

Table 20-1 Bourne shell redirection

Redirect	What it does
> file	Redirects all subsequent standard output from this command or any sub-shells it spawns into the named file. It always starts a new file, erasing the old content.
>> file	Redirects standard output as for a single caret but appends to the existing file. Creates a new file if it doesn't exist.
2> file	Redirects standard error output to a file. It always starts a new file, erasing the old content.
2>> file	Appends standard error to an existing file. Creates a new file if it doesn't exist.
>& 2	Writes to standard output (say with an **echo**) but redirects that standard output and any other output that needs to be passed through to standard error.
> file 2>&1	Redirects standard output to a file and redirects standard error to the same place.
< file	Takes the standard input from the named file. This is called a *here file*, as in "take your instructions from here."
<< keyword	This redirects input instructions, line by line, from the shell level (usually a script) that initiated the command. The input will stop when the keyword is on a line by itself. Within the sequence of instructions, parameter substitution, back-quotes, and backslash escapes, all work and are evaluated before handing the line to the process input. Beware of leading white space.
<& number	Standard input instructions are redirected from a previously opened file descriptor.
>& number	Standard output is redirected to a previously opened file descriptor.
<&-	Standard input is closed. Rarely needed.
>&-	Standard output is closed. Rarely needed.

This is how to redirect the output of an **ls** command into a temporary file:

```
ls -a > /tmp/filelist.tmp
```

Sub-Shells and Back Quotes

Everything that you can do on the command line can be spawned off into a sub-shell. That is a cloned version of the current shell running as a child process.

At the command line, this is done by enclosing a command in back quote (sometimes called *back tick*) characters (`'`). The command is executed by the sub-shell, and if it produced anything on its standard output, the parent shell takes that and substitutes it in place of the back-quoted command. This is useful in assignment expressions. This command line assigns the count of directory items to a shell variable:

```
COUNT=`ls | wc -l`
```

Useful Command Line Tools

UNIX comes with hundreds of useful command line tools. Some of them are particularly useful because they are available on all versions of UNIX. If you know that common subset, you can approach a system you have never used before and start producing useful work immediately. It is worth learning how they work. Table 20-2 shows a short list of useful UNIX commands.

Table 20-2 Useful UNIX command line tools

Tool	Description
at	Executes a command or shell script at a specified later time.
awk	Searches for patterns in a file and applies a process to them.
calendar	Presents reminders. This could be used to trigger a process on a date.
cat	A file catenator that is useful for displaying files onscreen or merging many files together into one.
cd	Change to another working directory.
cp	Can be used like **cat** but is intended to copy files. Copying files to the screen is how you display them.
cut	Select a column or field(s) and discard the rest. Applied line by line.
date	Displays the date in a widely variable formatted presentation.
df	Displays available disk space.
diff	Compares two files, looking for differences.
du	Displays disk usage information.
echo	Like a print statement, it takes literal text and displays it onscreen.

Table 20-2 Useful UNIX command line tools (continued)

`expr`	Evaluates an expression.
`find`	Locates files within the file system.
`grep`	This is a fantastically useful tool. You can build a regular expression as a search key and then filter huge amounts of data to find exactly the one line you want.
`head`	This displays just the first few lines of a file.
`ls`	List the files in a directory. Often used as the starting point in a watch folder handler.
`man`	This the online help. On UNIX systems, this is an incredibly deep and rich resource of information about commands and API calls.
`mkdir`	Make a directory. We would use this to create a temporary folder to work in.
`more`	A paging program. It displays just one page at a time of its input on its output. You'll see why this is so neat if you use it in a piped arrangement with the output of a cat command that views a log file.
`mv`	We don't rename files in UNIX, we move them.
`od`	Dumps a file out in formats other than its current physical form.
`ps`	Displays process status information.
`rm`	Remove (delete) files. Be very careful.
`rmdir`	Remove directories. Be careful with this too.
`sed`	This stream editor is useful when driven with scripts to create editing filters.
`sort`	Command line driven sorting is hugely powerful when used in a pipe.
`tail`	This displays just the last few lines of a file, but you can make it follow the file as it is written and watch what your application is writing to its output files.
`tar`	Useful for packaging and unpacking archives.
`tee`	Splits one input into two outgoing pipes.
`uname`	Tells you what flavor of UNIX you are using.
`uniq`	Sorts a file and displays exactly one instance of each different line. This has some useful extra counting facilities.
`vi`	A visual editor that drives a terminal interface. You can customize this with macros and drive it with an automated interface from scripts.
`wc`	Word counter. This counts all sorts of things as well as words.
`zip`	A useful packager for compressing and storing data. Use this to create ODT files for Open Office. The **unzip** tool does the reverse and unpacks a zipped archive. **gzip** and **gzcat** are variations written in open source.

Keep an extra terminal session window open to check the **man** page for the command. This is a good way to learn what the commands are capable of doing. To lean about the **ls** command, type **man ls** and press return.

These commands are at their most powerful when piped together into a compound filter.

Regular Expressions

Regular expressions are useful for matching patterns of letters and numbers. Throughout the tutorials in Part 2 of this book you will see how Regular Expressions can solve a complex pattern matching problem with ease.

Pay particular attention to the metacharacters. The ^ symbol matches the beginning of a line and **$** matches the end. With these, you can achieve positional accuracy in the pattern matches. You can also match empty lines using the pattern **'^$'** that describes the line beginning and end with nothing in between. This kind of matching is very powerful.

Appendix E lists some more useful regular expression patterns. There are other examples throughout the tutorials in Part 2.

Summary

We have only taken the briefest look at UNIX command lines here. We will develop that in the coming chapters as we look at Power Tools first and then shell scripts, which exploit the command line and the power tools.

Power Tools

Leverage

Building workflow components is easier with tools that are more powerful. Think of these as power tools. If you want to do something complex with text, then Perl and Python are great tools that give you more leverage than using shell scripts or writing in ANSI-standard C. In fact, Perl is a combination of the capabilities of the Bourne shell and the C language. If you are familiar with either Bourne shell or C, then you will find the transition to Perl comes quite easily.

Perl and other power tools can be built into web servers, which makes it easy to build distributed workflows. If you add a hypertext preprocessor (PHP) to the mix, then you can build web pages that dynamically query the internals of the remote system and present formatted output to the calling client.

Power Tools Compared

These are Power Tools that you can download and install at no cost or you can purchase them cheaply with added value services. They are all worth checking out and getting to know. A few hours spent learning one of these tools will save you days or weeks of effort trying solve a problem using the wrong technology. Table 21-1 lists some popular tools.

Table 21-1 Power tools compared

Technology	Strengths
UNIX shell + C	Manipulating text character by character in the shell script environment is painful. You often have to resort to writing other scripts that you call in as utilities. C language components help, as do the wide variety of other commands. The strength of the shell is in its use of pipes but these are designed around a line-by-line process. Dealing with characters, words, sentences, paragraphs and other non line-oriented constructs is tricky. Multiple line operations are especially hard to do.
Perl	Good for a wide range of general purpose tasks. Especially good for text processing. Based on C, but with language additions from Bourne Shell, **sed**, **awk**, and the Lisp language. Supports procedural and object-oriented coding and has many extra third-party modules that can be loaded as language extensions.

Table 21-1 Power tools compared (continued)	
Python	A dynamic programming language capable of many general-purpose tasks. The language is more compact than Perl. It also supports run-time (late) binding of method and variable names. Very extensible and useful for a variety of tasks, and often used in place of Perl.
Ruby	A wholly object-oriented, general-purpose language similar to Perl and SmallTalk, but somewhat different from Python.
Tcl	Tcl was originally devised as a Tool Command Language development kit. It is a scripting language used for rapid prototyping of user interfaces. Tcl is often combined with the Tk GUI toolkit. The syntax is quite easy to use and compact. You can do a lot in just a few lines of code.
Expect	Designed for controlling user interfaces through scripts. Wrapping existing applications in an Expect script would make them easier to integrate with your workflow. Designed to do things that shell scripts cannot, such as responding to login and password entry. It is an extension to Tcl and has been ported to Python and Perl.
MySQL	A useful and capable database, which is handy for general-purpose data storage and workflow content management. There is no reason why you shouldn't use other SQL databases, but MySQL often comes packaged with Apache and PHP in a ready-to-run configuration.
PHP	Designed for dynamic web page creation. It lives most comfortably in the request-response loop of a web server. Fast and flexible, PHP has a huge range of API calls – the manual is approximately 6,000 web pages long!
AJAX	Asynchronous JavaScript and XML is a technique where transactions are moved between a client web page and a server using XML, but the content is then put into a page that remains on the screen. It depends on the JavaScript code extracting content from the XML DOM and putting it into the browser DOM in the current view.
WebObjects	This software used to cost tens of thousands of dollars, but now it is shipped free with the Mac OS X development environment (Xcode). It is a good way to build dynamic web sites and is used behind some of the world's leading online sites. It abstracts the business logic in a clean way, unlike all the other dynamic web site builders, which mix business logic in the same file as HTML.

There are many other languages available. See the shootout page on Debian for a list of some candidates and some performance comparisons.

Debian shootout page: http://shootout.alioth.debian.org/

Portability Issues

Choosing to implement important parts of your workflow with these power tools frees you from dependence on any one particular platform.

If you implement something with AppleScript, then your component can only run on Mac OS X, and if you use PowerShell it will only run on Windows. You may require more choices than either of those solutions provides. Select Perl or Python and your tools should run anywhere. They may still need an occasional tweak but that's easier than a complete rewrite.

Embedding the Interpreters

Because many of these power tools are available as open-source kits, some applications developers are embedding them inside their applications to provide a level of internal scripting. This is certainly happening with Perl, Python, and JavaScript. In fact, JavaScript is used in many places you wouldn't expect. The ActionScript used in Flash is JavaScript-derived, as is the forms language in PDF. Dreamweaver supports customization of its user interface with JavaScript.

You should look at all your major application tools to see if they support some measure of internal scripting through one of these embedded interpreters. You could unleash some amazingly useful creativity.

Extensions

A language on its own doesn't accomplish much; it is effectively some procedural glue. Most power tools support some kind of extensibility. They are called many different things but are capable of enhancing the way a power tool works:

- Extensions.
- Plug-ins.
- Modules.
- Units.
- Libraries.

The power of the language comes from the addition of libraries of extra functionality. It is popular to publish an extension API and allow third parties to develop plug-in extension modules. Perl and PHP benefit from having a community of developers underpinning them.

When Adobe Photoshop started supporting plug-ins, other applications adopted the same API. If you have a Photoshop plug-in available, it might work in other applications too.

Adobe After Effects certainly supports plug-in enhancements. The Profound Effects plug-in has a Python interpreter built in and there are probably others with similar capabilities.

Hex Dumps and Recompilers

Being able to dump a file out in hex or other expanded text-based formats is useful. Being able to edit and recompile it back to a binary form allows you to apply fine-grained fixes to the data passing through your workflow. This is all part of your toolkit. Figure 21-1 shows what a hex dump might look like.

```
Ch_001.doc – Data
Len: $00013800 | Type/Creator: W8BN/MSWD | Sel: $00000000:00000000 / $00000000
00000C70: 74 6C 79 0D 33 2E 09 50 72 6F 74 6F 74 79 70 65  tly.3..Prototype
00000C80: 20 61 6E 64 20 74 65 73 74 20 6E 65 77 20 69 64  and test new id
00000C90: 65 61 73 0D 34 2E 09 42 75 69 6C 64 20 63 6F 6D  eas.4..Build com
00000CA0: 70 6F 6E 65 6E 74 73 0D 35 2E 09 54 65 73 74 20  ponents.5..Test
00000CB0: 74 68 65 6D 0D 36 2E 09 49 6E 74 65 67 72 61 74  them.6..Integrat
00000CC0: 65 20 74 68 65 20 73 79 73 74 65 6D 0D 37 2E 09  e the system.7..
00000CD0: 54 65 73 74 20 61 67 61 69 6E 0D 0D 0D 4E 6F 74  Test again...Not
00000CE0: 69 63 65 20 74 68 61 74 20 74 68 65 20 77 6F 72  ice that the wor
00000CF0: 64 20 74 65 73 74 20 6F 63 63 75 72 73 20 69 6E  d test occurs in
00000D00: 20 73 65 76 65 72 61 6C 20 70 6C 61 63 65 73 2E  several places.
00000D10: 20 20 54 68 69 73 20 69 73 20 76 69 74 61 6C 2E   This is vital.
00000D20: 0D 0D 54 68 65 20 62 6F 6F 6B 20 69 73 20 64 69  ..The book is di
00000D30: 76 69 64 65 64 20 69 6E 74 6F 20 74 77 6F 20 6D  vided into two m
00000D40: 61 69 6E 20 70 61 72 74 73 2E 20 20 54 68 65 20  ain parts.  The
00000D50: 66 69 72 73 74 20 70 61 72 74 20 69 73 20 6D 6F  first part is mo
00000D60: 72 65 20 70 68 69 6C 6F 73 6F 70 68 69 63 61 6C  re philosophical
00000D70: 20 61 6E 64 20 64 65 73 63 72 69 62 65 73 20 77  and describes w
00000D80: 68 79 20 6D 65 74 61 64 61 74 61 20 73 79 73 74  hy metadata syst
00000D90: 65 6D 73 20 6E 65 65 64 20 74 6F 20 62 65 20 63  ems need to be c
00000DA0: 61 72 65 66 75 6C 6C 79 20 63 6F 6E 73 74 72 75  arefully constru
00000DB0: 63 74 65 64 2E 20 20 41 20 66 65 77 20 69 6C 6C  cted.  A few ill
00000DC0: 75 73 74 72 61 74 69 6F 6E 73 20 61 72 65 20 75  ustrations are u
00000DD0: 73 65 64 20 62 75 74 20 6D 61 6E 79 20 6F 66 20  sed but many of
00000DE0: 74 68 65 6D 20 61 72 65 20 63 6F 6C 6C 65 63 74  them are collect
```

Figure 21-1 An example hex dump

Your hex dump tool needs to allow you to patch and modify the files and should display things in several ways. Having some intelligence built-in helps as well.

Some tools can examine a resource file to extract icons, text strings and other objects. The Quadrivio General Edit tool is particularly useful for examining files and understanding their internal structure.

Table 21-2 summarizes a list of useful decompile/recompile formats where you might insert an editing operation between them. These are analogous to the effects insert (send and return) connections on an audio mixing desk. You get access to each channel to tweak its characteristics but the overall mixing framework does not need to be modified. These might be generically referred to as transformers.

QuadrivioGeneral Edit: http://www.quadrivio.com/

Table 21-2 Data filter inserts

Filter	Useful for
Hex dump	Patching individual bytes at the physical level. This is a completely unstructured edit but handy for applying a patch.
Hex recompile	The complement of hex dump but you could use this to synthesize a new binary image. Manufacturing small GIF files is easy.
SQL to TSV	Inserting data into applications that can't connect to databases is facilitated if you can extract the data into a form they can manage.
TSV to SQL	Taking arbitrary TSV data files and massaging them so they can be imported into a database.
Shell query	SQL-like queries that you can apply to TSV and other data file formats. Useful for building macro commands to examine logs and saves constructing huge complex piped commands.
XQuery	This hasn't become as popular as it should have. Being able to operate on an XML file from the command line can be very useful.
XML to TSV	Apps that can't deal with XML might cope with TSV.
TSV to XML	Using these tools in nonsymmetrical ways allows you to take SQL through a TSV format, change the data and convert it to XML. Package that as a macro and you have an SQL to XML conversion with a filter in the circuit.
String extractor	Yields the contents of a binary file as a series of text strings. The strings commend will do this but it strips off the binary information in between. If we can preserve that somehow and edit the text as text (as opposed to hex) we should be able to recompile the file afterwards. Similar to URL escaping in web browsers perhaps.
SVG decompile	Convert an SVG file to more easily read drawing instructions.
SVG recompile	Convert a series of vectors and drawing instructions into SVG.
Get from remote	Use `curl`, `ftp`, HTTP or SOAP (or whatever you like) to download something.
Send to remote	This starts to extend the reach of things you can do. Similar ideas allow you to drive serial ports and control hardware systems.
Others	Any file format you pass through your workflow is a candidate for building a transformation tool like this. This could apply to audio, video and image data too although the extracted formats might not be text. Transforming a video clip into an image sequence and back again would be useful.

JavaScript Bookmarklets

When debugging web systems, a little known JavaScript technique can help. You will be familiar with **http:** URLs, but your web browser can respond to a variety of other types of URLs. The **https:** protocol is used for secure servers, and **ftp:** is for fileserver access. You might have noticed **JavaScript:** showing up in the location bar. Most often, you will see this when a URL is coded to call a local piece of JavaScript, perhaps to check a form.

If you make a bookmark of that, the JavaScript is embedded in the bookmark. You can embed quite lengthy and complex scripts in there. Here is one that validates the current page with an online validation service:

```
javascript:void(document.location='http://validator.w3.org/check?uri='+document.location);
```

Here is a list of other possibilities:

- Display the names and contents of all form fields.
- Dump out all the scripts on the current page.
- Execute arbitrary scripts.
- Show DIV borders.
- Show DIV borders with their ID values.
- Show tables.
- Validate CSS for current page.
- Check links for current page.
- Show all images for the current page.

These can be used in a similar way to Microsoft Word macros. You may even be able to hack your browser to attach them to function keys. The preferred length of bookmarklets is 255 characters or less, because of the buffer limitations on some browsers. Your browser may allow longer bookmarklets.

Here is one that sets your browser window size:

```
javascript:self.moveTo(0,0);self.resizeTo(800,screen.availHeight);
```

Bookmarklets.com: http://www.bookmarklets.com/

MacWorld article on bookmarklets: http://www.macworld.com/2004/02/secrets/marchgeekfactor/

Safari developer site: http://developer.apple.com/internet/safari/faq.html

Apple bookmarklets: http://www.apple.com/applescript/safari/bookmarks.html

PHP and MySQL

A major advantage of PHP and MySQL is that they are free to download and install. MySQL is a popular database with plenty of support available. Because it is an open-source project, you can run MySQL on any platform, which also makes it a great candidate technology for integration into larger OEM and VAR scenarios. MySQL is only one of many SQL database alternatives so it is mentioned here as a representative of all free and open source SQL RDBMS projects.

All SQL databases adhere to a basic set of functionality. Often they implement some specific unique features, but provided you avoid those proprietary extensions, your SQL code and hence your database schema will work on any SQL database platform.

Therefore, within a constrained feature set, you could prototype on MySQL and then migrate to SQL Server or Oracle, or vice versa if the need arises. Oracle is a huge product with many features that support large databases and which you won't find in smaller products, but the open-source community is improving MySQL and its counterparts all the time.

PHP is a useful alternative to using Cold Fusion. For some projects, it might even be better suited than WebObjects. The feature set in PHP is huge. The documentation amounts to some 6,000 web pages, most of which are dedicated to describing API calls on a one-per-page basis. This is a lot of functionality to assimilate and understand. You won't grasp it all at once.

PHP is a great way to learn how content can be stored in databases and it works well with MySQL. You will often find them both packaged together with an Apache web server.

HyperCard: Still Useful After All These Years

In the same way that Windows Visual Basic is still a useful tool after many years, HyperCard and its derivatives are useful too. Even though it has not been supported for a long time, HyperCard still runs on current PowerPC-based systems in the Mac OS Classic environment. In fact, it runs faster than it ever did before.

HyperCard is a handy tool for all kinds of small data cleaning jobs. The newer Mac OS X Intel architectures are unable to run the old Mac OS Classic environment. Regrettably, HyperCard's days are numbered now. It still comes in useful from time to time and it is worth maintaining a legacy machine running an old operating system version to use it occasionally. Windows users may have similar legacy applications and tools that are useful and need to maintain some ancient systems to run them on.

Because you can build a form layout quickly, tools like HyperCard and Visual Basic are good for putting together a data cleaner in no time at all. The hierarchical nature of HyperCard allows you to deal with different kinds of data on different template backgrounds but refer to the processing scripts with the same names. Then you can iterate through all the cards picking up a code stub that is specific to a background or even an individual card.

Macintosh, Apache, Mysql and PHP (MAMP): http://www.mamp.info/

The HyperCard application is not a database. It doesn't do SQL. Nor is it a spreadsheet. HyperCard does lend itself to exchanging its data with all of these. If you import and export between HyperCard, Excel, and MySQL, you have a powerful set of tools. Swap Visual Basic for HyperCard, and the same applies for Windows users.

The trick is to integrate several applications together. Sometimes that is all you need. It is still a workflow, even though it is simple.

With a combination of HyperCard and Excel and a data transport between them (TSV files), I have cleaned 8,000 names and addresses and corrected about 30,000 formatting errors in a contacts database imported from raw TSV data—in less than a day.

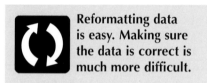
Reformatting data is easy. Making sure the data is correct is much more difficult.

With that same configuration, I processed 1,000 food recipes into individual ingredient and instruction components and output it as 30,000 records of SQL code with complex relational joins between records—in 2 days.

Designing effective workflow techniques is about attaining leverage so that you can apply filters and cleaning processes across the whole data set without destructively altering the data. If you can find the right tools, you can do this on any platform.

Tools for Proprietary Formats

Using PDF files as part of your workflow is becoming increasingly popular. Apart from the obvious Adobe software products, many third-party plug-ins and auxiliary tools create or process PDF files.

Check Wikipedia for a list of PDF tools that you may not already know about. The DMOZ Open Directory Project web site has a useful page that lists PDF software tools. This is a useful place for finding information on a variety of document formats and how to work with them. The entire Open Directory Project site is worthy of full exploration if you have the time.

Recommendations

Building workflow solutions with these power tools is cost-effective and sometimes better than a proprietary solution. The open-source alternatives are now so robust that it is difficult to justify paying huge license fees for applications and web development kits.

Use the tools listed in Table 21-3 for different purposes, with an emphasis on portability. Use proprietary and native technologies such as Xcode and Visual Studio or AppleScript and PowerShell where it makes good business sense.

Open directory PDF tools: http://dmoz.org/Computers/Data_Formats/Document/Publishing/PDF/Software/
DMOZ Formats: http://dmoz.org/Computers/Data_Formats/
Search Wikipedia for: "list of PDF software"

Table 21-3 Power tool application summary

Tool	Application strengths
Perl	For general-purpose workflow components.
Python	As a backup to Perl.
Tcl	Portable user interface design.
MySQL	Or other free/shareware/open source RDBMS for general-purpose storage and dynamic publishing systems.
PHP	For dynamic web content and distributed services.
Expect	For components of the workflow that need to solve authentication access problems but embedded within Tcl, Perl, or Python frameworks.

Summary

This was a brief introduction to some of the power tools we can use to accelerate the construction of our workflows. Next, we shall start to put some of these ideas together, starting in the next chapter with shell scripts.

22

Automation with Shell Scripts

Script-Driven Tools

In Chapter 20, we examined UNIX command line tools. Everything that you can type in a shell to use those tools can be captured into a text file and replayed, just like a Visual Basic Macro in Office. These text files are called *shell scripts*.

When a script executes a command, that command usually passes a return value or result code back to the calling shell. It is tedious typing extra lines to inspect those status values, so you rarely bother to check them when you are operating the command line manually. In a shell script, we can exploit them to test whether the command was executed correctly and take some remedial action if it wasn't. DOS scripts used on Windows do a similar thing, but they are called *batch files*. PowerShell and AppleScript both call them scripts.

Shell scripts are specific to a particular shell type. You can't run a Korn shell script in a C Shell environment. Aside from it not working correctly, it may damage your system. To protect you against this happening, the first line of a shell script uses a special format. We will cover that piece of magic shortly.

Writing Shell Scripts

Building reliable shell scripts is quite straightforward. Good programming practices apply as much to shell scripting as they do to writing the C or Java source code for a compiled application.

In shell scripting in most shell environments, your variable names need to be prefaced with a dollar sign. They can also optionally be enclosed in curly braces. This helps to disambiguate the variable name from any other keyword that the interpreter might recognize. You can represent the **PATH** variable as **$PATH**, but it is more reliable to refer to it as **${PATH}**.

You should work through some solid tutorial exercises to learn and understand the syntax rules. Certain constructs such as square brackets (**[...]**) need careful construction. White space is important and needs to be put in exactly the right place. Shell scripts do not like the syntax to be collapsed and white space removed.

Sometimes you will need to escape something. This can get complicated if you have multiple levels of wrapping and escaping going on. Start at the innermost level. Construct a basic command and, if necessary, escape any special meta-characters within that command when you wrap it in the first level of quote characters. Then look again at the command and escape anything that might be affected by a higher level of quotation. Certainly, the quote characters themselves will need to be escaped. Perhaps some of the escape characters themselves will need to be escaped again. This is all necessary, because at each level of evaluation, the escaping is removed and replaced with the substituted characters. That must preserve the escaping that is required for the next level down.

This happens much more frequently than you might imagine. If you build a **grep** command with a regular expression in quotes, you can store that command in a variable and invoke it several times by using variable substitution. To assign it to a variable, it must be quoted again at a higher level. The content of that variable will need to retain its own internal quotes around the regular expression. They must be escaped during the assignment. Similar things happen when you use back-quote characters to execute a command, and substitute its output in place of the back-quoted string.

Escaping is sometimes tricky and requires some experimentation. Working outwards and adding the escaping one onionskin layer at a time is the best approach. It forces you to work backwards from the end of the process, but it does the trick.

Dealing with escapes will probably be different for each shell that you use. Understanding complexities like this is the sort of thing that discourages you from learning a new shell when you have already made the investment in the one you use regularly.

The Bolthole web site illustrates how scripts might be written by programmers with different levels of experience.

Shell Switching Strings

Shell scripts are designed to run in one particular shell interpreter. It is vitally important that they run in the correct context. Early shell development engineers implemented a neat solution that still works wonderfully well today.

If the first line is a comment character followed by an exclamation mark and the path to a shell command executable, the script will run inside that shell. The first line of the script indicates exactly what shell the script is designed to run in, such as this example for the Bourne shell.

```
#!/bin/sh
```

This is necessary, even if we abide by conventions when naming our shell scripts. There is nothing in the shell that makes file associations the way that Windows Explorer or the Mac OS X Finder does. They both ensure that the correct application is started when you double click on a document icon. Shell command interpreters do only what you tell them to do, even if it is completely stupid!

If the path is not correct for your operating system you will need to edit the script to run the correct shell. Some manufacturers change this sort thing for no apparent reason but there are a limited number of alternative paths they use. It isn't usually difficult to figure this out.

Bolthole scripting examples: http://www.bolthole.com/solaris/ksh-sampleprog.html

Way back in the past when there was only one shell (Bourne) and it was convention to create UNIX command names that were only a couple of letters long, these special codes used to be called *octographs*. When command and shell names became longer than 8 characters following the comment, that didn't make sense any more. Now they are commonly called *shebangs*, probably because an exclamation mark is sometimes called a bang and "shebang" sounds a bit like hash-bang or sharp-bang or even shell-bang.

Every script should begin with **#!** followed by the path to the correct interpreter for the script. The command executive can then, if necessary, perform a shell switch before running the script. This keeps everything nicely under control.

If you leave off that special piece of code, your script will try to run in the current shell. If the shell misunderstands some of the command syntax, it could misinterpret the commands and do something dangerous—even something as dangerous as going to the top-level directory and deleting all the files. That is not likely to happen by accident, but an important file could be damaged accidentally and you wouldn't know until it was too late.

Table 22-1 summarizes some shells and their shebang switching strings:

Table 22-1 Shell switching strings

Switch	Description
`#!/bin/sh`	The original Bourne shell, always available everywhere.
`#!/bin/ksh`	The Korn shell is a compatible upgrade to the Bourne shell.
`#!/bin/csh`	The C Shell is an alternative shell written by Bill Joy of Sun Java fame.
`#!/bin/tcsh`	The Tenex C shell upgrades the standard C Shell with file-name completion and command-line editing.
`#!/usr/bin/bsh`	A variant of the Bourne shell found on some IBM systems.
`#!/bin/bash`	The Bourne again shell is an open-source upgrade to the original Bourne shell.
`#!/usr/bin/expect`	Expect is a GUI automator tool built with Tcl.
`#!/usr/local/bin/expectk`	The ExpecTk interpreter supports Expect running within the Tk GUI design environment.
`#!/bin/zsh`	Z Shell is yet another compatible superset of **sh** and **ksh**.
`#!/usr/bin/perl`	The Perl script interpreter. Add a **-w** flag to turn on warnings. Perl may be installed in a variety of different locations. Check yours and alter the scripts accordingly.

Table 22-1 Shell switching strings (continued)

`#!/usr/bin/python`	The Python script interpreter. This might also be run via the **env** command.
`#!/usr/bin/env tclsh`	Used at the head of a Tcl script to invoke Tcl via the **env** command.
`#!/bin/awk`	Run the script in the **awk** tool. An optional **-f** flag can be added to pass parameters to the **awk** command.

If we can switch a shell inside a script as soon as it starts executing, then we can run shell scripts written in any language from whatever shell we are used to having on our desktop.

This is a great thing for workflow development. For instance, you might need the capabilities of Expect to deal with a remote login that a Bourne shell script would not be able to cope with. Wrap the login in an Expect script and call it from your Bourne shell environment. This is neat, and it is a particular trait of the UNIX system.

Windows users also have powerful tools and can acquire some of these UNIX capabilities by running Microsoft Services for UNIX on a Windows workstation.

Another reason why these strings at the top of a shell script are useful is that a text editor like BBEdit or TextWrangler will sense that they are present and switch on some helpful syntax coloring for you. This helps to visually indicate missing quotes and other incorrect syntax in your script files.

Building an Environment

When tools connect together in a workflow, building an environment for them to operate in reduces the maintenance overhead. An environment is a set of pre-defined references to such things as locations in the file system. Certain commonly used strings, such as access codes and other things that might be required in several places, can be kept in a central location.

As part of that environment, you can create some commonly used tools and utilities that accelerate the process of writing a script. Some of these tools and environment components might be inherited from other projects. Soon, they build into a standard kit that you use to start new projects.

The environment should be described in a file that can be invoked at the start of a shell script. This file is pulled in from a single instance and ensures that every script-based utility in your workflow inherits the same environmental setup. Any executable applications that are run from within those scripts will inherit that environment too. It is similar to using "include" files in C language or Java. It keeps things consistent.

Simple things like setting the ${PATH} variable are important so that you can refer directly to the commands by name and not worry about where they have been installed. This all helps to make your workflow components more portable, since you only have to alter the environment setup script to port the workflow to a completely different machine and installation setup.

Chapter 28 expands on this with a worked example based on a web server farm.

Flow Control

Building scripts requires branching, decision-making, and flow control. You will soon learn some language constructs that help you build the decision-making capability that you need. There are a few important caveats that you need to learn as well. This isn't a complete course in shell scripting, but the following few sub-sections talk about real problems that cropped up during workflow development projects.

The Case of the Badly Formed Switch

If you implement some branching logic that chooses from one of several different alternatives, you might at first implement that with **if ... else** logic. After a few items have been added, this starts to get unwieldy and it looks nasty.

Use a **switch ... case** mechanism instead. These are commonplace in many languages but the syntax is always just a little different. Some require a **break** command on the end of each clause, while others require two semi-colons (**;;**). Check your documentation. This Bourne shell example uses a hostname commend and defines system types based on their names.

```
case 'hostname'
     in
          huey)      SYSTEM_TYPE="DEV"      ;;
          louie)     SYSTEM_TYPE="LIVE"     ;;
          dewey)     SYSTEM_TYPE="LIVE"     ;;
          www)       SYSTEM_TYPE="LIVE"     ;;
          ora)       SYSTEM_TYPE="LIVE"     ;;
          minnie)    SYSTEM_TYPE="BACKUP"   ;;
          *)         SYSTEM_TYPE="DEV"      ;;
esac
export SYSTEM_TYPE
```

Sometimes, you may want more than one **case** to have the same value. In the script example, several machines are defined as live machines. If your switch handler allows it, you might leave off the break (double semi-colon) terminator and let the cases fall through to the next active item. You must properly terminate the last one.

```
case `hostname`
     in
          louie)
          dewey)
          www)
          ora)      SYSTEM_TYPE="LIVE"    ;;
          minnie)   SYSTEM_TYPE="BACKUP" ;;
          huey)
          *)        SYSTEM_TYPE="DEV"     ;;
esac
export SYSTEM_TYPE
```

This doesn't always work, and it looks a little slap-dash. The safer option more in keeping with systems administration good practice is to go with the first example. The second one has some potential for error and it is harder to maintain. To make **huey** into a live machine requires the line to be moved. In the first example, the value being assigned needs to be altered.

While You Were Reading

Piping values from one command to another is powerful. Sometimes you want to operate on each line one-by-one with a **while** … **read** loop. This is an area where scripts are flexible enough to be useful, but so bad in performance terms that once you have the logic sorted out, you should re-implement the tool in a compiled language. If saving time is unimportant, then it doesn't matter which route you choose. Scripting is a neat way to prototype something first before writing it in C.

```
df -m -i $1 |
tail -1     |
while read FSYS BLKS USED AVAIL X IUSED IFREE Y MOUNT
do
    echo "File system ........... : " ${FSYS}
    echo "Disk space available ... : " ${AVAIL}
    echo "I-nodes available ...... : " ${IFREE}
    echo ""
done
```

This script example pipes a line of space-separated words to a **while** loop that reads them line by line. Because we know there are nine separate items, we can **read** them into different variables. We only want to output three of them each time round the loop.

In general, UNIX is great at dealing with things line by line in a horizontally oriented processing regime. It is quite a bit harder to do anything with columns of data. Using **while** loops is one way of handling columns of data, albeit with moderate-to-severe performance issues. For larger data sets, it might be quicker to use the **cut** command to extract a column or load a SQL database and query out the data we need.

Empty Is Not the Same as Nothing

Getting a null response is not the same as getting no response. An empty string is not equivalent to no string at all. This kind of logic can bomb out your conditional tests in shell scripts.

Condition testing is done with the square brackets operator. This is a pseudonym for the **test** command, and we use it with the **if** … **then** construct. This is the general form:

```
if [ VALUE1 condition VALUE2 ]
then
...
```

If condition is **−eq**, then we are testing for numeric equality. Strings of nonnumeric values cause an error.

To compare two strings, the operator is an equals sign (**=**). This is fine, provided the strings genuinely contain something. If either one of them is empty, we get some weird and syntactically wrong script lines.

Let's assume that the variable called **$VALUE1** is empty. That's perfectly reasonable. We might have executed:

```
VALUE1=`ls fred`
```

If the file **fred** didn't exist then **$VALUE1** will be empty.

The **if** script line is parsed and some substitutions happen inside the shell interpreter. What it tries to execute is:

```
if [ = $VALUE2 ]
then
...
```

The equals operator must have two arguments or the test command throws an error.

First, let's make sure that variables always have braces (**{** … **}**). It won't solve this problem, but it does help the parser evaluate some complex script lines.

Next, we can place these variables in quotes. That doesn't fix it either, but now we can place some extra characters inside the quotes so that if the variables are empty, the quoted strings now contain something tangible and don't get parsed to a nonexistent argument.

The correct way to do this kind of test is like this:

```
if [ "|${VALUE1}|" = "|${VALUE2}|" ]
then
...
```

We could have gotten away with a single vertical line, but the symmetry is good.

Now we can build tests for empty strings like this:

```
if [ "|${VALUE1}|" = "||" ]
then
...
```

The braces are required because the variable names wouldn't parse correctly if they had a vertical bar immediately following the variable name.

Summary

Shell scripting is useful for knitting tools together. The tutorials in Part 2 illustrate practical shell scripting techniques. Chapter 28 shows how shell scripts can be used to create work-flow environments.

 Becoming a skilled scripter requires practice. Once you have written a few lines of shell script and spent a little time debugging them, this sort of thing comes as second nature to you. It's hard-won knowledge, but well worth the effort.

In the next chapter, we will look at a different kind of scripting, AppleScript on the Mac OS X operating system.

Automation with AppleScript

AppleScript—Mac OS X on Autopilot

If you are building a workflow on the Mac OS X operating system, you can exploit the capabilities of AppleScript. It is designed around a model that depends on the application developers providing support while Apple engineers the framework. Some applications are better supported than others. There is a great deal of help online, with many sample scripts to mine for ideas that you can recycle in your own designs.

There are some pitfalls, too. Beware of gradual changes to the AppleScript dictionaries. Replacing an application with a later version will affect your AppleScript code in ways you may not expect.

Heritage

AppleScript was originally developed on the Mac OS Classic operating system and was closely related to the HyperCard project. The HyperTalk language was one of the easiest to learn and use, and it was implemented on HyperCard in a way that was at the time revolutionary and has never been matched for its simplicity of use.

AppleScript was added to HyperCard to enable it to do things with operating system resources that previously required extensions to the HyperTalk language to be coded in C or Pascal and installed as plug-ins.

At that time, the Open Scripting Architecture was developed on Mac OS Classic, an architecture that is still evident in the names of some system calls. Where you see the term **osascript**, you now know that it comes from those old golden days of HyperCard and Mac OS Classic.

Dictionaries

AppleScript-equipped applications include a dictionary of available objects and properties with descriptions of the methods that can be used with them. These dictionaries are used to augment the basic syntax of AppleScript. It becomes extensible by calling an application within a **tell application** … **end tell** structure.

Various suites of functionality are standardized (to some extent) and can be overridden within the application. A basic suite might allow you to **open**, **close**, **save**, and **quit**. These commands are augmented according to what the application can do.

The best place to start when working with a new application is its AppleScript dictionary. This illustrates how extensive the AppleScript support is in that application.

If only the most basic support is provided, you may have to resort to GUI-interface programming, which is a series of point-and-click events generated by the script.

The major shortcoming of dictionaries is that you have to sit and decode the language to some degree. Where the HyperTalk language used to be very easy to understand and debug, AppleScript seems to be much harder to assimilate. The editor also modifies a few things for you. Things change while you are looking at them—this is annoying sometimes. The AppleScript editor must complete a successful syntax check before saving the file as a script, which makes it difficult to leave a script partly unfinished. It is also very easy to save a script in a 'Run Only' form that you cannot open again for editing. This can be frustrating after spending some hours developing a script only to find it works but cannot be altered. Keep backup copies between edits.

Recording Scripts

A quick way to learn the AppleScripting capabilities for a new application, provided it is scriptable and recordable (not all apps are) is to open the script editor, turn on the script recorder, and then perform the task manually. At the end, stop the recording and inspect the script that the script editor has created. Sometimes there is nothing there because the application is not recordable. Sometimes it is complete rubbish and throws errors if you try to run it from the editor. Anything that is recorded usually gives you some helpful clues though.

Automator

Not all applications are scriptable. Increasingly, the scripting capability is becoming part of the core operating system.

Mac OS X 10.4 (AKA Tiger) introduced the Automator tool. This is a powerful workflow editor that lets you build on the capabilities provided by AppleScript. Automator provides some additional architecture.

Application developers can supply plug-ins that Automator can use to exploit their internal code. The user can drag-and-drop them into a series of process steps. This is easy, because the connections between each step are somewhat intelligent. A built-in help facility is provided to guide you when necessary.

Automator is a much easier way to build scripts than to sit and write them out in source form. Automator was designed specifically to aid the creation of workflows. The systems designers clearly see this as most applicable to a single-user scenario, but you can extend the idea and build server like processes.

You can use the Automator design protocols and create your own extensions to the Automator environment.

Apple Developer Connection: http://developer.apple.com/

Figure 23-1 Automator workflow builder

UNIX Shell to AppleScript Calls

Calling graphical user interface scripts from the UNIX command-line shell revolves around the **osascript** command. This is a means of calling AppleScript from UNIX. GUI applications can provide the output that we expect from normal UNIX command lines.

This example extracts address data from the Mac OS X address book application but makes it accessible to scripts running in the UNIX command line environment:

```
osascript -e 'tell app "Address Book" to get the name of every person'
```

That script line returns a comma-separated list of the name fields in every vCard in the address book application. A small downside to this is that the GUI application needs to be fired up and draws its UI on the screen. This is not strictly necessary and wastes CPU capacity, graphics memory, and time. It is also unattractive to see apps flash up and disappear while a script is executed. Developers have asked Apple to make AppleScript hide things like this. Maybe we'll see that in a new version one day.

Tutorial 59 uses UNIX shell code to search Word documents for a key string. Tutorial 59 bridges three worlds because it contains Visual Basic code wrapped in AppleScript, which is called from UNIX. Tutorial 61 exploits that and wraps it in GUI so you can use it from your desktop.

AppleScript to UNIX Shell Calls

Working in the opposite direction from the AppleScripts running in the GUI environment of Mac OS X, we can include a command in the AppleScript source code that will call a command-line utility in the UNIX shell. Here is an example:

```
do shell script "cd ~; ls"
```

There are important considerations here with regards to what environment is created when the script is executed. You should never assume what the default environment is going to be. Instead, explicitly build the environment you want. See Chapter 28 for environment-building advice. Include a separate script that is used by all of the tools and centralizes the environment construction into one source script file.

The important thing is to design everything to be modular, reusable, predictable and reliable in execution.

XML and SOAP

AppleScript is now capable of manipulating XML files, communicating directly with a SOAP server, and aggregating the results with the rest of an AppleScript. You don't need to know XML to do this, since it is all buried inside the OS support for AppleScript. This is an example based on the Apple documentation, which you can download:

```
set myText to "My frst naem is John"
tell application "http://www.stuffeddog.com/speller/speller-rpc.cgi"
set returnValue to call xmlrpc {method name:"speller.spellCheck",¬
parameters: {myText} }
end tell
```

The **returnValue** variable in this case contains a list of candidate misspellings and replacements with the character position where they are located:

```
{{suggestions:{"fast", "fest", "first", "fist", "Forst",
"frat", "fret", "frist", "frit", "frost", "frot", "fust"},
location:4, |word|:"frst"}, {suggestions:{"haem", "na em",
"na-em", "naam", "nae", "nae m", "nae-m", "nael", "Naim",
"nam", "name", "neem"}, location:9, |word|:"naem"}}
```

AppleScript developer pages:

  http://developer.apple.com/documentation/AppleScript/Conceptual/AppleScriptX/Concepts/work_with_as.html
Making XML-RPC and SOAP Requests With AppleScript (HTML):

  http://developer.apple.com/documentation/AppleScript/Conceptual/soapXMLRPC/index.html

Microsoft Office and AppleScript

Although Word and Excel have scripting capabilities internally by virtue of their embedded Visual Basic for Applications Edition interpreters, you can still do some cool things from the outside. Office 2004 represents the current state-of-the-art, but Office version 12 for Mac OS X (due out in 2007) will no longer have Visual Basic embedded. It will be interesting to see what the replacement is. The integration with AppleScript should improve still further. This would make the Microsoft Office suite a very useful and important text-processing factory.

If you design AppleScript code for Office version X (as opposed to version 2004), you will have to resort to some bridging to call Visual Basic. You can do this by putting a fragment of Visual Basic code into a string and getting AppleScript to pass it to the Office app with a **do Visual Basic** command.

```
do Visual Basic "ActiveDocument.SaveAs"
```

When Office 2004 for the Macintosh was released, some of the AppleScript support was revised and you will need to resort to the Visual Basic code far less often to drive the application. However, you will need to fix up your older scripts to make them work once more. You will need to do this again when the next version of Microsoft Office is released too.

It is possible to do some powerful things with this interface, but there isn't a great deal of help around. There is a large reference document for each Office application. It is good place to start learning about the scripting capabilities of your applications. Refer to Tutorial 56 to see how to make a spreadsheet with AppleScript driving Excel 2004 directly. Tutorial 57 shows how to do the same with Word 2004 and create a document from a script that could be generated dynamically.

It is possible to create huge and complex documents in this way, but it probably isn't the best way to publish large bodies of content. Instead, it is better to dynamically create SYLK files and import them into Excel. You can add style with AppleScript once the data is there. Likewise, with Word, create an RTF file and import it; you can include all the styling you need. For large projects, create DocBook XML files, convert them to RTF with XSLT transforms, and then load them into Word with AppleScript for conversion into MS Word Doc format. Another alternative is to create Open Office ODT files, which are probably the best supported XML format for documentation by virtue of the Open Office application suite.

Adobe Applications and AppleScript

Using Photoshop to create an alpha channel and saving it in a file is a useful step when building workflows to add titles to video clips. Tutorial 58 demonstrates this concept. Driving Adobe Illustrator and InDesign is just as straightforward.

Summary

Writing AppleScript is a useful skill to have if you want to exploit the power of applications that only work on Mac OS X. Some of Apple's own professional audio and video tools such as Soundtrack Pro and Shake are scriptable. These are powerful applications and are available at economic prices. Processing a collection of audio files through Soundtrack to remove noise and artifacts is something that you wouldn't want to do manually on thousands of files.

Shake could be useful for automating multilayer compositing jobs. Normally it is used on feature films, but there is no reason why it should not be used on TV production now that the price has been reduced to a few hundred dollars.

AppleScript is only applicable to the Mac OS platform. Its one of the few proprietary scripting tools you can't use everywhere. Microsoft also has some scripting tools that you can only use on the Windows platform, and the next chapter briefly examines what they can do.

24

Script Automation in Windows

Opening Windows

If you are building your workflow components on a Windows platform, then you can wrap some script control structures around the tools available there. There is considerable support for scripting applications on Windows.

A variety of different scripting languages have been developed by Microsoft over the years, all of which continue to evolve and become more sophisticated with each new variant of the operating system that is introduced. Most of these languages are aggregated together under the heading of "active scripting."

Whatever scripting languages you may be using on Windows, it is likely that PowerShell will take their place when it is released. The enthusiasm for PowerShell amongst developers is growing as we anticipate the release of Vista. Microsoft has put immense effort into PowerShell, and it should elevate scripting on Windows to be on a par with what we can already do on UNIX.

MS-DOS batch and interactive command lines are still used with the Windows operating system. Whether they continue to be available when PowerShell is in public use remains to be seen.

MS-DOS batch files are executed in the **COMMAND.COM** shell. This is a command-line interpreter that was introduced for DOS when Windows 95 was being developed. The shell is used for both interactive user-typed commands and for automated batch execution. DOS is fundamentally the same sort of thing as a shell in the UNIX operating system, but its capabilities are limited when compared with all the I/O redirection and process control available in UNIX.

Table 24-1 lists a few equivalent commands between DOS and UNIX command lines. Because the operating systems work so differently, there are only a few genuine matches. The entire philosophy is different. DOS users are allowed to do things that UNIX systems administrators would never allow a normal user to do (such as locking disks).

Table 24-1 DOS and UNIX equivalent commands

DOS	UNIX
DIR	ls.
CD, CHDIR	cd.
COPY	cp.
REN, RENAME	mv.
DEL, ERASE	rm.
MD, MKDIR	mkdir.
RD, RMDIR	rmdir.
VOL	df, du.
LABEL	no direct equivalent.
VERIFY	no direct equivalent.
TYPE	cat.
BREAK	kill.
CTTY	Use I/O redirection.
DATE	Get times and dates with the **date** command; only systems administrators can set the date.
TIME	Get times and dates with the **date** command.
ECHO	**echo** plus I/O redirection.
LH, LOADHIGH	Real virtual memory systems don't need the user to control this.
PATH	**${PATH}** environment variable.
PROMPT	Use **${PS1}** environment variable; the exact method depends on the shell.
SET	**set** or **env**.
VER	uname.

Windows Script Host (WSH)

Windows Script Host (WSH) is an environment within which the scripts for Windows applications automation can run. It supports JScript and VBScript by default. Other scripting engines can be added by installing additional software.

WSH annoynaces: http://www.annoyances.org/exec/show/wsh

Dev Guru Introduction: http://www.devguru.com/Technologies/wsh/quickref/wsh_intro.html

Iopus guide: http://www.iopus.com/guides/wsh.htm

WSH and Perl: http://www.xav.com/perl/Windows/windows_script_host.html

Windows Script File (WSF)

You can store scripts in files, with language-specific filename extensions, or in **.wsf** files, which can contain script code of any kind, possibly even mixed languages in the same file.

The **.wsf** files place scripts into containers in a similar way to putting a script into an HTML page. The **<script>** tag in those containers has similar syntax to that used in HTML, and scripts can be included or referenced in external files. The files are structured in an XML fashion.

```
<package>
 <job id="Describe the the job here">
  <runtime>
     Security certification here
  </runtime>
  <script language="VBScript">
     Visual Basic script source here
  </script>
  <script language="JScript">
     JScript source here
  </script>
 </job>
</package>
<package>
…
</package>
```

The **<package>** containment is only necessary if more than one job is being described in the script file. The **<resource>** tag can be added to store shared text and graphics resources that don't need to be repeated in multiple **<script>** blocks. The **<reference>** tag can call in shared libraries of code and values to achieve some re-use.

WSH Security Issues

WSH scripts often require access to file system resources, which means that some attention must be given to security if you expect to import workflow components from other sources. Recent versions of WSH support a script-signing capability. This can be checked by the operating system to ensure that only signed and approved scripts are executed.

The signature encodes some information about the source script body. If the signature is tampered with or the script body changes, they won't match anymore and the script will be inhibited from running. This information—with details of the certificate, the author and the source code—is embedded in the **<runtime>** element of the **.wsf** file.

Microsoft scripting guidelines:

  http://msdn.microsoft.com/library/default.asp?url=/library/en-us/dnanchor/html/scriptinga.asp

WSH scriping: http://www.wshscripting.com/

Win scripter: http://www.winscripter.com/

Rob Vanderwoude scripting guide: http://www.robvanderwoude.com/index.html

Windows scripting group: http://groups.msn.com/windowsscript/_homepage.msnw?pgmarket=en-us

In the documentation examined while writing this book, every Microsoft scripting technology came with a warning about being subverted by virus writers. You must be diligent in making sure your workflow system is secure and all access to it is closed to anyone who should not be logged in. You should not accept any unsigned scripts and certainly never execute a script that is carried by e-mail unless you have a completely closed infrastructure over which you have 100% secure control.

Active Scripting

Active Scripting, sometimes called *ActiveX Scripting*, is used to build component-based script systems. It has descended from the ActiveX/COM system and provides a way to install user-defined scripting engines.
Typical Active Scripting engines are:

- JScript (installed by default).
- VBScript (installed by default).
- ActivePerl.
- ActivePython.
- ActiveTcl.
- HaskellScript.
- PerlScript.

JScript and VBScript are integral to the operating system. The other possibilities listed above need to be purchased and added on. You probably won't come across them as often, and then only if you have purposely installed them.
Active Scripting is becoming less popular with the introduction of PowerShell on the horizon. Variations of the Active Scripting languages are available via .NET but there are subtle differences and you need to be aware which you are authoring for.

JScript

JScript is based on ECMAScript. It is often said to be standardized. Only those parts of JScript that correspond to ECMAScript are genuinely standard and compatible with JavaScript. That is known as core JavaScript and it is a tiny fraction of what JScript supports. The rest is somewhat like JavaScript but certainly couldn't be called standardized. The marketeers are being every economic with the truth when they say JScript is a standards compatible language.
More language syntax is added as somewhat JavaScript-compatible support. Significant amounts of proprietary syntax are also present. It is probably a waste of time trying to achieve complete portability between JScript and JavaScript. Unless you are embedding the script into web pages intended to be viewed by the public on all browsers.

Active State: http://www.activestate.com/

Visual Basic Script Edition (VBScript)

Visual Basic Script Edition (VBScript) is one of the Active Scripting languages managed under the Windows Script Host framework. It is a variation on the classic Visual Basic programming language.

VBScript can be used to automate systems administration tasks, which it has done successfully as a replacement for the older MS-DOS batch files. It can also be used inside the Internet Explorer web browser in place of JavaScript (or JScript, if you prefer) and in stand-alone HTML applications.

Windows PowerShell

Windows PowerShell is a new command-line interface (CLI) shell being developed for the Vista release of Windows. The influence of UNIX on the design is clear, but it adds an object-oriented flavor and integrates with the .NET framework. PowerShell is designed to be more extensible than any previous Microsoft scripting language.

At the time of writing, PowerShell is still a relatively new technology and still being developed. It is likely to become the primary workflow scripting and control environment on Windows workstations and servers. It runs within an architecture that Microsoft is calling Windows Workflow Foundation, which is designed to give us a standardized framework for building workflow systems.

PowerShell will be available for Vista but may be delivered separately as an additional installation. PowerShell will also be supported on Windows XP, Windows Server 2003, and Windows Server.

PowerShell is built from small components that can be combined as complex workflows, similar to the way UNIX allows you to construct workflows from simple commands.

PowerShell components come in several different types, listed in Table 24-2:

Table 24-2 PowerShell components

Component	Description
Commandlets	Commands that are based on methods operating on .NET classes.
Providers	Virtual drives that drill down into .NET classes.
Scripts	Text-based shell scripts that can masquerade as commands.
Snap-ins	Packages of functionality containing all the other three components in a bundle.

Commandlets (or cmdlets) can be used to create a pipeline in the same way that UNIX pipes text from one command to another. The difference is that PowerShell commands will pass objects to one another, instead of text streams. This could turn out to be an extremely powerful technique if Microsoft can make it easy to learn and use.

Provider modules are used to access data sources such as files or registry entries. These are extensible, and user-defined providers can be snapped in as needed.

PowerShell features that have already been announced in publicly accessible documentation include several important functions:

- Programming can use a language style that is similar to C#.
- Flow of control via **if** and **switch-case** style constructs.
- Loops with **for**, **foreach**, **while**.
- Regular expressions.
- Array-slicing tools.
- Support for hash tables.
- Self-modifying code and **eval()**-like support.
- Variable scoping chains.
- User-defined functions.
- The cmdlets support hooks that can delegate control to the user.
- Command-line abbreviation to the shortest unique string that represents a command.
- Tab auto-completion everywhere.
- The results of a command can be assigned to variables similar to the back-quoted execution model in UNIX.

PowerShell Compatibility

PowerShell provides functionality that looks similar to UNIX. It is feasible to add aliases to your PowerShell environment that mimic the corresponding UNIX functionality.

The fine points, such as command-line flags, might not be reproducible but certainly, commands like **more** appear to already have aliases provided by default. Whether this is a good thing or not is open to question. PowerShell is such a different environment that it may be better to force yourself to learn the new syntax. It will likely never be possible to run UNIX shell scripts directly in PowerShell.

It might be possible to run a Perl script initiated by PowerShell and passed to Perl. If it is possible to spawn a compatible shell using the hash-bang technique, we might be able to carry out some interesting portability experiments.

Microsoft PowerShell: http://www.microsoft.com/powershell

PowerShell info: http://www.microsoft.com/technet/scriptcenter/hubs/msh.mspx

PowerShell developer team blog: http://blogs.msdn.com/powershell/

PowerShell Security Policies

Having developed a security model for Windows Script Host, the PowerShell development team knew from day one that security policies would be required. You can use the `Get-ExecutionPolicy` cmdlet to tell you which of the four possible execution policies is currently in force. The Windows PowerShell execution policies include the security settings listed in Table 24-3:

Table 24-3 PowerShell security policies

Policy	Description
`Restricted`	No scripts can be run at all. Windows PowerShell can only be used in interactive mode.
`AllSigned`	Only those scripts that are signed by a trusted publisher can be run.
`RemoteSigned`	Downloaded scripts must be signed by a trusted publisher before they can be run. Until then, they will not work.
`Unrestricted`	No restrictions; all Windows PowerShell scripts can be run. This is a dangerous setting with no protection whatsoever.

The current execution policy can be seen by running this command:

```
Get-ExecutionPolicy
```

To change the execution policy, use the **Set-ExecutionPolicy** cmdlet like this:

```
Set-ExecutionPolicy RemoteSigned
```

PowerShell Examples

Here are a few examples of simple PowerShell commands. The **PS>** string is the PowerShell prompt; you don't need to type that if you see it in any example listings. These also show the piping mechanism, which will be familiar to UNIX users.

This example stops any processes that contain the text '**httpd**'. These might be web server processes:

```
get-process *httpd* | stop-process
```

Given a string object, change it to all uppercase:

```
"hello powershell!".ToUpper()
```

Modify a string object by inserting a string into it:

```
"The Grouse".Insert(4,"Famous ")
```

Test to see if there are any Windows Media Audio (**.wma**) files in a target directory:

```
Test-Path c:\mediafiles\*.wma
```

Get the current version number of Windows from the registry:

```
Test-Path HKCU:\Software\Microsoft\Windows\CurrentVersion
```

Write some data out to a text file:

```
Set-Content c:\temp\sample.txt "This is some sample data"
```

Use **Add-Content** to append more data to the same file.

Grab a listing of the processes running in the computer and output them to a file. This is roughly equivalent to the UNIX **ps > /tmp/process.txt** command, which captures the same kind of information.

```
Get-Process | Out-File c:\temp\process.txt
```

If you want that output in XML form, then use this modified version:

```
Get-Process | Export-Clixml c:\temp\process.xml
```

An HTML version is easy:

```
Get-Process | ConvertTo-Html | Set-Content c:\temp\process.htm
```

Comma-separated format is done like this:

```
Get-Process | Export-Csv c:\temp\process.txt
```

The XML files can be imported back into a PowerShell object, which can be used for something else like this:

```
$myProcessList = Import-Clixml c:\temp\process.xml
```

Converting from XML to comma-separated format goes like this:

```
Import-Clixml c:\sample.xml | Export-Csv c:\sample.txt
```

These import mechanisms also support filtering. The matching lines can be imported and the others ignored. Using this for workflow creation could be quite rewarding.

This is a fragment of script which lists information about all the audio and video codecs installed on a computer. It is based on one at the PowerShell resources web site provided by Microsoft (see the web link).

```
$colItems = get-wmiobject -class "Win32_CodecFile" -namespace "root\CIMV2" `

foreach ($objItem in $colItems) {
  write-host "Description: " $objItem.Description
  write-host "Last Modified: " $objItem.LastModified
  write-host "Manufacturer: " $objItem.Manufacturer
  write-host "Name: " $objItem.Name
  write-host "Version: " $objItem.Version
  write-host
}
```

Scripting Applications in Windows

Adobe supports scripting of the InDesign, Illustrator, and Photoshop applications with JavaScript or Visual Basic in Windows. Most scripting of Adobe applications (with only a few exceptions) is done with JavaScript.

The major difference from scripting with Mac OS X AppleScript is that the JavaScript and VB scripts that are shown as examples in the Adobe documentation and elsewhere on the web are all run from inside the application. This makes it a bit more difficult to build workflows unless you can trigger those scripts from outside the applications.

You can find examples of running things from outside an application if you dig for long enough on the web. This is based on an example that Microsoft provides to show how to create an object that represents Excel. The script creates a new instance of Excel, then makes a new workbook and locates the first sheet.

```
Set objExcel = CreateObject("Excel.Application")
objExcel.Visible = True
Set objWorkbook  = objExcel.Workbooks.Add
Set objWorksheet = objWorkbook.Worksheets(1)
```

Making objects that refer to other applications is done like this:

```
Set objReference = Wscript.CreateObject("Word.Application")
Set objReference = Wscript.CreateObject("InternetExplorer.Application")
Set objReference = Wscript.CreateObject("Scripting.Dictionary")
Set objReference = Wscript.CreateObject("Wscript.Network")
```

Next, we need to work out the object model of the application internals. This example stores values in three cells, then adds a formula to sum them. The cell containing the formula is formatted and colored.

Microsoft PowerShell examples: http://www.microsoft.com/technet/scriptcenter/topics/msh/cmdlets/index.mspx
Microsoft Script Center: http://www.microsoft.com/technet/scriptcenter/hubs/msh.mspx
PowerShell samples: http://www.reskit.net/monad/samplescripts.htm
Resource kit: http://www.reskit.net/

```
Set objExcel = CreateObject("Excel.Application")
objExcel.Visible = True
Set objWorkbook = objExcel.Workbooks.Add
Set objWorksheet = objWorkbook.Worksheets(1)
objExcel.Cells(1, 1).Value = 10
objExcel.Cells(1, 2).Value = 20
objExcel.Cells(1, 3).Value = 30
objExcel.Cells(1, 4).Formula = "=sum(A1:13)"
objExcel.Cells(1, 4).Font.Bold = TRUE
objExcel.Cells(1, 4).Font.Size = 24
objExcel.Cells(1, 4).Font.ColorIndex = 3
```

This example from the Microsoft scripting web site shows how to append text to a document.

```
Const END_OF_STORY = 6
Const MOVE_SELECTION = 0

Set objWord = CreateObject("Word.Application")
objWord.Visible = True

Set objDoc = objWord.Documents.Open("c:\scripts\word\testdoc.doc")
Set objSelection = objWord.Selection
objSelection.EndKey END_OF_STORY, MOVE_SELECTION

objSelection.TypeParagraph()
objSelection.TypeParagraph()

objSelection.Font.Size = "14"
objSelection.TypeText "" & Date()
objSelection.TypeParagraph()
objSelection.TypeParagraph()

objSelection.Font.Size = "10"
```

Many more scripts are provided for you to enjoy at the Microsoft TechNet script center.

Scripting Multimedia Tools

If you install QuickTime 7 for Windows and add a Pro license to a Windows machine, you can access the QuickTime tools from scripts. This makes it much easier to create media management workflows. At the time of writing, there isn't yet any PowerShell support for QuickTime, but it is not a vast stretch of the imagination to see that it is likely be there in due course.

Right now, you can automate your QuickTime workflow with the Active Script support.

Microsoft TechNet script center: http://www.microsoft.com/technet/scriptcenter/scripts/office/

Windows Scripting Filename Extensions

Table 24-4 lists the file extensions, which you should check and validate the source of before running them in your workflow environment.

Table 24-4 Windows scripting file extensions	
File type	*Extension*
JScript	`.js`, `.jse`
VBScript	`.vbs`, `.vbe`
Vanilla WSH script containing any language	`.wsf`, `.wsh`
Signature certificate files	`.cer`
Stand alone HTML applications	`.hta`
MS DOS batch files	`.BAT`
PowerShell scripts	`.ps1`

Summary

Now that PowerShell is on the horizon, scripting will get much more exciting on Windows. Virtually everything that you can do in UNIX shell scripting is possible with PowerShell. There are many similarities, but there are also a few subtle differences that you need to watch out for as you learn the language. There is no substitute for spending time and effort experimenting with it.

Elsewhere, I stated that you should look at the intent of the script examples and then implement them in your own preferred scripting language. Although I have described many examples in UNIX shell script terms, you should be able to implement them in PowerShell with little effort.

In the next chapter, we will look at compiled languages. these are a completely different way to build workflow components and you will most likely use compiled languages like C or Java to build plug-in tools rather than whole frameworks, which are best built with scripts.

Compiled and Interpreted Languages

Performance Products

We use compiled languages to build our major applications and content processing frameworks. It is where we can get closest to the machine and control things with the finest granularity.

For well-conceived workflow architectures, some component modules might be written in compiled languages. If you factor the design of the system carefully, you can use shell scripts to glue the whole system together and then call the compiled code when you need optimal performance. Using the shell scripts in this way allows you to bind things together in flexible ways. You can accomplish the same thing inside a compiled application, but it's difficult to reconfigure from the outside when you need to change something.

The right mix of compiled or interpreted vs. scripted implementation delivers the best of both worlds.

Tool Development

Learning a compiled language enables you to create some efficient and high-throughput tools to process the content.

Java is flexible and quite easy to learn and use, but C language is better performing by comparison (although even C doesn't achieve the performance of Assembler). Objective-C combines the benefits of both Java and C.

See Tutorial 35 for a description of a relative date tool (**theDate**) that is much easier to develop in a compiled language than in a scripting environment.

Compiled vs. Interpreted

It is important to understand the differences between compiled and interpreted languages. They are quite different things, and once you have processed the source code into its executable form, they operate in completely separate ways.

A compiled language distills the source down to the fundamental machine code level that is executed directly by the CPU.

Interpreted code is converted into tokens that need to be looked up and an appropriate handler selected at run time. That handler may need to move some things around or convert some values. The code is no longer being executed directly. The interpreter intercedes with the CPU on behalf of the code and adds some overheads and latency to the execution.

Table 25-1 lists some languages and describes whether they are interpreted or compiled.

Table 25-1 Interpreted and compiled languages

Language	Interpreted	Compiled
BASIC	Usually	Often possible
Java	By Virtual Machine (VM)	Possible but unlikely
JavaScript	Embedded interpreter (JIT)	Difficult to do
C	Occasionally	Always
Fortran	Rarely	Always
Pascal	Via p-code machine	Possible
Forth	Always	Rarely
PostScript	Always	Never
Cobol	Sometimes	Often
Visual Basic	Embedded interpreter	Possibly via Visual Studio
JScript	Active Scripting	Not practical
VBScript	Active Scripting	Not practical
PowerShell	Command line	Not expected to be
AppleScript	Yes	Yes

Which Language?

There are many hundreds of compiled languages, more than we can possibly discuss here. Some have come and gone over the years, and a few have survived from the earliest days of personal computers. Table 25-2 lists the important candidates for workflow implementation.

Table 25-2 Compiled languages for workflows

Language	Strengths and weaknesses
C	The C language is robust, mature, and well supported everywhere. It is available on every platform, and as with the common UNIX tools (**vi** and Bourne shell), you should know some C in order to cope in an emergency.
C++	A popular but sometimes unwieldy object-oriented extension to C language. Many useful API libraries have a C++ interface.
C#	A proprietary language available only on Microsoft platforms. This is targeted at Windows application developers and locks you in to that platform.
Java	An interpreted language useful for a wide variety of tasks. There are still issues with incompatible versions of the virtual machine, and by centralizing the VM, you could crash many processes at once if the VM goes wrong. It was supposed to be very portable, but there are exceptions.
Objective-C	An elegant extension to the C language to introduce new object data types into the core of the language. It is an open source language and available in the **gcc** compiler on all platforms. Mac OS X is built around this because of its NeXTSTEP heritage.
Pascal	Developed in the 1970s at the University of California, San Diego, this language became popular as a teaching tool in systems and programming courses. It is a good capable general-purpose language but is far less popular than it used to be.
Fortran	Designed for mathematical programming, this is still a popular language in scientific circles. In the 1970s and 80s, it was primarily used in graphics work. We would probably implement those solutions with C language now. Some useful legacy algorithms are still available in Fortran code libraries such as NAG and could be linked into a new application.
BASIC	Designed in the earliest days of computing. BASIC lives on as Visual Basic and Real BASIC. It is embedded into products such as Microsoft Office. It is worthy and easy to use and a useful extra tool to have access to.
Cobol	Designed for transaction processing and financial systems. Legacy implementations are still deployed but there doesn't seem to be much new development going on in Cobol.
Forth	A semi-compiled or interpreted language with a strange syntax. It uses a reverse Polish notation where the operands are described first and the operator is described last. The values are pushed onto a stack and pulled back off as they are processed with the result being pushed back on again. You need to be careful with tracking the current state of that stack. Strangely popular with astronomy experts and used quite frequently in boot ROM firmware.

Table 25-2 Compiled languages for workflows (continued)	
PostScript	An interpreted page-description language for imaging systems with much the same behavior as Forth. You can control the imaging down to a single pixel in a 1200 dots-per-inch laser photo setter. Useful for creating images, and because its raw source form is ASCII, you can dynamically generate the code. You can encapsulate in EPS and in PDF files or send it directly to a printer.
Assembler	Difficult to use, but the absolute ultimate in performance if done well. Almost completely nonportable, as you are writing directly to the machine architecture. You may be able to factor in some shared source code for use on other systems with the same kind of CPU.

Portability Issues

The same portability issues that we discussed for scripting will apply here. Using C# locks you into Windows operating systems, just as using Visual Basic locks you into Microsoft applications. It is less common to find a compiled language locked to a platform because the compilers are usually available from an open source.

While PostScript is an Adobe proprietary language, you can deploy it almost everywhere, because the PostScript readers are supported on all platforms and by many printers.

Structural Design

You have a wide variety of tried and tested approaches to building your workflow tools in a compiled language context. Here are some of the technical solutions you will use when you build an application.

Threaded Applications

If you run an application and split it into multiple, simultaneously running threads within the same process, they share the same resources. All of the threads run in the same process space and use a common pool of file buffers.

Sometimes the threads need to be interlocked to maintain synchronization. They might also need to communicate with one another. Search for these related topics to find advice and sample code to use:

- Event objects.
- Mutual exclusion (mutex).
- Shared memory flags.

Child Processes

If threads are too restrictive, you can spawn off separate processes in their own space. These child processes are forked from the original parent and inherit many of its qualities and its environment. Because they are processes in their own right, they don't suffer the shortcomings that threaded processes endure with shared resources.

Frameworks

Frameworks are a container within which your code can run. They create the context where you plug in code that is called as it is needed. This is sometimes called event-based coding, and is related to the general area of callbacks and plug-in design.

You rarely need to create the main control and event processing executive part of an application. Usually, it comes as a pre-built framework onto which you just add your code. Your Integrated Development Environment (IDE) will set this up for you when you start a new project. Xcode and Visual Studio are IDE tools on Mac OS X and Windows respectively.

Callbacks

A callback is a mechanism that the operating system exploits to ask your application for a decision about something. It is used to enhance sort and search algorithms with plug-in comparators.

You can register a function by providing a pointer to its executable code, and the operating system will then remember to call that function and pass it some contextual information. You must manufacture your function so that it conforms exactly to the expected parameter syntax or the callback won't work correctly.

Delegates

Object-oriented coding provides hooks that will call a specifically named handler that you provide. These are like callbacks, but the operating system is smart enough to know that if you don't provide them, it can cope without your input and will handle the request internally and in a default manner. These make use of the Objective-C runtime binding to extend the operating system behavior.

In the context of a web application running in the request-response loop, you might be called at various times in that handling process. You have an opportunity to modify something or access a database. You might even be able to modify a URL value and perform a redirection. You would then pass control back, possibly indicating a true or false status to tell the calling framework whether there is anything else to be processed or not. That status allows a chain of callback to be assembled, but any callback at a higher priority can cancel any further activity and inhibit lower-priority callbacks from ever being called.

Bindings

Bindings connect fragments of code to events and callbacks from a framework. Usually, the binding happens through you naming a function with a predictable name. The runtime environment identifies that name and binds your code to an appropriate place in the framework.

When you build applications and want more control over this binding, determine where in the framework your handler is going to be attached. You might bind your code to a button in a dialog and to a pull-down menu item.

Plug-in Design

Plug-ins are a form of callback but usually triggered by a manual or user-requested action of some kind. The plug-in code must adhere to a strictly defined calling syntax. The code to be executed is maintained in a separate file that is bound into the application at runtime, usually by being placed in a predictably named folder that the application checks automatically.

Libraries

Libraries are a counterpart to frameworks. A framework would call your code to do something based on a user interaction. You would call a library routine to do something that is generic and which is needed often enough that you don't need to reinvent it again.

The Model-View-Controller Paradigm

Building your applications using the model-view-controller (MVC) paradigm lets you factor the code into different parts of the design in a sensible and easily maintained fashion.

Often, we commence coding with no clear idea of what we want to achieve. We end up with a mess of code, some of which alters the database content, and then within the same functional call we update the screen display and collect a keystroke. This is a fundamentally bad way to design software.

In the same way that we spend time normalizing our database schema to ensure we avoid duplication, we factor our application design. The code relating to the business logic is placed together under the heading of model code. Anything to do with the display of that model, date, and time formatters, for example, is part of the view code.

If you recall our earlier discussion of date values, we discussed holding dates as millisecond count values and then displaying the human-readable form via a formatter. This fits precisely with the model-view approach.

The controller acts as the glue. In some cases, you don't have to write much controller code, as the framework can provide most of it. The framework might provide some of the view code too. This is good, because the model is where your intellectual property resides. That's where the value of your design is and should be.

MVC works for any kind of system, not just GUI-based designs. It might even be called server-client-controller.

Observer-Controller

Controllers don't just join your one model to the one view you have. They act as an intermediary between your model and all views.

If you have several windows open at once, or another application is watching your model values and waiting for a change, they can all register an interest with the controller. Then, when a value changes, the controller will alert any of those registered callbacks with an update message.

Those processes that have registered an interest are called *observers*. They need not all be in the same application.

This is only going to work if the controller is also involved with every change to the model. If you want to operate on your model, the external view asks the controller to perform a change on a model value. The controller knows who is interested in that update and advises them accordingly. Don't go round the back and modify the model directly. No one else will see the change. The model and all the views will then be unsynchronized. Do it properly or don't use the paradigm!

This behavior is visible when you run a shell script that puts a file in a directory where the Mac OS X Finder has a window open. You will see the new file appear almost instantly in the GUI view.

Inter-Process Communication

If you factor your workflow properly, you might have multiple processes all running at once. Some processes will be on the same machine and others distributed around the network. These processes will need to talk to each other somehow.

Controlling Processes with Signals

On the UNIX operating system, applications can send messages to each other in a variety of different ways. The traditional method is to use signals. This requires a signal handler to be created when the application starts up. It isn't hard to do and is well documented in the UNIX programming guidebooks and manuals. Only a few signals are supported on the Windows platform. Other techniques for messaging and sending events will be necessary. Table 25-3 lists the signals available for controlling your application, as well as noting which ones are supported on Windows. They are all supported on Mac OS X and Linux.

Table 25-3 Signals

No	Name	Description	Win
1	**SIGHUP**	Terminal disconnected but often used to force a soft restart within the app.	
2	**SIGINT**	Interrupt program.	YES
3	**SIGQUIT**	Quit program.	
4	**SIGILL**	Illegal instruction – halt.	YES
5	**SIGTRAP**	Trace trap.	
6	**SIGABRT**	Abort program.	YES
7	**SIGEMT**	Emulate instruction executed.	
8	**SIGFPE**	Floating-point exception.	YES
9	**SIGKILL**	Kill program.	
10	**SIGBUS**	Bus error – halt.	
11	**SIGSEGV**	Segmentation violation – halt.	YES
12	**SIGSYS**	Nonexistent system call invoked.	
13	**SIGPIPE**	Write on a pipe with no reader.	
14	**SIGALRM**	Real-time timer expired.	
15	**SIGTERM**	Software termination signal.	YES
16	**SIGURG**	Urgent condition present on socket—needs your handler.	
17	**SIGSTOP**	Stop (cannot be caught or ignored).	
18	**SIGTSTP**	Stop signal generated from keyboard.	
19	**SIGCONT**	Continue after stop.	
20	**SIGCHLD**	Child status has changed.	
21	**SIGTTIN**	Background read attempted from control terminal.	
22	**SIGTTOU**	Background write attempted from control terminal.	
23	**SIGIO**	I/O is possible on a descriptor.	
24	**SIGXCPU**	CPU time limit exceeded.	
25	**SIGXFSZ**	File-size limit exceeded.	
26	**SIGVTALRM**	Virtual time alarm.	
27	**SIGPROF**	Profiling timer alarm.	
28	**SIGWINCH**	Window size change.	
29	**SIGINFO**	Status request from keyboard.	
30	**SIGUSR1**	User-defined signal 1.	
31	**SIGUSR2**	User-defined signal 2.	
32	**SIGTHR**	Thread interrupt.	

Most of these signals will cause a process to halt provided they are received from a process that has authority to communicate them. Some require user-defined handlers to have any meaning. You can put handlers in for most, but signal **17** cannot be blocked. Otherwise, you might be able to create a process that cannot be stopped.

There are limits to what you can do during a signal handler, especially on Windows. Don't try to do any I/O because that could cause memory to be accessed or interrupts to be generated and if we are handling a signal, we are already in the midst of an interrupt. Allowing interrupt recursion can crash the operating system or at best, just your application process.

Controlling Processes with Apple Events

Another approach on Mac OS X is to send Apple Events to applications. This is effectively how AppleScript communicates with applications. On Windows, you may be able to accomplish something similar with .NET and COM interfaces.

There are other, more passive approaches, such as where the application is checking a watch folder. The presence or absence of a file can indicate whether the process should do something. That's a bit "old-school" now that we have better ways to do it. A similar technique inside the application is to use a shared memory flag. Setting it from outside is the difficult part but that could be done via signal handlers.

Pipes

Another means of inter-process communication is through pipes. These look like file buffers, and your sending process can write some bytes into its outgoing pipe, which is connected to the incoming channel on the receiving application. You need a pair of pipes if the applications must communicate and do any handshaking. These are sometimes called *named pipes*.

Sockets, Ports, Listeners, and inetd Services

Distributing processes around a network means that sockets, ports, and listeners are another possibility. You can communicate with processes on the same machine; they don't need to be running elsewhere. It is quite feasible to run a web server and SQL database on the same machine and test out a distributed web publishing service without needing three machines to do it.

If you attach a process to the **inetd** daemon by adding it to a list of services, that process will take its input from an incoming network connection and its output will be returned to the client application. This is neat, because you can write network responders without needing to know anything about writing socket handling code. Furthermore, the process is started when it is needed and does not need to be busy running when it isn't required.

Windows runtime document: http://msdn.microsoft.com/library/en-us/vclib/html/_crt_signal.asp

Summary

These are some useful principles to bear in mind when deciding whether to write script or code in a compiled language:

- Scripting is great for binding things together.
- Interpreted languages like Java run faster.
- Compiled languages C, Objective-C or C++ run faster still.
- Compiled code simplifies your scripts and hides complexity.
- Things that are difficult to do in script can be done with a small plug-in written in C.
- Compiled code cannot be changes as easily as scripts.

In the next chapter, we will take a brief look at GUI tools before starting to combine all the things we've covered into a workflow.

GUI Tools and Processes

Controlling GUI Applications

Many useful tools that we would like to use in a workflow have graphical user interfaces (GUIs). If the application has been designed to let you use automation systems to leverage its capabilities in a workflow then we can take advantage of that with a script.

Applications designed around the X-Windows system on a Linux or other UNIX workstation may be relatively easy to access using additional software such as Expect, ExpecTk, and Tcl, as well as X-Windows automation mechanisms.

Mac OS X has AppleScript support for automating GUI applications and Windows Vista has PowerShell for the same kind of script-driven control.

There have always been third-party solutions, too. These haven't always caught on, but occasionally you find a solution that is economic and easy to deploy.

Scriptable Applications

A scriptable application is one that you can control with a workflow framework such as AppleScript or Windows PowerShell. Applications that are designed to be scriptable support dictionaries or API implementations that provide entry points to the application's core functionality. If an application is not scriptable, then a GUI scripting front end might allow you to control the application via its user interface. The changes to the user interface introduced by a new version can compromise this method of driving the applications. You should always check your workflow scripts for compatibility after upgrading any application.

Recordable Applications

A recordable application is one in which you can set a macro recorder running, and then execute the task you want to automate. At the end of the task, you can stop the macro recorder and examine the script that it has generated.

Even if an application is scriptable, it may not be recordable. If it is, then recording it is an ideal way to understand the fine points of how to drive it within a workflow framework. AppleScript-recordable applications will show you how to do some extremely tricky things that you might never have discovered without spending an enormous amount of time trying to work them out. This functionality is now being wrapped in the Automator workflow framework, which makes it much easier to exploit. Nevertheless, if you want to build complex workflows, you eventually have to resort to code.

Using recordable applications is similar to putting a logger onto a terminal application and then editing the result to create a shell script. Recording a sequence of commands to make a script has always been quite straightforward with a command line interface such as the UNIX shells or even the old MS-DOS BAT files. Applications with GUI interfaces don't lend themselves to recording or scripting, hence the need for AppleScript and Windows PowerShell.

Sometimes the recorded script code is complete rubbish and doesn't work. That indicates that the developers didn't really understand how to make scripting work for their application.

Nonportability of GUI Scripting

By its nature, any kind of GUI scripting is bound not to be portable. Indeed, you may find that the scripts won't work if you change the screen size or resolution. This is because UI objects might have moved on the screen.

It is certainly not likely that a script wrapped around a Mac OS X version of Photoshop would function at all in a Windows environment even if the same version of Photoshop were available. You have to completely disregard the possibility of portability for GUI programming at the outset.

GUI Apps with No Scripting Support

Within the constraints of scripting applications on a single platform, you may be able to extend the operating system with a plug-in mechanism that supports GUI scripting. This can be accomplished by hooking into the mouse and keyboard input routines and emulating physical input devices.

It works, but it's not likely to survive an upgrade of the application. Often, some UI elements will move, be changed, or disappear altogether from one release to the next.

You may be able to make it work for the current version of the application. Be prepared to put in some extra work when you upgrade.

If the UI manipulation can be wrapped in an outer layer of scripting, you may be able to isolate yourself from changes and maintain a standard API to this workflow component. Then, changes can be carried out inside the wrapper; they won't disturb any external processes that call the wrapper.

Visual Basic and Office Applications

Microsoft Office applications contain the embedded Visual Basic interpreter for automation. This is primarily a means of writing macros to extend the capabilities of the individual applications within Office.

This level of scripting is document-centric and designed to execute inside Office applications. It is related to the Visual Basic available within Visual Studio as a tool for creating applications but it isn't the same thing.

Visual Basic scripting works on Windows and on Mac OS X for now. The next version of Office to be released will be Office 12 (due in 2007), and Visual Basic will only be available on the Windows version. It is not being taken forward for the next Mac OS X compatible version for technical reasons to do with porting it to the Intel CPU.

The AppleScript support in the Office 2004 software is much improved from the earlier versions and has minimized the need to call Visual Basic from AppleScript. Office 12 for the Mac should continue this trend, as it would significantly reduce the complexity of scripting Office apps on Mac OS X.

On the Windows platform, Visual Basic is hugely popular in the business community. It will be interesting to see what impact the PowerShell scripting tools have on the use of Visual Basic, but that scenario could take several years to unfold.

Scripting Other Windows Applications

Windows scripting can be done with a variety of different scripting tools. Windows Script Host (WSH) wraps several tools in a unified scripting environment that lets you add third-party script engines.

If you want to get a specific level of control, you can use C# and COM via the .NET technologies. You'll need to buy some developer tools. Most people will accomplish what they need with Active Scripting in JScript and VBScript.

Soon, PowerShell will be publicly available and deliver unprecedented levels of scripting capability to Windows.

Third-Party Support for Windows Apps

Table 26-1 is a summary of some possible scripting tools for automating the Windows GUI:

Table 26-1 Windows GUI automation tools

Tool	URL
AutoIt	http://www.autoitscript.com/autoit3/
Perl	http://www.pti.co.il/qa_automation.html
Python	http://sourceforge.net/projects/pywinauto/
Ranorex	http://www.ranorex.com/

GUI Tools in AppleScript

Before Mac OS X was developed, the third-party Frontier tools extended the Mac OS Classic UI so that it could be scripted. With the introduction of Mac OS X and the newer versions of AppleScript, that capability is available as a standard fixture in the OS itself.

GUI control is accomplished via the System Events application. AppleScripts tell the System Events application to intercede for them and operate the user interface on Mac OS X native (but not Mac OS Classic) applications.

This only works sometimes. Some companies develop applications that, in their view, cannot use the standard operating system menus and UI design. Instead, they go ahead and implement their own. Their application bloats up because it is carrying all that unnecessary overhead of menu handling and drawing code that it doesn't really need. Even worse, this stops the UI scripting mechanisms from working. There is very little you can do about this other than lobby the company concerned.

PreFab UI Browser

Apple's GUI Scripting has a flaw in that it is difficult to deduce the object hierarchy necessary in order to build a working UI script.

The PreFab UI Browser helps to explore, control, and monitor the user interface of most Mac OS X applications. It is always easier if you can exercise a UI and get the system to record the actions but it doesn't always deliver well formed scripts—that is when it works at all. Many applications are recordable. When they aren't, PreFab helps to solve the problem for as many apps as it can. It expects the user interface to be implemented using the standard kit of parts in Mac OS X. Some applications don't use the built-in UI tools and so PreFab cannot intercept the user actions and record them.

Summary

Turning your GUI applications into server-like black boxes isn't always easy, but it is worthwhile. You only have to do the work to solve the problem once; after that, you can repurpose the script wrappers many times over.

The next chapter looks at how we build tools and kits to use in our workflow architectures.

Prefab UI browser: http://www.prefab.com/uibrowser/

Building Tools

Component Architectures

Your workflow infrastructure falls conveniently into two main kinds of components:

- Frameworks that control things.
- Tools that do things.

The frameworks or control mechanisms decide what is processed, when it happens, and how it's done. The "how" part of the equation is implemented as a series of tools or components.

Microsoft PowerShell uses this approach where you can create commandlets, providers, snap-ins, or services. UNIX uses this approach by virtue of its command line utilities and pipes. Mac OS X uses its GUI applications as component tools that it can send AppleEvents via its AppleScript infrastructure.

The Importance of Sticking to Guidelines

If you are building your workflow around an existing infrastructure, then your components are only going to work properly if you adhere to the design principles and guidelines laid down by the operating system or infrastructure provider.

If you are building the entire workflow yourself, then spend some time thinking about standardized API call formats and data types. Try to make the components out of a standardized wrapper. Generic wrappers receive their input in a similar way and produce control output consistent with each other.

Separate the control from the data inputs. The command-line parameters might describe what needs to be done, but the standard input is where the data is "squirted" for processing. The standard output is the filtered or processed result, but an auxiliary output channel or file would pass on metadata and triggers.

Piped filters are probably not yet well-enough developed for processing graphical images and even less so for processing video—even though that is effectively how we process video when we connect together a rack full of hardware video-processing equipment.

Workflows that can process pictures, video, and sound as readily as UNIX shells process texts would be useful. Some open-source projects such as **ffmpeg** are making progress towards this goal.

PowerShell attempts to resolve this by passing objects from one process to another instead of text.

Developing Components

Simple text-processing components could be implemented in shell scripts, Perl, Python, or a variety of command line-driven tools. As always, you should stick to the same principles and make sure the input/output conforms to the designs you laid down when you designed the workflow.

You might enclose your compiled modules in a small shell script wrapper. This appears to be how Windows PowerShell delivers it snap-in modules.

Processing images and audio/video content will usually compiled code. It is impractical to directly manipulate video or pixel data with script. None of the normal command-line and text-processing tools are suited to processing video files directly although you may be able to extract fragments of text in a pinch or inspect the header, looking for metadata attributes.

Tools that can open a video file and generate a list of time codes or extract metadata that is bound to the file would be very useful. Then you can process it externally.

Compiled-language tools for embedding and de-embedding metadata will be vital. Real Networks Inc (formerly Progressive Networks) supplies tools like this that embed URL tracks into movies. When they play, the web browser is triggered to do something in another frame. You can even call JavaScript so that dynamic things happen on the screen when the movie is played.

You can only make that work, if you can produce the textual metadata track with the correct time codes and then merge it with the raw video.

QuickTime provides many of these facilities through the Movie Player application, which you can drive from AppleScript or Active-X (as long as you have a QuickTime Pro license).

Integrating All the Components Together

When you put your system together, think about where you are going to put things. Do all your users share a single version of the system? Do you want them to have private extensions that only they can access?

You can build your system so it has a hierarchical search for its component tools built into it. UNIX does this by virtue of the `${PATH}` variable, which is a list of folders to be searched for the binary executable for a command that has been typed into the command-line interface. The directory path that is earliest in the `${PATH}` variable will be searched first. Your `${PATH}` variable will contain a reference to the system-wide shared tools, but to the left of that reference might be a description of a local directory in your own home folder. If that contains a somewhat different version of the command, then that one will be used in preference.

It is not always a desirable thing to allow users to override systems behavior, and you may have security policies in place that guard against this sort of thing. Additionally, there may be tools for which you only have limited licenses available and you may not want all users to have the folder for them in their search path.

The control scripts that programmers use to build applications have evolved from a script, which was used with a tool called *make*. Now that we use Integrated Development Environments (IDE) this is all hidden 'under-the-hood'. Nevertheless, you will often hear developers talking about using a make script or 'doing a make' when they compile the application.

Put all your compiled tools in one place and set up your control scripts so that the building process will install new versions there when you build a final released version. Have a separate directory for prototypes and new tools under "test."

Keep the script in a different directory. Keeping it all well organized, consistently named, and (most importantly) well documented with user guides, **man** pages, and adequate version control all contribute to building a more reliable system.

Operating System Support

Let the operating system do as much work as possible; after all, that's what it is there for. If you don't look at the operating system to see what it can do for you, you might waste time and effort implementing a piece of not very robust code that reinvents one of its wheels.

It is amusing, intriguing, and somewhat alarming how many application developers port code from Windows to UNIX and feel obliged to bring along an implementation of the Windows registry—with somewhat disastrous results when the registry goes into a clean-up mode. This was the case with a well-known middleware product. Every few days, it would shut down for 90 minutes while it reconstructed the registry. During that time, the dynamic parts of the web site would not serve to the end users. If only the developers had used a few minutes of their development time to understand UNIX environment variables, they could have saved weeks of porting effort, not to mention that we would have had a web site that worked 24/7 and they would have had a better product.

If you look carefully when you are porting code, you can make decisions that build on what is already there.

Designing for Portability

Let me tell you about the time that I wrote the most portable application I have ever managed. Back in 1989, I needed to write an application that would be installed on VMS, Windows, Mac OS Classic, and half-dozen different UNIX variations. It would access indexes and data files in several locations, which I could have hard coded and had to build a dozen different versions of my application.

I looked at a number of factors before designing any code. At the outset, I decided to stick to ANSI standard C, without extensions but conforming to POSIX interfaces. This seemed to be supported everywhere. Then I considered the differences between the systems.

- Filename character sets.
- File extensions.
- Directory paths.
- Device names.
- Environment variables or their nearest equivalent.

As far as filename character sets were concerned, DOS and Windows are caseless. Filenames are (or were at that time) displayed in uppercase regardless of whether the shift key was down or not when the filename was defined. VMS is the same. UNIX is case-sensitive and case preserving. Provided I used uppercase characters only it would be consistent. Mac OS Classic is case preserving but case-insensitive (although this is a facet of the file system rather than the OS). Again I decided to stay in uppercase. This localized the problem. It meant that whenever I wanted to access the file system, I could create some helper routines that would force the filenames into all uppercase characters. DOS was the constraining OS as far as filename lengths were concerned. I needed to keep all my portable data file names to eight characters or less.

Then I thought about file extensions. DOS expects only three characters. VMS can cope with 3 characters and is happy to have more if required. Mac OS and UNIX consider the dot and file extension to be part of the file name. I elected to stick with 8.3 (pronounced 8 dot 3) for filename and extension, all in upper case (**NNNNNNNN.XXX**).

When I looked at directory paths, I saw that all of the operating systems are completely different. I really didn't want to have to mangle directory path names to convert between them.

Device names in DOS are single letters followed by a colon. In VMS, devices have longer names but are also terminated by a colon. The rest of the VMS directory is a dot-separated list of folder names with the whole enclosed in square braces. Mac OS uses a colons as the folder separator, UNIX uses a forward slash, and DOS uses a backwards slash. They are all different, although the differences are confined to the delimiters.

At this point, I resolved to store the paths to any directory I wanted to access in an environment variable and then use the **getenv()** call from C to extract that value. On UNIX this worked fine. VMS mapped **getenv()** to its system variables, so it was transparent. I had to simulate this in Mac OS and Windows. On the Windows platform there was support for **.INI** files. I wrapped that in some code so that it looked like a **getenv()**.

The result was that to open a file, I would get the directory path with **getenv()** call and append the filename to it. I needed to make sure that the installation processes created the right environment for the code to run in as part of the commissioning process. That was just a case of creating the **.INI** file on Windows and editing some shell scripts on the other platforms.

This was a moderately large application with several thousand lines of code. I developed it on a small Mac OS computer. I took it into the client and compiled it on VMS. Apart from a small issue with leading white space characters on compiler directives, it compiled without error and worked. I copied the source code to the UNIX systems. Apart from a result flag that needed to be inverted on a **getc()** call in IBM's AIX operating system, it all just worked. Then on Windows, it compiled and worked immediately.

I spent three months designing the code and one month writing it. Often we are tempted to start writing code at the outset of a project. I could have spent four months writing the code and then several more debugging it on all the different machines. In the end, the porting required no effort—beyond fixing two lines in VMS and one line in AIX—because I constrained the design to fit within the observed operating system behaviors.

It worked because I used what was there on each platform. I just made it look like a `getenv()` call on them all.

Open-Source Libraries and Tools

If you are setting out to build a system today, you have a huge variety of open-source applications you can access and modify. There are also many open-source libraries and software developer kits that save you from writing thousands of lines of code.

This is leverage! Because many people are using them, open-source library bugs are fed back and fixed quickly. The overall quality of the library code you are using is generally much better than that found in some of the libraries we used to buy for thousands of dollars.

Before starting that wheel-reinvention process, go and search the Internet to see if someone else already has a supply of wheels you can use over again. You know it makes sense!

Mac OS X, NeXT, and Rapid Tool Building

When Steve Jobs left Apple in 1985, he founded the NeXT Company, which set for itself the task of building the most efficient and structurally complete object-oriented software development environment.

NeXTSTEP—and OpenStep as it later became known—was renowned for its ease of use when developing applications. The object-oriented frameworks were far more advanced than what developers were used to using with the ANSI C standard library support.

Brad Cox's extensions to the C language yielded Objective-C, which was well designed because of Cox's earlier involvement with the SmallTalk team back at Xerox PARC.

Wind the clock forward to 1997 or thereabouts. Steve Jobs is back at Apple, and the OpenStep operating system is evolving rapidly to become Mac OS X.

If we only listen to the marketing hype, Mac OS X was born around 1998, so it's easy to think of it as a young operating system. Certainly much has changed, but a great deal of it is still classic NeXTSTEP and OpenStep framework code. Mac OS X is fundamentally an operating system that has evolved over about 20 years and not for the eight or so that we might assume. It is a more robust operating system because of that provenance.

In changing from NeXT to Apple, the OS hasn't lost any of its nice application development functionality. In fact, it has got even better.

The Xcode development tools, combined with the NeXT Interface Builder, can get you a significant way into building an application without writing a line of code. The drag-and-drop kits and controllers are so sophisticated that you can build a basic text editor, PDF viewer, movie player, or web browser without coding at all. Even save, load, and print are reasonably functional, and adding a toolbar is easy.

When CoreData, CoreVideo, and CoreImage were added, some sophisticated capabilities came with them. CoreData can build an object model by dragging an XML file onto a pane in the Xcode toolkit. You can then save that as a runnable application that can edit the data and save it to a file, still without writing any code.

CoreImage is a foundation not only for image filtering, but also a surface onto which movie playback is presented. You can produce live interactive effects on video with this technology. Building video filtering tools is easy by combining CoreImage with CoreVideo.

Because we have these toolkits, it makes the Mac OS X operating system an interesting place to develop advanced workflows for multimedia content. If you prefer, you can do this work on Linux and Windows. However, you might need to locate some supporting code libraries from other sources. Mac OS X has everything you need built-in already, which means that if a problem arises in the integration of those technologies, you only have to approach one company about getting it fixed. There is no arguing about which SDK developer didn't adhere to some arbitrary guidelines. There are no grey area's of responsibility. The buck goes back to number 1 Infinite Loop in Cupertino and stays there until it is fixed.

This default level of integration is what compels me to stay on the Mac OS X platform for my multimedia research projects.

Development Systems

You will need a development system on which to build your prototype workflow. This can be a reduced-performance version of your live system— you can cope with it having less memory, less disk space, and a slower processor—but it should be running the same operating system version and be configured as closely to the same software specification as possible. You will also have development tool licenses on it that are not on the live system.

Version Control

Keep everything in a source control system. Not only source code, but scripts and documentation, too. This allows you to revert to older versions and undo software changes. SourceSafe is one possible source control system. The open-source CVS is useful, as is Subversion. Perforce is becoming quite popular lately.

Keep your source code check-ins atomic; that is, never check back in a nonworking source. Check in when a single feature upgrade is completed, even if this means you need to check in and check out again immediately to continue working. If you do it like that, you can roll back individual feature upgrades without having to undo months of work.

Version Numbering

Work out a reliable version-numbering scheme. A four-part number separated by full stops works well.

A major rollout of the whole system should increment the most significant number. Rolling out individual tools might increment the second most significant number. Fixing a bug, but not adding any new features, should only increment the third most significant number. A fourth significant number could be reserved for field maintenance patch upgrades.

Incrementing any number should reset lower priority numbers to zero. The four-part number is constructed like this:

```
Version.Update.Revision.Patch
```

You might also want to include build numbers as a supplementary value, which could be held separately.

If you release prototype and test versions, distinguish between pre-alpha, which are hacked together and possibly crash prone, and experimental, alpha, beta, and candidate Golden Master (GM) releases. A pre-alpha release should never leave the lab. An alpha will be seeded within the team or organization. A beta might be seeded to selected outsiders but only if they have signed a nondisclosure agreement. Candidate releases can be supplied to trusted users.

Never be tempted to placate a difficult customer by giving them access to your alpha and beta test releases. It is guaranteed to end in tears.

When you roll out a major upgrade, make sure you do a clean and complete build. This brings all the components up to the same level of shared libraries, and it should reset their version number strings so the entire kit is version numbered consistently.

Releasing Strategy

Develop a mechanism for rolling out new versions of the workflow. Remember that these will be deployed to a system that is live and may not be stopped to allow you to carry out an upgrade.

Set up your environment and define a root directory in a single variable. Change that in a single place and you can rollout the upgrade to a secondary location, test it on the live service, switch over, and, if necessary, switch back to the previously working installation immediately.

Never overwrite a live system with a new version and obliterate your back-out contingency support.

Portable System Directory Structure

Organize your project directories sensibly. Keep similar things together. If you have executable binary applications that have been compiled, store them in a folder together. It makes pathing to them easier.

Sometimes you have a product that runs on multiple operating systems. You will need to build a special binary for each OS. You cannot run an IBM UNIX binary on a Sun operating system. You cannot run an Intel Linux binary on a Linux system installed on a PowerPC machine. There might be problems with different distributions of the Linux operating system running on the same hardware (or it might work—but check first). There are two ways to organize this, the hard way and the easy way.

The hard way creates a separate version of your product that is shipped to customers with specific hardware. You must make sure that they get the correct version and that the binary executables are stored in the same folder location in all variants. The only difference between each version is that there are different binaries. This approach creates huge amounts of extra work for everyone in the company.

The easy way is to add another level of folders to the directory where the binaries live. Those extra folders are named according to the results of the **uname** command on the target system. Then you make sure that a **uname** is executed during the environment-building process. The value creates a pointer to the folder that is relevant to the current machine. This means you ship both the Sun OS and Mac OS X executables in your IBM UNIX installation kit, but the IBM system never sees them because it only looks in its own executables directory. It is a little wasteful of disk space but your installer could throw them away once it has finished.

 Apple calls this technique *Universal Binaries*. It is a legacy of the original NeXTSTEP system, which was designed to support multiple architectures in a single distribution from the outset. Mac OS X has always been able to support different architectures too. It was just a well-kept secret.

This works even if you port to nonUNIX architectures, because you can simulate the effect of a **uname** command on Windows or VMS or any other OS.

Template System Design

Create these top-level folders. Use your own names if you prefer. These folders live in the version numbered master folder for this release:

- Executables (including all the different binaries).
- Object_Code (only on the development system).
- Source (only on the development system).
- Configurations.
- Tools.
- Data.
- Logs.
- Temporary_Files.
- User_Files.

In the **Executables** folder, create a folder that corresponds to the **uname** command on all the target OS architectures you plan to use. Wrap that **uname** command in some script that creates a string with no spaces and takes account of different CPU types.

For example, **uname** on Mac OS X replies with "**Darwin**;" **uname -m** on some systems says "**Power Macintosh**," while on others it will say "**Intel Macintosh**." If you aren't making a universal binary, you'll need to know the difference. A "**DarwinPowerPC**" and "**DarwinIntel**" directory would be called for. If you wrap the **uname** in a script you can cope with minor differences as the OS is upgraded and chooses to spell things differently, or you can add extra differentiation for kernel versions, etc. This is a concept, not a set of hard and fast rules.

The **Object_Code** folder is only used during system compilation and building. You might store libraries there, or you can create a top-level directory for them if it is merited. If you share directories across different machines so you can build multiple versions, the **uname** technique would apply here and to the optional **Libraries** folder, too.

Your **Source** folder should be a single version for all architectures with conditional compilation where necessary. This directory is bound to your source control system and is where you check out the source for editing and building.

The **Configurations** folder is where you store files that control the way the system works, such as web server **httpd.conf** files. These may need to be copied to a **/etc** directory in a live installation, but you can build scripts to manage all that. This is your master copy.

The **Tools** folder is where you put scripts and workflow support components. You might segment this by different parts of the workflow. For a small workflow project, you won't need sub-directories. For a big system, you might create folders for Video Tools, Audio Tools, Text Tools, and so on. It is a method of keeping things neat and tidy. Being well organized like that is good practice and makes the maintenance task easier. It doesn't require any significant extra effort.

The **Data** folder is where you put your SQL database or the TSV files that the workflow might use, such as lists of day and month names, catalogs, and look-ups. This is data for the workflow system; user data goes somewhere else.

The **Logs** folder is a centralized place where you journal what happens and collect metrics and performance data.

The **Temporary_Files** folder might use a working directory somewhere else in the OS. Often called **/tmp**. Keeping all the temporary files in one place makes it easier to clear out the trash.

The **User_Files** folder is where anything that relates to systems administration users or workflow operators is stored. Perhaps they have customized user environments or favorite colors. That all gets stored here.

Summary

Now that we can plan our systems-building process, we are ready to start constructing a workflow. That's what we'll do in the next chapter.

Keep It Moving

Building Workflows

A workflow system by definition, organizes a flow of information through a series of steps where some work is done on the data as it proceeds from one step to the next. Sometimes that processing can happen automatically, while at other times it might require some human intervention.

Keeping control of that work and tracking the media assets or metadata entities requires considerable organizational skill. If we were trying to do all of these things manually, we would inevitably make mistakes and lose things along the way. Automation is all about saving you effort and improving the reliability of what you produce. Then you can concentrate on the quality of the knowledge you distil into the content (essence data and metadata).

Systems Building Plan

Database-driven and dynamically generated web sites use techniques that can be applied to other forms of content. Those techniques have been extended to video and audio through media asset management systems, and interactive content can be published in the same way. Regardless of the type of content, the steps are more or less the same:

- Understand your content.
- Understand your incoming source formats.
- Understand your outgoing target formats.
- Develop the transformation algorithms.
- Design your model.
- Build your database.
- Build your input and ingest tools.
- Build your editorial tools.
- Build the distribution and syndication mechanisms.
- Build the publish and export sub-system.
- Integrate.
- Test.
- Deploy.

Think of this set of requirements as a set of columns arranged horizontally.

Content Design

Architecting a system to build a workflow requires the content to be divided into several disciplines, which helps to reduce the complexity of the problem:

- Creating textual content.
- Creating structured data/informational content.
- Creating graphics.
- Creating animations.
- Processing audio content.
- Processing video content.
- Creating metadata to describe all these assets and all the implications thereof.
- Aggregating content together into presentations.
- Adding interactive controls.
- Storing content into containers.
- Publishing each kind of content.
- Distributing content.
- Broadcasting content.
- Implementing rights management.

Managing these different content types will require a system that knows about the provenance, rights issues, and formatting processes for each kind of asset. We also need to control editorial ownership, revision control, creation, and editing as well as re-formatting for alternative outlets. To manage data effectively, we need to understand how to manage metadata. That is data about the data.

Think of this as a set of rows arranged vertically.

The Matrix Overview

Taking the systems building plan and the content design, you can now create a matrix that generates a set of tasks, one per box. The breakdown of tasks can be put onto your project plan and delegated to your engineers.

As tasks are completed, the matrix gradually fills up with ticks in all the boxes. When the last column is complete, the system is done. Figure 28-1 shows a sample matrix. You will need to create one that is appropriate to your project.

	Understand					Build					Rollout		
	Content	Source formats	Target formats	Transforms	Model	Database	Ingest tools	Editorial tools	Distribution mechanisms	Publish system	Integrate	Test	Deploy
Text													
Data													
Pictures													
Animations													
Audio													
Video													
Metadata													
Aggregation													
Interactivity													
Containment													
Publishing													
Distributing													
Broadcasting													
Rights													

Figure 28-1 Matrix planner

Advancements Required for Interactivity

Advances in open standards such as the MPEG-4 BInary Format for Scenes (BIFS) and its latter counterpart MPEG-4 Lightweight Scene Representation (LASeR) suggest that a new generation of interactive TV services could be emerging. This would play well on IPTV platforms and gradually migrate to replace the existing technologies as they reach the end of their lifecycle. The content creation systems need to produce much richer and deeper user experiences and need to manufacture the content in industrial quantities.

To do that, we need to build content management systems that model interactivity in ways that allow the authoring process to be better distributed and far less of a technical exercise. Interactive authoring tools are generally built as single-user applications. By applying dynamic web site publishing techniques, we can leverage large teams of content experts without the need for them to learn UI design and interactive authoring skills. This approach worked well for web-based content where broadcast journalists would create content for the BBC News web site. The same idea should work as effectively for interactive TV applications, provided we build the systems carefully.

There are several problems we need to address:

- Author once, play everywhere.
- Platform-neutral (TV, web, mobile phone, PDA, Mac OS X, Windows, Linux).
- Rich media (pictures, text, animation, video).
- Nonproprietary containers.
- Can be broadcast in a transport stream.
- Can be requested via a web server.
- Compact.
- Packaged so that it arrives complete.
- Secure.

Your System Already Does Some of This

Bear in mind that there may be places in your operating system where you can hook scripts to automate a workflow with minimal effort. As always, don't spend any time reinventing something that is already there.

Look especially for those hooks where the OS can have a script attached. Delegates, agents, schedulers, and rules that run a script are all useful. Check out your mail and diary applications to see what they can do already.

Going the Open-Source Route

You can buy or build your workflow infrastructure. You have to justify which is the priority: money or time. Somewhere between those extremes lies the decision to use an open-source application that someone else built but gave you the parts to assemble your own version. The Plone content management system is an example of the open-source approach. Consequently, the functionality of Plone can be extended quite easily.

If you are building a web development workflow, you should also check out the Apache Cocoon project. This is another open source framework that might save you some development time.

Buying Off the Shelf

Large, monolithic, proprietary systems are available. They are capable but very expensive to purchase and license widely enough across the organization. They also tend to be somewhat rigid and hard to adapt to the specifics of your business process. This forces companies to change their business process to suit the way the system has been designed. Because it has been designed by someone completely unfamiliar with the business, this can sometimes lead to problems.

Plone content manager: http://plone.org/

Cocoon web development framework: http://cocoon.apache.org/

By purchasing smaller, modular components from your suppliers, you can knit (integrate) them together with scripts and control the process in a way that is much more sympathetic to your existing business model.

Some purchased solutions are custom-built solutions that are supplied by service companies whose expertise is engineering instead of product. These may prove to be a quite expensive way to do things and don't guarantee a pain-free deployment. Nevertheless, paying someone else to take the risk is a way to solve your problems by delegating them. The downside is that you sacrifice the hands on control at the same time.

Many systems are available off the shelf. Some will allow a huge amount of configuration to select the components needed for your deployment. That approach isn't quite bespoke; it is just finely grained configuration. You also need to be diligent with your selection process to avoid issues with unsupported data formats.

 If you do buy a system, make sure the company is still going to be around when you need them. Companies are bought by bigger companies or by their competitors. If they are bought by their competitors, look out! Support and upgrades for software you bought from them could likely be curtailed.

When selecting systems primarily for asset creation, management, and distribution, reject solutions that appear to be play-out and broadcast automation systems with MAM facilities added on. Systems that were designed for MAM first, with play-out added later, will likely be more in the spirit of what you require.

Whether you buy a complete system or build something, you will have to integrate it with the rest of the world. If something is going to go wrong, the focal point of that integration is the most likely place for it to happen.

Search Tools (Spotlight, Google Desktop)

If you are building a standalone workflow that runs within single workstations, you might be able to take advantage of desktop searching mechanisms. An SDK is available that lets you leverage the Apple Spotlight API; Google Desktop is an alternative for portable designs across several platforms. Windows Vista will have a similar API in the fullness of time.

The Mac OS X Spotlight system has an importer plug-in design that allows you to create your own metadata generators. You can even create metadata plug-ins for files that are already processed but don't extract all the information you need. Spotlight is an interesting architecture because it is built into the core of the OS and is extensible.

Microsoft has a similar concept under development for launch in due course. It will require a file-system upgrade, but looks quite interesting as a means of adding searchability to the operating system. This will be introduced as an add-on to Vista after it is released.

Round-Tripping

If you work with any quantity of video, then integration with the nonlinear editing (NLE) applications running on desktops and provided by third parties (e.g., Apple Final Cut Pro, Avid Xpress Pro, Adobe Premiere) is important. Some MAM systems roundtrip to an NLE better than others. Most of them (if not all) are able to do it to some extent, and those that don't might be configured to support the NLE as an external third-party system during the commissioning process. You should expect to see this capability demonstrated when evaluating your potential suppliers.

Moving Data from Place to Place

If you are moving files around between systems, you have several approaches you can use:

- Share in the target directory and mount the share so that you can copy the file onto it. Make sure you copy files instead of writing them line-by-line on an incoming share.
- Write to a folder on a local drive and share it so the remote system can mount it. This avoids I/O blocking on a shared in disk.
- Sharing works best if both systems are the same OS. If they aren't, you could use FTP.
- If security is an issue and you have a corporate firewall, consider web uploads or downloads for file transfers.
- If the data is small and text-based, then in a pinch, you could e-mail it from one system to another to get round some overly strict security blocks.
- Find out how to implement watch folders with the minimum CPU overhead. You should hook into the file system update mechanism to generate an observer trigger. It is more efficient than being busy watching the folder.

The Implications of File Systems

If you write to files as part of your output from a workflow filter or processing tool, be sure to write onto a local hard disk. If you write onto a shared disk that is mounted across the network, the performance of your output routines will be drastically reduced because every buffer full of content to be written must be transferred across the network and acknowledged. This might I/O-block your next processing cycle. Writing line-by-line can significantly slow your processing.

Write it to a local disk and then at the end kick off a file copy process. That file copy can transfer the file one data block at a time instead of one record at a time. It is far more efficient.

Also, beware of file system differences. Some file systems have a limited filename length. We don't often fall prey to the DOS limitation of 8.3 filename and extension anymore. Still, it is common to find applications that can only cope with a 31-character file name, and some legacy file systems may limit your filename length accordingly.

This may lose data because the uniqueness of a filename from one file to another is usually at the end of the filename. That bit is most likely to be truncated. The truncated filename might collide with one already in existence and overwrite it.

Some operating systems can only store truncated names but provide an extension mechanism that is used when browsing. This is dangerous, because the filename that is used for the physical storage is rarely the same as the one you thought you were creating. It is unhelpful having this mechanism interfering with the workflow.

You can avoid these issues by keeping your work-in-progress filenames short and succinct.

Queuing Jobs to Run Sequentially

Way back, when there was a company called the Digital Equipment Corporation, we used to use computers called VAX 11/700 series. These ran an operating system called VMS (Virtual Memory System). It was architected by Dave Cutler, who later went on to develop the Windows NT architecture. VMS had some nice features. Although its I/O was slow when compared with UNIX, it supported several useful capabilities:

- Shared and well-managed batch queues.
- Shared, managed print queues.
- Useful lexical functions in its command shell.
- ACL-based security models.
- A good semi-compiled object code system for its compiled code.
- Sophisticated shared-shareable library support.
- 1000 simultaneous users on quite modest hardware. More on bigger systems.

Many of these features have found their way into contemporary operating systems. Unfortunately DEC is now long gone, having been absorbed by a competitor (Compaq) that itself has disappeared after being bought by HP.

The batch queues were interesting. They worked within the Access Control List (ACL) security model. You could allow users to add jobs but not change their priority. Certain users could stop and start queues, and so on. The queues could run with varying levels of CPU attention. The system administrator could throttle the amount of work done to control the throughput or this could be controlled automatically by a monitoring process.

Scheduling with cron

In UNIX (unless you install extra software), the nearest equivalent to a VMS queue is the **cron** process. The **cron** utility is a scheduler and not a queue manager. A scheduler is designed to run things on a regular basis. The **cron** scheduler is flexible, but it is only granular down to 1-minute intervals.

The **cron** utility lets you schedule regular jobs for execution at one-minute intervals, once a year, or anything in between. This is useful for building polling loops that check something every minute. The downside is that the computer is busy waiting. It can be a simple way to implement a watch folder mechanism.

Various systems administration tasks are run by **cron** on a regular basis; you can add others. Typical things might be to check the disk usage with the **df** command and watch for disk full situations. The script that **cron** runs can send an e-mail report to the system supervisor. Because **cron** creates sub-processes with almost no environment defined by default, you need to include your environment setup code to allow the **cron**-executed jobs to interact with the rest of the workflow.

If you implement your queue mechanism around a **cron** scheduler doing a watch folder-like activity every minute, you first have to put a lock on to prevent it from firing a second job too early. Second, when the job finishes, **cron** might waste a minute before it cycles round and starts another.

VMS batch queues worked much more efficiently than that. As soon as a job finished, the next one started. This kind of behavior is still available. Indeed, it ships as part of the Apple professional video-processing suite. It was developed as part of the Shake compositing application and is called QMaster. The queue manager ships with a variety of Apple Pro apps. You can install other third-party queue managers on any operating system.

Scheduling Jobs to Run at Intervals

A batch queue is the wrong solution for a job that needs to run regularly. You might want to periodically schedule a job to be added to the queue. That queuing operation might check to see if the job has already been queued. You might only want one instance queued at a time.

Already you can see that the deferred-action mechanisms are many, and you might want to use scheduling and queuing in a variety of different ways.

Use the **cron** scheduler on UNIX to control regular processing. It is quite easy to add new jobs to the **cron** process. The format of the control file is a little arcane, but there are third-party GUI tools that make it easier to manage the **crontab** file.

The **crontab** files are created on a per-user basis with the one belonging to the system **root** user taking on housekeeping tasks for the whole system. The jobs in the **crontab** will be run under the user account to which the **crontab** belongs.

Modern **crontab** files support the definition of environment variables that will be inherited by the processes activated by **cron** in addition to the ones it defines already. You should still pay some attention to setting up the environment correctly, as the defaults may not be what you need. An environment variable is defined on a line by itself.

```
name = value
```

On each job-specification line in **crontab**, five fields define a date and time value. The remainder of the line describes what the job is. Date and time is arranged in this order:

```
<minute> <hour> <day of month> <month> <day of week> <command>
```

Commands can be scheduled to run at these times:

```
<month><day of month><hour><minute>
<month><day of week><hour><minute>
@<special event>
```

The time and date field ranges are listed in Table 28-1:

Table 28-1 Dates and times for crontab

Field	Values permitted
Minute	0 - 59
Hour	0 - 23
Day of month	1 - 31
Month	1 - 12 (Or three-letter names)
Day of week	0 - 7 (Or three-letter names)

Notes:

- All fields can be replaced by asterisks to match all possible values.
- Inclusive ranges of numbers indicated by two numbers separated with a hyphen are permitted. Adding a slash and a number defines a step interval.
- Steps are also permitted after an asterisk. If you want to say "every two hours," use "*/2."
- Lists of values or ranges separated by commas are legal.
- Some operating systems allow Sunday to be defined as 0 or 7, while others only allow 0.
- The rest of the line specifies the command to be executed.
- Percent-signs (%) in the command will be changed into new line characters, unless they are escaped with backslash (\). All data after the first % will be sent to the command as standard input.
- The day of a command's execution can be specified by two fields <day of week> and <day of month>. If a value is specified in both, the command will run when either matches. Both are active.

Table 28-2 lists some example time settings.

Table 28-2 Example cron times

Settings	Time
* * * * *	Every minute
0 0 1 1 *	Once per year
0 0 1 * *	Once per month
0 0 * * 0	Once per week
0 0 * * *	Once per day
0 * * * *	Once per hour
5 0 * * *	Five minutes after midnight every day
15 14 1 * *	2:15 p.m. on the first of every month
0 22 * * 1-5	10 p.m. on weekdays
23 0-23/2 * * *	23 minutes after midnight, 2:23 a.m., 4:23 a.m., etc. everyday
5 4 * * sun	5 minutes after 4 a.m. every Sunday
30 4 1,15 * 5	4:30 a.m. on the 1st and 15th of each month, plus every Friday

Events vs. Polling

Build your system so that it is event-driven rather than using a polling approach to check for new content. It is a far more efficient approach. Suppose you have a five-step workflow, with jobs being dropped into folders where the next stage of processing will pick them up. In the worst-case scenario, each job might arrive in the next stage's folder a second after the workflow manager has polled for new work to be done. You'll waste 59 more seconds before it is seen. Jobs going through your workflow will potentially take almost five minutes longer than they might have otherwise. If the process steps are executed quickly, then that delay time could significantly slow down your potential throughput.

You can work around that to some degree by controlling the whole process within one script, but that may not give you the flexibility you want. You really need to implement a series of batch queues that can feed each other or use an event trigger to start a process running. You could trigger the next stage by initiating it as a background job and detaching it from the current one. Then it will run in a separate process space. Some operating systems or workflow frameworks will provide all this event management and control for you. Luckily, if you do have to build it for yourself, it isn't very hard to do.

Job Control Examples

Table 28-3 lists a summary of some different kinds of scheduled activity.

Table 28-3 Job control scenarios

Frequency	Job
At midnight	Rollover some log files so that they start accumulating in a new file. Initiate the log analysis of "yesterday's" log file.
Once an hour	Check the available disk space. Add current usage to a history table to work out a trend. Predict the usage and calculate when the disk will be full. Send a warning if necessary.
Once a minute	Check your web services backend process. Look out for abnormally high numbers of child processes.
Once a minute	Check the latency of some key performance indicators. Look for five successive "out of spec" results and only then trigger the sys-admin pager. Make sure you turn a lock on so that you don't trigger the pager every minute thereafter. Provide a means for the supervisor to unlock the pager messaging without needing to remember how.
Once a day	Run system cleanup to get rid of unwanted caches.
On arrival of a file	Process it immediately, having responded to an event. Generate a trigger event for the next stage of processing.
Once an hour	Back up incremental data to a local disk.
Once a day	Back up incremental data to a remote disk.
Once a week	Run a complete backup of the data areas to tape.
Once a month	Run a full system backup of the OS, applications, and data.
On finishing maintenance	Run a backup of the affected disks.
On completing a major data import	Schedule an incremental export and backup of the parts of the database that are affected.
Every night	Export and backup your SQL database.
On reboot	Run cleanups to remove temporary working files and start up your queue managers and event listeners.
On wake-up-from sleep	Re-initialize drivers, remount disks, and (if necessary) stop and restart processes that don't cope gracefully with sleeps.
On power fail detected	Save the vital information in nonvolatile storage.
On intrusion detection	Lock down the system. Alert sys-admin. Intrusion detection might be triggered via the authentication system or regular monitoring of network stats, login histories, and checksum comparisons on critical files.

Multiple Threaded Workflows

If you have a mix of jobs going through the system, you might want to separate the large from the small to ensure the system can still process the work quickly.

Consider the workflow shown in Figure 28-2. It could be implemented as a series of watch folders, event triggers, or queues. The boxes represent a process.

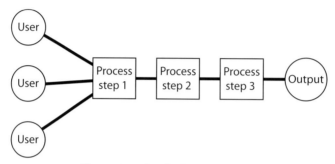

Figure 28-2 Single thread workflow

Now, we could provide three alternative routes as completely parallel chains. More than three would be even better. See Figure 28-3.

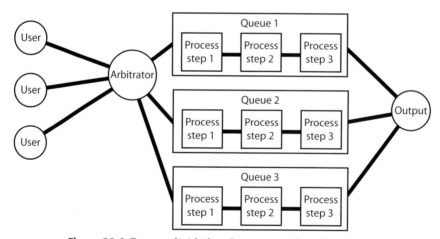

Figure 28-3 Queues divided at the start, combined at the end

This would be better, but three large jobs would clog this up as surely as they would a single-path model.

The model in Figure 28-4 was proven on a large distributed plot-rendering system. The plot files needed to be processed through several stages. The queues were split and merged at each stage. That system had five routes through each stage.

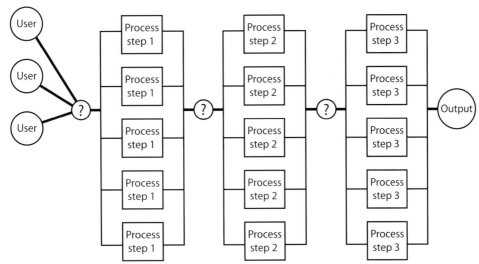

Figure 28-4 Staged split-and-merge queues model

Think of it as a five-lane highway. Jobs are queued to thread 1–5 according to a measurement and estimation about how much work they would require. One queue in each stage runs at high priority but will only accept small jobs. This is the fast lane. The lowest-priority queue gets somewhat less CPU priority and only gets the largest jobs queued.

There is a selection process going on here that assigns a lower priority to bigger jobs.

The net effect is that jobs progress through each stage and, according to the amount of work they require, they might overtake slower running jobs. The intent in this case is to keep the spooler queues at the end fully loaded with jobs waiting to be plotted. This maintains the plotters at 100% duty cycle. The system in use before this one was implemented lost 75% of the jobs through timeouts, and the plotters were sitting idle 90% of the time because jobs were being processed through a single thread.

This would work effectively for a distributed graphic rendering system or video compression farm.

There Can Be Only One!

Inconsistencies creep into workflows when a value is defined in more than one place. Implement a way to store values centrally, and then refer to that master definition when you need to. Otherwise, some parts of your system look at copy 1 of a value, while others look at copy 2, and some may have a private copy of their own. Modify one and the others remain unchanged.

This shows up every day in news stories where the number of survivors of a disaster or an amount of money stolen in a robbery changes constantly, and each outgoing news feed reflects a value that depends on how often someone updates it. Keep the value in one place, set up observers that trigger a republish when the value changes, and let the system take care of it for you.

Building an Environment

On a UNIX system, the environment can be built with environment variables that are inherited downwards as child shells and processes are spawned. On Mac OS X, values can be written to the defaults database and then they are accessible to other applications not necessarily parented by the same shell process. They are also persistent. The same is true of the Windows registry where similar persistent storage of environment data can take place.

Managing Multiple Servers

When you build an environment, a typical scenario might be one where you have a development machine and a live machine. Often there will be others. You might name the machines uniquely but want to store a value in an environment variable that represents a certain type of machine, having deployed several machines with identical configurations.

This is an extract from a **.profile** login script that determines what sort of UNIX machine we are running. Later on, that can be used to select a different web server configuration file to start your Apache server.

```
case 'hostname'
     in
          huey)     SYSTEM_TYPE="DEV"      ;;
          louie)    SYSTEM_TYPE="LIVE"     ;;
          dewey)    SYSTEM_TYPE="LIVE"     ;;
          www)      SYSTEM_TYPE="LIVE"     ;;
          ora)      SYSTEM_TYPE="LIVE"     ;;
          minnie)   SYSTEM_TYPE="BACKUP"   ;;
          *)        SYSTEM_TYPE="DEV"      ;;
esac
export SYSTEM_TYPE
```

That system-type value can now be used to configure other things. Here is a command-line prompt setup that uses it:

```
case ${SYSTEM_TYPE}
     in
          DEV)    PS1='$ '        ;;
          LIVE)   PS1='LIVE$ '    ;;
          BACKUP) PS1='BACKUP$ '  ;;
          *)      PS1='? '        ;;
esac
export PS1
```

Next, we set up the **${PATH}** variable based on our system type.

```
case ${SYSTEM_TYPE}
     in
         DEV)
             PATH=/usr/ccs/bin:${PATH}
             PATH=/usr/local/bin:${PATH}
             PATH=/usr/local/scripts:${PATH}
             PATH=${PATH}:.
             ;;

         LIVE)
             PATH=${PATH}:/usr/local/bin
             PATH=${PATH}:/usr/local/scripts
             PATH=${PATH}:.
             ;;

         BACKUP)
             PATH=${PATH}:/usr/local/bin
             PATH=${PATH}:/usr/local/scripts
             PATH=${PATH}:/usr/ccs/bin
             PATH=${PATH}:.
             ;;
esac
export PATH
```

For a web server farm, all the administrative tools were designed so that the prefix of their directory paths came from an environment variable. The next step is to define that root variables. In this example, there is an admin tools tree, a log files directory, a place where web sites store their **htdocs** folders, and a scratch workspace directory. These are all in a different place in each of the three types of machines:

```
case ${SYSTEM_TYPE}
     in
         DEV)
             ROOT_ADMN=/admin
             ROOT_LOGG=/www/logs
             ROOT_SITE=/www/sites
             ROOT_WORK=/www/logs/_scratch
             ;;

         LIVE)
             ROOT_ADMN=/apache/assets/admin
             ROOT_LOGG=/apache/logs
             ROOT_SITE=/apache/assets/sites
             ROOT_WORK=/apache/logs/_scratch
             ;;

         BACKUP)
             ROOT_ADMN=/app/admin
             ROOT_LOGG=/www/logs
             ROOT_SITE=/www/sites
             ROOT_WORK=/app/_scratch
             ;;
esac
export ROOT_ADMN
export ROOT_LOGG
export ROOT_SITE
export ROOT_WORK
```

A line in the Webmaster's login script sets up access to the web server manager tools. It uses an already defined value so the path it creates is localized to a specific machine but now we only need to configure the common parts of the environment because we dealt with the differences already:

```
WSRV_MNGR=${ROOT_ADMN}/Apache_manager
```

Within the web server manager's tool kit, an auxiliary environment is created for the web server in a setup file that is included into all the tools. This sets up specific environment values that are only needed by the these tools but which need to be consistent across all of them:

```
INSTALL_APACHE=/usr/local/apache

FILE_WSRV_MAST=${WSRV_MNGR}/httpd.conf.${SYSTEM_TYPE}

FILE_WSRV_BADD=${INSTALL_APACHE}/etc/httpd.conf.bad
FILE_WSRV_MAKE=${INSTALL_APACHE}/etc/httpd.conf.new
FILE_WSRV_SAFE=${INSTALL_APACHE}/etc/httpd.conf.safe
FILE_WSRV_CONF=${INSTALL_APACHE}/etc/httpd.conf
FILE_WSRV_BINX=${INSTALL_APACHE}/sbin/httpd
FILE_WSRV_PIDS=${INSTALL_APACHE}/var/run/httpd.pid
```

Note how we define **${FILE_WSRV_MAST}** to point at a master **httpd.conf** file that is specific to the system type we are running on using a variable to complete its name.

These **httpd.conf** files are stored in the working directory:

```
httpd.conf.BACKUP
httpd.conf.LIVE
httpd.conf.EXPERIMENTAL
httpd.conf.DEV
```

We have managed to completely decouple ourselves from knowing the machine name and type ever since we first ran that login script at the start of the environment construction process.

Now we can build the web server manager's tools. This one takes one of the **httpd.conf** templates, stamps it with tomorrow's date, and then overwrites the live **httpd.conf** file in the **/etc** directory. Note how it also makes a backup copy. If the subsequent server restart fails because the conf file is broken, the safe copy gets rolled back in automatically.

```
# --- Build the environment
      . /etc/profile
      . ${ROOT_ADMN}/_create_environment.bsh
      . ${WSRV_MNGR}/_setup.bsh

# --- Create paths to temporary files
      TEMP=${ROOT_WORK}/tomorrow.sedf.$$

# --- Work out the date stamp for tomorrow
      FILE_STUB=`thedate TOMORROW FILE_STUB`

# --- Create the sed filter for processing the conf file
      echo "s/\~{YYYY_MM_DD}\~/${FILE_STUB}/g" > ${TEMP}

# --- Preserve the currently working safe copy of the conf file
      cp ${FILE_WSRV_CONF} ${FILE_WSRV_SAFE}

# --- Parse the master conf file to put in the date stamps
#     and make a new one
      rm -f ${FILE_WSRV_MAKE} > /dev/null
      echo "# DO NOT EDIT THIS FILE"        >> ${FILE_WSRV_MAKE}
      echo "# EDIT \"${FILE_WSRV_MAST}\"!" >> ${FILE_WSRV_MAKE}
      echo ""                                >> ${FILE_WSRV_MAKE}
      cat ${FILE_WSRV_MAST} |
      grep -v "^#"          |
      grep -v "^$"          |
      sed -f ${TEMP}                         >> ${FILE_WSRV_MAKE}

# --- Move new conf onto old one ready for a hup
      mv ${FILE_WSRV_MAKE} ${FILE_WSRV_CONF}

# --- Clear up the garbage
      rm -f ${TEMP} > /dev/null
```

The configuration file for the web server has been marked up with tags that represent the date stamps. These are replaced by the **sed** commands in the script shown above. At the same time, an edit warning message is prepended to the output. Any comment and blank lines are also removed. Anyone opening the file for editing will not mistake it for the master copy:

The lines in the master start out looking like this:

```
CustomLog /logs/ /Online.xlf.~{YYYY_MM_DD}~.extended
```

But end up like this after the script has processed them:

```
CustomLog /logs/ /Online.xlf.2007_02_04.extended
```

Soon after rewriting the live **httpd.conf** file, the server is kicked with a **kill -1** command. The script that does that knows which process to kick because the script that originally started the server noted the process ID (PID) in a known location for it to pick up and use.

Wrappers

Using the wrapper concept we discussed earlier, you can wrap your GUI applications in such a way that they can be hosted on another machine while a stub running the local machine can communicate across the network to the hosting machine. This allows you to use GUI applications like Photoshop or Illustrator as if they were a server process.

You might need several layers of script to accomplish that. One example is shown in Figure 28-5:

- Start with Photoshop, running on a Macintosh.
- Wrap it initially in some AppleScript so that you can pass control parameters to it from an external script.
- Call that AppleScript layer from a Perl scripting environment and set that up as a listener service.
- On a remote Linux or Windows machine, write the dispatcher in Perl so that it will pass parameters to the connection it makes to the remote machine.
- Build your workflow by calling those stubs, which send and retrieve work to and from the remote machines.

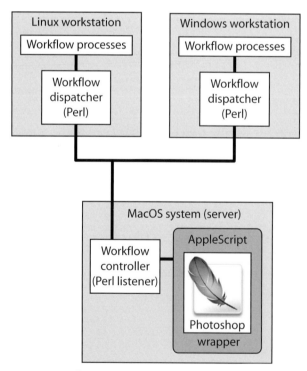

Figure 28-5 GUI apps as services

There are many different ways to build this sort of distributed processing. The important thing is that by exploiting the portability, you are freed from being locked into one operating system or application. You can aspire to a workflow that at any point in the process has the optimum system selected based on its fitness for the task. That is quite different from the "let's do it all in our one favorite operating system with our favorite application" approach.

Summary

In the end, with a workflow that is this flexible, who cares if you do it with Windows, Linux or Macintosh? Your users can use any desktop machine they like and the various processing stages are just ports and IP addresses on your network.

Mac OS X fits my needs best. You might like Windows or Linux. Neither of us should dictate to the other what they should use and neither should be disenfranchised and unable to use the workflow because we use the 'wrong' desktop operating system.

These are some initial ideas for building your workflow environment. We did it here on UNIX with environment variables. The examples were from a Solaris system but the concept works with Windows registry values just as effectively.

If you need to add a publishing pipeline to the workflow, we will look at that in the next chapter.

Publishing Systems

Dynamic Content Creation

Large web sites need to be data-driven. The HTML being browsed by the end user is a view of the database content, which has been rendered via a publishing system. Can we apply this same approach to producing content for other outlets, such as Interactive TV?

Clearly, XML and HTML fall into the same category as far as publishing is concerned. Since they are text files, they are both readily published by a content system. XML provides a means to describe graphics, and with a suitable graphics tool, we can import data and create dynamically generated images. Adobe Photoshop and Illustrator each support a rich scripting library and can be driven by automation to accomplish anything you need to do with pictures.

Publishing Logic

The logic behind a publishing pipeline is straightforward, and the arguments in favor of creating dynamically generated interactive content are equally clear:

- HTML is a text-based format for describing the content of a web page.
- It is in fact a subset of XML, which itself is a textual representation.
- There are many applications available for manipulating XML.
- Many other applications use XML for storing their project information, and more are adopting the technique as they are upgraded. Microsoft is using XML to store Word documents. Open Office already does this more effectively from the outset.
- Many industries have developed XML variants to describe their industry-standard entities (ChemML, MathML, NewsML, etc.).
- Entire books can be described in XML with DocBook.
- Illustrations can be described in XML using SVG.
- Multimedia can be described in XML using BIFS derivatives (XMT), VRML, and MPEG-4.
- If we can create an XML file of any arbitrary kind, we can push it through other applications (or XSLT parsers) to transform it in some way or perhaps to render it into a binary form.

Can It Be This Simple?

The key here is that the content is ASCII (or Unicode) text-based. We don't need to understand complex binary file formats for every tool we are trying to build (although that is sometimes helpful).

There are other useful ASCII and Unicode formats we can use as intermediate or source file formats:

- RTF.
- SYLK.
- PDF.
- SQL.
- Script source code.
- Compilable source code.
- TSV, CSV and other arbitrary data formats.

We need a system that can dynamically generate text files based on a static template plus data from an SQL database.

That sounds like a description of a classic web production system. Therefore, as a technology, it is well-known and easy to understand. Who would think to use it to create source files that can be rendered into a binary format as a GIF image further downstream in the publishing pipeline? Not many people, apparently. I've presented such a system proposal to clients, and they are completely amazed that it is even possible. But it's certainly not rocket science.

The Proposition

Think laterally about the data upon which you are operating. Use the applications for purposes for which they might not have been conceived. Then you can build workflows to dynamically create and render any kind of data you need to. Because you are predominantly operating on text files, these can be archived in your source code repositories such as CVS or Perforce. Then you gain all the benefits of automated version control.

Mixed-media content creation is reduced to a process that is mechanically similar to software development. Think of applications like Illustrator or Photoshop as image compilers, since the image is now described in source form in our database or script.

This suggests that we could even use **make** to control the dependencies and use other software IDE tools such as Visual Studio or Xcode to create templates.

This concept works for the dynamic generation of image files by directly creating pixmap values. I have embedded this technique inside an Apache module and generated images algorithmically within the request-response loop without ever referring to a cached image file.

A better solution nowadays might be to create a script that can instruct Illustrator to draw a vector diagram or manufacture an SVG file (another XML format). That vector image can then be loaded into Photoshop to create a pixmap, if that's the format you need.

You may not even need Illustrator or Photoshop, if your needs are modest and can be met by the utilities already built into your operating system or available as open-source projects.

These solutions are amenable to deployment on distributed computing systems. For heavyweight processing you can create a farm of machines with some queue management to distribute the work.

Refer to Part 2 for tutorials that show you how to dynamically generate Excel Spreadsheets (Tutorials 52 and 56), Word Documents (Tutorials 53 and 57) and SVG image files (Tutorial 54). Tutorial 58 shows how to create an alpha channel in Photoshop under script control.

Redaction Tools

As you process your content, certain parts of it may be removed by your publishing system based on conditional switches and appropriate markup. You may have generated a master document that describes every optional feature. That document needs to be edited on a per-customer basis based on the options they have bought. You don't want to tell customers about features they haven't purchased. Your publishing workflow needs to efficiently and completely remove the unwanted sections.

This process is called *redaction* and it needs to be applied to Word documents and PDF files as well as other kinds of content too. Redaction may also be used to remove text styling, macros or deleted content.

Redaction is necessary because deleting a paragraph of text in a word processor doesn't always physically remove it from the document. It just hides it from view. The fast save and automated backup routines will not spend the time cleaning out this deleted text. Instead, they append new content to the end of the file and move a few pointers around. The old content is still there. Anyone curious enough to hack open your files can find it. A full Save-As will sometimes redact any invisible content but you should check this to see what level of redaction is carried out.

You can perform redaction manually by saving files in different formats after you have edited them to remove the unwanted sections. The file formats available on the export menu are more likely to do a better job of this because only the currently visible content will make it through the exporter.

As you edit a document more, its internal structure becomes ever more complex. This can cause some problems with continued editing. Sometimes the word processor will crash just as you do something very simple. Then it may be time to save the document into a new file. Use the Save As command rather than just a plain save. Then put it in a new location so that word processor can create a clean copy. You should notice the performance increases because anything it has to do on the text now is straightforward and doesn't involve a lot of navigation backwards and forwards between many small fragments of text.

You can test the quality of the redaction by removing some content, saving the document and then opening it in a raw viewing application such as the text editor of an IDE or a hex dump tool. If the deleted content is still visible, the redaction is not working well enough.

Summary

Publishing systems are now a well-understood part of the content management scenario. Some of the more esoteric formats, such as video and interactivity, offer additional challenges, but companies are working on solutions to deliver those formats.

We don't want to live a life ruled by workflow systems that need constant attention. In the next chapter, we shall look at monitoring, measuring, and making the systems clever enough to look after themselves.

Adding Intelligence and Metrics

Taking Care of Business

As workflow systems designers, we have a responsibility to consider the smooth running of the systems and not create additional burdens for the systems administrators who have to look after the systems we deploy. Indeed, some of these systems might be replicated dozens of times in large installations. and the systems administrators will already be busy keeping everything working.

Be Kind to Your Sys Admin

It is important to go the extra mile when we can to make life easier for our customers. That means thinking about how the system will withstand the daily grind of processing the content.

Consider what happens to the disk capacity on your system. There is a condition called *software rot* that systems suffer from over a long period. This is when gradual accumulations of temporary files and manual deletions of rubbish, coupled with an occasional hand edit of a configuration file, eventually renders a system prone to crashing. You see evidence of this if you install an operating system, then add dozens of haxies and extenders from less-than-reliable sources, and then run a half-dozen upgrades. The system becomes unstable and crashes for no apparent reason. Running a major OS upgrade doesn't seem to fix it. In fact, it might even make things worse.

This happens because installers don't always clean up, or they overwrite a later version of a `.dll` file or kernel extension with an older one, or perhaps they leave some file permissions set to the wrong value.

Running disk repairs periodically is sometimes helpful, but in the end, you have to reinstall the operating system from scratch, even though that should always be the last resort.

 A useful adage is often found at tourist locations and it applies to us too: "Only take pictures, only leave footprints."

Consider all this, and don't add to the system administrator's burden by contributing to the mess. Make sure your installers are well-tested, and make optimal decisions with graceful bailouts that put everything back the way it was.

Collecting Metrics and Measurements

At various points during the workflow, you'll automatically capture some system metrics without realizing it. Don't throw the information away when you are done. Passively gathering system metrics can build up an audit trail and provide useful evidence to a systems administrator.

Think Like an Astronomer

Sometimes the thing you are trying to measure is hard to get a handle on. When you are debugging Apache modules, they run in a detached process space that you can't see directly. Getting any kind of debugger attached to them is a genuine 'pain.'

Astronomers have the same problem. They can see stars that are millions of light years away but they can't observe the planets that orbit round them. Instead, they look for the characteristic slight wobble to the position of the star that indicates the gravitational effect or an orbiting planet.

Apply this technique and observe the effects that a detached process has on your system. Perhaps it writes temporary files to a known location or the process can be observed with the **top** utility to ascertain how much CPU time it is getting. If you have access to source code, then getting the invisible application to write a log file that you can watch is a great help.

Date and Time Records

You might be tracking resource utilization in order to work out trends or recording system performance metrics. These might be processed to report on system availability and throughput. You need to work in the context of physical time when you do this. Avoid storing DST- and time zone-corrected values. Instead, store the UTC date/time values measured in milliseconds directly from the system clock. Then you can apply arithmetic to them and merge the metrics from several systems that may be geographically separated and operating in different time zones without needing to compensate for the localized time conversions.

If you want to display time zone- and DST-corrected values, it is much easier to add a time formatter to the output routines to avoid having to code around the DST changes. That formatting capability has already been built into the operating system and you don't need to duplicate code that is already there.

Often there is a temptation to store date/time values in a character-formatted field, but this is usually the wrong thing to do unless it is part of an export mechanism or if you plan to parse the data with text processing tools. Web servers do this and it causes problems twice a year when the clocks are adjusted for DST because it is hard to compensate for the change with shell script code.

On the other hand, a textual representation in a log file is much easier to process with UNIX command line tools. Weigh up the alternatives and record things in a way that allows you to process the metrics to yield the measurements you need.

Monitoring Disk Usage

Measuring disk space, counting processes, taking snapshots of start and finish times, and evaluating whether the system is gradually slowing down can all contribute towards a metrics system that can be probed and inspected by automated agents or systems administrators. This shouldn't make your system any more complicated if you design it in from the beginning.

If you copy files across the network with an FTP protocol, you could wrap the transaction to steer it with a "here" file. This is a set of instructions that you manufacture and pass to the **ftp** client to execute. You might measure the file size and ask the remote system if it has enough disk space. To provide an answer, it must measure the available space and reply yes or no. As it measures the space, an extra line of code can log the resulting space with a date and time.

In case there is very little traffic, you might also call the same disk space measurement code on a scheduled basis every hour.

Whenever you move a file to the destination system the available space is checked. If there is insufficient space to store the new file, the system that is trying to send it can abort the copy gracefully and queue the transfer for later when there might be enough space. This will avoid crashing the remote system by filling its disk. Because the remote system is watching the available disk space the monitoring software can send a warning if the available space falls below a predefined threshold. Indeed, it may be able to make some decisions about backing up and removing some files or perhaps when some work has been processed, the temporary files are removed. Either of those possibilities would free up some much needed space. When the system that attempted to copy the file tries again, there may be enough space to copy the file this time. This automated, self-managing approach is an opportunity to introduce all manner of housekeeping scripts that sweep up old core dumps and purge the log files.

You have just made your systems much more resilient as the expense of a few milliseconds of process time and a couple of quite short pieces of script code. And it all happens automatically.

Watching for Boundary Conditions

Boundary conditions are where odd things happen. Perhaps a date value changes in length from nine characters to ten. Perhaps disk space falls below a value where the operating system needs to create a temporary file periodically and no longer has the space. These faults are hard to detect, because the cause and effect are separated by some time.

Certain dates cause problems. Daylight savings time switchover dates give you 23- and 25-hour days. These can throw an unwelcome spike into statistical measurements.

Exceeding internal buffers—creating one more user than a table is able to maintain, opening one too many file buffers, allocating storage beyond some pre-allocated memory size—is a classic security exploit, and should always be guarded against.

Testing for boundary conditions is quite arduous, because there are so many possibilities. If some metrics have been logged, then you can inspect those periodically to see if any resources are getting scarce.

Rotating and Truncating Logs

Log files tend to grow until someone or some process does something about rotating them. This is something that crops up in web site operations more often than it does anywhere else, because we take the server access logs and analyze them on a daily basis to ascertain the traffic levels to our sites.

This is easy to solve. There may be some internal mechanism that the server supports to rotate the logs itself. Failing that, you can modify the **httpd.conf** file so that log file name contains a date stub.

Instead of naming the access log file **access.log**, call it **access.2007_01_01**, where the date is coded as **YYYY_MM_DD** format (see ISO 8601). By using some shell scripting magic, you can modify the **httpd.conf** file and store a copy as a template. The date stubs would all be edited to be a consistent **YYYY_MM_DD** format. Then you create a shell script that can manufacture a new date stamp, build a global search replace filter to change **YYYY_MM_DD** to the correct date stamp, and run that on the **httpd.conf** file template to rewrite the **httpd.conf** file every night, immediately after midnight, scheduled by **cron**. Refer to the example shell script near the end of Chapter 28 for an example of how this is done.

This problem led directly to the creation of **theDate** utility (see Tutorial 35). It was designed so that the automation could pre-roll that log turnover process and use the command line "**theDate tomorrow**" to yield the time stamp. The scripts would edit the **httpd.conf** file just before midnight and then, exactly at midnight, send a signal to the web server with a **kill –1** message. This tells it to restart and reread its configuration file but not throw any client sessions offline.

Soon after that, the log analyzer can commence processing the log files. By then, it is past midnight. Tomorrow, in fact. All the relative dates have changed in the meantime. To find the correct one, the date stamp is selected by using "**theDate yesterday**." This utility was a neat and compact piece of C code that does useful things with dates. Those things were incredibly difficult to do in shell scripts otherwise. For a brief description of this, see Chapter 31.

Watching for Systems Failures

If you are collecting the metrics about your system, you need to monitor them to watch for systems failures. I once had a web server that routinely crashed catastrophically every few days, always late in the afternoon. Something cumulative was happening.

By counting child processes and logging them by time of day into a monitoring file, I started to build a picture of what was happening. After a few days, it was evident that the child process count was steady most of the time. About 20 minutes before the server crashed, child process counts started to increase. Because this was exponential, the increase was slow and almost insignificant at first. The increase in processes got worse and reached a point where the entire machine was so busy that no new processes could be started. Plotting the process count showed a rising curve, followed by an instant drop where the server was rebooted.

Establishing a pattern creates a curve that can be profiled. The next step is to build a mechanism that observes process counts and looks for the onset of this problem. In the case of my web server, after proving that it could be detected by generating alarms, I introduced some code to signal the web server to restart about 15 minutes before it would have crashed. This cured the symptoms of the problem, and we didn't suffer any further outages while we investigated the cause of the problem. Further investigation pointed to a memory leak in a shared Java VM that was used system-wide as a possible culprit.

This is an example of systems that are designed to self-monitor and heal themselves. We gradually added more of this sort of code as we learned more about the system and how it might fail.

It is a straightforward technique:

1. Measure.
2. Log.
3. Analyze.
4. Detect the trend.
5. Set the threshold.
6. Test the assertion.
7. Find a cure.
8. Apply the cure automatically.

If you go through this stage-by-stage approach and look at all your systemic failures in this sort of structured way, you will soon have a sweetly running server and workflow.

You should be focusing on the things that are causing the most serious problems first and then gradually work down to the minor issues.

False Positives

This subsection could have been called "Alarms that aren't and warnings that don't."

Sometimes when you build metrics and monitoring systems, you can get a false trigger. This might be OK if it only results in an extra e-mail being sent to a systems administrator. You don't want this to happen in the middle of the night if it is going to ring a pager.

Eliminating false positives requires a little extra testing. A useful approach is to use a voting technique. Monitor the system behavior in several different ways, and if they all indicate a failure mode, then log that as a genuine failure. But don't yet go for the pager. Wait one minute and measure again. Measuring every minute for five minutes before alerting with a pager is about right. Your circumstances may be different, and you might allow more or less time. For my pager to be triggered, I had to have five successive failures. If I got a success then another failure, that single success reset the counter. This was implemented as a five element shift buffer. New readings were pushed onto one end and the one at the other fell out. A simple test then checked to see if there were five failures in total.

If you search the Internet (and you don't need to look far), there are monitoring tools that you can download at no cost. They may not be as powerful as a commercially purchased product but if they have the functionality you need then you haven't had to purchase a large system to only use 5% of its capabilities.

Open Source Solutions

Tobi Oetiker's MRTG—the Multi Router Traffic Grapher—is one of the tools that systems administrators find useful. These tools can highlight a serious router problem well before your users notice anything is wrong. Another example is RRDTool which you can also download and compile from the source code. If you run these tools in a command line environment, they generate graphs of system performace. Then you can use something like GeekTool to regularly fetch and display them on your desktop.

Summary

Most of this is common sense and second nature to experienced systems administrators. It just requires a little time and effort.

Throughout this book, I've encouraged you to think "outside the box." Thinking laterally is what the next chapter is all about.

MRTG: http://oss.oetiker.ch/mrtg/

RRDTool: http://oss.oetiker.ch/rrdtool/

GeekTool: http://projects.tynsoe.org/en/geektool/doc.php

Lateral Thinking

Using Applications in New Ways

Lateral thinking describes how the process of innovation and invention happens. It is a combination of serendipity (chance), synchronicity (things happening at the same time) and having a broad knowledge of many different fields. Lateral thinkers will take a solution from an existing context and apply it in a completely original way in a new context.

Buy or Build?

When selecting tools and components to build your workflow, you can choose to buy cheap or expensive products. If products aren't available that meet your requirements, you'll have to build. That can get expensive if you try to solve too many problems at once and build a system that is too large and complex. Sometimes you can save yourself unnecessary effort developing tools from scratch if you take the tools you already have and see if there is a way to use them to solve your problem by applying them in a different way. This is the lateral thinking approach. What follows are some examples of lateral thinking that should suggest new "outside-the-box" solutions for your challenges.

Using Web Browsers as Control Rooms

It has become fashionable to create 'mash-ups' of several information sources to build a new online service from the merging of existing content. This often uses a combination of RSS and AJAX approaches to construct entertainment web sites. Why not use the same techniques to create a master control surface for a workflow system?

The problem with web browsers as control surfaces is that they don't maintain state very well. AJAX exploits the techniques that had already emerged as the best solutions for this, namely asynchronously downloading messages and extracting information from them.

From a technical standpoint, this is somewhat inelegant, as we are pushing the web browser toward its limit in terms of supporting libraries of JavaScript code to simplify the AJAX process.

In time, this problem may evolve into purpose-built browse clients with AJAX interfaces built in.

Using Excel to Steer Workflows

Use Excel spreadsheets to collate a sequence of tasks and drive a workflow with the spreadsheet content. This was at the heart of the Showtime channel's automation system for creating stings and trails.

The Excel spreadsheet was accessed with AppleScript, which then used the data to steer Illustrator, Photoshop and the Video 100 NLE software.

Triggers via PHP

The PHP software integrated with Apache can execute all kinds of processes on a remote machine. Normally, you would use PHP to create a dynamically generated response to make a web page on the fly.

In Tutorials 52, 53 and 54, see how PHP can be used to publish a file on the remote machine. The only reason it sends anything back in the web page is to say the publish operation was OK.

Distributing parts of your workflow around the network and controlling them by activating PHP is an interesting idea.

Manipulating Text and Data with Web Tools

Understanding the transformation capabilities of all your tools means you use them to process data in new ways. We need a workbench for data cleaning where we can move data around and operate on it with remote processes and tools.

- When manipulating information to write books or clean data, you can use JavaScript in a web page to generate tabulated indexing sequences of numbers and data.
- Loading HTML or XML and exploring the DOM is something that JavaScript is useful for.
- Collecting data in a MySQL database and pulling it out in a structured way with PHP is another example.
- Upload content to a web service, get the result back, and then use it somewhere else.

Using PDF for Forms Handling

Don't neglect the possibility of taking dumb forms and adding sophisticated forms handling to them. This might be web-based, Flash-based, or achieved with PDF forms. With Adobe's acquisition of Macromedia, some powerful forms handling capabilities are bound to emerge with a combination of web and Flash being embedded in PDF. The integration of the online video chat software with the PDF tools takes Acrobat in a completely new direction. This approach is bound to pervade the rest of Adobe's products. Adobe needs to be careful not to overload the applications with too much unnecessary functionality.

The Power of Three

Using three applications in a tightly coupled manner seems to be a magic combination. A text editor, FTP client, and command-line interface on a remote system form a powerful combination. If you can use scripts to tie them together more intimately, then you are componentizing application functionality and building meta-applications.

Adding a script to the text editor menu to send the file via FTP and then remotely executing it speeds up your development and testing process. This the sort of thing that Dreamweaver does with web site content.

Edit-save-run cycles, which you perform iteratively, apply the leverage of script wrappers.

Dynamically Generating Configuration Files

Use a templated approach for more than content production. Build your server configuration files in the same way. Because configuration (and **.INI**) files are textual representations, we can mark them up and run them through a template parser to instantiate them, as long as we are careful to observe the syntactic construction.

This worked well on a web server project where the daily rotation log depended on this technique. That web server configuration file became the center of the entire log-analysis process, because the presence of a virtual site also determined whether a management report was generated. Various other parameters were extracted from the configuration file as well. Some of these were embedded in comments so that they didn't affect the configuration in any way. They would have been syntactically incorrect otherwise. By embedding them in comments but structuring them so the logging complex could read them, every aspect of the site's service, maintenance, and reporting could be controlled from a single block of configuration data wrapped as a virtual host specification.

If that virtual host specification itself became a component stored in a separate file, we could then build an editor that could maintain the **httpd.conf** file in fragments which are then assembled and aggregated into a complete **httpd.conf** file before parsing to stamp the dynamic values in there.

 Content creation and workflow converge using the same technologies and techniques for essence data and metadata.

The next logical step is to provide an admin user interface to create new sites by cloning a master virtual host fragment file, and then enter the details with a simple form.

Mining for Data

Occasionally, we are faced with the prospect of processing huge data sets. This is when we apply the leverage of SQL databases and clients that help us sculpt that data into a useable form.

Mining for valuable data in this way can produce some amazingly valuable content. Until it is extracted and refined, it is of no use at all. The process is exactly similar to that of finding minerals and turning them into useable material. Organizations which have been in existence for many years will have untapped resources like this that can be turned into valuable assets.

This process needs to be carried out in several carefully ordered steps.

1. Locate the source media.
2. If it isn't already in a digital form, then digitize it.
3. Clean it up so that it can be processed.
4. Break it down into component documents.
5. Break the documents into records.
6. Analyze the records to understand the applicable structure.
7. Build the structure containment.
8. Process the records to distribute values amongst the structure fields.
9. Clean the data by sorting, inspecting, and then editing.
10. Export the data for deployment.

These operations work differently for text, pictures, and moving images. We also need to be careful not to damage the originals. There is an aspect of conservation that is involved. Sometimes the cleaning process may require a little repair to be carried out without damaging the original files.

For text, use a combination of OCR and scanning tools, Excel, a text editor, HyperCard, MySQL, Quadrivio General Edit, and UNIX shell scripts. On a Windows platform, you wouldn't have HyperCard available but might substitute Visual Basic and use PowerShell in place of the UNIX command line. There is probably a vast range of other "text-cutting" tools you can use. You don't always have to roll your own.

For graphics, use Photoshop and Illustrator, but also consider the shareware application called Graphic Converter, the Portable Bit Map (PBM) format, and possibly some hand-built tools for special fixes. Sometimes an OCR application can help extract images. If you have PDF files, you'll find that even though an image might look small on the screen, there may be a full-resolution version inside the PDF. Having access to Acrobat Professional is helpful for image extraction, provided the PDF is not locked and rights-protected.

For video, you have a range of possible tools, including some proprietary tools like Apple Final Cut Pro, Adobe Premiere, or AVID Xpress Pro. Kino is useful for Linux users. The **ffmepeg** tools are open source and available cross-platform. Movie Maker, QuickTime Movie Player, iMovie, and Motion are useful for a quick cutting or correction jobs.

You can do time-base correction and gate weave fixing in Adobe After Effects. In a pinch, saving an image sequence and using Photoshop is OK for short sequences. Sometimes, you have to use the tools that are available, even if it takes a long time.

You should build up a toolkit of applications that can help you clean and transform content. It takes time and costs money, but if each job you do for a client funds a new tool, your arsenal will soon start to become more impressive and allow you to take on bigger jobs.

Maintaining Your Custom Enhancements

If you routinely import code or data from a third party but need to custom-modify it, then the last step of your deployment process should be to difference compare your deployed copy against their original. This will give you a self-documenting list of deltas, which you will need to apply at the next release.

If you embed some comments in your modified copy, then those comments will be differenced out with the actual code changes. It really is easy to maintain a record of your custom changes and keep track of your edits.

Differencing to a text file, which you keep with the maintenance documents, provides something you can cut-and-paste when you next apply the deltas for a subsequent release.

If you are fixing bugs, then some of your deltas may no longer be necessary if the supplier incorporates your changes into the shipping code or text.

Visualizing Data

Understanding the data set and what is hidden in it is often helped by visualizing the data in a graphical form. The usefulness of 3D, color and lightness cannot be underestimated.

One of the finest examples of data visualization is the map of Europe showing Napoleon Bonaparte's march on Moscow. The width of the line at any point in the route is proportional to the strength of his army. This data visualization technique was developed by Joseph Charles Minard and can be found online or in the books by Edward Tufte.

Visualizing Web Log Data

Analyzing web log data yields graphs showing traffic statistics. Showing this in a single linear graph is useful, but plotting it as a 3D surface chart is sometimes more useful, because you can see what happens as the weekly pattern is repeated.

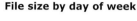
File size by day of week

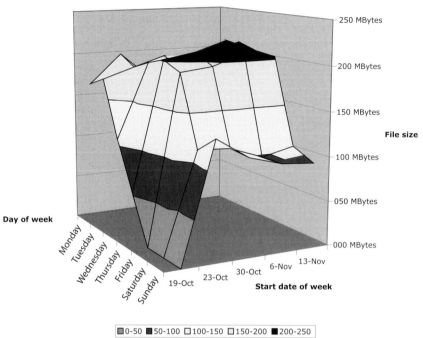

Figure 31-1 Visualizing web log data in 3D

Summary

Useful insights occur when we challenge the traditional way of solving a problem and use a new approach. Combining data items that don't seem to be related and using imagery to look for patterns are both examples of lateral thinking.

One of the most innovative text searching systems is the Spire application by Pacific Northwestern Labs. The software analyzes text for semantic meaning and plots the results out on a graphical display. From this it generates spatial maps of large numbers of documents. Finding related texts is now a spatial problem, rather than a semantic, problem.

Fast-Talk developed a speech-searching tool that breaks audio down into phonemes. By recognizing phonemes and matching 8 out of 10, you get a robust audio search tool that is resilient to background noise.

That is innovation and demonstrates lateral thinking.

32

The Bottom Line

Keep the Customer Satisfied

Building workflows for essence data and metadata (content) involves attention to quality for both kinds of information. It is waste of time building a great system to maintain high-quality metadata if the essence data you are managing is full of errors. Likewise, if you have top-quality essence data but your metadata is unreliable, you'll never be able to do anything with your essence data, however good it might be.

Fixing the systems and building efficient workflows is only part of the problem. All the time, there is a human being in the loop, and if you are expecting them to perform like an automaton you are going to be disappointed somewhere along the line. People function at their best when their job is interesting and absorbing. If they are faced with sheer boredom, they are going to get things wrong.

This should be a guiding principle in the design of your metadata and essence data workflow systems. Don't make them hard to use or boring to sit in front of.

General Good Practice

These are key design principles that are important for any systems you design, but especially the systems used for creating metadata, because the results of any errors are likely to be seen by many millions of people. Good design principles include these attributes:

- Ensure that your user interface responds within half a second at worst.
- Provide contextual help.
- Warn about potential duplication.
- Provide helpful assistance to the user but don't get in their way.
- Ask "are you sure" before initiating a destructive request.
- Ask "are you sure" before opening too many windows onscreen. The user may have accidentally selected too many items.
- Always provide undo and redo capability.
- If possible, provide multiple-level undo/redo.
- Mandate that important metadata be filled in.
- Let the users tune their UI and make fonts bigger or alter color schemes.
- Make sure your system behaves predictably.
- Your system should look nice.
- Provide a novice and expert behavior and let the user judge how much they want to hide the novice help bit by bit with checkboxes in a preferences pane.

Likewise, there are things you should avoid:

- Don't expect the user to remember important systems values that are meaningless in human terms.
- Don't force them to look up a primary key ID value and then type it elsewhere.
- Don't cascade delete things (EVER!).
- Don't recycle primary key values.
- Don't ever delete anything. Instead, mark it as inactive. You can undo the change.
- Don't do modal dialogs.
- Don't flash the screen unnecessarily.
- Change the software not the hardware. Yes, it does happen the other way round sometimes and it is wrong.
- Don't patronize your user.

Interactive TV UK: What We Learned

Digital TV has been available in the UK for many years. In that time, we have learned many useful lessons about systems design and how to cope with three completely different platforms, commercial models, and formats.

There were many differences between the three platforms that needed to be managed by the workflow systems and which weren't all discovered until broadcasting started:

- Functionally different authoring languages.
- Different color palettes.
- Different drawing primitives.
- Different typographic metrics, even though the same font was available.
- Different menu handling.
- Different image decoding capabilities.
- Structurally different graphical overlays.
- Video frame buffer scaling was not possible on all platforms.
- Video display buffer scrolling was not possible or consistently supported on all platforms.
- STB memory might be too small, leading to cache issues.
- Not enough bandwidth available to reduce carousel times to a reasonable minimum.

A significant overarching problem has been how to deliver a truly interactive service to set-top boxes that have virtually no memory. This results in a service that carousels so much data that latency becomes a problem.

What Might Happen Elsewhere

Other regions such as the U.S., Asia, Australia, and the rest of Europe will benefit by learning what worked and what didn't during the UK rollout.

There are technologies available now that weren't ready to use 10 years ago; in particular, the IPTV technologies, which suit a market like the U.S. very well because there are many cable TV networks there. IPTV can be used to leverage interactivity that does not need to be carouselled but instead can be delivered on a demand-driven basis. The video programming can be delivered on demand too. This could free up valuable bandwidth in the broadcast service. All it needs to do is deliver crosslinks, similar to the old analog WebTV system that Microsoft were trialing in the late 1990s.

The missing piece of technology is the interactive protocols. The Digital Satellite interactive services in the UK are based on Open TV which has the most fine grained and detailed control but is anything but open. The MHEG standard used on Digital Terrestrial TV is challenging to learn and the implementations are not all identical leading to inconsistent user experiences. The HTML-based middleware in Digital Cable receivers is easy to develop for but the service providers don't willingly open up the services to outsiders.

Which one of these "big 3" interactive TV platforms that were rolled out in the UK is appropriate for IPTV? Any of them? None of them? The most important thing we learned is that you only want one platform. We have two platforms too many to support already and the situation would be better with only one alternative across all three platforms (four if you include IPTV).

The interactivity needs to be achieved in an open-standards way with affordable licenses. MPEG-4 would have been ideal, but its licensing is putting people off the idea. Some kind of HTML-based mechanism might work well with IPTV but it is hard to produce a televisual appearance with attractive transitions and visual effects.

The merger of broadband with PVRs is beginning to deliver some useful services to the end user. TiVoCast looks very interesting.

If we are going to deliver next generation interactive services, we shall need to produce interactive content in industrial quantities. That can only be done with publishing systems with great workflow tools and metadata handling built in.

Standards

Standards are not forced upon us. We have to choose to use them. The benefits of interoperability that we gain are significant. We also save ourselves the trouble of having to invent and document our own internal proprietary standards, which might not be of as high a quality. We certainly could not devote the same amount of time to develop a better solution.

Selecting an international standard has become more difficult in the last several years. Large companies have proposed proprietary technologies that have been adopted into the standards. Although the standard is ratified, it is not open because no one can afford to use it. This is a completely ridiculous situation. It has probably already delayed the deployment of MPEG-4-based interactive services by four years.

It is not surprising that other groups set up competing standards processes to create genuinely open and free standards.

Optimal Data Formats

If you want to build a modern workflow system for managing and creating content, then you need to select the technologies carefully. An open-standard, open-source, and license-free approach is best.

Table 32-1 lists what I think are the optimum candidate technologies and formats for exchanging content around the workflow.

Table 32-1 Recommended essence data and metadata technologies

Data type	Portable formats
Names and addresses	vCard version 3 or better.
Dates and times export	iCalendar.
Dates and times import	vCalendar and iCalendar.
Date and time values	UTC microsecond counter for internal local representation. ISO date for export. Character string format for exchange purposes.
E-mail content	US ASCII 7-bit quoted printable.
Currency codes	ISO 4217.
Country codes	ISO 3166.
Schedule data	TV-Anytime (although in the U.S., SMPTE standards might prevail).
Object model design	Erich Gamma's patterns and Unified Modeling Language methodology.
Interactivity	No single model for describing it yet exists; Flash is widely available but not ubiquitous. MPEG-4 is ideal, but adoption has been slow.

Table 32-1 Recommended essence data and metadata technologies (continued)

Text	Unicode UTF-8, unless foreign language dictates UTF-16 or UTF-32.
Word processed docs	ODT or RTF for exchange. PDF for short term and publicly accessible archives. Consider Open Office's ODT format or DocBook XML for long-term storage into databases via an object model. Consider the Apache Jakarta POI technologies for publishing DOC files.
Spreadsheets	SYLK for dynamic publishing and long-term storage and Excel for publishing. Also consider the Apache Jakarta POI technologies.
Raw data	Tab separated values for record and field structured table data.
Numerics	IEEE 754 and its successors.
Booleans	Explicitly use the default TRUE or FALSE symbols as predefined by your development tools.
Raster images	TIFF, JPEG-2000.
Vector images	SVG.
Moving video	DV25 or better for archive. H.264 for distribution. Manage in QuickTime containers or use MXF wrappers.
Metadata schemes	Dublin Core Metadata Initiative is a large standard with more than most people need. The same is true of SMPTE 330M. Use a subset and cherry-pick the things you like.
Publishing frameworks	PHP attached to Apache for dynamic HTML and XML creation from database content. Apache Jakarta POI for publishing directly to Microsoft Office file formats. There are many other useful projects, platforms and tools at the Apache Org web site.
OS functionality	Stick to using POSIX-compliant APIs and tools.

Summary

Metadata quality can be compromised at several important points. The accuracy of the data itself is important as a priority. The metadata formatting needs to be carefully considered to avoid corruption. The storage and transfer need to be resilient against the possibility of damage in transit. The human element introduces uncertainty in the form of mistakes made during entry or choices not to enter the metadata. Our systems need to guard against all of these in order to run reliably.

Successfully build a system that can achieve all of that, and you should be justifiably pleased with yourself.

Part 2

Tutorials

About the Tutorials

Part 2 of this book is a collection of tutorials that illustrate pitfalls, work-around solutions, components, and algorithmic ideas that are useful when building workflow and media management systems.

To make sure the tutorials are as useful as possible, I have purposely kept the coding of any scripts or source code quite simple and straightforward. You can add the "bells and whistles" to your own implementations.

Upgrade your parameter-collecting support via **getopt()** calls, or range-check all the input arguments as well as redirecting errors to silence any unnecessary warnings.

Most of these tutorials are implemented with UNIX shell commands and some with AppleScript. A few mix in some Visual Basic where it is necessary to control Microsoft Office apps.

Don't get bogged down in the choice of implementation language; instead, look at the underlying philosophy. Try to build small compact components that can be used many times over. I try to solve one problem with each tutorial. Large industrial systems are held together with humble nuts, bolts, and washers. Without them, even the biggest of machines cannot be assembled. You can implement the same functionality as I describe here in Perl or PowerShell if that is your preference.

The tutorials are grouped together under these general headings with an icon at the head of each one to indicate its general theme:

Table 1 Tutorial icons

Icon	Description
	Bridging from one language to another.
	Systems administration and log processing.
	File management and storage.
	Solving problems at the design stage.
	Making searches work better.

Table 1 Tutorial icons (continued)

	Data cleaning.
	Reformatting data.
	Regular expressions.
	Data recovery.
	Dealing with dates and time values.
	Geographic Information Systems (GIS).
	Extracting metadata and labels.
	Handling web URLs.
	Cross referencing and links between data.
	Publishing content.
	Power tools.

Bridging

Bridging from one environment to another is a critical technique. If you can call out to another environment, then all the capabilities of its tools are available to repurpose and exploit. Often, this means you can design tools in the optimum environment and benefit from efficient design. You should work out your bridging strategy before building the main workflow. Do this in isolation so that you have solved how to access one language or environment from another. Then you aren't trying to get something difficult to work under the time pressure of your workflow implementation. Here, I talk about bridging Java, C, Shell and AppleScript. You an bridge anything to anything. It's Simply a Matter of Programming (SMP).

Systems Administration

Log everything that you think might be useful. This will provide evidence in case of failure, and you can run processors on the logs to gain an understanding of your resource utilization or to perform diagnosis when the system is down.

Anything you can do to automate the systems administration process is useful, particularly if you need to run dozens or even hundreds of computers single-handedly. It is a lonely job, and a feeling of paranoia goes with the territory, but why make matters worse by requiring the sys admin to type the same thing 500 times as well?

File Management

File management is about the movement of work or finding which files to work on. The system manages many files for you. The workflow process needs to facilitate the creation, movement, and editing of content (almost always in files).

Data Design

Designing your data structures carefully will save you hundreds of hours of problem solving later on. It will save you time and money. Guaranteed.

Searching

Building better search mechanisms facilitates better productivity for your content editors and eventually your end-users.

Data Cleaning

If you put poor-quality data into your media asset management system, it will materially affect how your business processes function. If people don't fill out metadata fields when ingesting new material, how will anyone ever find that footage again? Searching by date is not the answer. Clean it or lose it.

Data Conversion

A great deal of the work that a content management, and workflow system does is data conversion. It is constantly changing data from one format into another. Pay attention to any performance gains you can make here.

Regular Expressions

Up to this point, the examples are unsophisticated in the amount of pattern matching they need to do. That is going to change with the subsequent tutorials, and they will rely significantly on regular expressions. Refer also to Appendix E for some additional information on regular expressions.

Data Recovery

Sometimes things go wrong and files get corrupted. Sometimes, you have an unrecognized file containing some text or pictures that you need to recover. Either way, data recovery is not always as hard as you might expect. But sometimes it is hard. Very hard. Occasionally it is impossible.

Date and Time

Date and time is a complex subject on its own. We need a variety of small and nimble tools for manipulating date and time values.

Geographic Information Systems (GIS)

Most metadata systems are concerned with where things are placed—or where they originated—geographically. The same issues crop up whether the database is being designed for direct marketing or managing news footage being ingested from on-location shoots.

Extracting Metadata and Labeling

There are tools for managing metadata in media asset management systems, as well as mechanisms for inspecting embedded metadata in Microsoft Office applications or Adobe products. Although the metadata schemas and implementations are different, the tools are there and available for use. We cannot always integrate the tools we might want to use with our workflow framework. We need to resort to other tactics.

URLs

Many kinds of data have URLs embedded. We need to extract and reorganize them and most importantly, we need rapid checking mechanisms to winnow out the failed and broken links.

X-Ref

Cross referencing between one data set and another is a useful facility. Those references don't have to be between local systems. Use remote methods to link to networked services.

Publishing

The output part of a workflow results in publishing some content that is driven by our publishing systems. These tutorials show how to publish formats that are not often considered because they are thought to be "too hard" to exploit. They turn out to be easier to use than they appear to be at first. They also remind me how utterly awesome PHP is and how useful it can be for things other than web site publishing. These tutorials publish from a local template to a local output file, but they could be triggered by a remote system calling a specific URL to activate the PHP process. Powerful!

Power Tools

Sometimes you need the additional leverage that a power tool brings to bear. These tutorials show you some examples.

Calling Shell Commands from AppleScript ▬▬▬

Bridging between different environments opens up the power of already-implemented tools that can be repurposed or bound into a workflow. If you build a workflow in AppleScript, you might exploit some significant performance improvements by calling down into a UNIX command line environment, especially if you want to process large quantities of text. This is not difficult to do.

1. First, construct your shell script. Parameterize any variable behavior as command line arguments.
2. Make sure the shell script sets up the necessary environment internally. Never assume that an environment is anything more than a basic default. Set your **${PATH}** variable, any other environment variables, and command aliases as required.
3. Formulate your command line as a string.
4. In AppleScript, work out how to assign that string to a variable so it can be passed to the **do shell script** command.
5. Choose an unambiguous path to where the shell script is stored. Remember that AppleScript can use UNIX and Mac OS X path construction formats (slashes or colons as separators).
6. Test the calling with a dummy script that gives a predictable response.
7. Now use your AppleScript skills to compose the parameter values that you want to pass to the script.
8. Concatenate the shell script path with the parameter values. You can do this into another variable if you want to call it multiple times or assemble the component strings with the **do shell script** command.
9. Add code to process the result, and you are ready to test it.

Converting from Mac OS colon-delimited paths to POSIX slash-delimited paths is done like this (where **HD** is the boot disk):

```
POSIX path of file "HD:shellscripts:test.sh"
-- result: "/shellscripts/test.sh"
```

These commands call the **ping** command without wrapping it in a script:

```
set hostname to "www.apple.com"
do shell script "ping -c1 " & hostname
```

This command calls the shell script and passes the same parameter.

```
do shell script "/shellscripts/test.sh " & hostname
```

Some useful advice is available in Apple technical note TN 2065.

Apple technical note TN 2065: http://developer.apple.com/technotes/tn2002/tn2065.html

2

 Calling AppleScript from Shells ▰▰▰▰▰▰▰

Calling AppleScript from your UNIX shell environment helps you build a workflow that is controlled from the UNIX environment but can still exploit any GUI-based applications in the desktop world. Realistically, AppleScript is the only language supported under the Mac OS X Open Scripting Architecture by default. The **osalang** command will reveal the available open scripting interpreters:

```
osalang -L
```

Which produces the following result:

```
ascr appl cgxervdh  AppleScript (AppleScript.)
scpt appl cgxervdh  Generic Scripting System
                    (Transparently supports all installed
                    OSA scripting systems.)
```

There are a few different ways to call AppleScript from the command line. Either the AppleScript command is passed in a file containing some AppleScript source text or it can be passed as a quoted parameter string.

Assuming you have the AppleScript source code in a text file, call it like this:

```
osascript myScript.txt
```

You can compile that script so it will run a little faster. Saving the script from the GUI script editor compiles it first. Compile it from the command line like this:

```
osacompile -o myScript.scpt myScript.txt
```

Now it can be called like this:

```
osascript myScript.scpt
```

You can enter the script manually by typing **osascript** and pressing the return key. Continue typing in lines of script separated by return keys. The script will be cached and executed when you press control-D to exit after the last line is entered. It might be easier to paste in a block of script code.

This uses the standard input hooks so you can pass the source from a "here" file using standard input redirection. For most situations, that doesn't offer anything more than you get by referring to the script file directly.

Communicating feedback to the user who may be working in the GUI environment is quite easy. This fragment of AppleScript will display a message through the Mac OS X Finder's **display dialog** support.

```
tell app "Finder"
   display dialog "My processing has finished."
end
```

Generate a **display dialog** message dynamically during the script execution to report progress and call it when necessary.

The same thing is possible on one line when you use the **osascript** command with the **-e** flag. In the **bash** shell, you can embed Macintosh newline characters (**\r**) between each line of script to put them all into a single parameter string:

```
osascript -e 'tell app "Finder"\rdisplay dialog "Finished."\rend'
```

In the Bourne shell, you need to work your quotation escaping differently and you can use multiple **-e** flags to simplify the escape processes:

```
osascript -e "tell app \"Finder\"" -e "display dialog \"Finished.\"" -e "end"
```

Escaping the quotes is probably where the most complex issues are going to be. The way you do that will be dependant on the shell you use.

When you call GUI applications that generate lists of values, you get a single level, comma-separated list of values. Include a **-ss** flag on the **osascript** call if you need the nested curly brace notation that AppleScript normally presents in its native mode.

The UNIX environment treats newlines differently than does the Mac OS X environment; Windows approaches them differently from either.

Convert all your Mac OS newlines to UNIX compatible newlines with a pipe like this:

```
<AppleScript process> | tr "\r" "\n" | <subsequent UNIX processes>
```

If you want to pass arguments into an AppleScript, you need to write a **run** handler in the script to take the parameters.

The general structure of your script should look like this:

```
on run argv
   return "parameter accepted, " & item 1 of argv & "."
end run
```

Call the script like this and pass in the additional parameter after the script name:

```
osascript myScript.scpt parameterValue
```

This also illustrates how an AppleScript can return values to the UNIX environment. A return value means you can use AppleScript call outs in the same way as any other shell script or command whose result you can test for success or failure.

For further information check out the **man** page for **osascript**, either with the **man osascript** command either in your terminal session or at Apple's developer web site.

Mac OS X UNIX man pages online: http://developer.apple.com/documentation/Darwin/Reference/ManPages/

Calling Visual Basic from AppleScript

When calling Visual Basic from AppleScript there are some minor things to be aware of.

You can often record the script in the script editor, but sometimes you'll find that the recorded script does not run and throws a compile error in the Office application. This is usually because the line breaks in the Visual Basic script cause completion errors in the VBA compiler.

This script code listing shows parameters spread over several lines to improve readability, but you should remove the line breaks if you experience this problem. Your experience may depend on the vintage of Visual Basic support, which Office application you are driving, the specific call you are making, and how you manufactured the script.

Concatenating the parameters into a string variable may be more convenient.

```
tell application "Microsoft Word"
    do Visual Basic "ChangeFileOpenDirectory \"HD:Users:piglet:Desktop:\""
    do Visual Basic "ActiveDocument.SaveAs
        FileName:=\"simple_000.rtf\",
        FileFormat:=wdFormatRTF,
        LockComments:=False,
        Password:=\"\",
        AddToRecentFiles:=True,
        WritePassword:=\"\",
        ReadOnlyRecommended:=False,
        EmbedTrueTypeFonts:=False,
        SaveNativePictureFormat:=False,
        SaveFormsData:=False,
        SaveAsAOCELetter:= False,
        HTMLDisplayOnlyOutput:=False"
    close document 1 of window 1
    quit saving no
end tell
```

Try placing each parameter assignment on a line by itself and execute it as an individual Visual Basic call. In the case of an object structured property assignment, a **with** structure is created by recording the script but the result is syntactically incorrect when executed in Visual Basic. You need to unroll the **with** block and apply the prefix to each property being assigned. You can see that this is a series of separate assignments, which is not the same as the multiple parameter function call shown above.

```
do Visual Basic "Selection.Find.ClearFormatting"
do Visual Basic "Selection.Find.Text = \"search_key_string\""
do Visual Basic "Selection.Find.Replacement.Text = \"\""
do Visual Basic "Selection.Find.Forward = True"
do Visual Basic "Selection.Find.Wrap = wdFindContinue"
do Visual Basic "Selection.Find.Format = False"
do Visual Basic "Selection.Find.MatchCase = False"
do Visual Basic "Selection.Find.MatchWholeWord = True"
do Visual Basic "Selection.Find.MatchWildcards = False"
do Visual Basic "Selection.Find.MatchSoundsLike = False"
do Visual Basic "Selection.Find.MatchAllWordForms = False"
do Visual Basic "Selection.Find.Execute"
```

Calling Visual Basic from UNIX ▄▄▄▄▄▄▄▄▄

If we can call Visual Basic from AppleScript and we can call AppleScript from the UNIX shell, then chaining the two together allows us to call Visual Basic from the UNIX shell. Like this:

```
echo  "tell application \"Microsoft Word\""            >> myScript.txt
echo  "do Visual Basic \"Selection.Find.ClearFormatting\"" >> myScript.txt
      <... set up the rest of the find parameters ...>
echo  "do Visual Basic \"Selection.Find.Execute\""    >> myScript.txt
echo  "end tell"                                      >> myScript.txt

osascript myScript.txt
```

You could drive Excel, PowerPoint, or any other scriptable component of the Office suite like that too.

5

 Calling UNIX Shell Commands from C

Use the **system()** function to pass control to the shell environment that a C language application is running in. Here is a minimal source script listing that executes a command to list a directory into a temporary file:

```c
#include <stdio.h>
#include <stdlib.h>

main(void)
{
    char command [80];

    sprintf(command, "ls /working_dir > /tmp/xxx.txt\n");

    system(command);

return(0);
}
```

Also check out the **fork()** and **exec()** function calls in the standard library if you want to create multiple processes running in the background.

Calling Java from C Language

You may have some utilities written in Java that you want to embed into an application written in C. Sometimes it is worth the effort to translate or port the code from one of these languages to the other. Then, everything is running wholly in Java or C. Occasionally it isn't worth it, or perhaps you have a Java application but no source for it.

The big difficulty here is that you need to construct a Java environment and run up a VM for it to execute the Java code in. This not hard and there is some online advice about how to do it. Search Google using the string "calling Java from C" will yield many helpful articles.

The best source of example code is the JNI (Java Native Interface) Java Launcher, which is written in C. This open source project is available as part of the Sun Java SDK.

Getting this to work is a nontrivial exercise but fortunately for us, other developers have already trod that path and published their guidelines. Here are the main steps that are required, but don't try to reinvent this, take the code from the Sun Java SDK:

1. Create the execution environment.
2. Dynamically load the JVM.
3. Prepare the runtime options for the JVM.
4. Create the JVM.
5. Load the target class into the JVM.
6. Call the main method of the target class.
7. When it returns (if it does), shutdown the JVM.
8. Cleanup and exit.

On Mac OS X, you can use the Java Bridge. This is one of many bridges in the Cocoa development environment which also provides routes from Objective C to JavaScript, Python and any other languages you are likely to need when building and integrating your workflows. Technologies like this come and go and you sometimes find that they wither and are deprecated, only to be replaced by something else more powerful. Java Bridge may become deprecated in later versions of Mac OS X.

Sun Java SDK: http://java.sun.com/j2se/1.4.2/download.html

JNI how to article: http://webservices.sys-con.com/read/45840.htm

Sample source code: http://res.sys-con.com/story/45840/Havey0908.zip

JNI development on Mac OS X: http://developer.apple.com/technotes/tn2005/tn2147.html

Cocoa language integration guide:

  http://developer.apple.com/documentation/Cocoa/Conceptual/LanguageIntegration/index.html

7

Calling C from Java

This is also nontrivial and not for the faint of heart. Many examples are available online and once again the JNI support comes in useful. If you are planning to bridge between Java and any other Native language, you should thoroughly investigate and understand JNI first.

Here is an outline of what you need to do in order to call C from Java:

1. Design the application and clearly define the interface boundary taking care to factor things into the Java or C language portion sensibly.
2. Write your Java application and declare the native methods.
3. Compile the code to produce a class file.
4. Create a header file (`.h`) from your compiled class file by executing the **javah -jni "classname"** command.
5. Open the `.h` file it just created, and copy the signature definitions to your C language source code file.
6. Referring to these signatures, write the native C code that implements the required functionality.
7. Use the JNI support functions access the method arguments supplied with the Java method call.
8. Create a shared library that contains your C language handlers.
9. Test and debug your program.
10. If you get an linker errors, your paths or method signature names are incorrect.

As you can see, this is quite challenging to build. But once you have got a test version working, you may be able to wrap that up as generic code with some supporting build scripts so you don't have to work so hard to do it next time.

On the Windows platform, check out the Cygwin tools when you need to do Java to C and C to Java bridging.

What Your Web Server Log Can Tell You

Web servers tell us an amazing amount about the general health of our systems, provided we are prepared to do the forensic analysis. For commercial purposes, we can analyze the logs to produce visitor traffic metrics that we can publish to our clients and attract more advertising revenue. From a workflow and systems engineering point of view, the error logs and failed requests tell us what we need to fix in our content system.

Automate the creation of content maintenance requests by scanning the web server logs for errors. Quite separately from the normal traffic analysis, you can scan for 404 errors. These were requests for pages that don't exist. You should have your logging set up with an extended log format that records referrers, user agent strings, and cookies, as well as the usual access log data. Then, for any 404 errors in the log, you can check the referrer data. If the page being viewed prior to the error is within your web site, it is a good candidate for further investigation to fix up a bad link.

The bad link shouldn't have been there in the first place. Since it has been discovered by one of your customers, you should rectify it immediately. You haven't done the diligence you should have if it shows up again for a second customer. This is not hard to do. It is basic level of quality and attention to detail that all of your customers can reasonably expect.

Analyzing the user agent strings is important, because it will tell you whether robots and spiders are probing your site. They don't always honor the **robots.txt** instructions. Check and compare against an authoritative list on a regular basis.

Measuring the network bandwidth requires sophisticated packet monitoring techniques. Summing the file sizes of requests that have been served by the web site and plotting these on a graph may indicate whether some bandwidth limitations are being reached. If the curves are not all smooth and rounded, but instead have flat tops with a consistent maximum level, you may be saturating your network capacity. It is time to make the "pipes" fatter. If you don't, your users will either not be able to connect at all or will get slow performance, which is bad for your site's reputation.

Looking outside your site, the referrer data can tell you about the sites that are linking to you. The Google search parameters should be evident in the referrer. From the search parameters, you will be able to deduce the search keys that people use to find your site. This applies to other search engines too.

9

 Monitoring Your Operating System Logs ▬▬▬▬▬

Your system logs will tell you whether your computer is degenerating or perhaps subject to unwelcome intrusion from outside.

You should design logging into your workflow to augment whatever the operating system already does by default. Occasionally it helps to have an audit trail that you can check to see whether files were transferred to your clients and a record of when that happened. This is especially important if you are providing a service that customers are paying for. If they claim not to have received the files, you may be able to find the evidence if you have added logging stubs to your file transfers.

This is an added benefit of wrapping an FTP file transfer in some script (see Tutorial 12). The same wrapper can be used for transfers with a copy command onto locally mounted disks that are shared in from an external server. The logging stubs work as a compliance-recording process.

Most system logs are maintained in the **/var/log/** directory on a UNIX system. We'll show that on the first example command line but omit it thereafter. Windows systems might store them in **C:\WINDOWS\System32\LogFiles**, but your system might be configured differently

Running this command when you log in to a UNIX system tells you whether authentication failures have happened. These relate to users who already have login access to your system. Other external intrusions may be logged separately by your security systems.

```
cat /var/log/secure.log | grep -i "failed"
```

As a systems administrator, you would certainly want to see a filtered version of this information viewed on a daily basis across all the systems for which you are responsible. It could indicate some casual (and possibly benign) intrusions.

This yields a quite wordy log output, but a few piped commands in the UNIX command line will make short work of that.

Stacking up the **grep** commands and switching their sense to "true" or "false" with the **-v** flag is quite powerful and easy to learn. These two command pipelines list two mutually exclusive sets of lines from the log file:

```
cat secure.log | grep -i "failed" | grep -v -i "user"
cat secure.log | grep -i "failed" | grep -i "user"
```

The first one tells you what kind of intrusions happened. The second tells you who has been trying and failing to authenticate what they are attempting to do.

This tells you how many application crashes have occurred:

```
cat crashreporter.log | wc -l
```

This variation generates a list of applications that have crashed:

```
cat crashreporter.log | cut -d: -f5 | sort | uniq
```

Adding a **-c** to the **uniq** command adds a leading column with a count of how many times the unique line occurred. Following that with a **sort** **-r** to reverse the order of the sort will rank your most failure prone application to the top of the list.

```
cat crashreporter.log | cut -d: -f5 | sort | uniq -c | sort -r
```

When we are applying effort to solving our workflow problems, we get the maximum gain from fixing the problems that occur most often. This crash reporter log analysis would indicate which application we could fix to benefit the most users right away.

Putting the piped commands in the correct order makes some difference to the processing time.

Both of these commands will tell you the date and time when you last ran the software update:

```
cat install.log | tail -1 | cut -d' ' -f-4
cat install.log | cut -d' ' -f-4 | tail -1
```

For a log file containing 5000 lines, the first example command line is back with an answer instantly; the second one took almost a second. The second one applies the **cut** command 5000 times and throws away all but one of the results. The first one looks at the file, and locates the last line, and applies the **cut** just once only.

Think carefully about how you organize your analyzers to make the most efficient use of the computing power available.

Keeping an eye on the **/var/log/system.log** file is useful. If your system is exhibiting some odd behavior, there may be some evidence in there. That log will be rotated quite frequently, and it is where many processes will naturally record their performance problems.

Measuring and Monitoring Disk Usage

When you build a workflow system, you need to capacity-plan the disk space you require. Estimate how much data or how many assets you are going to create each day. Then multiply the estimate by a factor depending on your storage format.

This tutorial specifically addresses disk usage but consider the larger picture. This kind of approach to monitoring can be applied to measure what is happening all over your system (or systems).

This seems straightforward but it rarely turns out that way. Perhaps because more people use the system than you expected, or more assets are being stored than anticipated. It could be that the amount of storage you originally planned for was too expensive and you had to scale it back to meet your budget allocation.

Inevitably, you are in a situation where disk space could run out. You need to monitor the space being used and watch the trend. You must predict how quickly it is being consumed in order to add more capacity before it gets full and the system crashes.

On a UNIX-based system, even on a Mac OS X server, I would deploy a shell script to do this, mainly because it doesn't need a user interface for the data collection. Windows users will be able to accomplish something similar with PowerShell.

A simple monitoring script will measure and record the disk space whenever it is called.

To make the script more flexible, the name of the disk drive is passed as a parameter so it can be called for any drive on the system. Two command line flags are added to the **df** command to modify the output format. One normalizes the block sizes to measure disk capacity in 1MB increments, and the other adds a count of inodes. The inodes are directory slots that are also prone to run out and cause disk-full conditions even when the physical space is partly empty.

The **df -m -i** command lists all the disks when we don't indicate a specific disk. The **$1** parameter will be supplied from the command line when our script is called. We get this output when manually specifying a disk drive:

```
df -m -i /Volumes/WORK

Filesystem     1M-blocks Used Avail Capacity iused      ifree %iused  Mounted on
/dev/disk0s10     40820  597 40222      1%  153023 10296895    1%   /Volumes/WORK
```

We only want the last line. We can pipe the **df** command into a **tail** command to discard the unwanted output and keep the last line.

Now we need to split the arguments and create a formatted output line. If the output of the **tail** command is piped to a **while** block, we can **read** the individual items on the incoming character stream as if they were separate arguments. By giving them sensible names, we can easily manipulate them inside the **while** block. Here is the shell script so far:

```
# Measure the disk space for the indicated disk
# Use the -m flag to force the default block size to 1Mbyte
# Add the -i flag to measure inode usage
df -m -i $1 | tail -1 |
while read FSYS BLKS USED AVAIL X IUSED IFREE Y MOUNT
do
    echo "Disk space available ... : " $AVAIL
    echo "I-nodes available ...... : " $IFREE
done
```

Now we want to gather the measurements into a file. Measurements like this are best accumulated separately, and for the measurement to be useful, we need date and time records.

The **date** command on its own will give us a date and time value, but we should always avoid using defaults. We should give it a specific format to get predictable results. Read the manual pages with a **man date** command to find out all about this. For now, we will use a formatter string that yields an ISO-standard date and time like this:

```
YYYY-MM-DD HH:MM.
```

We can build a format and put it into a quoted string as a parameter of the **date** command. Unusually for UNIX, we use the plus sign (**+**) to delimit the format parameter.

```
date +'%Y-%m-%d %H:%M'
```

Note how **%m** and **%M** are both used. Case is important at all times when writing shell scripts.

We need this value stored in a variable. Another useful power user technique in UNIX is to enclose a command in back quotes. That will spawn a sub-shell, execute the command, and return its output text as a substitute for the back-quoted string. If that back-quoted string is on the right hand side of an assignment, we can assign the result of executing the **date** command to a variable and use it several times later on without needing to re-compute the time.

```
MYDATE=`date +'%Y-%m-%d %H:%M'`
```

Note how we have different kinds of quotes being nested here. Sometimes we may need to escape the inner quotes. For this tutorial, it is fine as it is. Our shell script has grown a little more complex:

```
#!/bin/sh

# Save the current date/time in a variable
MYDATE=`date +'%Y-%m-%d %H:%M'`

df -m -i $1 |
tail -1     |
while read FSYS BLKS USED AVAIL X IUSED IFREE Y MOUNT
do
    echo "Disk space available ... : " ${MYDATE} ${AVAIL}
    echo "I-nodes available ...... : " ${MYDATE} ${IFREE}
done
```

Now there is a "shebang" at the top to force the script to run in a predictable shell environment. This also switches on syntax coloring in the script editor (if your script editor supports it). The **date** and **tail** commands have been put on separate lines so we can easily modify the pipeline if we need to. The date value stored in the variable is echoed with the measured disk usage. The variables have also been enclosed in curly braces. This is optional but reduces the ambiguity when the shell parses the script lines to decide what to do. It helps to make things work more predictably, which is always a good idea. The output looks like this:

```
Disk space available ... :  2006-07-31 11:09 40221
I-nodes available ...... :  2006-07-31 11:09 10296830
```

We have three space-separated values that are ready to be written to the log files. The spaces will help us import the logged data into Excel.

When you output any text, it will normally be sent to the standard output. If it is a warning or error message, it will go to standard error. These two streams of text are separate and can be redirected. The **echo** command by default goes to standard output too.

We redirect in slightly different ways according to the shell we are using. Here, I am using a basic Bourne shell, because I know that it is available almost everywhere. Where it isn't available, the bash shell provides a compatible environment. Some of the other shells might need to be added separately. Modern operating systems come with most of them pre-installed.

Bourne shell redirection is accomplished with the **>** or **>>** meta-character sequences. There are a few different ways to use these redirects, as shown in Chapter 20. We need the standard output to be appended to the log files.

Setting up some default variables identifies the log files at the outset of the script. For illustration purposes, we will use an include file to create an environment that can be shared consistently between many commands.

In Bourne shell we can run that include file as if it were being executed in the current shell level. If we executed it like a normal script, it would set up any commonly used variables but create them in a sub-shell. When it finished, the sub-shell would die and return control to the calling shell, discarding any changes that happened to the environment in the sub-shell. Variable values can be inherited downwards by child processes but cannot be propagated upwards to parents. Dot-running the script runs it in the context of the current shell.

We need a script that assigns some variables with paths to the directory and filename where we want the log files to be created. This script is intended to be included, therefore it doesn't need the "shebang" at the beginning.

You need to consider variable name collisions and use names that won't be used anywhere else. Adding a prefix on is a sensible precaution. I used the word **COMMON**. Here are the contents of the **common.sh** file.

```
# Create shared commonly used pointers to directories and files
COMMON_DISK_SPACE_LOG="/log_files/disk_space.txt"
COMMON_NODE_USAGE_LOG="/log_files/inodes_used.txt"
```

Now we need to call this into our script with the dot command. In this tutorial, the script lives in a folder called **shared_files**. We add this line to the top of our script, immediately after the "shebang."

```
. /shared_files/common.sh
```

Here is the finished script, shortened for convenience and with the human-readable text removed from the logging output.

```
#!/bin/sh

# call in the shared common variable values
. /shared_files/common.sh

MYDATE=`date +'%Y-%m-%d %H:%M'`

df -m -i $1 |
tail -1     |
while read FSYS BLKS USED AVAIL X IUSED IFREE Y MOUNT
do
    echo ${MYDATE} ${AVAIL} >> ${COMMON_DISK_SPACE_LOG}
    echo ${MYDATE} ${IFREE} >> ${COMMON_NODE_USAGE_LOG}
done
```

When you run this, two files should appear. They are called **disk_space.txt** and **inodes_used.txt** respectively. At this point (having run the script just once) they each contain a single log line. Here is the disk space file (the inodes file is very similar).

```
2006-07-31 13:59 40221
```

Now all you need to do is attach the script to a **cron** scheduler to execute on a cyclic basis. Once a day is probably sufficient. You could enhance this script to make some decisions every time it is run. That might lead to a warning e-mail being sent to the system supervisor's mailbox. If you prefer, you could log the percentage value and generate a warning when there is only 5% free space. That is not as efficient as measuring the actual space. You can calculate the percentage value if you need it.

After a few days, your files will start to build an interesting picture of your disk usage patterns. You can plot these out on a graph to see the trends.

On a Mac OS X system you can use a fragment of AppleScript to display the results in a graph with Microsoft Excel. If this script is saved as a compiled application, you can double-click on it to bring up a graph whenever you want to. Excel doesn't even have to be running for this to work.

```
tell application "Microsoft Excel"
    OpenText "LOGS:log_files:disk_space.txt" ¬
        Origin xlMacintosh ¬
        StartAtRow 1 ¬
        DataType xlDelimited ¬
        TextQualifier xlDoubleQuote ¬
        FieldInfo {{1.0, 5.0}, {2.0, 1.0}, {3.0, 1.0}} ¬
        with TreatConsecutiveDelimitersAsOne, ¬
        TabDelimiter ¬
        and SpaceDelimiter ¬
        without SemicolonDelimiter, ¬
        CommaDelimiter ¬
        and Other
    Select Range "C1:C3"
    Create New Chart
end tell
```

The '¬' character indicates that the line is continued without a return and allows us to format the line more attractively for print. You can modify the script to draw different kinds of graphs and change the style as you wish.

Starting the AppleScript editor and telling it to record while manually opening the file in Excel created this script without having to enter it by hand. A few extra lines were removed to pare it down to the minimum. The AppleScript support in Excel is extremely powerful. This bodes well for us using Excel as a general-purpose mathematical tool in our workflows.

Doubtless the same level of interaction is available when using PowerShell on Windows Vista, but the syntax will be different.

Wrapping FTP Transfers in a Script

We frequently need to move files from one machine to another. That's easy when the file systems on the remote machines are shared out and we can mount them locally. That isn't always possible, sometimes for security reasons and other times because the sharing mechanisms aren't compatible. Perhaps we are delivering content to a customer's server.

Moving files around a workflow needs to be done carefully. Avoid moving a file to a target machine that has insufficient space if possible. The sending script might bail out, having transferred an incomplete file and crashed a remote server. It might assume that the server is getting on with the job and delete the file at the client end to save space. This whole scenario could be problematic and lead to data loss.

First, check that you can do something, then do it, and then afterwards check that it was done properly and completely.

Rather than call the FTP tools directly from my shell scripts, I built a framework for the FTP client to run in. This framework set up the copy and checked that the file had arrived at the destination server afterwards. It also provided feedback mechanisms for reporting and compliance.

Because I created a wrapper for the FTP command, I could take advantage of that checking process every time without needing to implement dozens of line of code for every copy operation I wanted to implement.

We use the **ftp** command to run a client that opens a session with a remote server. Provided we have set up a **.netrc** file with the correct access permissions, our FTP client will have automatic remote access. At that point, some of the things we type will happen locally, while others will happen remotely. There are four commands we'll use right now:

Table 11 FTP commands

Command	Description
binary	Makes sure that files are not converted with text translators.
put	Delivers a source file to a target location.
ls	Lists the directory in the target remote machine.
bye	Closes the connection and exits.

To get FTP under automated control, we can use redirection techniques. This time we want to redirect its command input so the instructions come from a "here file." We will use the keyword "**EOF**" to denote the end of our "here file." Instead of manually opening the **FTP** session, we use the input redirector to drive it automatically.

```
ftp target_machine <<EOF
binary
put local_file.xxx remote_file.xxx
ls remote_file.xxx
bye
EOF
```

Those filenames need to be defined by parameters with the "here file" created dynamically. Wrap the FTP example we just developed in some **echo** commands and redirect their output to a temporary file. The first empty line is necessary to force the file to be purged if it has been used before. The last empty line ensures there is a carriage return to complete the command.

```
echo ""                                    >   temp.sh
echo "ftp target_machine <<EOF"           >>  temp.sh
echo "binary"                             >>  temp.sh
echo "put local_file.xxx remote_file.xxx" >>  temp.sh
echo "ls remote_file.xxx"                 >>  temp.sh
echo "bye"                                >>  temp.sh
echo "EOF"                                >>  temp.sh
echo ""                                    >>  temp.sh
```

Now we can put this into a scripting framework and replace the hardwired filenames with variables that are generated from passed in parameters. Here is the finished script:

```
#!/bin/sh
# Define the temporary file name for the here file
# The $$ is a meta string that is unique for the
# current process
FTP_DRIVER=/tmp/ftp.$$

# Define a temporary file for the ftp result output
FTP_OUTPUT=/tmp/output.$$

# Use command line parameters to indicate names of source
# and target files
SOURCE_FILE=$1
TARGET_FILE=$2

# Define the remote machine's network address
REMOTE_CPU="huey"

# Make the here file
echo ""                                    >   ${FTP_DRIVER}
echo "ftp ${REMOTE_CPU} <<EOF"            >>  ${FTP_DRIVER}
echo "binary"                             >>  ${FTP_DRIVER}
echo "put ${SOURCE_FILE} ${TARGET_FILE}"  >>  ${FTP_DRIVER}
echo "ls ${TARGET_FILE}"                  >>  ${FTP_DRIVER}
echo "bye"                                >>  ${FTP_DRIVER}
echo "EOF"                                >>  ${FTP_DRIVER}
echo ""                                    >>  ${FTP_DRIVER}

# Ensure the here file is executeable
chmod +x ${FTP_DRIVER}

# Run the here file with a dot command and redirect any
# output from it to a temporary output file
. ${FTP_DRIVER} > ${FTP_OUTPUT}
```

```
# Inspect the result. Filter in the remote file name.
# Filter out error messages. Note the use of backquotes
# and pipes.
ARRIVED=`cat ${FTP_OUTPUT}                       |
         grep "${TARGET_FILE}"                   |
         grep -v "No such file or directory"  |
         grep -v "Permission denied"`

# If the file arrived, display a suitable message
if [ "|${ARRIVED}|" != "||" ]
then
    echo "${SOURCE_FILE} - UPLOADED"
else
    echo "${SOURCE_FILE} - UPLOAD FAILED"
fi


# --- Collect up the trash
       rm -f ${FTP_DRIVER} > /dev/null
       rm -f ${FTP_OUTPUT} > /dev/null
       rm -f ${FTP_NETRC}  > /dev/null
```

Note how the **if** test is constructed. Because the **=** character is used, the comparison is string-based. There is a possibility that the variable could be empty, and in certain circumstances an empty string with two quotes is "cleaned-up" by the shell interpreter. This leads to a difficult-to-diagnose syntax error in the **if** test evaluation logic. Placing vertical bars on either side of both operands being compared allows the test for equality to work, but it ensures that the quotes are never empty and won't be misinterpreted.

To measure the remote disk space, we need to perform a **df** commend in the server and get its results back to the client. You will require authenticated access to execute a command remotely. Provided you have access, you can execute a command on the remote machine with the **rsh** command.

```
rsh target_host df
```

This command would present the results of the **df** command so you can parse them locally. This should be checked before you attempt to **FTP** the file to the remote system.

For this tutorial, we only check that the file arrived. The remote machine dictates how much information is supplied by the **ls** command. It may be more or less verbose than you expect. The remote FTP server may be a different version than what you expect as well. More recent implementations of the FTP server and client support more features, such as requesting the actual size of the remote file. This can be compared with the size of the local file and, if they aren't identical, then truncation has occurred.

You have to read the **man** pages on the local and remote machines to check the fine details.

Once it is all set up and working, transfers will go smoothly unless either system is changed.

As alternatives to FTP, there are other tools such as **curl**, **wget**, and **smbget**, which will pull files across from a remote machine using **HTTP:** or **SMB:** protocols. These are useful, but you need to know the file is there to be requested in the first place.

The **curl** tool is especially powerful and is available as an open-source project that has been ported to every operating system. It is also bound into other tools such as PHP and Perl.

Wrapping gzip in a Shell Script

Here is a sample script that uses the **gzip** command-line tool to compress a file. Because it is wrapped in a script, we can add a check that the file was compressed properly by uncompressing it again and comparing the result with the original. If the compression was successful, the original file is removed. Otherwise, the abortive compressed file is discarded.

```
SOURCE_FILE=$1

gzip -9c ${SOURCE_FILE} > ${SOURCE_FILE}.gz

LINE_COUNT=`cat ${SOURCE_FILE} | wc -l`
ZIPP_COUNT=`gzip -dc ${SOURCE_FILE}.gz | wc -l`

if  [ ${LINE_COUNT} -eq ${ZIPP_COUNT} ]
then
    rm ${SOURCE_FILE}
else
    rm ${SOURCE_FILE}.gz
fi
```

Although this might seem wasteful, it performs some useful validation. Firstly, it checks that the archive is good and that it is not corrupted in any way. Because we now know that the archive is reliable, we can safely delete the original knowing that we can retrieve it again.

Many-to-Many Relationships

Using a foreign key to reference another table satisfies the one-to-one and one-to-many cases. Many-to-many is a little bit more difficult, unless you place foreign keys in both tables. There is a significant problem with this approach because you have introduced a cross-dependency that is hard to maintain.

A clever solution is to create a small table whose sole purpose is to join the two tables together. You place the foreign keys in that table and remove them from the main two tables being joined. Yes, it is that simple.

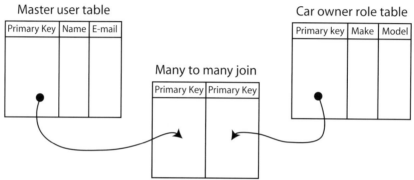

Figure 13 Many-to-many mapping

Phonetic Searches

Sometimes your user types almost the correct thing and expects the command line interface you created to understand what they meant to type. The same thing applies to searching databases. Entering the correct spelling is sometimes quite difficult. Wouldn't it be better if the software could read our minds and understand what we meant to type?

Way back in 1989, I found a magazine article written by Ben Franklin that set out an approach that I have found works even now, 25 years later. It is quite simple, really.

Use phonetic rules to degenerate the command or search key. If the reference you are comparing against has also been degenerated using the same technique, the two will converge and, in most cases, they will intersect, giving a match. This is a sort of fuzzy matching that is quite useful.

To deploy it, you use your normal techniques to search and match. You only wield the phonetic technique when the standard approach results in no matches at all. It is helpful before you apply the phonetic degeneration technique to convert any numbers to spelled out text strings. The string "**42**" should be rendered as "**Forty Two**" before applying the phonetic degenerator to the keys in the database and the query key at run time.

Here are a series of steps that describe changes you make to the key values. These are applied one word at a time and only work reliably for English. Your national language may require completely different rules for contraction, but the general technique should work:

1. Spell out any numbers first.
2. Remove any punctuation either collapsing the space or replacing with a space to separate into words.
3. Change the letter **C** into an **S** if it is followed by **E**, **I**, or **Y**.
4. Otherwise change **C** into **K** unless it is followed by a letter **H**.
5. Change **G** into **J** if it is followed by **E**, **I**, or **Y**.
6. Change any remaining **GH** pairs to **H** (deleting the **G**).
7. Change **PH** into **F**.
8. Change **Q** into **KW**.
9. Change **TI** into **SH** if it is followed by a vowel but leave it alone if it is at the beginning of a word.
10. Change **X** into **KS**.
11. Change **Y** into **I** unless it is the first character of the word.
12. Change **Z** into **S**.
13. Change any remaining double consonants into a single instance of the character.
14. Delete all but the last vowel of a consecutive run of vowels.
15. Remove all spaces.

Some of the transformations are extreme, and you may find for some vocabularies it is necessary to tweak some of the transformation rules listed above.

Nevertheless this would correctly match **PENNSYLVANIA** with **PENCILVANEYA** because both will converge on **PENSILVANA**.

We can loosen the matching algorithm a little by allowing a percentage of characters to match between the two transformed strings.

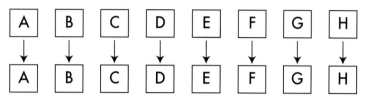

Figure 14a Perfectly matching keys

We can also allow a diagonal match between a character and the ones either side in the other string.

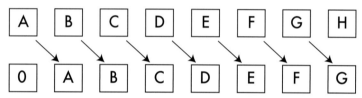

Figure 14b Imperfectly matching keys

The matching techniques can be applied and ranked in order to arrive at what is considered the closest match. Pre-processing rules to correct common misplacements would help to avoid incorrect transformations.

- **OIN** at the end of a word should become **ION**.
- **HP** in the middle of a word could be changed to **PH** and the match retested.
- **EI** should be changed to **IE** except after **C**.

Fuzzy Searching and Sorting

On at least five database-oriented projects that I have worked on with different clients, I have suggested and implemented the same phonetic searching and hidden sort-ordering tables in the database for making sure that data sequencing and location works properly. Only the first column in Table 15 is visible to the end user. The second column ensures that the items are sequenced correctly. The third is a search key that has been degenerated according to phonetic rules. By degenerating the query key, you can run a second query on the phonetic field if searching the main (visible) key field doesn't yield any meaningful results. The results of both queries are then merged, de-duplicated, and ranked before presentation.

Table 15 Sorting and sequencing with hidden data

Visible data	Sequence ordering	Phonetic search
Level 42	Level Forty Two	levelfortitwo
Maroon 5	Maroon Five	maronfive
M-People	MPeople	mpople
McCartney	MzzzMcCartney	mkartni

16

Finding Buffer Truncation Points ▬▬▬▬▬▬▬▬

When building your data model, you may need to use systems that have already been implemented but for which there is limited documentation. Here is a systematic process for testing string buffer lengths to allow you to limit buffer sizes and avoid truncation problems.

```
AAAAA00000BBBBB11111CCCCC22222DDDDD33333
```

Figure T-16 Source test data

1. Create a source-data buffer longer than you suspect the target field is capable of storing.
2. Create another buffer to retrieve the result into.
3. Fill your source-data buffer with a pattern of data that is structured so that it is easy to measure by eye.
4. Groups of five alphanumeric characters are useful, because you can see where the truncation point is (See Figure 16).
5. Store the source value into the target field or storage mechanism you are testing.
6. Read the stored value back into the result buffer.
7. Compare the two buffers. If the result buffer is shorter, then it is truncated. If they are still the same length, grow the source buffer and test again.
8. When you get a truncation, you know you have reached the buffer size limit.

If you need to do this on many data fields, build a test harness. It is worthwhile because it will exercise your import/export code, and it is useful to have as a regression test later on when the component parts of your system are being integrated together.

Cleaning Unstructured Data

When ingesting data from an unstructured source, we must clean it up to make it record-structured. This unstructured data might have been generated by an OCR process, which is at best only 90% accurate. There is usually a significant amount of cleaning up required.

This process is mainly about the physical organization of the data. Until we have been able to load it into a database and operate on the data values, it is hard to ensure the data is coherent. We can't do that level of checking until this physical cleanup has been done, because the database import mechanisms are uncompromisingly dumb. They expect everything to be presented in a strictly ordered and syntactically correct fashion.

This cleaning process digests the raw unstructured data to make it fit the shape of the model we have defined. Certain kinds of data will proceed through this stage without any trouble, while others will present numerous difficult challenges.

Name and address information is straightforward. However, you will find exceptions that force you to reconsider the field organization of your address database store. Refer to Appendix C for a catalog of object formats you could use to start building your object model.

18

Sorting Out Address Data

Cleaning address data is challenging, because the address information is divided across multiple lines. This is a real problem, because the delimiters may be tabs, commas, or line breaks, and the number of lines is variable and so too is their positional order.

Automating the whole process is not easy because of the widely variable formatting. Parts of it may yield to some scripting. Unless the dataset is extraordinarily huge, you might find that loading the address data into Excel and manipulating it there makes for a handy "workbench." We might start with something like this:

```
Rye House, Whitehart Road, Crowborough, East Sussex, TN7 1NU
16 Darley Road, Tunbridge Wells, Kent, TN1 1LX
Unit 32, Camcenter, Harcourt Industrial Estate, Elliot Road, Fairford, Glos, GL7 4SX
Downscote, 3 Kingsmartin Close, Steyning, West Sussex, BN34 3QS
Apartment 4, 15 Pollards Pine Crescent, Hurst Green, Oxted, Surrey, RH6 0FG
```

Figure 18a Raw address data

First, apply some straightforward delimiter detection to split the raw addresses into fields like this. Note that in the figure, the records are arranged vertically to illustrate how they line up and so we can illustrate them within the format of a book. Normally they would be arranged horizontally across the worksheet:

Record 1	Record 2	Record 3	Record 4
Rye House	16 Darley Drive	Downscote	Apartment 4
Whitehart Road	Tunbridge Wells	3 Kingsmartin Close	15 Pollards Pine Crescent
Crowborough	Kent	Steening	Hurst Oak green
East Sussex	TN1 1LX	West Sussex	Oxted
TN7 1NU		BN34 3QS	Surrey
			RH6 0FG

Figure 18b Delimited into fields and records

After cleaning, everything should be lined up like this:

Record 1	Record 2	Record 3	Record 4
			Apartment 4
Rye House		Downscote	
Whitehart Road	16 Darley Drive	3 Kingsmartin Close	15 Pollards Pine Crescent
			Hurst Oak green
Crowborough	Tunbridge Wells	Steening	Oxted
East Sussex	Kent	West Sussex	Surrey
TN7 1NU	TN1 1LX	BN34 3QS	RH6 0FG
UK	UK	UK	UK

Figure 18c Sorted into correct fields

Spreading the records across the screen in Excel so they are one address per row with as many fields as we need is straightforward. It happens automatically as we read in the source data and detect the delimiters.

Some cleanup may be required before we can even attempt to load the data into Excel. The delimiters must be consistent. A script-driven filter or global search-and-replace in a text editor will fix any gremlins and remove leading and trailing space either side of the delimiter. I would suggest using a tab character to separate the fields.

Here are the fields we intend to categorize the data into:

- Apartment number.
- House name.
- Street address.
- Village.
- Town.
- County.
- ZIP or postal code.
- Country.

Here is a systematic process:

1. Remove leading spaces from all lines.
2. Remove trailing spaces from all lines.
3. Remove leading tabs from all lines.
4. Remove trailing tabs from all lines.
5. Remove empty lines.
6. Look for gremlin characters and fix them.

7. Unfold any multiple-line items so the whole record is visible on one line.
8. Import into Excel using text formats to avoid corrupting any data values.
9. Count how many fields there are in each line and fix any missing fields.
10. Remove any leading white space from all the fields.
11. Remove any trailing white space from all the fields.
12. Our longest example address was six fields, but collectively the addresses require eight fields. Foreign address formats might increase the number of fields even more.
13. Sort on the ZIP/postal code field. This will organize all the records with an empty postal code to one end. Secondary sort on the county field.
14. Now you can drag any incorrectly positioned ZIP/postal codes to the correct column.
15. Repeat, with secondary sorts moving leftwards until you have all the ZIP/postal codes in the correct column. Some order should already be starting to appear.
16. Now, it is easier to move the county values into the correct column.
17. Repeat for towns, then villages.
18. Sometimes I find it helpful to separate the street number from street name, in which case you need to add a column and then use some Excel formulas. The `LEFT()`, `MID()` and `RIGHT()` functions slice the data but they aren't very smart about it. You can search for an offset to a space character and build a more complex formula around the result. If you are very careful, you can copy a whole column to a text editor, work some filter magic, and then paste it back in. You must make sure that the exact same number of lines is moved back and nothing has moved vertically. Introducing extra tabs means that pasting back in requires more columns. That is fine, provided you have anticipated it. If you haven't, it will paste over something important.
19. Some fields contain values that should have been split by the tab delimiter but there wasn't one there. Now that things are largely in the correct columns, sorting by each column in turn will make the bad items show up very clearly.
20. Now look carefully for bad ZIP/postal codes. These will show up if you sort by county and then by town as a secondary sort. There will probably be obvious typographic mistakes in the first few characters. Any lower-priority mistakes will be very hard to detect.
21. Fix broken telephone area codes by sorting on town name or postal codes to spot spurious or missing values.
22. At this stage, you can also fix misspelled town and county names.
23. Fix capitalization and any other typographic errors. Excel provides some filtering functions that you can apply. Add a spare column, put in the formula, and duplicate it vertically. Then copy the column to the clipboard and paste special to put back the values to replace the formula. Then you can remove the original column.
24. Correct or remove any unwanted abbreviation.

25. Correct any misspellings.
26. You might already have spotted some duplicates and zapped them. This is also something that Excel is good at. Add a column and use an `if()` function to compare a cell with the one above. The `if()` can display an asterisk if there is a duplicate and a space or empty value if not.
27. Check for any fields whose data length is longer than the model allows for.
28. Export to a format for further use, perhaps XML or CSV/TSV. Another option is text with CSV tags for further editing to create SQL for loading the database.

This is a remarkably quick way to clean and sort thousands of address records in only a few hours. Everyone who does any data cleaning should have a copy of Excel.

19

♻ Time Data Cleaning

If you take care, time values can be cleaned independently of date values. In order to perform arithmetic, we need to ensure the time zone offset is consistent. This is usually a value in brackets that indicates hours and minutes. The time should be converted to UTC with a scanner function. The time scanner will usually scan a variety of different formats and understand them, making compensations where necessary. Then the correct GMT time value can be used to calculate time zone offsets.

Cleaning time values only becomes problematic if we try to do arithmetic with a text-based approach. This is only going to work if we are doing a minor reformatting operation to add a leading zero or convert between 24- and 12-hour representation for display purposes.

Anything requiring adjustment for daylight savings time, offsets from GMT, etc., needs to be done in UTC millisecond count values, because changing the time value might roll over into the next or previous day.

Excel manipulates time values in a convenient way. Alternatively, a short C language filter tool might do what you need, given that it can break the time structures down into components, fix them, and reassemble a time value. Perl will provide a viable solution, too. There are many powerful Perl extension modules for date-time processing. You don't need to implement your entire system in Perl. Just create a short Perl script that you can call when needed. The shebangs will take care of switching the right parser in.

Removing Duplicates

Solving problems like duplication sometimes requires some lateral thinking. Occasionally, you need to transform the data set in a way that appears to be moving it further away from where you want to get to. However, this will give you some leverage to solve the problem a different way.

De-duplicating a single column is easy. Use **sort** and **uniq** commands in a UNIX shell. It becomes more difficult if we want to find and merge duplicate records based on a name or e-mail field.

Removing duplicated information requires that you step through the data set one item at a time. Then go and examine all the other records to see if they are the same. Some performance gains are possible because as we walk through the data set, by implication, we will already have compared any items prior to the one we are currently indexed to.

This is not very a satisfactory solution. It takes a long time.

If we sort the data set using the key field we are interested in, then duplicates should be adjacent. That makes them much easier to find if we are only considering that one field. Sorting with a compound key will order sub-sorted items together, and we should be able to check several fields and still find duplicates. Compound keys are not a recommended approach when using relational databases for performance reasons. Nested sorting with a secondary and even a tertiary sort order based on additional keys accomplishes the same thing. Excel does this very well.

If we want to do something a little fuzzy, perhaps looking for things that are similar or represented in a slightly different form, it gets a little harder. For example, person names where the middle name is optionally present, person titles (Mr. vs. Mister), or numbers (42 vs. Forty Two).

Add a temporary column and transform the values you are looking for into the same format. Then sort on that column and search for duplicates as before. For all records that have field 1 set to "Mr.," set field 6 to "Mister." Apply this in a case-less fashion. Then repeat for all records that have the string "Mister" in field 1. Now sort the data set using field 6 instead of field 1. When you have found and processed any duplicates, field 6 can be removed, leaving the original values intact.

21

Converting TSV to XML

For this tutorial, assume that we have a tab-separated file with three columns of data: name, age, and country of residence. We will use a short file with those field names in the first record and three subsequent records with genuine data. The listing shows what our source data looks like. The tabs have been replaced with asterisks so that they are visible in print:

```
Name*Age*Country
Tom*25*United Kingdom
Dick*33*USA
Harry*78*Denmark
```

Figure 21 Raw TSV data

We will create some minimal XML. This isn't a course in XML, just a brief demonstration of how to create the somewhat different structure of an XML file from records and fields.

Here, we know that there are three data fields in each record. The field names are picked up from the heading line and used to build the DTD and as tag names.

Here is the shell script that converts the TSV file to XML:

```
#!/bin/sh

# --- Set up storage
INPUTFILE=$1
TEMPFILE=/tmp/$$.tmp

# --- Extract tag names
cat ${INPUTFILE} |
head -1           |
tr [:upper:] [:lower:] > ${TEMPFILE}

FIELD1=`cat ${TEMPFILE} | cut -f1`
FIELD2=`cat ${TEMPFILE} | cut -f2`
FIELD3=`cat ${TEMPFILE} | cut -f3`

# --- Write header & embedded DTD
echo "<?xml version=\"1.0\"?>"
echo "<!DOCTYPE peoplelist ["
echo "<!ELEMENT peoplelist ANY>"
echo "<!ELEMENT person ANY>"
echo "<!ELEMENT ${FIELD1} (#PCDATA)>"
echo "<!ELEMENT ${FIELD2} (#PCDATA)>"
echo "<!ELEMENT ${FIELD3} (#PCDATA)>"
echo "]>"

echo "<peoplelist>"
```

```
# --- Ignore first line and extract data lines
cat ${INPUTFILE} |
tail +2           |
while read DATA1 DATA2 DATA3
do
  echo "<person>"
  echo "<${FIELD1}>${DATA1}</${FIELD1}>"
  echo "<${FIELD2}>${DATA2}</${FIELD2}>"
  echo "<${FIELD3}>${DATA3}</${FIELD3}>"
  echo "</person>"
  echo ""
done

# --- Write trailer
echo "</peoplelist>"
```

And here is the XML file that is created from the original data we started with:

```
<?xml version="1.0"?>
<!DOCTYPE peoplelist [
<!ELEMENT peoplelist ANY>
<!ELEMENT person    ANY>
<!ELEMENT name      (#PCDATA)>
<!ELEMENT age       (#PCDATA)>
<!ELEMENT country   (#PCDATA)>
]>
<peoplelist>
<person>
<name>Tom</name>
<age>25</age>
<country>United Kingdom</country>
</person>

<person>
<name>Dick</name>
<age>33</age>
<country>USA</country>
</person>

<person>
<name>Harry</name>
<age>78</age>
<country>Denmark</country>
</person>

</peoplelist>
```

Running this through the STG validator tells us that it is valid XML, even if it isn't very pretty. You can access the validator for your own XML code to test it.

STG validator for XML files: http://www.stg.brown.edu/service/xmlvalid/

22

 Removing Macros from Word Documents ▬▬▬▬▬▬

Sometimes, older RTF formats will not support features of the word processor that you want to use. While saving into this format may lose some data, it can also be an advantage sometimes, such as when you have some style settings that are implemented in Word using macros. Opening the document will kick in the macro virus protection.

Saving the document as an RTF file and then re-importing it back into Word and saving the file again as a DOC file again seems to cure this, but at the expense of losing all the macros in the document. This is a desirable outcome if you wanted to clean the document of any macros, but the version of Word and the RTF version support may affect whether this is possible.

It isn't documented very well, but it is certainly true of Microsoft Word version X on Mac OS X. Run some tests to see if it works with your version of Word.

Removing all Hyperlinks from Word

If you select and copy text in a web page or load a URL in Word, you get many hyperlinks embedded in your text. It can be extremely distracting when you inadvertently click on one and it opens a web browser.

Even after a heavy editing session, these hyperlinks remain intact, hidden under punctuation characters and any words that you had typed over the original hyperlink. Removing all of these by hand is quite monotonous, especially if there are many of them. They are very hard to find unless you use the "View Field Codes" command. Even then, you can't see the visible result text. If you remove the hyperlink while the field code is on view, the result text disappears as well.

There is a quick way to remove them that is more convenient than editing each hyperlink by hand and turning it off. Because they are implemented as a kind of field code, you can manipulate them with the field code tools associated with the [F9] key. Various combinations of [control]/[command]/[alt]/[option] and [shift] with the [F9] key manipulate the field code in different ways. Generally, on Mac OS the [command] (clover leaf) key corresponds to the [control] key on Windows. The [option] key on Mac OS corresponds to the [alt] key on a PC keyboard.

The unlink command will render the field and produce the result value, which it will substitute in place of the field code. If you know the region that contains the hyperlinks, select it and press [command]+[shift]+[F9] on Mac OS X. On Windows, [control]+[shift]+[F9] does the same thing.

This clears all hyperlinks and leaves behind the result text. Any field that was a placeholder for a formula and didn't display anything will disappear.

If you don't know where your hyperlinks are, you can select the entire document. This is dangerous, however, because it will clear all field codes in the selected region.

Using field codes is a quite obscure technique. Unless you have inserted one of the automatically updating codes or put in some mail merge and dynamic fields of your own, the hyperlinks are probably the only thing in your document anyway. Knowing that you can remove hyperlinks like this is useful. A better technique is to paste the original web page into a temporary document and apply the field code-cleaning technique before cutting and pasting it into your target document.

Now that we know how hyperlinks are implemented in a Word document, it should be feasible to write scripts to locate them and remove them without affecting other field codes. They are certainly visible in RTF files. We would need to write a Word macro if we wanted to do this inside Word or an AppleScript/PowerShell script to do it from outside. We could write a UNIX shell script to process RTF files.

Putting URL links back in is not as easy. Converting the document to the ODT file format with Open Office renders it in a form (XML) that you can access as a data file instead of a word-processed document.

Recognizing U.S. ZIP Codes

Matching U.S. ZIP codes for syntactic correctness is straightforward. They are composed from a string of numeric characters. Any nonnumeric character is an error, except for the dashes in ZIP+4 codes.

To match the standard 5-digit ZIP code we could use this regular expression:

```
[0-9]{5}
```

The "+4" part of the extended ZIP code is a variation with a "**4**" in the braces. Combined, we get this for the whole ZIP+4 combination with its embedded dash:

```
[0-9]{5}\-[0-9]{4}
```

This will also match a ZIP code with too many digits in either half. We need to delimit the ZIP code and allow either of the two forms. In this case, we will assume that the check is on a field. The beginning and end of the line can be used to mark the extent of the code. You did already clean the leading and trailing white space, didn't you? This won't match otherwise.

```
^([0-9]{5} | [0-9]{5}\-[0-9]{4})$
```

Recognizing UK Postal Codes

It is not as easy to match the UK postal codes as it is the U.S. ZIP codes, because the codes in the UK always include both letters and numbers.

To match "**TN7 2NE**" we can break this down into three parts as per the UK Post Office specification.

- Incoming code (**TN7**),
- A space character,
- Outgoing code (**2NE**).

We can also use some position matching at the start and end of the line. The "**TN7**" incoming code should match this:

```
^[A-Z]{2}[0-9]*
```

The "**2NE**" outgoing code at the end of the line should match this:

```
[0-9][A-Z]{2}$
```

We can use a space character or a dot to match the gap. Our whole regular expression pattern would be:

```
^[A-Z]{2}[0-9]*.[0-9][A-Z]{2}$
```

Let's try and use that in a PHP script with a slight variation.

```php
<?php
$sourceValue = 'TN7 2NE';
$pattern = '^[A-Z]{2}([0-9]{1}|[0-9]{2}).[0-9][A-Z]{2}$';

// This pattern also works
//$pattern = '^[A-Z]{2}([0-9]{1,2}).[0-9][A-Z]{2}$';

if(eregi($pattern, $sourceValue))
{
   print "TRUE";
}
else
{
   print "FALSE";
}
?>
```

407

26

 Finding Variable Names in Source Code

Sometimes we find ourselves in the middle of a job, unable to sort out a simple syntax problem. Regular expressions can be useful in many ways. If you wanted to locate references to variables in a PHP script, you could use a regular expression in your text editor to search for them. But how do you do that when you don't know what the variable names are?

This regular expression matches all variable names in PHP. They always begin with a dollar and then a letter, but never a number:

```
\$[a-zA-Z][a-zA-Z0-9]*
```

Note the two ranges, the second one being repeated as many times as required until we reach a nonalphanumeric character or white space.

Finding Double-Quoted Strings

Searching for a double-quoted text string is tricky. The quotes get in the way, but they are the specific characters that delimit the text we are searching for.

Here is a sample regular expression that matches double-quoted strings. These have a quote at each end but may not contain a quote:

```
"[^"]*"
```

Note the character range value is everything except a quote character and is repeated until we match a quote character.

28

 Finding Single-Quoted Strings

Searching for a single-quoted text string is even more difficult, because single quotes are often used to delimit a regular expression in place. Sometimes you can use the same regex format as the double-quoted method and enclose the whole regex in double quotes. If you can't, then the single quotes will need to be escaped as well.

Here is a sample regular expression that matches single-quoted strings. These have a single quote at each end but may not contain a quote. This search pattern is escaped so that it can be embedded into a regex that is enclosed in single quotes:

```
\'[^\']*\'
```

Note the character range is everything except a quote character and is repeated until we match a quote character.

Finding Currency Values

Matching currency values in text files as they are ingested is a useful technique. Regular expressions are ideally suited to this.

Here we match a currency value with an optional pence amount:

```
\£[0-9]+(\.[0-9][0-9])?
```

The **£** symbol implies this must be a Unicode string. The **+** operator means we must have at least 1 digit after the **£**. The brackets atomize the decimal point and pence value that is optional or instantiated only once because of the **?** operator. We could use the bounds operator like this to mean the same thing:

```
\£[0-9]+(\.[0-9]{2})?
```

30

 Finding Time Values ▬▬▬▬▬▬▬▬▬▬▬▬▬▬▬▬

Time values are tricky. They should fit this format, although the 12- and 24-hour versions are different:

```
00:00 xx
```

But we must take account of the range of values. The trick is to divide and conquer. The leading zero is optional, so the **?** operator helps with the first digit. The second digit is problematic, but this will match **0** to **23** including whether we also have **00** as well:

```
[01]?[0-9]|2[0-3]
```

The minute values range from **00** to **59** and are matched with this:

```
[0-5][0-9]
```

Putting it all together with the colon and adding seconds values we get this:

```
([01]?[0-9]|2[0-3]):([0-5][0-9]):([0-5][0-9])
```

For a 12-hour clock with am/pm we could use this:

```
(1[012]|[1-9]):([0-5][0-9]):([0-5][0-9]) (am|pm)
```

Recovering Text from Corrupted Documents

The ingest processes are quite straightforward when they work correctly. Everything runs predictably, and the content flows through the system. Occasionally, you get a rogue document. Perhaps it was saved incorrectly or a computer crashed while producing it. There may be some content there, but the editing application won't open it.

Some document formats will allow you to extract some or even all of the text from a damaged file. A few document formats are so heavily compressed or tokenized that this is not feasible. You can approach this at different levels depending on the format of the file and the tools you have available.

Some document formats store older versions of the text as well as the current version. Microsoft Word does this provided the text has not yet been redacted. On the upside, this might give you two or more opportunities to recover a particular fragment of text, but the downside is that you have some copy that is not required. It isn't easy to tell which is which.

There may be commercial recovery services that can help, or tools you can buy commercially. You wouldn't want to spend money on that if you can solve it yourself.

This is an outline of a recovery process that I apply in these circumstances.

1. I prefer to use a UNIX system to analyze text files like this. There are tools to view the file in a variety of different formats, and I can make new ones with shell scripts and pipes.
2. Make a safety copy of the file to be worked on. This avoids damaging the original. This should be copied to a separate physical disk drive with some space to extract the contents to separate files.
3. Try opening the document with an older version of the editor. If we are rescuing content from Word documents, then try other versions of Word on Macintosh or Windows machines.
4. Forcing the application to open the file in the wrong format might send it through some different file-recognition logic. Sometimes this bypasses a piece of code that might reject the file at the outset. Although this is exploiting a potential bug in the application, it works for our purpose. You can force this by manually altering the file extension.
5. Open the file in a raw text editor. It might present a complete or semi-complete transcript with no styling but the text is accessible for cut and paste.
6. If the text editor won't open the file, try using the **strings** command from the UNIX command line. This will scan the file, looking for printable characters. It is a bit nicer than dumping the entire file out. The filter in the **strings** command removes text that is nonsense to humans. For many cases, this is all you need to do. The second example adds an offset into the file where the line occurred.

```
cd /working_directory

strings ./damaged_file.doc > ./extracted.txt

strings -o ./damaged_file.doc > ./numbered_extracted.txt
```

Other approaches involve variations on the **od** command that dumps characters in various forms (octal, hex, ASCII, etc.). This is a more raw form of extraction that needs some work to be done on its output. You might find this helpful when trying to extract image or numeric data.

Software probes like General Edit by Quadrivio provide a mechanism for deducing the file contents byte-by-byte and building a C language structure definition, which it can then compile. This is a powerful tool and supports complex numeric extraction rules.

Finally, as a last resort, you can send the file off to a consultant or service company to do their best. They may have some heavyweight tools and software that they have specially developed for this purpose. It won't be cheap, but the content might be worth it.

Extracting Text from PDF Files

Pulling text and graphics out of PDF files is possible provided the files have not been encoded and locked. Even then, it may be possible to grab screen shots.

Third-party PostScript tools are useful for processing PDF (PostScript) files. GhostScript and the PDF kit embedded within Mac OS X are good examples. This is not for the fainthearted, but developing applications around their APIs in a compiled language like C or even Java may be the route to binding PDF documents into your workflow.

You can obtain some developer support from Adobe, but you need to subscribe for a fee. An SDK for Acrobat is available for a reasonable price.

Getting Acrobat to save files from AppleScript has proven to be difficult (for difficult, read impossible). Extensive web searching doesn't reveal any solutions. This presents a challenge.

You can set up a batch processor inside Acrobat professional. There is by default a batch-control script already set up to save PDFs as RTF. You can create an input and output folder and then manually run the batch job. If we could run that from outside Acrobat, the solution might be workable, but that too seems to be problematic. At times like this, you can resort to UI scripting, but even then you need the application to have implemented its UI with the standard operating system tools. In this case, the UI appears to have been coded separately. Consequently, UI scripting doesn't work. It is possible to drop files into the Acrobat input bin and grab them using watch-folder techniques, but we can't run the batch automatically. It requires human input to select a menu and provide two mouse clicks. Workflow implementation can be frustrating at times.

Windows users have a selection of shareware and commercial tools available that will solve the PDF-to-RTF problem. Some have batch processing, and in time many of these are likely to be available as PowerShell plug-ins.

Another approach is to capture a screen shot and then OCR the text. This is not to advocate piracy. You should always honor the intent of any licensing or supply of documentation you have been given. OCR software does a good job, but is difficult to automate since it requires user interaction to select the scanning zones.

By adding third-party applications, you may be able to construct something that does the job. Here is a hybrid AppleScript and Visual Basic solution that works well with MS Office version X once you install the shareware TextLightning application made by MetaObjects.

```
tell application "Finder"
    open document file "HD:Input:simple.pdf" ¬
    using application file "HD:Publishing tools:TextLightning:TextLightning.app"
end tell

tell application "Microsoft Word"
    do Visual Basic "ChangeFileOpenDirectory \"HD:Input:\""
    do Visual Basic "ActiveDocument.SaveAs
        FileName:=\"simple_000.rtf\",
        FileFormat:=wdFormatRTF,
        LockComments:=False,
        Password:=\"\",
        AddToRecentFiles:=True,
        WritePassword:=\"\",
        ReadOnlyRecommended:=False,
        EmbedTrueTypeFonts:=False,
        SaveNativePictureFormat:=False,
        SaveFormsData:=False,
        SaveAsAOCELetter:= False,
        HTMLDisplayOnlyOutput:=False"
    close document 1 of window 1
    quit saving no
end tell
```

Although this does the job, the TextLightning software will only extract the text. You are subject to the quality of your PDF conversion tool at this point. Other, more industrial-strength tools might be substituted, or you might custom-build something yourself if you have access to GhostScript or the Mac OS X PDF kit.

MS Office version 2004 supports a better AppleScript dictionary, and the next version of MS Office will not support Visual Basic at all. Then you will have to use AppleScript. On the downside, where Word version X was recordable, Word 2004 isn't. This makes it harder to decide how to write a script. What Word X recorded as scripting source code wasn't always syntactically correct and required some fix-up to make it work anyway. Here is a substitute **save as** handler for Word 2004.

```
tell application "Microsoft Word"
    Change File Open Directory path "HD:Input:"
    save as active document file name "simple_000.rtf" file format format rtf
    close active window
    quit
end tell
```

The syntax for Word version 2004 is cleaner and more compact. It doesn't require the embedding of the Visual Basic code and is the direction that Microsoft are likely to continue with the next version of Word which will not have any Visual Basic support at all. The code is leaner because we are assuming the default settings are OK. That isn't always a good idea and in scripts it costs you nothing to explicitly set up all the default values to make sure the files are saved exactly as you want them to be.

MetaObjects TextLightning: http://www.metaobject.com/

Mail and HTTP Header Removal

Mail messages and web page downloads are constructed in a similar way. The original RFC 822 format for document structures with headers and bodies seems to appear in a variety of places. It has been superceded by RFC 2822. Having some tools to extract or remove headers is useful. The headers in some instances are folded to fit a constrained column width. They need to be unfolded before you can do anything with them. Depending on the mail client you use, extracting raw mail messages might have folded or unfolded headers.

This utility is written in ANSI standardized POSIX compatible C. This guarantees that it is portable to any operating system. It is designed for a command-line environment and reads the input one line at a time. Folded lines look different from the start of a new header. The tool senses that and unfolds them. The null line between the header and the body throws a state switch that is initially set to indicate we are processing the header. If the command line argument is "**HEAD**" then the output only displays the header lines. Alternatively, "**BODY**" discards the header and only starts output after the state switch.

```c
#include <stdio.h>

#define BUFFER_SIZE 32000
#define STATE_HEADER 1
#define STATE_BODY   2

char Buffer[BUFFER_SIZE];
char Accumulator[BUFFER_SIZE];
char command[256];
int  length;
int  state;

/* Main entry point */
int main(int argc, char **argv)
{

/* Setup */
int ii;

state         = STATE_HEADER;
Accumulator[0] = 0;

/* Collect command line args */
if (argc == 2)
{
    strcpy(command, argv[1]);
    for (ii=0; ii<strlen(command); ii++)
    {
        command[ii] = toupper(command[ii]);
    }
}
```

```
/* Read the standard input and loop to handle each line */
while (fgets(Buffer, BUFFER_SIZE, stdin) != NULL)
{
    length = strlen(Buffer);
    if (Buffer[length-1] == '\n')
    {
        Buffer[length-1] = 0;
    }

/* Switch states to BODY on first null line */
    if (Buffer[0] == 0)
    {
        state = STATE_BODY;
    }

/* Handle HEADER or BODY states and unroll folded HEADER lines */
    if (state == STATE_HEADER)
    {
        if (Buffer[0] != 9)
        {
            if(strcmp(command, "HEAD") == 0)
            {
                printf ("%s\n", Accumulator);
            }
            Accumulator[0] = 0;
        }
        else
        {
            Buffer[0] = ' ';
        }
        strcat(Accumulator, Buffer);
    }
    else
    {
        if(strcmp(command, "BODY") == 0)
        {
            printf ("%s\n", Buffer);
        }
    }
}
return(0);
}
```

I compile this source code into an executable called rfc822. Because it reads from standard input, you can pipe the raw message source into it via the command line. You can choose to keep either the header lines or the source lines. This also works on raw HTTP content (combined header and body) as well:

```
$ cat my_message.txt | rfc822 HEAD | grep "^Subject:"
$ cat my_message.txt | rfc822 BODY
```

You can redirect the output of these tools to a file by appending the > character and adding the destination file name.

ISO 8601 Date Format Output

Here is the ANSI C code for getting the current date and printing it in ISO form:

```c
// Create time storage structs
time_t now_t;
struct tm now;

// Read time value from system clock
time(&now_t);

//Convert to broken down time structure
now = *localtime(&now_t);


// Display formatted output
printf("%4d-%02d-%02d",
       now.tm_year+1900,
       now.tm_mon+1,
       now.tm_mday);
```

If you prefer to use Perl, here is the code for presenting the current date and time in UTC form:

```perl
($sec,$min,$hour,$mday,$mon,$year,$wday,$yday,$isdst) = gmtime(time);
$t = sprintf "%4d-%02d-%02dT%02d:%02dZ\n", 1900+$year,$mon+1,$mday,$hour,$min;
print $t;
```

Portable JavaScript and *JScript* code that constructs an ISO 8601 date looks like this:

```javascript
function fixForY2K(aYear)
{
    // Co-erce the parameter to a numeric
    aYear = aYear - 0;

    // Compensate for Y2K
    if (aYear < 70) return (2000 + aYear);
    if (aYear < 1900) return (1900 + aYear);
    return aYear;
}


function outputISO8601Date()
{
    // Grab a date and time value for 'now'
    var today = new Date();

    // Zero pad the day value
    var dd  = today.getDate();
    if(dd < 10) dd = '0' + dd;
```

```
    // Zero pad the month number
    var mm = today.getMonth() + 1;
    if(mm < 10) mm = '0' + mm;

    // Fix up the year (it comes back as a 4 digit value)
    var yyyy = fixForY2K(today.getYear());

    // Create the output string
    return (yyyy + '-' + mm + '-' + dd);
}
```

Use this format with the **strftime()** function:

```
"%Y-%m-%dT%H:%M:%SZ"
```

When configuring server-side includes, this should define an ISO-standard date and time in the outgoing HTML, but you should check that it works on your implementation:

```
<!--#config timefmt="%Y-%m-%dT%H:%M:%SZ"-->
<!--#echo var="DATE_GMT"-->
```

If you only want the date with no time value, use this:

```
<!--#config timefmt="%Y-%m-%d"-->
<!--#echo var="DATE_GMT"-->
```

For PHP implementations, write the date and time in ISO format like this:

```
$now = substr_replace(strftime("%Y-%m-%dT%H:%M:%S%z"), ":", -2, 0);
echo "ISO date and time is ", $now;
```

Relative Date Tool (theDate)

Determining when special dates occur can be quite tricky, especially when using scripts. Relative date computation is difficult to implement in shell scripts. The solution is to create a small C language command line tool (I called it **theDate**).

The ANSI-standard C library's calls for time computation let you break down the time into a structured set of values and then add increments to them before reassembling the components back into a binary time. To compute yesterday's date, we get the time now, break the time down into components, subtract 1 from the day number within the month, and build a new time. This is smart enough that if our day number is zero or negative, it will compute the correct relative date/time.

Finding next Monday, the first of this month, or next New Year's Day becomes quite easy.

The tool expects a variable number of arguments. One is a keyword that selects a relative computation, which uses the numeric value that is passed in another argument. Another keyword is a date output format selector. Sometimes, a count value is indicated too.

This is the syntax:

```
thedate [<count>] [<date_selector>] [<format_spec>]
```

In the shell script, it looks like this:

```
$ thedate file_stub
1997_06_10

$ thedate day_name
Monday

$ thedate 1 week_ago month_name
June

$ thedate yesterday
1997_06_09

$ thedate tomorrow day_of_year
162

$ thedate last_christmas_eve day_name
Tuesday

$ thedate first_day_of_next_month dd_mm_yyyy
01-07-1997

$ thedate 10 years_time date_n_day
2007_06_10 Sunday
```

It works best when it is used in back quotes to assign its resultant value to a variable that can be used elsewhere in the script.

When I developed this, the problem couldn't be solved efficiently in the shell-scripting environment of 1998. We have many other tools available now, but this is still a hard problem to solve.

These are the date selector keywords:

```
TODAY                              <n> MONTH_HENCE
YESTERDAY                          <n> MONTHS_HENCE
TOMORROW                           <n> MONTHS_TIME
FIRST_DAY_OF_LAST_YEAR            <n> YEAR_HENCE
FIRST_DAY_OF_THIS_YEAR           <n> YEARS_HENCE
FIRST_DAY_OF_NEXT_YEAR          <n> YEARS_TIME
FIRST_DAY_OF_LAST_MONTH        LAST_SUNDAY
FIRST_DAY_OF_THIS_MONTH        LAST_MONDAY
FIRST_DAY_OF_NEXT_MONTH        LAST_TUESDAY
LAST_DAY_OF_LAST_YEAR          LAST_WEDNESDAY
LAST_DAY_OF_THIS_YEAR          LAST_THURSDAY
LAST_DAY_OF_NEXT_YEAR          LAST_FRIDAY
LAST_DAY_OF_LAST_MONTH         LAST_SATURDAY
LAST_DAY_OF_THIS_MONTH         NEXT_SUNDAY
LAST_DAY_OF_NEXT_MONTH         NEXT_MONDAY
<n> DAY_AGO                        NEXT_TUESDAY
<n> DAYS_AGO                       NEXT_WEDNESDAY
<n> WEEK_AGO                       NEXT_THURSDAY
<n> WEEKS_AGO                      NEXT_FRIDAY
<n> MONTH_AGO                      NEXT_SATURDAY
<n> MONTHS_AGO                     LAST_CHRISTMAS_EVE
<n> YEAR_AGO                       LAST_CHRISTMAS_DAY
<n> YEARS_AGO                      LAST_NEW_YEARS_EVE
<n> DAY_HENCE                      LAST_NEW_YEARS_DAY
<n> DAYS_HENCE                     NEXT_CHRISTMAS_EVE
<n> DAYS_TIME                      NEXT_CHRISTMAS_DAY
<n> WEEK_HENCE                     NEXT_NEW_YEARS_EVE
<n> WEEKS_HENCE                    NEXT_NEW_YEARS_DAY
<n> WEEKS_TIME
```

In C, you get the current date as a UTC value. Then you break it down into a **struct** that contains year, month, day, etc., in separate variables within that **struct**.

If you set the numbers to out-of-range values, and remake the UTC time, it will calculate what the correct date and time would have been.

Therefore, March the 0th is the last day of February, and it works for leap years as well. You don't have to work out whether there is a leap year; the operating system libraries do it for you. Just increment or decrement the day, month, or year value. The date one week ago is today's date minus 7 days. If that happens to be November, the minus 4th it will fall four days back into October.

Last Christmas Eve is easy—you decrement the year and force the month to be 12 and day to be 25.

After you remake the UTC time, you can then output the relative date using a date formatter. This is where the second keyword argument comes into play and selects an output handler accordingly.

ZIP/Postal Code-to-Location Mapping ▬▬▬▬

I worked on a project for a client who had three separate Web sites, and each one needed to cross-link to pages in the others in an intelligent way. Each site maintained separate metadata systems, although they were implemented on the same servers.

Because we designed these systems from the ground up, we were able to dictate a common location policy for geographic information.

We wanted to connect together cinemas from the film listings service with restaurants in the food web site's metadata system. This would provide a way to book a whole evening out, have a meal, and then watch a movie (or vice versa).

The problem is, if you ask someone where they are, they give you a street address within a town and county. That isn't going to be easy to search and match with a street nearby.

The postal systems in most countries use ZIP or postal codes. These are designed to route mail from one distribution center to another. They help us with our problem because they have a standardized format that you can check for accuracy. You can obtain databases that map the ZIP/postal code values to a geographical location (for a fee).

In our metadata schema, we created a relational join from the postal code value in the cinema address table and use that as a foreign key to access the postal code to geo-reference a coordinate converter. Then, that single coordinate is expanded to describe a box. A circle would be better, but SQL databases don't understand spatial coordinates in quite that way. Now we use that box to range-limit a search for viable ZIP/postal codes within a reasonable catchment area. Those can then be used as seed keys to search the restaurants database. If we are lucky, some of them will hit, and we should get a list of restaurants that are near the cinema. A degree of fuzziness is required to make this work. Fuzziness is something computers aren't adept at. In this case, fuzziness is applied by trimming the postal codes. We only search for part of the key and wildcard the rest.

This worked pretty well, in fact, provided we allowed the box to be large enough.

We ran into some minor problems on this because we made assumptions about the geo-ref coordinate and the size and shape of the postcode zone. The zones are mostly a sensible shape. But a few are not. Some are oddly shaped, long and curved round so that if you work out the center point, it sometimes falls outside the boundary of the zone represented by the postal code. This only really turned out to be a problem when we worked on a fine grid at individual street level or when we tried to aggregate several zones to form a shorter code. The zones are not mapped like that.

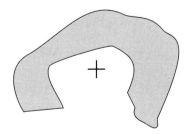

Figure 36 Centroid of an oddly-shaped zone

Shortest Distance Between Two Towns

The shortest distance between two nodes in a network may not be a direct connecting line. This happened on the project that connected cinemas and restaurants.

If you know the geography of the UK, you'll remember that in the west of England, the river Severn separates it from Wales. This is a very wide estuary and is quite a barrier to travel as far up as the Severn Bridge, and there are not many other crossings until you get to Bristol.

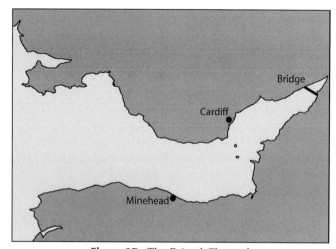

Figure 37a The Bristol Channel

If you have a series of unconnected points, some in Wales and some in North Devon, without seeing where they are with respect to the coastline you might make a false assumption about traveling between them. This is exactly what happened to us.

Customers complained that they could find a cinema in Cardiff, Wales but that nearby restaurants included establishments in Minehead, North Devon. The distance was probably only 20 miles. However, to drive between the two would be a journey of more than 80 miles.

Dealing with the Bristol Channel problem is quite a challenge unless you spend time correcting the node connections. This problem shows up in dozens of places around the coastline of the UK and is likely to affect the mapping of any coastal regions wherever you are in the world.

If we take all of the nodes (cinema and restaurant locations) and draw a polygon around them, we get the effect of stretching a rubber band around the points. This is called a *convex hull*.

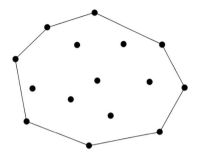

Figure 37b Convex hull around outer edges

Now place this in the context of the physical geography. Minehead and Cardiff should not be joined directly, because we must remain on dry land. Aside from all the other points, there are two nodes on the bridge across the estuary. Cardiff connects to one and Minehead to the other. We need to pull that boundary in and create a concave hull. The algorithms usually triangulate the points and knock out the offending spurious joins. The revised diagram shows the old (removed) joins as dotted lines. Some points (a) give us a problem. We might knock out either of the lines going away from it. We can't leave any orphans, and no lines are allowed to cross.

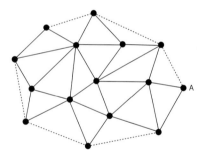

Figure 37c Concave hull around outer edges

We can't casually eliminate joining vectors. The dotted lines indicate where we need to make choices. Computer graphic systems do it all the time when they draw polygons and create surfaces.

Our network of nodes needs to be augmented by a coastline polygon that surrounds them. Then we can use a generic polygon-drawing routine to test whether the line between any two points crosses the boundary of the polygon. If it does, it will go into the sea. We must reject any of those node connections, because they are spurious.

This was all implemented using a stored procedure inside the Oracle database. We compared the stored procedure against an external computation, and the stored procedure technique turned out to be as fast so there was no loss of performance. Considering that we hit it with a single query and got back the matching establishments as a set of records, this was a good solution, and was much faster than getting back a larger set of records and calculating intersections manually. It was also a better structural design from a software architecture point of view.

38

 Dealing with Islands

The same flaw in the search of related establishments showed up with the Isle of Wight and the mainland. That journey requires a ferry trip and cannot be made other than at scheduled times.

We needed to solve this in a generalized way because the resources were not available to look at the connectedness of any point with respect to another. In fact this appears to be the same as the Minehead–Cardiff problem but isn't. There is no land bridge between the two.

Step one is to identify islands. Establishments on the Isle of Wight, Isle of Man, and the Channel Islands need to have a value that identifies which island they are on. The mainland of the UK is considered to be another island, and Ireland is another. Add a column to the database, examine the postcodes with a script, and define the value in the island column accordingly.

Our search algorithm can now eliminate any matches that are not on the same island as the starting point. This is easily accomplished by extending the SQL query.

Calculate Centroid of Area

There are some complex formulae and the engineering approaches that are well suited to handling regular shapes that can be simplified.

For a postal region, the irregular shape can be divided into a low-resolution grid and the average worked out in X and Y using a numerical method. We can grid this as shown in Figure 39.

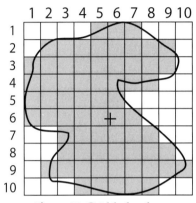

Figure 39 Gridded polygon

First we can consider the horizontal. The top row has cells 5, 6, and 7 filled. The total is 18 and the average is 6. We add all the horizontal coordinates together and divide by the cell count to get a horizontal average. Then we do same for the vertical axis. This yields a block address that is the centroid of the area.

The 68 filled cells add up to 351 in the horizontal axis and 379 in the vertical. This averages to 5.16 and 5.57, respectively, which determines the X-Y point where the centroid crosshair is placed in the illustration.

Use a polygon scan line fill algorithm to convert the outline to a set of filled pixels and then calculate the average. Lowering the resolution speeds up the computation, but sacrifices accuracy.

## 40

Extracting Text from Illustrator ▬▬▬▬▬▬▬

Sometimes you have to get devious in order to extract or convert essence data or metadata. An ideal solution is one that doesn't require any preset configuration of the tools. You use the application in its normal, out-of-the box installation. Sometimes, you can allow the installation of a plug-in, but you want to avoid any manual intervention, otherwise your solution isn't a closed-box scenario.

Exporting text from Illustrator so you can reuse any legends or other texts in the image can be done with a technique that involves setting up a predefined action and then calling that with a **do script** command.

This approach has a downside. The file name that it is saved as is hardwired into Illustrator because it is a parameter, which is saved in the action. OK, we could cope with that by gathering up the file after triggering the action. The next problem is the GUI dialog that needs a manual click to prevent it blocking. This is hard to process because the GUI uses nonstandard UI kit components and the AppleScript UI scripting won't talk to it. Sometimes, you have to go back to square one and try a completely different approach.

Dialogs like this may respond to you adding the "**showing dialogs never**" post-script to your AppleScript command. If the application responds to this, it won't prompt the user for help and your script can continue uninterrupted.

The Adobe Illustrator AppleScript reference describes a better way to export.

This still won't allow us access to an "**Export as Text**" option but it will allow an "**Export As SVG**" instruction that contains the text in a form we can extract. Because an SVG file is XML-structured, we can access the text with an XML tool or as raw text. We have to do it this way; the PDF files that Illustrator normally creates are compressed, so we can't grab the text directly from them.

Use this AppleScript to save the file:

```
tell application "Adobe Illustrator"
    open file "B_001.ai"
    export current document to "metaexperiment.txt" as SVG
    close document 1
end tell
```

The lines we are interested in as far as extracting the text look like this. In fact, we want to get just the word "**Arts**" from the file:

```
<text transform="matrix(1 0 0 1 171.5684 129.2324)" style="font-family:'Myriad-Roman';
font-size:76;">Arts</text>
```

We could certainly fire up some powerful XML editing tools, but because this is text, sometimes the old ways work as effectively (in this case, even better).

This fragment of shell script will extract just these lines and trim off the vestigial XML markup tags.

```
cat metaexperiment.svg |
grep "<text"           |
sed 's/<\/text>//'     |
sed 's/<text.*>//'
```

The result is the text on its own, with each item on a separate line—and we used tools that are about 30 years old. Who says UNIX is obsolete!

This was tested on version CS2 of Illustrator, things could change with CS3 and there may be better ways to do things as applications evolve. Keep notes of places like this where you may want to go back and refine something when an application is upgraded.

We can extract some interesting document properties such as size and color depth without needing to save the file. Both Illustrator and Photoshop have rich enough scripting interfaces to yield lots of useful information. This could help us quickly populate a media asset management system if all we knew about the images were their file names and locations in the storage silo. We can also use the same scripting interface to set metadata information inside the files. This is a good way to add copyright information. Illustrator and Photoshop present this information in the XMP dialog where you can edit the metadata properties manually if you prefer.

Adobe Illustrator AppleScript reference:

http://partners.adobe.com/public/developer/en/illustrator/sdk/AICS2-AppleScriptGuide.pdf

41

 Generating Candidate Keywords ▰

This is useful for locating misspelled words in documents or creating indexes and keywords for adding to a metadata block associated with a document in a media asset manager.

Given an arbitrary block of text in a file, this UNIX script will transform the text file into a sorted list of unique words. A list of stop-words is maintained in a separate file that is applied to the output list to remove unwanted keys.

If the stop list contains words like "**the**," "**and**," "**of**," etc., then the result is a candidate list of keywords for indexing.

If the stop list contains all the words from a previously spell-checked document, then the result will be a list of words that have not been used before or are potentially misspelled.

You may have other keywords that you want to exclude. If you are running a discussion board and archiving the transcripts, you might be able to detect profanity and remove it from the keywords.

The stop lists themselves can be fed by your editing process to expand their vocabulary and can be passed through a "**sort | uniq**" pipe to remove duplications after adding new vocabulary to them.

This uses some quite advanced transformation and regular expression matching. After examining the script, you can read the line-by-line commentary about how it works.

```sh
#!/bin/sh

SOURCE_FILE=$1

cat ${SOURCE_FILE} |
tr "\r\t\n" " " |
tr ".,:;\"|()^#!$\{\}\\<>/=" "\n" |
tr "ABCDEFGHIJKLMNOPQRSTUVWXYZ" "abcdefghijklmnopqrstuvwxyz" |
sed 's/ /\
/g' |
sed "s/^'//g"      |
sed "s/'$//g"      |
grep -v "^[0-9]*$" |
grep -v "^.$"      |
grep -v "^$"       |
grep -v "^\-.$"    |
grep -v "n't$"     |
sort |
uniq |
while read KEYWORD
do
  if [ "|`grep "^${KEYWORD}$" ./stop_list.txt`|" = "||" ]
  then
      echo "${KEYWORD}"
  fi
done
```

Here is how it works:

1. We retrieve the source file from a command-line argument.
2. The first **tr** command replaces any tabs and new lines with a space character. This removes any hard line breaks.
3. The next **tr** removes punctuation and forces a new-line instead. Punctuation must be a word separator.
4. Then there is a **tr** that makes everything lower case to avoid duplicate entries in upper case.
5. The first **sed** command replaces embedded spaces with newlines. By now, every word is on a line by itself.
6. Next, we remove single-quote characters if they are at the start of a line. A corresponding **sed** on the next piped command removes the quote at the end of the line. We couldn't do that earlier, because it would have removed embedded single quotes in the middle of a word. We might want to keep those.
7. The **grep** command removes any line that is composed entirely of numeric characters.
8. Then, we discard any line that has a single character. By now, that is likely to be an alphabetic letter by itself, which is no use to us as a keyword.
9. Any lines that are empty are removed.
10. Any lines that start with a dash and are followed by one single character before the end of the line are discarded. They are probably UNIX command-line flags left over from code listings. They wouldn't show up in the text of a romantic novel, but they are all over the place in a technical document about UNIX scripting.
11. The last **grep** is there to deal with apostrophe style abbreviations such as "**can't**" and "**won't**".
12. The resulting list of keywords is sorted and then de-duplicated with a **uniq** command.
13. The new, much shorter list of keywords is piped to a while loop that compares each word against the stop list and only echoes it to the output if the word is not stopped. Note the back-quoted **grep** that uses a regular expression to search for the keyword delimited by the line start and end. If you don't use a regex like this, you will get spurious matches where the keyword is included within another word.

When you break the task down into small steps, it is not hard to see the power of the UNIX command line. It appears complex when you see the whole script, but each line on its own does something quite basic and simple.

42

Extracting Metadata from Word Documents ▬▬

You can inspect the document properties manually in Word. This provides access to the document metadata through a nice GUI. It's not easy to integrate that into a workflow.

If we export as RTF, we can inspect the resulting source file to extract the properties but RTF syntax is hard to understand and parse.

A neat way to solve this is to open the document with Open Office and save as an ODT file. Then unpack the document container it creates to extract the metadata XML file.

Here is a systematic process:

1. In Word, save the document as a normal DOC file.
2. In Open Office, open the DOC file.
3. Save the file as an ODT document.
4. In your command line or GUI environment use unzip to convert the zipped archive back to an uncompressed folder full of files.
5. Parse the **metadata.xml** file with XSLT to convert it to SQL.
6. Load the content database with that SQL script.

At the moment, scripting Open Office is unproven but the application is open source and it may be possible to deconstruct it to make a command line tool that does the conversions.

Alternatively, you can investigate using Apache Jakarta POI tools to access the DOC file with some custom written Java code.

Extracting Metadata from Image Files ▬▬▬▬

This tutorial shows how to detect the endianness of a TIFF file. The general principle applies to a variety of other header data that you can extract from any kind of file. The idea is to open a data file, pick out some binary-coded information from the header, and format the result.

In this case, we will use a command in the UNIX system called **od**. It is named after the Octal Dump facility that it provides, but it extracts and displays file contents in many other formats. This is useful for accessing the contents of binary files.

The shell script dumps the first few bytes of the file and extracts the Byte Order Marker (BOM), which should be either "**II**" or "**MM**." This principle can be extended to find out image dimensions, comments, and whether the file is color or monochrome. These are all things you might want to know when ingesting files into a media asset management system.

```
#!/bin/sh

SOURCE_FILE=$1

BOM_TAG=`cat ${SOURCE_FILE} |
        head -1               |
        od -h                 |
        head -1               |
        tr -s ' '             |
        cut -d' ' -f2`

case ${BOM_TAG} in

    '4d4d') echo "Big-endian";;

    '4949') echo "Little-endian";;

        *) echo "Invalid TIFF";;
esac
```

The BOM_TAG variable is assigned with the results of a back-quoted command. The source file is truncated by a **head** command to improve performance. This saves the following **od** command from processing more data than is necessary. The second **head** command discards all but the first line of the hex dump. A **tr** is necessary to collapse the multiple spaces that format the listing. This helps the **cut** command find the correct space delimited field.

A simple case switch handles the two valid possibilities and flags any others as errors.

Tools like this are useful when you are presented with a legacy repository of content that has not been metadata-indexed properly.

You can wrap these tools in a shell script loop that works its way through an entire archive and runs quietly in the background with only a small CPU loading.

Refer to Tutorial 45 for an alternative way to discover the endianness of a TIFF file in a single line with file magic.

Extract Metadata from a QuickTime Movie ▬▬▬

The QuickTime movie player application has a useful scripting interface for examining metadata and any other video, audio or data tracks in a movie.

This fragment of AppleScript presents the image rectangle for a video clip:

```
tell application "QuickTime Player"
    set myMovieSize   to natural dimensions of front movie
    set myMovieWidth  to item 1 of myMovieSize
    set myMovieHeight to item 2 of myMovieSize
    display dialog myMovieWidth
    display dialog myMovieHeight
end tell
```

Note that we measure the natural dimensions. Omitting the word natural yields the current playback size instead of the source dimensions of the clip.

These are a few of the metadata related properties that you can access for a Movie track when ingesting. There are many others (73 in total):

Table 44a Movie track metadata properties

Property	Description
data rate	Data rate (bytes/sec) of the movie.
duration	Duration of the movie.
href	Internet location to open when clicking on the movie (overrides track hrefs).
id	ID of the movie.
index	Index of the movie.
live stream	Is this a live streaming movie?
max time loaded	Amount of time loaded in a fast start movie.
name	Movie asset name.
natural dimensions	Dimensions the movie has when it is not scaled.
original file	File containing the movie.
poster frame time	Time of the poster frame for the movie.
preferred rate	Preferred rate of the movie.
presentation background color	Background color (default is black).
presentation mode	Mode in which the movie will be presented.
presentation size	Size at which the movie will be presented.
preview	Start time and end time of the movie preview.
stored stream	Is this a stored streaming movie?

Table 44a Movie track metadata properties (continued)

`streaming status code`	Streaming status code of the movie.
`streaming status message`	Streaming status message of the movie.
`time scale`	Time scale of the movie.
`pan range`	Minimum and maximum values for pan value.
`tilt range`	Minimum and maximum values for tilt value.
`field of view range`	Minimum and maximum values for field of view value.

These persistent playback controls can be set and saved with the movie:

Table 44b Persistent playback controls

Property	Description
`auto close when done`	Will the movie automatically close when done playing?
`auto play`	Will the movie automatically start playing?
`auto present`	Will the movie automatically start presenting?
`auto quit when done`	Will the player automatically quit when done playing?
`controller type`	Type of controller associated with the movie.

Because Movies are stored in tracks within a QuickTime file, additional properties can be enquired at the track level:

Table 44c Track properties

Property	Description
`audio channel count`	How many channels in the audio.
`audio characteristic`	Can the track be heard?
`audio sample rate`	Sample rate of the audio in kHz.
`audio sample size`	Size of uncompressed audio samples in bits.
`chapterlist`	Text track to use as a chapter list for this track.
`data format`	Data format.
`deinterlace fields`	Is the visual track deinterlaced?
`enabled`	Should this track be used when the movie is playing?
`high quality`	Is the track high quality?
`is video gray scale`	Is the video gray scale?

Table 44c Track properties (continued)	
`kind`	Name of the media in the track, in the current language (e.g., 'Sound', 'Video', 'Text', ...).
`mask`	Mask of the track.
`layer`	Layer of the track.
`position`	Position of the track.
`single field`	Is the visual track single field?
`type`	Type of media in the track (e.g., 'soun', 'vide', 'text', ...).
`video depth`	Color depth of the video.
`visual characteristic`	Can the track be seen?

Because QuickTime is a foundation or framework and not only a video file format, it can do things that other video containers cannot. The richness of the interface available from AppleScript is also accessible from application development languages such as C, C++ and Java. It is accessible via the plug-in from JavaScript. The same level of access should be available via Windows PowerShell although nothing has yet been publicized (at the time of writing).

We might construct all kinds of metadata extractions for a large variety of different file formats. That would be a big project and the coding would require specialist knowledge.

If we are prepared to forego a little performance in the metadata extraction and allow the files to be imported into QuickTime, we can use it as an enquiry mechanism. Instead of opening an MPEG file to rip through the binary and discover the movie dimensions, it might be more convenient and less effort to open that MPEG movie in QuickTime player and talk to QuickTime.

This is a nice solution because it generalizes our interface to multimedia assets and for any that we find QuickTime does not understand, we could examine the binary directly. That would require approximately the same amount of knowledge that writing a custom media handler requires. If we write a custom media handler, we can add any kind of data file to QuickTime.

45

Discovering Formats with File Magic

Sometimes you are presented with a data file to be imported and you don't know what it is. It may have an unrecognizable file type extension or it could be already associated with an application but that application does not recognize the file format.

In the UNIX operating system, there has for years been a useful command called **file**, which is available at the command line. The file command is smart enough to check the file using a series of cascaded tests. The first one to succeed will yield a decision about the file type. The tests are done in this order:

1. Is the file empty?
2. Is it a special system file?
3. Is it a socket, symbolic link or named pipe defined in **sys/stat.h**?
4. Is it an object or executable file recognizable by a 'magic number at a known location'?
5. Is it a recognized data file defined by the magic number byte codes in the file **/usr/share/file/magic**?
6. Is the file a text file conforming to a recognizable code set?
7. If a recognizable code set is used, what is the computing language?

The **/usr/share/file/magic** file contains over 10 thousand lines of tags and byte values to describe 170 different special file types. You can add your own by recompiling this file if you need to. The command is simple to use:

```
file myfile.xxx
```

Running the command on a Word document using version 4.10 of the file command like this:

```
file /WORK/ZZ_imaging.doc
```

Yields an output like this:

```
/WORK/ ZZ_imaging.doc: Microsoft Office Document
```

This is another powerful metadata extraction tool that is useful when building an ingest workflow.

46

 Extracting Hyperlinks from Word Documents ▬▬

If you have a Word document containing many hyperlinks that you want to test with a URL checking application, you need to extract them first.

Here is a fragment of UNIX shell script code that does the job.

```
#!/bin/sh

cd /working_directory

strings Ch_001.doc |
sed 's/ /\
/g'                  |
grep "HYPERLINK"     |
cut -d\" -f2 > extracted_links.txt
```

This provides a list of URLs that you can insert into a database or run through an automated checker. Only hyperlinks will be extracted. URLs in the body of the text that are not activated hyperlinks will not be detected.

There are some caveats related to this approach. We aren't fully exploring the **HYPERLINK** field code syntax within a Word document. We are exploiting the fact that Word inserts some extractable text. The hyperlink data is embedded within a more opaque field. This is accessible if we convert to RTF and then locate that fragment within a **/field** structure. It will need some decoding.

Nevertheless, this seems to work for the documents I examined. You should always test and investigate these mechanisms thoroughly to see if they do what you want. Don't just blindly use them without any checking first.

Extracting URLs from Raw Text ━━━━

The **HYPERLINK** data in Microsoft Word documents is formatted as field codes. When they are note activated as **HYPERLINK** fields, they appear as simple body text. If we save the Word document as a plain text file, we can process it with a filter that is a general-purpose URL extractor.

This script will pull the URLs from a raw text file and sort them into order.

```
#!/bin/sh

SOURCE_FILE=$1

cat ${SOURCE_FILE} |
tr "\r\t\n" " "    |
sed 's/ /\
/g'                |
grep "://"         |
sed 's/\.$//'      |
tr -d "()"         |
sort               |
uniq
```

After preserving the input filename, the file is pushed through a series of piped filters. Here is a systematic description of what happens:

1. Convert any new lines or tabs to space characters.
2. Convert spaces to line breaks. A URL cannot contain any spaces. You wouldn't expect it to be part of a word, therefore it is probably between two spaces. Converting the spaces to line breaks gets them all onto a line on their own.
3. Using **grep**, we search for a string that is guaranteed to show up in all URLs. "**http**" would miss some. "**://**" is present whatever the protocol used but might not catch **mailto:** links. They should have an asterisk (**@**) in them.
4. In the test data, a spurious period appeared at the end of a line containing a URL. That is removed by the **sed** command.
5. Likewise for a pair of round brackets.
6. Finally we **sort** and **uniq** the list of URLs and output it to the screen.

48

 Testing URL Hyperlinks ▬▬▬▬▬▬▬

It is still amazing how many public-facing web pages include dead links in their related pages list. If you have your links in a database and publish your site through a content management system, then removal of dead links should be wholly automated.

On finding a dead link, a report should be sent to the editorial team to check it out. The report should also include a list of pages that refer to it so that they can be republished without the offending link. This is the sort of thing that human beings find boring but computers are adept at coping with.

Given a list of URLs in a text file, perhaps generated by the extraction mechanism illustrated for Word, this script will test each link and generate a report indicating whether it is good or bad.

This script uses the **curl** utility available on all platforms. In this case it is wrapped in a UNIX shell script. The **curl** utility is available as an extension to all the popular tools such as Perl and PHP. You can apply it to building mash-up aggregators and automated report-generating systems.

```sh
#!/bin/sh

# Source the link testing from our list of URLs
# Eliminate JavaScript calls as they can't be tested like this
cat extracted_links.txt |
grep -v "^^javascript:"   |
while read URL_TO_TEST
do
    # Inspect the first line of the request headers for its HTTP status
    PAGE_STATUS=`curl -i -s ${URL_TO_TEST} | head -1 | cut -d' ' -f2`

    # Some malformed URLs result in a nul string being returned
    if [ "|${PAGE_STATUS}|" = "||" ]
    then
        PAGE_STATUS="999"
    fi

    # Categorsie the responses - add your own here
    # Unrecognised codes will insert the HTTP status value instead
    # You can then decide if it is good or bad and update this list
    case ${PAGE_STATUS} in

        '200') RESULT="OK ";;
        '301') RESULT="OK ";;
        '302') RESULT="OK ";;
        '404') RESULT="BAD";;
        '999') RESULT="BAD";;
            *) RESULT="${PAGE_STATUS}";;
    esac

    # Now write the output report line
    echo "${RESULT} - ${URL_TO_TEST}"
done
```

Now you have a report that lists which URLs need to be further inspected and corrected or removed from your document.

Dictionary Lookups via Dict.org ▬▬▬▬▬

This is how you can request the dictionary entry for a keyword using the **curl** utility and some shell commands to clean up the resulting response from the **dict.org** server.

```
#!/bin/sh
SEARCH_KEY=$1

curl -i -s "dict://dict.org/d:${SEARCH_KEY}:" |
grep -v "^150" |
grep -v "^2"   |
grep -v "^$"   |
sed 's/^151 //'
```

The **DICT:** protocol is described in RFC 2229. Many other resources are available at the Dict Org web site.

Add tools to the user interface you provide to your journalists so that they can access this useful resource too.

Dictionary Org web site: http://www.dict.org/

Lookup the Online Dictionary from a Web Page ■■■ ■■

This is a JavaScript bookmarklet that takes a word that is selected within the current page and looks it up on **Dictionary.com**. You need to collapse it down to this form and insert it in your web browser.

```
javascript:i=window.getSelection();if(!i){void(i=prompt('Word...',''))};if(i)
{void(window.open('http://www.dictionary.com/cgi-
bin/dict.pl?db=*&term='+escape(i),'_blank',''))}
```

This is what the code looks like in a more human-readable form (line breaks added to help readability):

```
javascript:
i=window.getSelection();
if(!i)
{
 void(i=prompt('Word...',''))};
 if(i)
 {
 void(window.open(
'http://www.dictionary.com/cgi-bin/dict.pl?db=*&term='+escape(i),
'_blank',''))
 }
```

Check for Editorial Integrity

Imagine a scenario where you have a package ready for airing on a prime-time news program. It follows a journalist in a war zone, and the camera's GPS annotated the footage. Your broadcast system pulls that annotation off and automatically converts it to an onscreen graphic with the text "**Live from <...>**" where the **<...>** is replaced automatically by a lookup mechanism.

Your NLE operator didn't like the visual appearance of one of the shots, and usually works in the drama department. All the fine points of news integrity are not taken into consideration due to lack of experience. As a consequence, a substitute segment of footage was edited in because it "looked nicer."

The GPS tagging on that footage was a completely different country, unconnected to the news story. The viewer sees the package being broadcast and sees the legend change from "**Live from Afghanistan**" to "**Live from Turkey**."

Your editorial supervisor might have previewed the package and signed off on it visually, but unless the preview mechanism correctly previews the metadata as well, its effects on the downstream broadcast infrastructure won't have been editorially approved.

Your integrity as a news provider just took a severe hit because the metadata was unmonitored. The metadata might have been put there automatically by a machine, but the error was human. Don't forget to check the metadata before you ship the video to the play-out system.

Publish a Spreadsheet SYLK File ▄▄▄▄▄▄▄

Running systems-monitoring processes and needing to generate reports means that at some stage you might have to produce an Excel spreadsheet. Excel worksheet files are a completely opaque binary format. We need a textual version.

Now, we could do that with XML, but there are alternatives to the obvious solutions. Older technology solutions might deliver what you need with less complexity and a smaller performance impact on your servers. There is an old format left over from the days when Microsoft shipped a spreadsheet called Multiplan. Fortunately, Excel can still read and write these old-style SYLK files. They are exactly what we need for this task.

Follow this sequence of arguments to see how to create Excel spreadsheets dynamically. Note that this is one of several possible ways to create Excel documents. This approach is attractive if you already have a publishing pipeline for web content:

1. Content management and publishing workflows were originally deployed most widely in the generation of dynamically created web sites.
2. Web sites are constructed using HTML and CSS that are fundamentally (in their physical realization) a plain text file format.
3. XML files are likewise a plain text file format and have been proven to be as easy to generate as dynamically created HTML.
4. Excel spreadsheets are not a plain text format. We might be able to add rendering support to a publishing pipeline but significant code changes might be necessary in order to incorporate templating and dynamic tag markup.
5. We need a spreadsheet exchange format that is clear text but which can describe the 2D structure, all the formulae and most importantly the cell-to-cell linkage.
6. If we can describe a spreadsheet in this way, we can tag it up and provided our publishing pipeline is designed to replace tags with arbitrary content that is dynamically produced and it does not care about the context of those tags then we could publish these textual spreadsheet files.

First you create a model of your spreadsheet, starting with a simple cellular layout in Excel.

	Column 1	Column 2	Total column
Row 1	{aaa}	{bbb}	0
Row 2	{ccc}	{ddd}	0
Row 3	{eee}	{fff}	0

Total row	0	0	0

Figure 52 Simple spreadsheet cell layout

Although all the summing formulae are in place, the data cells are filled with values that we can find when we create a SYLK file. Because they are text, they have a value of zero. If we put braces on them, they will appear as markup that our publishing system can replace. Once we have the model completed, we export it. Most of the preamble in the file is unnecessary. It defines formats we haven't used. They are omitted from this listing, but you don't have to remove them.

```
ID;PWXL;N;E
P;P0
F;P0;DG0G10;SM0;M260;N3 10
B;Y6;X4;D0 0 5 3
O;L;F;D;V4;K47;G100 0.001
F;SLRTBM0;Y1;X2
C;K"Column 1"
F;SLRTBM0;X3
C;K"Column 2"
F;SLRTBM0;X4
C;K"Total column"
F;SLRTBM0;Y2;X1
C;K"Row 1"
F;SLRTBM0;X2
C;K"{aaa}"
F;SLRTBM0;X3
C;K"{bbb}"
F;SLRTBM0;X4
C;K0;ESUM(RC[-2]:RC[-1])
F;SLRTBM0;Y3;X1
C;K"Row 2"
F;SLRTBM0;X2
C;K"{ccc}"
F;SLRTBM0;X3
C;K"{ddd}"
F;SLRTBM0;X4
C;K0;ESUM(RC[-2]:RC[-1])
F;SLRTBM0;Y4;X1
C;K"Row 3"
F;SLRTBM0;X2
C;K"{eee}"
F;SLRTBM0;X3
C;K"{fff}"
F;SLRTBM0;X4
C;K0;ESUM(RC[-2]:RC[-1])
F;SLRTBM0;Y6;X1
C;K"Total row"
F;SLRTBM0;X2
C;K0;ESUM(R[-4]C:R[-1]C)
F;SLRTBM0;X3
C;K0;ESUM(R[-4]C:R[-1]C)
F;SLRTBM0;X4
C;K0;ESUM(R[-4]C:R[-2]C)
E
```

The first line is an ID. It must be present. The second is the only cell formatter remaining in this interchange file. The **B** line defines the cellular area, and the **O** line is an option provided specifically for Excel. The lines with leading **F** characters define formatting information, but they also control the layout of the **C** lines that describe the cell contents. The **F** and **C** lines go in pairs.

Braces are ideal for this sort of tagging, because they are distinct from the left and right caret symbols used to mark up HTML and XML. Choose something different so that you can operate on attributes within tags. It avoids creating templates that are invalid XML.

Having put in the "**{aaa}**" cell values, we can see exactly where we need to do some string replacement.

Here is a PHP loader that will read the source template, replace some strings, and save the result. It also echoes the finished translation to the screen for the web browser to display.

```
<html>
<body>
<?php
$mySylk = file_get_contents('./BaseModel.slk');
$mySylk    = str_replace('"{aaa}"', "10", $mySylk);
$mySylk    = str_replace('"{bbb}"', "20", $mySylk);
$mySylk    = str_replace('"{ccc}"', "30", $mySylk);
$mySylk    = str_replace('"{ddd}"', "40", $mySylk);
$mySylk    = str_replace('"{eee}"', "50", $mySylk);
$mySylk    = str_replace('"{fff}"', "60", $mySylk);

$myFile = fopen('./BaseModel1.slk', 'wb');
fwrite($myFile, $mySylk);
fclose($myFile);

print("******<br /><pre>{$mySylk}</pre><br />******\n");
?>
</body>
</html>
```

Note in particular how the double quotes as well as the braces are replaced. If you omit the quotes, any numeric values will be quoted and will be assumed to have a zero value by the **=sum(**...**)** formulae.

You need to watch for type and creator codes to be set correctly for Mac OS systems. PHP doesn't do this automatically. You can fix this by changing the output file type to **.xls** in the **fopen()** call. Then Excel is quite happy to open the file. It correctly deduces that it is really a SYLK file.

Windows users will probably not experience any trouble with loading the output files directly into Excel.

You can find out more about SYLK on Wikipedia.

Search Wikipedia for: "Symbolic Link SYLK"

Publish a Word RTF Document ▬▬▬▬▬▬▬

RTF files are to Microsoft Word what SYLK files are to Excel. They are a text-based exchange format. They are well-understood, and many applications can read and write them. Microsoft Office is moving towards an XML format for storing its documents. This is a positive step for interchange mechanisms, provided the XML is described openly.

RTF makes liberal use of the braces that we used as a delimiter for the SYLK solution. Make sure any tagging and markup that might be conveniently edited in Word doesn't appear confusing or get broken by the RTF formatting.

Instead of using **{tag}** as a markup, here we will use **[tag]**, because it works better in an RTF context.

If we mark up our document in Word and save it as an RTF file, we can look at it in a text editor. This is interesting, because any formatting that takes place in the RTF domain is ignored provided the RTF syntax is honored. We can introduce line breaks wherever there are braces and semi-colons, and then inspect the file. Patterns quickly emerge.

There is a heading block where we can put document info. It looks like this:

```
{\info
    {\title [ChapterHeading]}
    {\subject [Subject]}
    {\author [Firstname1] [Surname1]}
    {\keywords [Keywords]}
    {\doccomm [Comments]}
    {\operator [Firstname3] [Surname3]}
    {\creatim\yr2006\mo8\dy2\hr1\min54}
    {\revtim\yr2006\mo8\dy2\hr1\min54}
    {\version2}
    {\edmins0}
    {\nofpages1}
    {\nofwords15}
    {\nofchars114}
    {\*\manager [Firstname2] [Surname2]}
    {\*\company [Company]}
    {\*\category [Category]}
    {\*\hlinkbase [HyperlinkBase]}
    {\nofcharsws114}
    {\vern16521}
}
```

Not all of these values are present in the RTF file until you have filled in the document properties dialogue. Some, you shouldn't interfere with at all. This section of the file is the result of filling in the document properties with recognizable tag values that we can replace with a publishing tool. The operator value does not appear to have a UI cell for the content to be entered but there is a metadata property that identifies the person who last saved the document.

None of the user-information properties in this block are placed in automatically. The metadata records are only present if custom property values are specified from within Word. That won't prevent us from placing them there as part of our publishing pipeline.

```
{\*\userprops
    {\propname Checked by}       \proptype30{\staticval [CheckedBy1]}
    {\propname Client}           \proptype30{\staticval [Client]}
    {\propname Date completed}   \proptype30{\staticval [DateCompleted]}
    {\propname Department}       \proptype30{\staticval [Department]}
    {\propname Destination}      \proptype30{\staticval [Destination]}
    {\propname Disposition}      \proptype30{\staticval [Disposition]}
    {\propname Division}         \proptype30{\staticval [Division]}
    {\propname Document number}  \proptype30{\staticval [DocumentNumber]}
    {\propname Editor}           \proptype30{\staticval [Editor]}
    {\propname Forward to}       \proptype30{\staticval [ForwardTo]}
    {\propname Group}            \proptype30{\staticval [Group]}
    {\propname Language}         \proptype30{\staticval [Language]}
    {\propname Mailstop}         \proptype30{\staticval [Mailstop]}
    {\propname Matter}           \proptype30{\staticval [Matter]}
    {\propname Office}           \proptype30{\staticval [Office]}
    {\propname Owner}            \proptype30{\staticval [Owner]}
    {\propname Project}          \proptype30{\staticval [Project]}
    {\propname Publisher}        \proptype30{\staticval [Publisher]}
    {\propname Purpose}          \proptype30{\staticval [Purpose]}
    {\propname Received from}    \proptype30{\staticval [ReceivedFrom]}
    {\propname Recorded by}      \proptype30{\staticval [RecordedBy]}
    {\propname Recorded date}    \proptype30{\staticval [RecordedDate]}
    {\propname Reference}        \proptype30{\staticval [Reference]}
    {\propname Source}           \proptype30{\staticval [Source]}
    {\propname Status}           \proptype30{\staticval [Status]}
    {\propname Telephone number}\proptype30{\staticval [TelephoneNumber]}
    {\propname Typist}           \proptype30{\staticval [Typist]}
    {\propname [MyCustomData]}   \proptype30{\staticval [YYYY]}
}
```

Knowing about these and making sure the relevant blocks are present in our RTF template means we can populate the file with useful metadata that will be carried with the file wherever it goes. Because it is integral to the file, it can't get lost.

This makes RTF a suitable file format for production use. If we can solve the workflow issues of publishing RTF documents into PDF formats (which might require them to be converted to an XML document along the way), we should be able to construct a really efficient pipeline.

Here is the PHP code, which modifies the template that was created:

```php
<html>
<body>
<?php
$myRTF = file_get_contents('./SampleDoc.rtf');

/* Fill in content texts */
$myRTF    = str_replace('[ChapterHeading]',  "Example Chapter", $myRTF);
$myRTF    = str_replace('[SectionHeading]',  "Section One", $myRTF);
$myRTF    = str_replace('[BodyText]',        "We could put a lot of body text here. PHP
could load in a file and use that if we wanted. Or it could get it from a database or
external web site and do a mash-up.", $myRTF);
```

```
/* Fill in table cells */
$myRTF   = str_replace('[Column1]',          "Name",                  $myRTF);
$myRTF   = str_replace('[Column2]',          "Place",                 $myRTF);
$myRTF   = str_replace('[Column3]',          "Instrument",            $myRTF);
$myRTF   = str_replace('[aaa]',              "Stu",                   $myRTF);
$myRTF   = str_replace('[ddd]',              "Crowborough",           $myRTF);
$myRTF   = str_replace('[ggg]',              "Guitar",                $myRTF);
$myRTF   = str_replace('[bbb]',              "Pete",                  $myRTF);
$myRTF   = str_replace('[eee]',              "Hadlow Down",           $myRTF);
$myRTF   = str_replace('[hhh]',              "Drums",                 $myRTF);
$myRTF   = str_replace('[ccc]',              "Andrew",                $myRTF);
$myRTF   = str_replace('[fff]',              "Rye",                   $myRTF);
$myRTF   = str_replace('[iii]',              "Keyboard",              $myRTF);


/* Fill in metadata */
$myRTF   = str_replace('[Subject]',          "Example",               $myRTF);
$myRTF   = str_replace('[Firstname1]',       "Cliff",                 $myRTF);
$myRTF   = str_replace('[Surname1]',         "Wootton",               $myRTF);
$myRTF   = str_replace('[Keywords]',         "Metadata, Workflow",    $myRTF);
$myRTF   = str_replace('[Comments]',         "A book about workflow", $myRTF);
$myRTF   = str_replace('[Firstname3]',       "Angelina",              $myRTF);
$myRTF   = str_replace('[Surname3]',         "Ward",                  $myRTF);
$myRTF   = str_replace('[Firstname2]',       "Eric",                  $myRTF);
$myRTF   = str_replace('[Surname2]',         "Schumacher-Rasmussen",  $myRTF);
$myRTF   = str_replace('[Company]',          "Elsevier",              $myRTF);
$myRTF   = str_replace('[Category]',         "Publisher",             $myRTF);
$myRTF   = str_replace('[HyperlinkBase]',    www.elsevier.com",       $myRTF);
$myRTF   = str_replace('[CheckedBy1]',       "Eric",                  $myRTF);
$myRTF   = str_replace('[Client]',           "Focal Press",           $myRTF);
$myRTF   = str_replace('[DateCompleted]',    "Oct 2006",              $myRTF);
$myRTF   = str_replace('[Department]',       "Broadcasting systems",  $myRTF);
$myRTF   = str_replace('[Destination]',      "Amsterdam",             $myRTF);
$myRTF   = str_replace('[Disposition]',      "Finished",              $myRTF);
$myRTF   = str_replace('[Division]',         "Focal Press",           $myRTF);
$myRTF   = str_replace('[DocumentNumber]',   "00-234-999",            $myRTF);
$myRTF   = str_replace('[Editor]',           "Eric",                  $myRTF);
$myRTF   = str_replace('[ForwardTo]',        "Angelina",              $myRTF);
$myRTF   = str_replace('[Group]',            "Focal US",              $myRTF);
$myRTF   = str_replace('[Language]',         "English",               $myRTF);
$myRTF   = str_replace('[Mailstop]',         "Burlington",            $myRTF);
$myRTF   = str_replace('[Matter]',           "Metadata",              $myRTF);
$myRTF   = str_replace('[Office]',           "HQ",                    $myRTF);
$myRTF   = str_replace('[Owner]',            "Cliff Wootton",         $myRTF);
$myRTF   = str_replace('[Project]',          "Pushing The Envelope",  $myRTF);
$myRTF   = str_replace('[Publisher]',        "Focal Press",           $myRTF);
$myRTF   = str_replace('[Purpose]',          "Book manuscript",       $myRTF);
$myRTF   = str_replace('[ReceivedFrom]',     "Cliff",                 $myRTF);
$myRTF   = str_replace('[RecordedBy]',       "Cliff",                 $myRTF);
$myRTF   = str_replace('[RecordedDate]',     "July 2006",             $myRTF);
$myRTF   = str_replace('[Reference]',        "MS in progress",        $myRTF);
$myRTF   = str_replace('[Source]',           "Original",              $myRTF);
$myRTF   = str_replace('[Status]',           "In progress",           $myRTF);
$myRTF   = str_replace('[TelephoneNumber]',  "555-413-234",           $myRTF);
$myRTF   = str_replace('[Typist]',           "Cliff",                 $myRTF);
```

```
$myRTF    = str_replace('[MyCustomData]',      "StatusCode",            $myRTF);
$myRTF    = str_replace('[YYYY]',              "Pending",               $myRTF);

$myFile = fopen('./SampleDocOut.rtf', 'wb');
fwrite($myFile, $myRTF);
fclose($myFile);

print("******<br /><pre>{$myRTF}</pre><br />******\n");
?>
</body>
</html>
```

The finished document looks like this when it is loaded into Word:

Example Chapter¶
¶
Section One¶
¶
We could put a lot of body text here. PHP could load in a file and use that if we wanted. Or it could get it from a database or external web site and do a mash-up.¶
¶
¶

Name¤	Place¤	Instrument¤	¤
Stu¤	Crowborough¤	Guitar¤	¤
Pete¤	Hadlow Down¤	Drums¤	¤
Andrew¤	Rye¤	Keyboard¤	¤

¶
¶

Figure 53a An auto published Word document

Here is the summary properties page, showing the metadata properties that were published into the file.

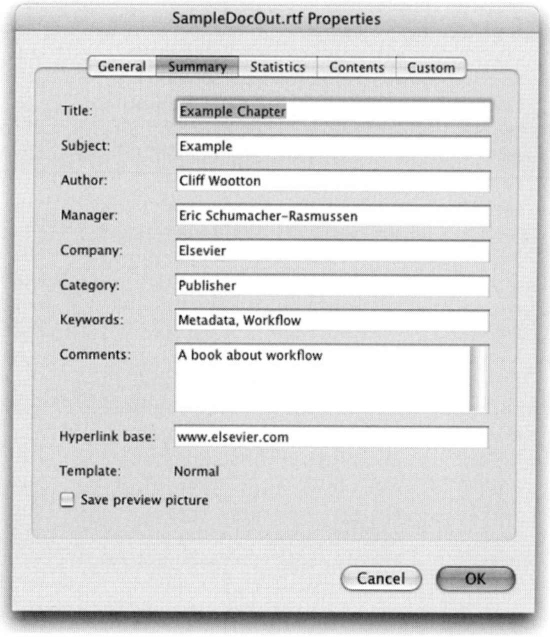

Figure 53b Document properties

And this is the custom user-defined properties page:

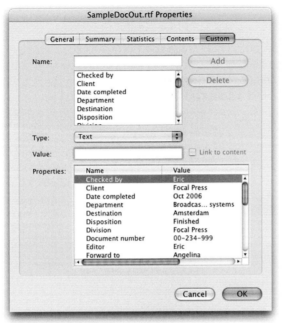

Figure 53c Custom properties

Publish an Adobe SVG ▰▰▰▰▰▰▰▰

We would want to use a drawing application like Illustrator to create our SVG diagrams from scratch. We can use the finished SVG files that Illustrator creates as a template. It is quite feasible to publish these files completely from scratch.

A useful benefit of using Illustrator is that it embeds a font in the SVG file, saving us trouble, subject to the embedding rights we have for fonts installed on our system. Illustrator interrogates the Adobe font file permissions and acts accordingly.

Here is the sample file with some brace tags added that we will replace with a PHP publisher.

```
<?xml version="1.0" encoding="iso-8859-1"?>
<!-- Generator: Custom Written Publisher)  -->
<!DOCTYPE svg PUBLIC "-//W3C//DTD SVG 1.1//EN"
"http://www.w3.org/Graphics/SVG/1.1/DTD/svg11.dtd" [
       <!ENTITY ns_svg "http://www.w3.org/2000/svg">
       <!ENTITY ns_xlink "http://www.w3.org/1999/xlink">
]>
<svg   version="1.1"
       id="Layer_1"
       xmlns="&ns_svg;"
       xmlns:xlink="&ns_xlink;"
       width="550"
       height="300"
       viewBox="0 0 500 500"
       style="overflow:visible;enable-background:new 0 0 500 500;"
       xml:space="preserve">
<style type="text/css">
<![CDATA[@font-face{font-family:'Myriad-Roman';src:url("data:;base64,\
T1RUwADACAAQA
*** Font data removed here to save space ***
                         QBpAD4AdwB3AD8=")}]]>
</style>

<path style="fill:#{FillColor};stroke:#{StrokeColor};stroke-width:{StrokeWidth};"
d="M 50,50 H 400 V 150 H 50V 50 z"/>

<text transform="matrix(1 0 0 1 75 120)"
       style="font-family:'Myriad-Roman'; font-size:70;">
{TextToReplace}
</text>

</svg>
```

Now we can construct a similar parser to the one we used for SYLK and RTF.

```
<html>
<body>
<?php
$mySVG = file_get_contents('./madeUp.svg');
$mySVG    = str_replace('{FillColor}',      "F0E0C0", $mySVG);
$mySVG    = str_replace('{StrokeColor}',    "773388", $mySVG);
$mySVG    = str_replace('{StrokeWidth}',    "8", $mySVG);
$mySVG    = str_replace('{TextToReplace}', "New Text", $mySVG);

$myFile = fopen('./madeUpOut.svg', 'wb');
fwrite($myFile, $mySVG);
fclose($myFile);

print("******<br /><pre>{$mySVG}</pre><br />******\n");
?>
</body>
</html>
```

When we run this, we get an SVG file that we can load into Illustrator.

This is interesting, because it closes the loop on Illustrator. We can export via SVG, and import via SVG, too. Once the SVG is opened in Illustrator, we can use scripts to save it in other formats.

There are many ways to exploit this to our benefit. We could embed tagging information to identify version numbers and identifying database primary key ID values in the visible portion of the document. Then when the illustration is used in a document we have tagged the original source. The color of that text could be the same as the background to create an invisible watermark. Drawing offices place complex borders round illustrations with sign-off and version control. We can add or remove that extra layer of management data with tools outside of the Illustrator application.

55

◯ Converting XML to HTML with XSLT ▰▰▰▰▰

This tutorial shows how to convert a raw XML document in XHTML. First, we start with a simple XML file (**superhero.xml**) that contains a link to the transformation stylesheet.

```
<?xml version="1.0" encoding="ISO-8859-1"?>
<?xml-stylesheet type="text/xsl" href="superhero.xsl"?>
<league>
 <superhero>
   <name>Batman</name>
   <alias>Bruce Wayne</alias>
 </superhero>
 <superhero>
   <name>Superman</name>
   <alias>Clark Kent</alias>
 </superhero>
</league>
```

Now we need to create an XSL stylesheet (**superhero.xsl**) with transformation rules:

```
<?xml version="1.0" encoding="ISO-8859-1"?>
<xsl:stylesheet version="1.0"
xmlns:xsl="http://www.w3.org/1999/XSL/Transform">
<xsl:template match="/">
  <html>
  <body>
    <h2>Justice League Members</h2>
    <table border="1">
    <tr bgcolor="#9acd32">
      <th align="left">Name</th>
      <th align="left">Alias</th>
    </tr>
    <xsl:for-each select="league/superhero">
    <tr>
      <td><xsl:value-of select="name"/></td>
      <td><xsl:value-of select="alias"/></td>
    </tr>
    </xsl:for-each>
    </table>
  </body>
  </html>
</xsl:template>
</xsl:stylesheet>
```

Opening the **.xml** file in an XSLT-compliant browser will display the table with the two lines in it.

This line iterates through the XML file looking for matches:

```
<xsl:for-each select="league/superhero">
```

This is one of two matching rules that extract the content inside the matched tag:

```
<xsl:value-of select="name"/>
```

It isn't as hard as you might have thought. Complexity comes with using large schemas and complex output formats.

56

 Making Excel Spreadsheets with AppleScript ▬▬

Using AppleScript to create Excel 2004 spreadsheets is as simple as you want to make it. This tutorial stores some values in cells using different addressing methods, creates a formula, and saves the result.

```
tell application "Microsoft Excel"
   activate
   set newBook to make new workbook
   set update remote references of newBook to true
   set value of cell 5 of column 1 of active sheet to "Sales Figures"
   set value of cell 6 of column 1 of active sheet to 10
   set value of cell 7 of column 1 of active sheet to 20
   set value of cell 8 of column 1 of active sheet to 30
   set formula of range "A9" of worksheet "Sheet1" to "=SUM(A6:A8)"
   save workbook as newBook filename "Sales.xls"
end tell
```

You could call the UNIX shell environment from AppleScript to generate the values, or you could call this AppleScript code from the UNIX environment.

Making Word Documents with AppleScript ▬▬▬▬

Creating text and putting it into a Word document is quite easy with the enhanced AppleScript support in Word 2004:

```
tell application "Microsoft Word"
    activate
    set newDoc to make new document

    create range active document start 0 end 0

    set replace selection of settings to false

    type text selection text "Title"
    type paragraph selection
    type paragraph selection
    type text selection text "Body"
    type paragraph selection
    type paragraph selection
    type text selection text "Footer"

    set titlePara to text object of paragraph 1 of active document
    set name of font object of titlePara to "Futura"
    set font size of font object of titlePara to 24

    set bodyPara to text object of paragraph 3 of active document
    set name of font object of bodyPara to "Times"
    set font size of font object of bodyPara to 12

    set footerPara to text object of paragraph 5 of active document
    set name of font object of footerPara to "Helvetica"
    set font size of font object of footerPara to 8

      save as newDoc file name "Sample.doc"
  end tell
```

This could be driven from a content management and publishing system and is an alternative to creating RTF files. This is fine for small documents, memos, and reports but probably not ideal for large projects such as books.

Scripting Alpha Channels in Photoshop ■■■■

Here is an AppleScript that drives Photoshop, creates an alpha channel and saves the file:

```
tell application "Adobe Photoshop CS2"
   set myText to "Example Text"
   set myTempFileName ¬
      to "/Users/cliff/Desktop/PStest0010.psd" as string

   activate
   make new document

   set myTextLayer to make new art layer ¬
      in current document with properties {kind:text layer}
   set properties of text object of myTextLayer ¬
      to {contents:myText, size:64 as points, position:{100, 100}}

   select all current document

   copy
   set myAlphaChannel to make new channel ¬
      in current document with properties {kind:masked area channel}
   set current channels of current document to {myAlphaChannel}
   paste

   feather selection of current document by 1

   fill selection of current document ¬
      with contents {class:RGB color, red:255, green:255, blue:255} ¬
      blend mode normal opacity 100

   deselect current document

   set current layer of current document ¬
      to background layer of current document

   delete art layer 1 of current document

   set visible of every channel of current document to true

   set myOptions to {class:Photoshop save options, save alpha channels:true}
   save current document in file myTempFileName ¬
      as Photoshop format with options myOptions ¬
      appending no extension without copying

end tell
```

⚡ Searching and Editing Word Docs ▬▬▬

While writing and editing technical books like this one, I end up with many folders containing different incremental versions of the manuscript. I want to search these to find the chapters that contain a keyword and open only the ones I need to fix something globally. I want my search tool to check the latest version and only open documents that contain that keyword as a whole word.

I developed a hybrid solution that is a UNIX shell script, which generates some AppleScript that calls a Visual Basic command inside Word. It all works predictably but requires some tricky escape coding to ensure that characters are un-escaped in the correct interpreter. Missing an escape character would mean a quote character that is intended to be evaluated in Visual Basic is parsed by the UNIX shell script. The challenge was to write a single script that contains code to be executed in all three environments.

The first step is to build an environment in shell script variables by searching the directory for the latest version of the manuscript. The **${ROOT_PATH}** variable is the starting point. It points at a directory where all the versions are stacked. The latest version is alphabetically the last one. The **ls** command lists the directory and a **tail -1** command discards all but the last entry. This is back-quote assigned into the **${LATEST_VERSION}** variable. The **${SCRIPT_PATH}** variable is defined with a temporary filename based on the process ID. Then it won't clash with any other processes that use the same technique.

Now start a search process. We begin by using a **find** command and rooting that in the latest version folder. We could have used **ls**, but **find** gives us a list of files and their whole path, where **ls** only gives us file names. It saves us having to manufacture the path.

My moral is to always let the OS do the work if possible. Some people call it lazy; I call it being pragmatic. The computer is usually faster than I am too and doesn't get bored halfway through.

The **find** command lists some spurious files that we don't want. The ones we do want are all Word documents. Their file names should all end with **.doc** file extensions. The **find** pipes into a **grep** command to filter in only the matching files. The output of the **grep** drives a **while** loop where the search processing takes place on each file.

The search extracts readable text from the binary Word documents with the **strings** command. This is filtered through some **grep** commands built around the search key. The number of times the search key matches in the file is returned to the conditional test. We reject any files with no matches and only process files that contain the search key at least once. This matching uses a regular expression to ensure we match whole words only. The search also discards any matches where the keyword is embedded inside a **HYPERLINK**. We only want to search the body text.

We need to generate a colon-separated **MAC_OS_PATH** so it can be used to construct some AppleScript code to call Word and tell it to open the files we want to edit. The **echo** statements redirect their output to the scratch file to manufacture an AppleScript that we can execute with an **osascript** command.

Rather than tell Word to open the file, we tell the Mac OS X Finder to open the file with the Word application. Then we add some AppleScript that instructs Word to set up its search facility to find the first occurrence of the keyword. You can produce the code you need by starting an AppleScript recording in the script editor and manually executing the **find** instruction you want to control with a script. It creates a script for you, but the syntax is not quite correct. Without modification, it will throw a compiler error in Word. You must have a "**do Visual Basic**" command on every line that assigns a property value.

The AppleScript source that was created dynamically is executed with the **osascript** command. After that, we clean up the temporary file.

Here is the complete script with the corrected Visual Basic syntax and a check that ensures it exits when no search key is indicated:

```sh
#!/bin/sh

if [ "|$1|" = "||" ]
then
    echo "Command <search-key>"
    exit 0
fi

SRCH_KEY="$1"

ROOT_PATH="/Volumes/WORK/PTE Book 1/Manuscript"

LATEST_VERSION=`ls "${ROOT_PATH}" | tail -1`

SCPT_PATH="/tmp/$$.scpt"

find "${ROOT_PATH}/${LATEST_VERSION}" |
grep "\.doc$"                         |
while read FILE_PATH
do
 COUNT=`strings "${FILE_PATH}" |
        grep -v "HYPERLINK" |
        grep -i "[^A-Za-z:blank:]${SRCH_KEY}[^A-Za-z:blank:]" |
        wc -c |
        tr -d ' '`

 if [ "|${COUNT}|" != "|0|" ]
 then
  MAC_OS_PATH=`echo "${FILE_PATH}" | tr '/' ':' | cut -d':' -f3-`

  echo -n ""                                                         >  ${SCPT_PATH}
  echo "tell application \"Finder\""                                 >> ${SCPT_PATH}
  echo "open document file \"${MAC_OS_PATH}\""                       >> ${SCPT_PATH}
  echo "end tell"                                                    >> ${SCPT_PATH}

  echo "tell application \"Microsoft Word\""                         >> ${SCPT_PATH}

  echo "do Visual Basic \"Selection.Find.ClearFormatting\""              >> ${SCPT_PATH}
  echo "do Visual Basic \"Selection.Find.Text = \\\"${SRCH_KEY}\\\"\""   >> ${SCPT_PATH}
  echo "do Visual Basic \"Selection.Find.Replacement.Text = \\\"\\\"\""  >> ${SCPT_PATH}
  echo "do Visual Basic \"Selection.Find.Forward = True\""               >> ${SCPT_PATH}
  echo "do Visual Basic \"Selection.Find.Wrap = wdFindContinue\""        >> ${SCPT_PATH}
```

```
   echo "do Visual Basic \"Selection.Find.Format = False\""            >> ${SCPT_PATH}
   echo "do Visual Basic \"Selection.Find.MatchCase = False\""         >> ${SCPT_PATH}
   echo "do Visual Basic \"Selection.Find.MatchWholeWord = True\""     >> ${SCPT_PATH}
   echo "do Visual Basic \"Selection.Find.MatchWildcards = False\""    >> ${SCPT_PATH}
   echo "do Visual Basic \"Selection.Find.MatchSoundsLike = False\""   >> ${SCPT_PATH}
   echo "do Visual Basic \"Selection.Find.MatchAllWordForms = False\"" >> ${SCPT_PATH}
   echo "do Visual Basic \"Selection.Find.Execute\""                   >> ${SCPT_PATH}

   echo "end tell"                                                     >> ${SCPT_PATH}

   echo ${MAC_OS_PATH}

   osascript ${SCPT_PATH}
  fi
done

rm -f ${SCPT_PATH}
```

To solve this on Mac OS X, we use three different scripting environments. This is certainly going to be possible on Windows Vista with PowerShell, but on that platform, everything would probably be accomplished within the PowerShell script.

 Beware when you design script-based tools like this. You are searching the directory structure in a specifically alphabetic order. Mac OS X Finder (and Windows Explorer) will sensibly order your files when displaying the contents of a folder having filenames with numbers in them. The document whose name is "`file 98.txt`" will be placed before "`file 100.txt`" when you view it on the desktop. UNIX filename listings would order these two items the other way round because it has no sense of the numeric value. The character '1' comes before '9'. The last item in the list of files may not be the one you expect.

Check out Tutorial 61 for details of how to wrap this in an Automator workflow action. Then it becomes a desktop tool that you can double click on to enter the search key. Awesome!

60

 Creating a Script Wrapper for Microsoft Word ◼◼◼◼◼

This tutorial shows how to wrap Word in a script so that you can connect it into your workflow in a modular way. Decide on a format for your text file. Here, I will use just a title heading and a single body text paragraph. We go through these steps:

1. Write an AppleScript (or PowerShell script) to tell Word what to do.
2. Design the script so the key parameters are placed near the top.
3. Escape any quotes in that script.
4. Wrap the escaped script in echo statements that write it to a temporary file.
5. Embed dynamic script creator into an executive body that creates the script and runs it.
6. Connect the parameters in the script to the environment variables in the shell.

Here is how to write an AppleScript to command Word 2004. This script will create a new document, insert the text and save the file. Windows PC users can use PowerShell or one of the other scripting environments to do the same thing. The commands in this script might need to change if you go back to Word X. We don't know what they might be for the version of Word shipping in the next version of Office, but we certainly hope they will stay the same.

We need to use some AppleScript code like this:

```
tell application "Microsoft Word"

    set myTitle to "My Title"
    set myBodyText to "My Body Text"
    set myOutputFile to "Output.doc"

    set myBasePath to "G415:Users:cliff:Desktop:"

    activate
    set newDoc to make new document

    create range active document start 0 end 0

    set replace selection of settings to false

    type text selection text myTitle
    type paragraph selection
    type paragraph selection
    type text selection text myBodyText
    type paragraph selection

    set titlePara to text object of paragraph 1 of active document
    set name of font object of titlePara to "Futura"
    set font size of font object of titlePara to 24
```

```
      set bodyPara to text object of paragraph 3 of active document
      set name of font object of bodyPara to "Times"
      set font size of font object of bodyPara to 12

      save as newDoc file name myBasePath & myOutputFile

      close window myOutputFile
   end tell
```

In this form, we can run and test the script as it is, but we want to wrap this in some UNIX command-line script so that it can be called within the workflow framework. Copy the source from the script editor and paste it into a new text file. Use BB-Edit or TextWrangler or whatever other IDE editor you have. VisualStudio or Notebook is fine, but you must be able to save the file as an executable shell script.

Now, we must replace any quotes with escaped quotes. If we do this first, it won't cause any problems when we enclose the whole thing in a further layer of scripting.

Use your global search-and-replace tool to change every instance of a double quote (") with a backslash followed by a double quote (\"). Check that this is the correct way of escaping quotes and fix as necessary if you aren't using the Bourne shell.

Now prefix every line with an echo and a quote character. This time the quote is starting an outer layer of quoting. At the end of every line, place a closing quote, two carets for redirection, and a reference to the temporary script file that we shall create.

Each line should now look like this:

```
echo"<escaped original line content>"  >>  ${SCRIPT_PATH}
```

Now embed this into the scripting executive container and connect the parameters so that they can be defined in the UNIX environment but are reflected in the AppleScript that is generated.

```
#!/bin/sh

MY_TITLE="$1"
MY_BODY_TEXT="$2"
MY_OUTPUT_FILE="$3"

SCRIPT_PATH="/tmp/$$.scpt"

echo -n ""                                              >  ${SCRIPT_PATH}

echo "tell application \"Microsoft Word\""              >> ${SCRIPT_PATH}

echo "set myTitle to \"${MY_TITLE}\""                   >> ${SCRIPT_PATH}
echo "set myBodyText to \"${MY_BODY_TEXT}\""            >> ${SCRIPT_PATH}
echo "set myOutputFile to \"${MY_OUTPUT_FILE}\""        >> ${SCRIPT_PATH}
echo "set myBasePath to \"G415:Users:cliff:Desktop:\""  >> ${SCRIPT_PATH}
```

```
    echo "activate"                                                      >> ${SCRIPT_PATH}

    echo "set newDoc to make new document"                            >> ${SCRIPT_PATH}

    echo "create range active document start 0 end 0"                 >> ${SCRIPT_PATH}
    echo "set replace selection of settings to false"                 >> ${SCRIPT_PATH}

    echo "type text selection text myTitle"                           >> ${SCRIPT_PATH}
    echo "type paragraph selection"                                   >> ${SCRIPT_PATH}
    echo "type paragraph selection"                                   >> ${SCRIPT_PATH}
    echo "type text selection text myBodyText"                        >> ${SCRIPT_PATH}
    echo "type paragraph selection"                                   >> ${SCRIPT_PATH}

    echo "set titlePara to text object of paragraph 1 of active document"  >> ${SCRIPT_PATH}
    echo "set name of font object of titlePara to \"Futura\""         >> ${SCRIPT_PATH}
    echo "set font size of font object of titlePara to 24"            >> ${SCRIPT_PATH}

    echo "set bodyPara to text object of paragraph 3 of active document"   >> ${SCRIPT_PATH}
    echo "set name of font object of bodyPara to \"Times\""           >> ${SCRIPT_PATH}
    echo "set font size of font object of bodyPara to 12"             >> ${SCRIPT_PATH}

    echo "save as newDoc file name myBasePath & myOutputFile"         >> ${SCRIPT_PATH}
    echo "close window myOutputFile"                                  >> ${SCRIPT_PATH}
    echo "end tell"                                                   >> ${SCRIPT_PATH}

    osascript ${SCRIPT_PATH}

    rm -f ${SCRIPT_PATH}
```

After you save the script, make sure you alter its file protections so that it can be executed. Now you can call this script, passing in the title text in parameter 1, the body text in parameter 2, and the target filename in parameter 3. Make sure the title and body texts are passed as quoted strings. This is fine for short texts, but you may need to rethink this approach for longer body texts. Passing in a reference to another source text file or using standard input redirection are both viable alternatives.

Here is how you call it from a command line:

```
MS_Script_Wrapper.sh "Title text" "Body text here…" xxx.doc
```

To alter it so that a text file containing the title and body text is used, we can reduce the number of parameters, refer to an input and output file. The title is assumed to be in the first line, which we can extract with a **head** command, and the body in the rest, which is accessed with a **tail** command.

The top part of the script where the environment variables are defined would change to this:

```
#!/bin/sh
MY_INPUT_FILE="$1"
MY_OUTPUT_FILE="$2"
MY_TITLE=`head -1 "${MY_INPUT_FILE}"`
MY_BODY_TEXT=`tail +2 "${MY_INPUT_FILE}"`

SCRIPT_PATH="/tmp/$$.scpt"
```

The quoting inside the back tick quoted section is necessary to cope with the possibility that the file paths might contain spaces.

The input text file looks like this:

```
The Title Line
The rest of the file is considered to be the body text …
```

The command line now looks like this:

```
File_Based_Version.sh input.txt zzz.doc
```

Now we can put this into a workflow. To test the technique, capture a directory listing, put a title on the top, and then pass that to Word.

```
#!/bin/sh

TEMP_FILE_PATH="/tmp/$$.scpt"

echo "Directory Listing" >  ${TEMP_FILE_PATH}
ls -la                   >> ${TEMP_FILE_PATH}

File_Based_Version.sh ${TEMP_FILE_PATH} zzz.doc

rm -f ${TEMP_FILE_PATH}
```

This creates the Word document with a title and the directory listing output. The directory listing doesn't look quite right with a proportional font. For this application, we might want to modify the AppleScript to choose a Courier font to make the directory-listing look prettier. Because the body text is now a multiple-line body, we need to rearrange the styling and paragraph creation so that we can set the body text style and let new paragraphs inherit that Courier font.

These lines insert the heading and body but also interleave the styling instead of applying the style setting at the end of the insertion process:

```
echo "set titlePara to text object of paragraph 1 of active document"  >> ${SCRIPT_PATH}
echo "set name of font object of titlePara to \"Futura\""              >> ${SCRIPT_PATH}
echo "set font size of font object of titlePara to 24"                 >> ${SCRIPT_PATH}
echo "type paragraph selection"                                        >> ${SCRIPT_PATH}
echo "type paragraph selection"                                        >> ${SCRIPT_PATH}

echo "set bodyPara to text object of paragraph 3 of active document"   >> ${SCRIPT_PATH}
echo "set name of font object of bodyPara to \"Courier\""              >> ${SCRIPT_PATH}
echo "set font size of font object of bodyPara to 9"                   >> ${SCRIPT_PATH}
echo "type text selection text myBodyText"                             >> ${SCRIPT_PATH}
echo "type paragraph selection"                                        >> ${SCRIPT_PATH}
```

Eventually when we run the script we get this output:

```
Directory Listing

total 136
drwxr-xr-x   34 cliff   cliff    1156 Dec 29 15:09 .
drwxrwxr-t   10 root    admin     340 Oct  9  2005 ..
-rw-r--r--    1 cliff   cliff       3 Feb  6  2006 .CFUserTextEncoding
-rw-r--r--    1 cliff   cliff   15364 Dec 29 15:09 .DS_Store
drwxr-xr-x    3 cliff   cliff     102 May 31  2005 .MacOSX
drwx------    5 cliff   cliff     170 Apr 27  2005 .Metadata
-rw-------    1 cliff   cliff   19771 Dec 28 15:22 .bash_history
-rw-r--r--    1 cliff   cliff    1091 Nov 13 13:14 .bash_profile
-rw-------    1 cliff   cliff      65 Mar 17  2006 .mysql_history
drwxrwxrwx   55 cliff   cliff    1870 Dec 30 00:52 Desktop
drwxrwxrwx   15 cliff   cliff     510 Dec 29 16:21 Documents
drwx------   60 cliff   cliff    2040 Nov 20 16:50 Library
drwx------    5 cliff   cliff     170 Oct 10  2005 Movies
drwx------    5 cliff   cliff     170 Apr 25  2004 Music
drwx------    7 cliff   cliff     238 Feb  6  2006 Pictures
drwxr-xr-x    5 cliff   cliff     170 Jan  4  2004 Public
drwxr-xr-x    7 cliff   cliff     238 Apr  8  2006 Sites
```

Figure 60 A script-generated document

Note that if your script calls this command:

```
set replace selection of settings to false
```

Moreover, you are using the same copy of Word to edit text, the "**Typing Replaces Selection**" preference value will be reset. You need to execute the line again to set the value true or run this in another session during which you are logged in as a different user. You could read back the current setting and restore it on exit if you want to be kinder to your users.

Change your AppleScript to preserve the settings like this:

```
set myReplaceSettings to replace selection of settings
set replace selection of settings to false
```

Then place this at the end of the script to restore the original settings.

```
set replace selection of settings to myReplaceSettings
```

Our final shell script wrapper now looks like this:

```
#!/bin/sh

MY_INPUT_FILE="$1"
MY_OUTPUT_FILE="$2"

MY_TITLE=`head -1 "${MY_INPUT_FILE}"`
MY_BODY_TEXT=`tail +2 "${MY_INPUT_FILE}"`

SCRIPT_PATH="/tmp/$$.scpt"

echo -n ""                                                      >   ${SCRIPT_PATH}
echo "tell application \"Microsoft Word\""                      >>  ${SCRIPT_PATH}

echo "set myTitle to \"${MY_TITLE}\""                           >>  ${SCRIPT_PATH}
echo "set myBodyText to \"${MY_BODY_TEXT}\""                    >>  ${SCRIPT_PATH}
echo "set myOutputFile to \"${MY_OUTPUT_FILE}\""               >>  ${SCRIPT_PATH}

echo "set myBasePath to \"G415:Users:cliff:Desktop:\""         >>  ${SCRIPT_PATH}

echo "activate"                                                 >>  ${SCRIPT_PATH}

echo "set newDoc to make new document"                         >>  ${SCRIPT_PATH}
echo "create range active document start 0 end 0"              >>  ${SCRIPT_PATH}

echo "set myReplaceSettings to replace selection of settings"  >>  ${SCRIPT_PATH}
echo "set replace selection of settings to false"             >>  ${SCRIPT_PATH}

echo "type text selection text myTitle"                        >>  ${SCRIPT_PATH}
echo "set titlePara to text object of paragraph 1 of active document"  >>  ${SCRIPT_PATH}
echo "set name of font object of titlePara to \"Futura\""      >>  ${SCRIPT_PATH}
echo "set font size of font object of titlePara to 24"        >>  ${SCRIPT_PATH}
echo "type paragraph selection"                                >>  ${SCRIPT_PATH}
echo "type paragraph selection"                                >>  ${SCRIPT_PATH}

echo "set bodyPara to text object of paragraph 3 of active document"  >>  ${SCRIPT_PATH}
echo "set name of font object of bodyPara to \"Courier\""      >>  ${SCRIPT_PATH}
echo "set font size of font object of bodyPara to 9"          >>  ${SCRIPT_PATH}
echo "type text selection text myBodyText"                     >>  ${SCRIPT_PATH}
echo "type paragraph selection"                                >>  ${SCRIPT_PATH}

echo "save as newDoc file name myBasePath & myOutputFile"     >>  ${SCRIPT_PATH}
echo "close window myOutputFile"                               >>  ${SCRIPT_PATH}

echo "set replace selection of settings to myReplaceSettings" >>  ${SCRIPT_PATH}

echo "end tell"                                                 >>  ${SCRIPT_PATH}

osascript ${SCRIPT_PATH}

rm -f ${SCRIPT_PATH}
```

We have just turned Word into a server process that can run unattended and could be used in the middle of a workflow controlled by shell scripts.

61

⚡ Putting It on the Desktop

Going back to Tutorial 59 which searches Word documents for keywords, we developed a shell script that searches a directory for candidate documents, inspects them with a UNIX command line tool (**grep**) and any candidates with the keyword are opened in Word with a search being performed.

The downside is that we need to open a terminal window and run a script manually. We also have to type in the keyword as a command line argument and it all seems inconvenient because we have to go and find the script to run. I want a tool on my desktop or in the Dock that I can double click and enter the search key.

Using Automator on Mac OS X we can build a simple workflow. Check this out when you have PowerShell on Windows Vista—similar tools are expected to be available there.

We need to get the user's input and run the shell script. That is two Automator actions.

The first one is called "**Ask For Text**" and it lives inside the TextEdit collection in the explorer list on the left. Drag this into the workflow box. Enter your prompting text and a default search key. Leave it blank if you added missing argument support to your script. Check the box that indicates that you require n answer. This value will be passed onto the next item in the workflow.

The second component runs the shell script. Add a run shell script Automator action to the workflow. This one lives in the Automator container at the left. Go find the folder that contains your static and nonmovable copy of the shell script and drag the icon onto the script text cell within this Automator action. So that Automator can find this script, check to see if there are any spaces in the path it generates. Put a back slash in front of them to escape them. You need to pass the arguments from the previous action and present them on the script's command line when it is run. There is a special string that does this. Just put a quoted string containing **$@** after your shell script:

```
"$@"
```

The at sign (**@**) signifies that the arguments come via a redirection mechanism and we put the argument in quotes to preserve any embedded spaces. The quotes are eaten by the shell script. Select the "**as arguments**" option from the Pass Input popup at the top right of the shell script action box.

Now you can save this as a workflow document that you can reuse in other workflows or an application that you can run from the desktop.

Your workflow should look something like this:

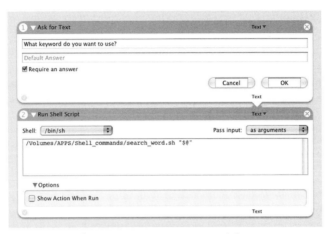

Figure 61 An Automator workflow

I saved this as an application, which I keep in the Dock so it is ready to use whenever I need it. You could attach it to a function key and call it that way. This is a massive speed improvement over searching 50 or more documents by hand.

62

 Remote Renderers and Compilers ▉▉▉▉▉▉▉

Winding the clock back to when we used large mini-computers, installing software licenses on every machine became too expensive. It is still expensive, and because we do much more on our desktop machines than we used to, license fees are a major problem for large enterprises.

I was maintaining an application that was mostly written in Fortran. A section of it needed to walk a tree-structured node hierarchy, and the original implementers couldn't get this to work properly in Fortran. Their solution was to implement this module in Pascal. I didn't have a Pascal compiler. Instead, I wrote some scripts to copy my Pascal source code to a machine in Alaska. The source was then compiled remotely and I could fetch back the object code that was produced. I could link that Pascal object code with my Fortran object code on the local machine.

This was possible, because my security permissions and access to the remote machine facilitated me doing it that way. In fact, after I wrapped it all in a script and aliased it to the Pascal compile command on my machine, you really couldn't tell this international journey was happening, apart from a slight delay with the Pascal compile command. It worked so well that the make scripts for the application build couldn't tell it was happening either.

Distributed compilation is built into development environments such as Xcode as a standard feature. Back in 1988 it was outrageously cool, now we take it for granted. We often need to do this sort of thing with graphics-rendering systems. Video-compression workflows present another task that is amenable distribution in this way. The requirements break down into some basic steps.

1. Identify the source content.
2. Identify the destination machine where the processing will take place.
3. Connect to the destination machine.
4. Deliver the source material to the destination machine.
5. Initiate the process.
6. Wait for the processing to complete.
7. Retrieve the processed output.
8. Clean up the garbage.

If we construct some command-line or GUI tools to dispatch these jobs, then we need to configure them with a list of target systems and the means of accessing them legally. That might be a text file with machine names, accounts, and login passwords, but now we have another problem: how do we hide those access codes so they can't be hacked? Some obfuscation is necessary; a little encryption should do the trick, with careful file ownership thrown in for good measure. A **.netrc** file can help solve this by giving individual users permissions without the scripts needing to contain any access codes. They don't work for users who lack the **.netrc** file.

The Expect tool might help us here if we need to use a login and password, or we might find a way to move the files to the remote system without needing to log in. Shared file systems, web server uploads, and FTP are all possible transport mechanisms. If you can do it by hand, then it also can be automated with some scripting ingenuity.

Initiating the remote process can be accomplished by having remote watch folders monitored by a server application, or we could kick a service listener on an **inetd** port to generate a trigger event. Using a PHP-driven web page or a CGI script, we can send triggers via **http:** as an alternative.

At the end of the processing run, the easiest way to get the output back again is to allow the remote system to send the results back when it is ready. It could use the same techniques as we did to deliver the files. We could continuously poll the remote server, but this is like having small child constantly tugging on your coat tails for attention. It ties up CPU effort with an unnecessary "busy checking" loop that wastes effort.

This distributed infrastructure works well when there is "intelligence" at both ends. The client script sends jobs out and initiates the processing with triggers. The server-based scripts run the applications to get the work done and send back the results. Garbage collection can then take place at the end of the script running in the remote server.

A

Data Exchange Containers

Moving Content

This appendix lists some useful file formats for exchanging content between applications.

Choosing the optimum file format for storing your content is critical. If you choose a format that applies too much compression and loses some of the information, it is gone forever. If you store this in your archives, you cannot recover that lost quality if you need to deliver to new platforms later on.

Video compression codecs are categorized as production and delivery codecs. Production codecs are lossless or so nearly lossless that the artefacts are invisible. Delivery codecs are able to sacrifice some data in order to achieve better delivery bit rates and reduced file sizes. Don't use a delivery codec for production or vice versa.

Your media asset management and storage system and any workflow processes should use uncompressed files. If compression is absolutely necessary in order to save space, then choose lossless data formats.

We have plenty of file formats to choose from for storing essence data. More recently the work has been focused on developing general-purpose containers, which can carry content (essence data and metadata), or on containers that can carry metadata alongside the essence data.

Some of your favorite formats might not be here because they are proprietary and not well suited to the exchange process. Some proprietary file formats are transparent enough that they can be used as open-exchange containers.

Essence Data File Formats

Interchanging arbitrary essence data (and metadata) between systems in structured containers can make use of use these file formats:

Table A-1 Essence data formats

Name	Description
CSV	Comma-separated data fields.
DIF	Data Interchange Format.
SQL	SQL script file for loading a database.
SYLK	Symbolic linked spreadsheet data files.

Table A-1 Essence data formats (continued)

TSV	Tab-separated data fields.
XLS	Excel spreadsheets.
XML	eXtensible Markup Language.

Text File Formats

These file formats are suited to exchanging text-based data, although some will require significant decoding work. PDF files are not nearly so easy to decode.

Table A-2 Text file formats

Name	Description
PDF	Adobe Portable Document File.
PS	PostScript page layout.
RTF	Rich Text Format file.
TROFF	Early runoff text markup formats.
XML	eXtensible Markup Language.

Graphics File Formats

These are containers for interchanging graphical content. Some are proprietary, some are lossy and some require significant decoding to extract the pictures.

Table A-3 Graphics file formats

Name	Description
DPX	Digital Picture Exchange Format.
GIF	Graphics Interchange File.
IGES	Exchange format for CAD graphical systems.
JPEG	Joint Photographic Experts Group image file.
PDF	Adobe Portable Document File.
PS	PostScript page layout.
PNG	'Ping' Portable Not Gif files.
PSD	Photoshop.
QuickTime	An object-structured container.
SVG	Scalable Vector Graphics.

Table A-3 Graphics file formats (continued)

BMP	Windows Bitmapped Pixels.
PhotoCD	A somewhat outdated format for storing 35mm film pictures onto CD.
SPIFF	Still Picture Interchange File Format Bitmap.
PPM	Portable Pixmap.
CGM	Computer Graphics Metafile (vector information).
PBM	Portable Bitmap.
IFF	Amiga Bitmap Graphic (not always used for pictures).
MIFF	Image Magick Machine Independent File Format Bitmap.
PCX	Run length-encoded image file.
TIFF	Tagged Image Format Files.
WMF	Windows Metafile.

Audio File Formats

Moving audio around in these formats may be useful, but avoid the highly compressed types for production use.

Table A-4 Audio file formats

Name	Description
AAC	Advanced Audio Coding offers high quality at low bit rates.
AAF	Advanced Authoring Format.
AIFF	Audio Interchange File Format—lossless CD quality.
ASF	Advanced Systems Format.
AVI	Audio Video Interleaved.
MIDI	Musical Instrument Digital Interface (sequences).
IFF	Amiga Sound File (not always used for sound).
MP3	Compressed audio file (not recommended for archives).
MPEG	Motion Picture Experts Group movie file.
MPEG-4	Based on, but not quite identical to, QuickTime.
MXF	Material Exchange Format.
QuickTime	An object-structured container.
WAV	Audio files with a file extension `.wav`.

Video File Formats

Some file formats are useful for moving both audio and video. They show up in both tables.

Table A-5 Video file formats

Name	Description
AAF	Advanced Authoring Format.
ASF	Advanced Systems Format.
AVI	Audio Video Interleaved.
DV	Digital Video (normally DV25).
MPEG	Motion Picture Experts Group movie file.
MPEG-4	Based on, but not quite identical to, QuickTime.
MXF	Material Exchange Format.
QuickTime	An object-structured container.

Multimedia File Formats

Multimedia is a combination of a variety of different media types. A file may contain images, audio, and video, with additional script-based playback and interaction instructions. These formats are containers or packages. They might be useful archive formats.

Table A-6 Multimedia file formats

Name	Description
MPEG-4	Based on, but not quite identical to, QuickTime.
PCF	Portable Content File.
QuickTime	An object-structured container.

Metadata File Formats

These containers are designed to transport metadata (with or without the essence data).

Table A-7 Metadata file formats

Name	Description
BWF	Broadcast Wave Format.
GXF	General Exchange Format SMPTE 360M.
MPEG-21	Emerging rights-control standard.
MPEG-7	Emerging metadata standard.
MXF	Material eXchange Format.
XML	eXtensible Markup Language.

Compressed Archive Packages

Packaging into an archive format might facilitate the delivery of multimedia content collections.

Table A-8 Compressed archive package file formats

Name	Description
ZIP	Compressed archive.
ARJ	An archiver designed by Robert Jung.
BZIP2	A high-quality, open-source data compressor.
COMPRESS	The compress tool creates `.z` compressed archive files.
GZIP	An open-source zip archiver.
JAR	Java archive files.
TAR	Tape archive files (from the UNIX heritage).
TAR.BZIP2	Tape archives subsequently compressed with bzip2.
TAR.COMPRESS	Tape archives subsequently compressed into z files.
TAR.GZIP	Tape archives subsequently compressed with gzip.

Other File Exchange and Data Formats

These containers are included because they are commonplace and may be useful in your workflow.

Table A-9 Other file exchange and data formats

Name	Description
TTF	True Type Font file.
BDF	Adobe Glyph Bitmap Distribution Format.

Mail Attachments

Transporting content from system to system via mail is not an ideal scenario, but it may be all that you have available.

It is quite feasible to create some content, package it, and attach it using the MIME extensions. You could build a web page and package the images it needs with it so that you know they are delivered. This makes an HTML e-mail safer to read than one that requires image downloads. Automatic image downloads should be avoided, as they are used by spammers to confirm that you are reading the message.

Mail can be sent through SMTP gateways by mail clients and retrieved by scripts that open and read a mailbox. Alternatively, with not too much difficulty, your applications can talk directly to an SMTP gateway to send and receive messages directly.

Internet standards are usually issued as RFC documents. Table A-10 summarizes a list of current RFCs that are relevant to mail transport in workflow scenarios. Older RFCs are obsoleted by these documents. All RFC documents are available at:

```
http://tools.ietf.org/html/rfcXXXX
```

Where **XXXX** denotes the RFC number.

Table A-10 Mail- and MIME-related RFC documents

RFC	Description
RFC 1847	Security Multiparts for MIME: Multipart/Signed and Multipart/Encrypted.
RFC 1870	SMTP Service Extension for Message Size Declaration.
RFC 2045	MIME Part One: Format of Internet Message Bodies.
RFC 2046	MIME Part Two: Media Types.
RFC 2047	MIME Part Three: Message Header Extensions for Non-ASCII Text.
RFC 2049	MIME Part Five: Conformance Criteria and Examples.

Table A-10 Mail- and MIME-related RFC documents (continued)

RFC 2231	MIME Parameter Value and Encoded Word Extensions: Character Sets, Languages, and Continuations.
RFC 2387	The MIME Multipart/Related Content-type.
RFC 2554	SMTP Service Extension for Authentication.
RFC 2821	The Simple Mail Transfer Protocol.
RFC 2822	Internet Message Format.
RFC 2920	SMTP Service Extension for Command Pipelining.
RFC 3030	SMTP Service Extensions for Transmission of Large and Binary MIME Messages.
RFC 3207	SMTP Service Extension for Secure SMTP over Transport Layer Security.
RFC 3461	SMTP Service Extension for Delivery Status Notifications.
RFC 3462	The Multipart/Report Content Type for the Reporting of Mail System Administrative Messages.
RFC 3463	Enhanced Status Codes for SMTP.
RFC 3464	An Extensible Message Format for Delivery Status Notifications.
RFC 3552	Guidelines for Writing RFC Text on Security Considerations.
RFC 3834	Recommendations for Automatic Responses to Electronic Mail.
RFC 4288	MIME Part Four: Media Type Specifications and Registration Procedures.
RFC 4289	MIME Part Four: Registration Procedures.
RFC 4409	Message Submission for Mail.

Compressed Archives

Compressed archives present us with some interesting interchange problems. Usually (but not always), they will be ZIP files. Instead, they might be self-extracting archive files. Those might also be compressed with the ZIP algorithm but with a fragment of additional code that will extract the archive from the file. A traditional ZIP unpacking application might open these self-extracting archive files. This certainly works for some self-extracting archives that only contain a Windows-based de-archive application. Using Stuffit or GZip on a Mac OS X system allows you to gain access to them.

Approaching this from a command-line point of view is probably the most valuable when building workflow systems. A GUI adds little in the way of help here.

In general, it is better not to use archiving unless you need to package a collection of items together. If you do need to do this, establish a compatible archive format that the source and target systems both understand and implement reliably. Avoid anything proprietary, and try to stick to default behavior. Unpack as soon as possible.

Web Archives

Microsoft Internet Explorer can package web pages into an archive format that contains the HTML and the images. Unpacking these archives is not difficult if you know how, but the knowledge is not widely publicized.

Resource Forks

The Macintosh operating system has always supported a special file format that is effectively two files attached to the same directory entry. The two files are referred to as *forks*.

 Because Mac OS files have two forks, some file manipulation tools only see one of them and don't correctly access the second. When you transfer a file or archive/dearchive files and folders, you must use a tool that is aware of Mac OS resource forks or risk losing some of the data. Pay special attention when using `tar`, `zip` and `rsync` tools.

The *data fork* is read and accessed like a normal file. C and other languages can open and read its contents with the standard portable calls provided by the standard libraries. The second file is called a *resource fork* and is structured internally as if an additional directory was used. It is designed to store objects or chunks of data. This concept has been reused and extended to provide flexible video storage files such as QuickTime and AVI. The resource fork should not be opened like a normal file, but instead it should be accessed via a resource manager.

Because the Macintosh operating system is based on UNIX, you might attempt to copy or archive any file you see. The UNIX operating system does not support resource forks. The result of copying a file with a resource fork using a standard UNIX utility is a file with the contents of the source data fork and NO resource fork.

There are resource fork-compatible counterparts for some of these commands.

Classic Mac OS (version 9 and older) used resource forks as described above. Mac OS X also supports a resource fork structure that is stored in a UNIX directory.

Packages in Mac OS X are implemented as a directory with a `.pkg` file extension. The same goes for applications, which are directories with a `.app` extension. In fact, this crops up in quite a few places such as Keynote presentations and installers.

You can open these folders by right-clicking or control-clicking on them. The contextual menu has an entry that says "Show Package Contents." Once opened, you can examine the internal folder structure as you would a normal folder.

 The simple solution is to copy resource fork files using AppleScript and the Mac OS X Finder. You can call this capability from a shell-script command line. Alternatively, search the man pages for resource fork-compatible versions of the commands you originally wanted to use.

Because these packages are accessible as simple UNIX directories, they can be created by publishing systems, and their contents easily accessed from a shell script.

The folder-structured resource forks are better supported on other operating systems and are more portable.

Metadata Standards

About the Standards

Some of the interesting metadata standards that I encountered during the research for this book are summarized here. You should consult the standards documents themselves for definitive element and attribute details.

Note also that new standards are emerging all the time and that this list is not exhaustive.

Reference tables of entities, identifiers and data sets in XML form with comparisons between EBU and other schemes are available at the EBU web site.

SMPTE 335M-2000 Metadata Dictionary

The SMPTE Metadata Dictionary Registry (RP 210) lists over a thousand different metadata elements organized under distinct class nodes, which are listed in Table B-1. The best way to obtain the SMPTE standards is to purchase the CD-ROM every year. It costs a several hundred dollars but it is worth it if you need to work with the standards.

Each metadata element is listed by Name, with a Definition of what it is, its data type, length, and reference to existing standards where appropriate. A full explanation is contained in SMPTE Standard "Metadata Dictionary Structure." This indicates the size of the elements in bytes that you will need if you are mapping the SMPTE scheme to your own metadata schema. Some elements are defined several times in alternative formats to allow them to represented in multiple formats.

If you want to know more about it, look at the SMPTE Metadata Registration Authority web site. There is a neat metadata dictionary browser provided by Metaglue Corporation.

Using the Diffuser tool, you can gradually unfold the dictionary class-by-class to drill down and examine the huge quantity of element and label names that have been defined. There are thousands of different items specified. You won't use them all on a single project. You might never use some of them and a few might be useful all the time. Diffuser is useful for helping you design your own scheme as a sub-set of the complete SMPTE registry. It works in conjunction with the AAFixer and MXFixer to validate AAF and MXF files against the registry.

Reference tables of metadata entities: http://www.ebu.ch/metadata/

SMPTE Metadata Registration Authority: http://www.smpte-ra.org/

Metaglue Corporation: http://www.metaglue.tv/smpte-ra/mg-diffuser.php

Download the final version of the specification from the SMPTE web site. The file with the complete list of element names and format descriptions, which you can load into Excel for inspection is called **RP210v8-final-040810MC.xls**.

Table B-1 SMPTE top-level metadata nodes

Node type	Description
1	Identification.
2	Administration.
3	Interpretation.
4	Parametric.
5	Process.
6	Relational.
7	Spatio-Temporal.
8	Unassigned.
9	Unassigned.
10	Unassigned.
11	Unassigned.
12	Unassigned.
13	Publicly registered.
14	Organizationally registered metadata.
15	Experimental use.

SMPTE UL (Unique Labels)

Metadata labels must be unique values within the scheme that is being used locally. For some items, they should be unique on a global basis. They are 16 bytes long with each byte having a specific meaning. Table B-2 lists the meaning of each byte.

Table B-2 SMPTE Unique Label (UL) long-form structure

Index	Meaning
1	Object identifier.
2	Label size.
3	ISO designator.
4	SMPTE designator.
5	Registry category designator. A value of **2** here indicates a KLV-encoded file.
6	Registry designator. A value of **5** here indicates that KLV packs have no length value and are fixed-length KV pairs. They are KV and not KLV in this case because they have a fixed length.
7	Structure designator.
8	Version number.
9	Item designator defined by the client organization.
10	Organization code. A value of **1** here indicates AAF.
11	Application. A value of **2** here indicates an MXF file.
12	Structure version.
13	Structure kind.
14	Set and pack kind. A value of **5** here indicates a primer pack containing local to global UL mapping schemes.
15	Primer version.
16	Reserved.

SMPTE UMID (Unique Material Identifier)

The SMPTE UMID is specified in SMPTE 330M. A Unique Material Identifier refers to a globally unique instance of audiovisual material. Because it is unique, the material can be linked unambiguously with its associated metadata. The UMID does not identify a finished program.

The UMID is constructed as an ordered group of components. These components identify individual parts of the audiovisual material:

- Picture.
- Sound.
- Video.
- Data.

A correctly generated UMID can be used as a globally unique dumb ID for that content.

A basic UMID contains the minimum components necessary for unique identification. As an alternative, the extended UMID is attached to a packed metadata set (source pack). This source pack contains the data for:

- Material Type code.
- Time.
- Date.
- Geo-spatial location.
- Country.
- Organization.
- User.
- Device.

The Material Type code identifies which material types are used by the content. This might describe a single material type, perhaps a mono audio track. The Material Type might also describe multiple material types in a single container, e.g., video plus surround-sound audio tracks.

While a UMID is globally unique, you would not be able to ascertain what a UMID represents without the registry belonging to the organization that created it. Since the UMID is designed to support production and post-production work, it describes fragments of programs down to a single frame. This is not the same as an ISAN value that describes a program once the production is completed.

Dublin Core Metadata Initiative (DCMI)

A wide range of skilled contributors and experts in different disciplines from a variety of backgrounds drove the Dublin Core Metadata Initiative forwards. Experts in all these fields presented ideas that were incorporated:

- Archiving.
- Traditional library management.
- Digital library systems.
- Content creation.
- Text-markup languages.

The DCMI delivers a range of standard descriptors to assist in searching for material across systems. The major descriptors that have been defined are listed in Table B-3.

Table B-3 Major DCMI descriptors

Label	Description
Title	A name given to the resource.
Creator	An entity primarily responsible for making the content of the resource.
Subject	The topic of the content of the resource.
Description	An account of the content of the resource.
Publisher	An entity responsible for making the resource available.
Contributor	An entity responsible for making contributions to the content of the resource.
Date	A date associated with an event in the life cycle of the resource.
Type	The nature or genre of the content of the resource.
Format	The physical or digital manifestation of the resource.
Identifier	An unambiguous reference to the resource within a given context.
Source	A reference to a resource from which the present resource is derived.
Language	A language of the intellectual content of the resource.
Relation	A reference to a related resource.
Coverage	The extent or scope of the content of the resource.
Rights	Information about rights held in and over the resource.

The Dublin Core Metadata Initiative scheme is designed to coexist with other metadata standards. It is quite feasible to use elements of DCMI with, the SMEF standard designed by the BBC. DCMI is simple scheme that won't support the advanced semantics that other standards do.

Dublin Core supports customized extensions that users can use in their implementations. These extensions can introduce new attributes at the highest level or but they add complexity to the scheme at a secondary level. More sophisticated schemes can be mapped to DCMI if required.

Details on the Dublin Core scheme can be found at their web site.

DCMI specifications: http://dublincore.org/

SMEF

The SMEF data model is large and complex. It is described as an *"Enterprise Semantic Data Model."* It is designed to support MAM deployment within large organizations having large data sets. Here are a few of its entity types.

Programs are represented by Editorial Objects. This would describe a complete program or a promotion or interstitial. In other standards, it might be called "a work" or "an episode." A series of programs would be an Editorial Object Group. This might also describe a season of programs or a series.

The Image Format type defines presentation characteristics of an image display. It also describes safe areas and aspect ratios.

A Media Object describes a component of an Editorial Object. It can represent audio, video, and subtitles. A Media Object must only be a single type. One Media Object represents the video and another represents the subtitles.

A Unique Material Instance (UMI) contains the attributes describing the storage or temporary existence of a physical Media Object. An attribute of a Unique Material Instance is the UMID (Unique Material Identifier) that references the SMPTE standard (330M) for the identification of material. The subtypes correspond to the "Material Type Identification" table in the SMPTE standard.

Related Media Objects are collected together as a Media Object Group. This might be a consequence of aggregating several clips during the editing process.

The UMI Usage entity maintains a provenance link to describe how instances (or copies) of a Unique Material Identifier have been used. A clip included within another must inherit some of the rights of the original parent clips, and this must be carefully maintained through a provenance hierarchy.

Other entities are provided to describe the storage format and location. Details of ingest sessions as well as physical devices used and device models, types, and manufacturers are provided in specialized entities design for that purpose.

Quite independently of the physical manifestation of the media, the ingest process, and storage location, we need to record data about what it is and who participates in it. For some clips, we will need to know details of the Content Location and what the story is about. Some kind of genre-classification scheme is also needed. All of these are used when cataloging and advertising the content. You probably wouldn't select a clip on the grounds of the device with it was ingested, but you would choose based on who was in it or the genre to which it belongs.

Story details and groups of related stories are aggregated to form Story Groups, which is particularly useful for News coverage. Editorial Description Terms describe the category or genre and might be nested to sub-divide each parenting category, as in Figure B-1:

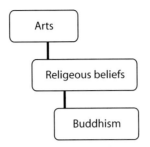

Figure B-1 Hierarchical tagging

Details of program production processes, transmission, properties of organizations, date, time, persons and places are also supported.

The entire SMEF schema comprises some Entity Relationship diagrams that span many pages in the SMEF specification. This allows the model to be traversed in a variety of ways. Having found a unique piece of media, in a complete implementation, you should be able to navigate through those relationships to find many other material identifiers that are related in different ways.

EBU P/META (European Broadcasting Union)

The P/META standard defines a set of Names and Identifiers that are explained in the standard with examples. There is no underlying model that organizes them into a hierarchy of nodes. It is probably better to think of P/META as a vocabulary. The first public version (1.0) of P/META was published in 2002. Many industry experts participated from a variety of organizations.

The EBU has sponsored the P/META Scheme as a set of definitions that provide a semantic framework for metadata that is exchanged with audio-visual material. The P/META standard creates a metadata exchange framework that is useful in a business-to-business scenario without requiring the disclosure of the participating organizations' internal business structures, workflows, and concepts. It shares the meaning of information that is useful for the commercial exploitation and exchange of program-related information and content.

Significant contributions were made by the BBC's Media Data Group that ensured that SMEF and P/META are compatible. This allows SMEF to be used inside the BBC and P/META to be used for exchanging information with other companies who may or may not be using SMEF.

Open source P/META tools: http://www.crit.rai.it/attivita/pmetatools/

P/META Scheme: http://www.ebu.ch/en/technical/metadata/specifications/notes_on_tech3295.php

The metadata descriptions identify concepts or subjects that cannot be divided into smaller components. This provides maximum precision of meaning, with maximum flexibility in the use and re-use of basic elements.

The P/META cross-industry trials make use of the MXF file format for transferring multiple essence streams with packaged metadata between systems built by different manufacturers.

One particularly attractive benefit of P/META is that both the P/META Scheme and the P/META XML Schema are offered by the EBU to users free of royalty fees and free of license to enable organizations wanting to exchange program-related metadata to share a common semantic scheme and a common technology for their metadata exchange. This is a welcome change from the recent standards processes that have been hijacked as a means of revenue generation by patent pools and licensing companies.

Details of the P/META Scheme and its XML Schema can be found at the EBU web site. Free, open-source Java-based tools for working with P/Meta and which will create the XML files are available.

EBU TN-3293

EBU Technical Note 3293 defines a simple set of metadata. This sub-set of the Dublin Core Metadata Initiative has been adapted for use in radio archives and is compatible with the main DCMI specification. It also harmonizes with metadata standards used by the broadcasting industry and which are standardized by EBU, SMPTE, and AES.

Details on the EBU Core Metadata Set for Radio Archives can be found at the EBU web site.

ISO Editorial Identifiers

SMEF recognizes three particular ISO identifiers and makes provision for them as attributes. SMPTE 330 refers to all of them; although the reference to V-ISAN isn't listed with the others, it may be implied as an extension of ISAN when V-ISAN is fully standardized. The editorial identifiers are listed in Table B-4.

Table B-4 ISO editorial identifiers

Identifier	Description
ISAN	ISO Audio-Visual Number.
V-ISAN	Version controlled ISO Audio-Visual Number.
ISBN	ISO Book Number.
ISSN	ISO Serial Number.
ISWC	ISO Musical Work Code.

EBU Core Metadata Set for Radio Archives: http://www.ebu.ch/CMSimages/en/tec_doc_t3293_tcm6-10494.pdf

Table B-4 ISO editorial identifiers (continued)

Identifier	Description
ISMN	ISO Printed Music Number.
ISCI	American Association of Advertising Industries Commercial Identifier.
ISRC	ISO Recording Code.
ISRN	ISO Report Number.
ISBD	International Federation of Library Associations and Institutions Bibliographic Descriptor.
ISTC	ISO Textual Work Code.

The ISAN, V-ISAN, and the ISRC used by SMEF are outlined below.

International Standard Audio-Visual Number (ISAN)

The ISO standard 15706:2002 which defines the ISAN format identifies an audiovisual work throughout its life. It should be used wherever precise and unique identification of an audiovisual work is required. As an identifier, it may be used for various purposes, such as to assist allocation of royalties among rights holders, to track the use of audiovisual works, for information retrieval, and for anti-piracy purposes such as verifying title registrations. It works in a way that is similar to an International Standard Book Number (ISBN).

The ISAN value can also provide a basis for identification systems such as:

- Product information for retail.
- Broadcast automation.
- Automated storage and retrieval systems.

The ISAN values can only be allocated by a designated ISAN registration agency. Like ISBN registrations, each ISAN is allocated on a one-to-one, permanent basis.

If you are provided with an ISAN value, you can look it up via a public registry. While ISAN and UMID values are equally unique on a global basis, a UMID is designed for internal use and an ISAN for public use.

Version-ISAN (V-ISAN)

The standardization process is underway to extend ISAN values to support version control. This will introduce a version identifier by extending the ISAN to include a version suffix.

ISAN web site http://www.isan.org/

V-ISAN working group (1): http://www.nlc-bnc.ca/iso/tc46sc9/wg1.htm

V-ISAN working group (2): http://www.collectionscanada.ca/iso/tc46sc9/15706-2.htm

Each separate version of the audiovisual work can then be registered with a V-ISAN. The original plan was to publish the V-ISAN standard separately as ISO 20925. It has now been aggregated as part two of ISO 15706.

This standard will have two parts. The first part specifies the identifier. The second part is the registration and resolution processes, along with the systems required to support its use.

The original ISAN specification defined an "audiovisual work" as "work consisting of a sequence of related images, with or without accompanying sound..." The V-ISAN standard is consistent with this, but with the added benefit that it can describe a version.

Where the sound track or the music video must be identified, the ISRC should be used to declare a unique reference to the audio material (see ISRC below)

International Standard Recording Code (ISRC)

The ISRC is a global method of uniquely identifying sound and music video recordings. Each ISRC is a unique and permanent identifier for a specific recording and can be encoded permanently into a product.

An ISRC is assigned to every different track of a recording where there has been new creative or artistic input. An unchanged track, when reused on a new album of recordings, will keep its original ISRC details for each track.

Details of the ISRC can be found at the International Federation of the Phonographic Industry (IFPI) web site.

MPEG-7

The MPEG-7 standard describes a "Multimedia Content Description Interface." It interacts closely with the MPEG-4 standard that describes the content and the MPEG-21 standard that describes the rights and ownerships.

In common with other MPEG standards that deal with video compression and multimedia, MPEG-7 is built around a set of tools. The available tools include:

- Description Definition Language (DDL).
- Visual descriptors.
- Audio descriptors.
- Generic entities.
- Multimedia Description Schemes (MDS).
- Generic description Schemes.
- Systems Tools.

IFPI – ISRC: http://www.ifpi.org/isrc/

MPEG-7 standard: http://www.chiariglione.org/mpeg/standards/mpeg-7/mpeg-7.htm

MPEG-7 overview: http://www.chiariglione.org/mpeg/tutorials/papers/IEEEMM_mp7overview_withcopyrigth.pdf

MPEG-7 defines a data model and is built around an XML format for describing the metadata.

There are several driving principles behind the MPEG-7 standardization process:

- A wide application base across live, stored, on-demand, online, or offline content.
- The metadata can be held separately, multiplexed and embedded, or linked to the essence data.
- A wide range of available data types for describing the metadata.
- Independent of any kind of media.
- Object-based.
- Independent of any storage format.
- Multiple levels of abstraction to provide a hierarchical model.
- Extensible enough to allow for future expansion.

MPEG-21

There is a symbiotic relationship between the three main MPEG standards emerging as a potential next-generation media infrastructure.

MPEG-4 describes the essence data. MPEG-7 is a metadata framework, which can be used to wrap the essence data so that it can be more easily managed. MPEG-21 completes the architecture by providing a way to find and rights-manage the content. The idea is to relate, integrate, and interact between the content, its metadata, the providers, and consumers.

Like most MPEG standards, the MPEG-21 standard is broken down into parts (listed in Table B-5):

Table B-5 MPEG-21 parts

Part	Description
1	Vision, technologies, and strategy.
2	Digital Item Declaration (DID).
3	Digital Item Identification (DII).
4	Intellectual property management and protection (IPMP).
5	Rights Expression Language (REL).
6	Rights Data Dictionary (RDD).
7	Digital Item Adaptation (DIA).
8	Reference software.
9	File format.
10	Digital Item Processing (DIP).

Table B-5 MPEG-21 parts (continued)

11	Evaluation methods for persistent association technologies.
12	Test bed for MPEG-21 resource delivery.

MPEG-21 is implemented using its own XML schemas and namespaces. Refer to the goals and aspirations document for an overview of how it is intended to work.

TV-Anytime

The TV-Anytime standard describes a mechanism for discovering programs using metadata-searching techniques. This yields a Content Reference Identifier (CRID) that is then resolved into a locator to find an instance that can be accessed. This is an ideal technology for PVR, DVR and IPTV platforms.

A CRID value is not the same as a UMID, although it is a unique reference to a program. The CRID is more like an ISAN than a UMID, because the public uses it. UMID values are used inside an organization and are kept confidential.

The TV-Anytime standards process is now complete, and the documents describing it are available from ETSI. It is attractive as a standard but is only gradually being adopted.

In the U.S., a competing standard (VOD Metadata) introduced by Cable Labs for Video On Demand applications is being rapidly adopted.

Digital Object Identifier (DOI)

The Digital Object Identifier (DOI) System is an identification system for digital media, originally developed by the American Association of Publishers and subsequently by the International Publishers Association. The International DOI Foundation is now working to extend the DOI to a wide range of digital content.

Other Models

The metadata standards listed in Table B-6 are additional documents that you may find interesting. Some of the documents belong to EBU member organizations and are listed on the EBU web site. Commercial licensing details for them may vary. Some of them may support the same open-availability models as the EBU.

MPEG-21 goals and aspirations: http://www.chiariglione.org/mpeg/tutorials/papers/MMpaper.pdf

TV-Anytime forum: http://www.tv-anytime.org/

VOD Metadata home page: http://www.cablelabs.com/projects/metadata/

DOI handbook: http://www.doi.org/handbook_2000/intro.html

Other specifications: http://www.ebu.ch/en/technical/metadata/members_specs/index.php

Table B-6 Additional standards documents

Specification	Description
DDV Metadata model	File-based program contribution provided by Beeld & Geluid.
DR Metadata standard	Metadata as used by DR (Danish broadcaster).
XTRADIO	Metadata used for Eurovision radio exchanges.
NMS	News Management System for use by Eurovision partners.
SVT Metadata model	Model used by SVT (Swedish television).
Escort 2006	EBU system for the genre classification of radio and television programs (2006 version).
Escort 2.4	EBU system for the genre classification of radio and television programs (earlier version).
PDC	ETSI standard EN 300 231 describes Program Delivery Control data which includes a genre tagging scheme.
PBCore	Public Broadcasting Metadata Dictionary.
Tribune	A commercial organization that supplies data for EPG listings.
MIME	Multipurpose Internet Mail Extensions.
IBTN	EBU International Broadcast Tape Number.
Dewey Decimal	A library cataloging scheme.
DMS-1	Library-oriented metadata standard.
LCMCS	Library of Congress Music Classification Schedule.
NLCS	National Library of Congress Scheme.
SMPTE RP 210	Metadata Dictionary.
DTV	Digital Television services describe packaging of data into a broadcast stream. Your metadata will end up here en route to the viewer.
EPG	Electronic Program Guides are available as embedded data streams that you can extract from the broadcast signal or as online services that can be downloaded. There are standards for the format and structure. Some data is available in nonstandard ways.
ATSC	Advanced Television Standards Committee is the U.S. equivalent of DVB for standardization of digital TV services.
PSIP	The Program and System Information Protocol standard describes how metadata is carried in an ATSC transmission.
DVB	Digital Video Broadcasting consortium. Primarily European standards-oriented. Some DVB standards work is applicable in the USA.
DVB-SI	The DVB equivalent to PSIP for carrying EPG metadata and service information. (ETSI EN 300 468).

Table B-6 Additional standards documents (continued)

MPEG-21	Rights-control metadata scheme.
IPTC	IPTC data is a method of storing textual information in images defined by the International Press Telecommunications Council.
XMP	Adobe eXtensible Metadata Platform for Photoshop and other Creative Suite tools.
ebXML	Electronic Business XML, an interchange mechanism for business and commerce.

Important File Formats

The file formats listed in Table B-7 are emerging as useful containers for exchanging data between systems:

Table B-7 Important file formats

Format	Description
EXIF	EXIF stands for Exchangeable Image File Format, and is a standard for storing interchange information in image files, especially those using JPEG compression. Favored by digital camera manufacturers.
TT AF	The W3C Timed Text Authoring Format represents text media for interchange between authoring systems. Timed text is textual information that is associated with timing information such as subtitles.
DFXP	Distribution exchange format profile.
AFXP	An enhanced exchange format for authoring subtitle content once and mapping it to many other outlets. Still in development and expected to support graphics as well as text.
MXF	Pro-MPEG Material eXchange Format.
GXF	The General eXchange Format was originally conceived by Grass Valley Group for the interchange of simple camera shots over data networks and for archival storage on data tape. Now standardized as part of SMPTE 360M.
	Be careful not to confuse this with other geographic file exchange standards that use the same three-letter acronym.
BWF	Broadcast Wave Format for storing audio.
BMF	IRT Broadcast Metadata exchange Format.
DPX	Digital Picture eXchange Format, designed to transport moving image representations in a file per frame structure.
AAF	Advanced Authoring Format.
ASF	Advanced Systems Format.

A Simple Metadata Dictionary

Metadata Object Examples

These are some basic designs for metadata objects. Think of these as starting points; you may want to add more properties. This doesn't conform to any particular metadata standard but draws ideas from them all. It's also not exhaustive and you need to design this around your own business model and its logic.

People

This object would be created as a master node to describe each person. They might have role objects attached. Joins to media would take place through a reference back to this object from the media objects.

Table C-1 Person object properties

Property	Format
Person name	Choose a length that is long enough to accommodate your longest expected name. Use this form if you don't want to break the name down into components.
Title	Mr., Mrs., Dr., Rev., etc.
First name	Given name.
Middle initial	This might be an initial or a name for more official data systems.
Surname	Family name.
Honorifics	Qualifications such as MD, PhD, etc.

Places

Location related data could be stored in a place object. This is abased around the concept of an address but other kinds of locations could be created. Locations and persons probably need to be linked in some way. Either by referring to the location from the person in the case of a home address or joining many persons to a location in the case of a business location where they all work.

Table C-2 Place object properties

Property	Format
Address structure	House name, number and street name, optional village, town, county, state, ZIP code. Note that additional lines may be needed to cope with apartments.
House name	Sometimes addresses are unnumbered, especially in rural areas.
Apartment number	Many buildings have been converted to apartments.
Village	Towns tend to be aggregated from several smaller villages.
Town	Collectively the town is the main postal area.
County	County names are helpful when sorting and checking. This might be replaced by a City name when dealing with urban areas.
Postal (ZIP) code	Postal codes must conform to a strict layout but that layout needs to be geographically relevant. It is different in each country.

Media Containers

This object describes the container in which some media is stored. Normalization suggests that it should just describe the container and noting about the program material.

Table C-3 Media container object properties

Property	Format
Clip ID	A UMID value that uniquely identifies the video or audio clip.
Title	A title for the clip.
Description	A descriptive paragraph of text.
Video clip	A reference to a file containing the essence data. This might need to include a machine name. Something formatted like a URI might be ideal. Ensure the space is big enough.
Audio clip	Similar to a video file. This also points at the essence data.
Image file	Pointer to an essence file.
Video browse	A low-res, low bit-rate copy of the master video file.
Image thumbnail	A reduced-size copy of the master image.
Video thumbnail	A reduced-size screenshot as a single picture.

Media Content

This object describes a program but has nothing to do with the way that it is stored. This record would be common to a VHS and DVD release of a program. Each of those releases would have a separate object to describe their specific attributes.

Table C-4 Media content object properties

Property	Format
TV program	An ISAN value that identifies a finished TV program.
TV series	An ISAN value that identifies a TV series.
Series name	A textual title for the series.
Season number	Which season of a multiseason series.

Content Owner

The rights owner is described in this object. There are many more properties we could add to this object.

Table C-5 Content owner object properties

Property	Format
TV channel air time	Details of the broadcast date and time.
Production company	Detail of the company that owns the video program.

Code Sets

ASCII Code Sets with Remapped Characters

Files using these formats require filtering because characters some 7-bit ASCII printable characters have been remapped.

Table D-1 ASCII-based code sets with remapping

Name	Description
ATASCII	Atari Standard Code for Information Interchange.
PETSCII	Commodore PET Standard Code of Information Interchange.
CBM ASCII	Another name for the Commodore PET Standard Code of Information Interchange.
ZX Spectrum	Sinclair special character set.
YUSCII	Yugoslav Standard Code for Information Interchange.
Galaksija	Character set of Galaksija kit computer.
ISO-646-DE	German DIN 66003 remapped ASCII.
ISO-646-DK	Danish DS 2089 remapped ASCII.
ISO-646-CA	Canadian CSA Z243.4 remapped ASCII.
ISO-646-CN	Chinese GB 1988-80 remapped ASCII.
ISO-646-CU	Cuban NC NC00-10 remapped ASCII.
ISO-646-ES	Spanish remapped ASCII.
ISO-646-FR	French NF Z 62-010 remapped ASCII.
ISO-646-HU	Hungarian MSZ 7795.3 remapped ASCII.
ISO-646-IT	Italian remapped ASCII.
ISO-646-JP	Japanese JIS X 0201 Roman remapped ASCII.
ISO-646-KR	Korean KS C 5636 remapped ASCII.
ISO-646-NO	Norwegian NS 4551-1 remapped ASCII.
ISO-646-PT	Portuguese remapped ASCII.
ISO-646-SE	Swedish SEN 850200 B remapped ASCII.
ISO-646-UK	British BS 4730 remapped ASCII.
ISO-646-YU	Yugoslavian JUS I.B1.002 remapped ASCII.

Latin Code Sets

These code sets are based on ASCII but have been augmented with other character encodings.

Table D-2 Latin code sets

Name	Description
ISO 8859-1	Latin-1. West European (Western).
ISO 8859-2	Latin-2. Central and East European.
ISO 8859-3	Latin-3. Maltese and Esperanto.
ISO 8859-4	Latin-4. North European (Baltic).
ISO 8859-5	Latin/Cyrillic for Slavic countries.
ISO 8859-6	Latin/Arabic. Middle East.
ISO 8859-7	Latin/Greek.
ISO 8859-8	Latin/Hebrew.
ISO 8859-9	Latin-5. Turkish.
ISO 8859-10	Latin-6. Nordic languages.
ISO 8859-11	Latin/Thai.
ISO 8859-12	Abandoned attempt to create a Devengari variant.
ISO 8859-13	Latin-7. Baltic Rim countries.
ISO 8859-14	Latin-8. Celtic.
ISO 8859-15	Latin-9. Modified 8859-1 to accommodate the Euro currency symbol.
ISO 8859-16	Latin-10. South Eastern Europe.

Partially Incompatible ASCII Code Sets

These code sets should be compatible as far as the lower 128 are concerned, but higher characters may differ:

- Extended ASCII.
- UTF-8.
- ISO 8859.
- ISCII.
- VISCII.
- Windows code pages.

Unicode Encodings

Table D-3 Unicode encodings

Encoding	Description
UTF-7	Variable-length encoding for ASCII compatibility.
UTF-8	Variable-length byte encoded.
CESU-8	A variant of UTF-8 used mainly for Oracle databases.
UTF-16	Variable-length 16 or 32 bits.
UCS-2	A limited subset of UTF-16.
UTF-32	Fixed-width four-byte representation.
UCS-4	An alias for UTF-32 that means the same thing.
UTF-EBCDIC	A means of representing Unicode in mainframe computers.
SCSU	Standard Compression Scheme for Unicode (not recommended for use).
Punycode	Special subset of minimal Unicode for non-ASCII DNS domain names.
GB 18030	Default Chinese national standard which is Unicode compatible.

Windows Code Pages

These are code pages that overlay the underlying ASCII coding scheme for international variants of the Windows operating system.

Table D-4 Windows code pages

Code page	Language
37	EBCDIC.
437	Original IBM-PC.
500	EBCDIC.
708	Arabic.
709	Arabic.
710	Arabic (OEM secondary).
720	Arabic.
737	Greek.
775	Estonian.
850	Western European languages.
852	Central European languages.
855	Cyrillic (MS-DOS).

Table D-4 Windows code pages (continued)

Code page	Language
857	Turkish.
858	Western European languages.
860	Portuguese (OEM secondary).
861	Icelandic (OEM secondary).
862	Hebrew.
863	Canadian (French and English).
864	Arabic (OEM primary).
865	Scandinavian (Icelandic, Finnish, Norwegian, Swedish).
866	Cyrillic.
869	Greek.
874	Thai text (see ISO 8859-11).
875	Greek EBCDIC.
932	Four-byte CJK (Japanese SJIS).
936	Four-byte CJK (Chinese GBK).
942	Japanese.
949	Four-byte CJK (Korean Hangul).
950	Four-byte CJK (Taiwan and Hong Kong Big5).
1026	EBCDIC.
1250	Central European Latin (similar but not identical to ISO 8859-2).
1251	Cyrillic text (similar but not identical to ISO 8859-5).
1252	Latin text (see ISO 8859-1).
1253	Modern Greek (similar but not identical to ISO 8859-7).
1254	Turkish (see ISO 8859-9).
1255	Hebrew (similar but not identical to ISO 8859-8).
1256	Arabic script (unlike ISO 8859-6).
1257	Estonian, Latvian and Lithuanian text (similar but not identical to ISO 8859-13).
1258	Vietnamese text (based somewhat on ISO 8859-1).
1361	Korean (OEM secondary).

Regular Expressions 101

Living Dangerously

Regular expressions are useful for matching organized patterns of letters and numbers. Throughout the tutorials in Part 2 of this book you will see that regular expressions can solve a complex pattern matching problem with ease.

There are some simple rules and some not-so-simple rules. The regular expression (or *regex* for short) is composed of meta-characters and literals. Meta-characters have special meaning, and if you want to use them as literals, they will need to be escaped. The regex is then constructed with framing characters that control the evaluation order. In many ways, they are like a mathematical expression, although they operate on strings of characters.

We will examine sufficient regular expression syntax to make a start and become dangerous. To find out how regular expressions work in detail, you can spend a whole month on your own tinkering with them at your own pace. It is worth the effort, because they are useful in Perl, PHP, and UNIX command lines, as well as find/replace boxes in text editors and command-line tools such as **sed** and **awk**.

Meta-Characters and Components

Table E-1 shows some simple regex components.

Table E-1 Regular expression meta-characters	
Meta	*Meaning*
.	A single full stop will match any single character at that point in the string.
*	Whatever character or meta-character is to the left of the asterisk will be matched from zero up to as many times as it is repeated.
+	Match at least one of the values to the left and also allow as many as are required to match the repeats.
?	Whatever character or meta-character is to the left may appear zero or exactly once only.
{n}	Used like the * operator but the value inside the braces specifies how many repeats. It is called the bounds operator.

Table E-1 Regular expression meta-characters (continued)

{n,m}	Indicate how many matching characters to the left. Minimum **n** characters, maximum **m** characters.
[ ]	Range specifiers.
[0-9]	A numeric character range list.
[a-z]	A lower-case letter range list.
[A-Z]	An upper-case letter range list.
[^ ...]	Matches any character other than those in the range.
\	Escape a meta-character so that it can be used as a literal.
( )	Brackets control precedence. The item in brackets is an atom.
\<	Matches the start of a word.
\>	Matches the end of a word.
|	Vertical bar separates alternative matches within a level of precedence.
!	A branch separator. The item to the left is matched first, and then, if true, the item to the right is matched. This is a multiple-layered match.
\1, \2, etc.	Matches the text previously matched in earlier sets of parentheses. Useful for matching duplicates of the same complex string within a line.

Regular Expression Examples

Using the meta-characters listed above, here are some simple regular expressions. These are the starting components for building bigger expressions.

Table E-2 Example regular expressions

Regex	Meaning
^.*$	Match the entire line regardless of how many characters are in it.
^.	Match only the first character in the line.
.$	Match only the last character in the line.
[0-9]	Match a single numeric digit.
[0-9]{5}	Match any sequence of five numeric digits.
^[0-9]*$	Match a numeric string rejecting any that contain non-numeric values.

Table E-2 Example regular expressions (continued)

`([0-9]|[A-F])`	Match a single numeric digit between 0 and 9 or a letter between A and F. This is hexadecimal.
`^$`	Empty line.
`()`	Empty atom.
`^([0-9]{5} | [0-9]{5}\-[0-9]{4})$`	USA ZIP code.
`^[A-Z]{2}[0-9]*.[0-9] [A-Z]{2}$`	UK postal code.
`\$[a-zA-Z][a-zA-Z0-9]*`	PHP variable names.
`"[^"]*"`	Quoted strings.
`\£[0-9]+(\.[0-9][0-9])?`	Currency values.
`\£[0-9]+(\.[0-9]{2})?`	Currency values (alternate form).

Here are two regular expressions that are too long to fit in the above table of examples. The first one is for a 24 hour clock time value:

```
([01]?[0-9]|2[0-3]):([0-5][0-9]):([0-5][0-9])
```

The second one is for a 12 hour clock time value:

```
(1[012]|[1-9]):([0-5][0-9]):([0-5][0-9]) (am|pm)
```

Glossary

Term	Definition
AAF	Advanced Authoring Format administered by the AAF Association. AAF is a file format that wraps essence data with its associated metadata to encapsulate them in one package.
AFXP	Authoring Format eXchange Profile. An enhanced version of DFXP for authoring subtitle content once and mapping it to many other outlets. Still in development, and expected to support graphics as well as text.
AJAX	Asynchronous JavaScript and XML is a technique where transactions are moved between a client web page and a server using XML.
Array	A collection of objects that is accessible by index number.
ASF	Advanced Systems Format.
Asset	An asset is some content plus its rights-management properties.
Atom	Atom Syndication Format.
ATSC	The Advanced Television Standards Committee.
Boolean	Represented as either **TRUE** or **FALSE**.
C	A compiled programming language.
Character	Individual character glyphs mapped into one of many alternative character sets.
ChemML	Chemical modeling Markup Language.
Content	Combining Essence data and Metadata together.
Creator	The author of the original content.
Curator	The agent of the owner who administers and looks after specific content on a day-to-day basis.
Custodian	The person who has official or technical responsibility for making sure a system works or content is available.
Data center	A data centre might be shared across an entire enterprise with multiple systems connected together passing work from one to another.
Data model	A model that describes how data is represented in an information system or a database in its abstract form.

Databases	A database containing many tables can have relationships constructed between the tables.
Date	Date and time are usually represented internally by a tick count resolved to millisecond accuracy.
DCMI	The Dublin Core Metadata Initiative.
DFXP	Distribution Format eXchange Profile.
Dictionary	A vocabulary that is organized with connected objects associated with each entry. See also Metadata Dictionary.
DocBook	Book manuscripts in XML form.
Domain	An information system is designed to function in a certain context. This is called its domain.
DPX	Digital Picture eXchange Format.
DTD	Document Type Definition. This is used by XML to control how the semantic content within the XML container is interpreted.
DTV	Digital TeleVision services describe packaging of data into a broadcast stream.
DVB	Digital Video Broadcasting consortium. Primarily European standards-oriented.
DVB-SI	The DVB equivalent to PSIP.
EBU P/META	The P/META standard defines a set of Names and Identifiers that are organized as a vocabulary.
Ecology	A collection of enterprises collaborating for mutual benefit.
Editor	The person responsible for making changes to content.
EPG	Electronic Program Guides.
Essence	The media or data that embodies the content.
Essence data	Describes the text, pictures, sound or moving images.
EXIF	EXchangeable Image File Format.
Expect	Designed for controlling user interfaces through scripts.
Fields	Strings of data with semantic meaning such as dates.
Floating-point number	Floating-point values can represent a wide range of values.
Geo-codes	Standardized country codes.
Geo-IP	The process of mapping an IP address to a geographic point.
Geo-location	Locating a point within the geography.
Geo-Ref	A military standard for locating points in battle planning.
GIS	Geographical Information System.
GML	Geography Markup Language.

GPS	Geographic Positioning System.
GXF	The General eXchange Format.
Information System	Interoperating components that represent, store and manage the information and knowledge relating to a domain.
Integer number	Integers are considered separately from floating-point values because they are a simpler data type.
ISAN	ISO Audio-Visual Number.
Join	A relational link between a record in one table and a corresponding record in another. Uses primary and foreign keys to make the join.
KLV	Key Length Value organization of parameters. The key is a named label while the data is described as a number of bytes following it.
Librarian	A person whose general duty is organizing assets and keeping a collection neat and tidy.
MathML	Mathematical formulae Markup Language.
Metadata	Describes the properties of the essence data.
Metadata Dictionary	A reference table of all the meanings for the metadata keys in a scheme. The consistency of the metadata can be improved by creating a dictionary and referring to it when needed.
Metadata Register	An alternative name for the Metadata Dictionary.
Metadata Scheme	A description of the organization of metadata in a collection. Pre-defined schemes such as Dublin Core Metadata Initiative can be used as a starting point when developing your own schemes. Implemented as a pre-defined dictionary of definitions with rules for how they can be combined.
Mob	A Metadata Object. This is the data structure that contains a fragment of metadata and labels it with a unique identifying name so it can be distinguished from other Mobs and referred to by reference.
MPEG-7	The MPEG-7 standard describes a "Multimedia Content Description Interface."
MusicXML	Music scores Markup Language.
MXF	Pro-MPEG Material eXchange Format. A file format that works similarly to AAF and can be used as an alternative packaging container. This is being integrated in a variety of broadcasting hardware and software.
MySQL	A useful and capable database, which is handy for general-purpose data storage and workflow content management.

NaN	Not a Number signifies the result of a calculation that generated an error.
NewsML	XML schema for Syndicated news stories.
Number types (other)	Fixed, financial, scientific octal, hex and other number bases (radix values).
Numbers	Numbers come in a variety of different formats. They can be represented as a binary value or a string of characters.
Object	A container for data.
ODT	XML document format used by Open Office Org.
Ontology	A collection of objects with some insights into their unique identity, existence, and classification.
Open eBook	An XML based format for producing eBooks.
Owner	Someone who receives monetary rewards for fee-based deployment of the content.
PDC	Program Delivery Control as specified by ETSI also describes a genre-tagging scheme.
Perl	A useful tool for a wide range of general-purpose tasks. Especially good for text processing. Based on C, but with language additions from Bourne Shell.
PHP	Designed for dynamic web page creation.
PSIP	The Program and System Information Protocol standard describes how metadata is carried in an ATSC transmission.
Python	A dynamic programming language capable of many general-purpose tasks.
RDF	Resource Description Frameworks.
Records	A collection of related fields.
Reference	A pointer to related information. Uses the ID associated with a Mob to point at another object.
Reference Data	A defined set of static values that can be referenced from other metadata objects.
Register	An alternative name for the Metadata Dictionary.
Registry	A repository or storage system with authority to mandate the meaning of items registered in it. Primarily used to ensure that registered entities to not duplicate or clash with one another and to ensure better interoperability.
Remote Sensing	Using satellite or aerial photography to map surface attributes and correlate them with a projected map.
RSS	Really Simple Syndication.

Ruby	A wholly object-oriented, general-purpose language similar to Perl and SmallTalk, but somewhat different from Python.
Schema	A formal description of the way data is organized in an XML document. Also used to describe the organization of a SQL database.
Scheme	A metadata scheme collects the model, vocabulary, and taxonomy together into a standardized structure. See also Metadata Scheme.
SMEF	Standard Media Exchange Framework, an "Enterprise Semantic Data Model," designed to cope with large data sets.
SMPTE 335M	The SMPTE Metadata Dictionary Registry.
Standing data	AKA: Reference Data.
Static data	AKA: Reference Data.
String	Character data is stored as a collection of characters that can be organized to mean something such as a financial value or a person's name.
Style Sheet	A CSS style sheet.
Stylesheet	An XML stylesheet.
SVG	Scalable Vector Graphic markup language.
Synonym	A connection between two separate metadata dictionary items that mean the same thing or something very similar.
System	A system is a connected set of applications that might operate on the databases and communicate with one another.
Tables	A table collects multiple rows together.
Taxonomy	An organized collection of data.
Tcl	Tool Command Language development kit.
Thesaurus	Like a dictionary but associates an item with synonyms.
TT AF	The W3C Timed Text Authoring Format.
TV-Anytime	The TV-Anytime standard describes a mechanism for discovering programs using metadata-searching techniques.
UL	Universal Labels are formed of a 16-byte number that can be used to construct a table of Metadata entities. subsets of these UL values are used in KLV coding within MXFG files.
UNIX shell	Command line environment for operating UNIX workstations.
V-ISAN	Version controlled ISO Audio-Visual Number.
Vocabulary	A genre-tagging scheme.
WebObjects	A good way to build dynamic web sites and is used behind some of the world's leading online sites.

Wrapper	Another name for the packaging of content with the wrapper being placed around Essence data and Metadata.
XBEL	Bookmark exchange in XML form.
XBRL	eXtensible Business Reporting Language.
XHTML	Web page content that is XML compatible.
XML Encryption	Defines the syntax and rules for encrypting XML document content.
XML Schema	The language used to describe the contents of XML documents. It normally designates a particular Schema definition, which describe the names and formats of entities in an XML document.
XML Signature	Defines the syntax and rules for creating and processing digital signatures on XML document content.
XPath	Refers to individual fragments within an XML document.
XPointer	Describes a system for addressing components of XML-based internet media.
XQuery	XML Query language.
XSL FO	eXtensible Stylesheet Language – Formatting Objects.
XSPF	XML Shareable Playlist Formal.
XUL	XML User Interface Language.
XUpdate	A lightweight query and update mechanism that has now apparently gone into hibernation.

Bibliography

Austerberry, David. *Digital Asset Management*. Focal Press, 2004.

Barber, Nan, Tonya Engst & David Reynolds. *Office X for Macintosh—Missing Manual*. Pogue Press, 2002.

Born, Günter. *The File Formats Handbook*. Thomson Computer Press, 1995.

Campesato, Oswald, *Fundamentals of SVG Programming*. Charles River Media, 2004.

Cichocki, Andrzej, Marek Rusinkiewicz and Darrell Woelk. *Workflow and Process Automation Concepts and Technology*. Kluwer Academic Publishers.

Cox, Mike, Linda Tadic and Ellen Mulder. *Descriptive Metadata for Television*. Focal Press, 2006.

Dolin, Penny Ann. *Exploring Digital Workflow*. Delmar Thomson Learning.

Dougherty, Dale. *sed & awk*. O'Reilly, 1992.

Friedl, Jeffrey. *Mastering Regular Expressions*. O'Reilly, 1997.

Gamma, Rich, Richard Helm, Ralph Johnson, & John Vlissides. *Design Patterns*. Addison Wesley, 1995.

Garnett, Walt. *Garbage In, Gorgeous Out: Text and Graphics Translation*. McGraw Hill, 1995.

Gilmer, Brad (Ed). *File Interchange Handbook*. Focal Press, 2004.

Gruber, Wolfgang. *Modeling and Transformation of Workflows with Temporal Constraints*. IOS Press.

Hupp, Toni. *Designing Work Groups, Jobs, and Work Flow*. Pfeiffer & Company.

Jackson, Michael and Graham Twaddle. *Building Workflow Systems*. Addison-Wesley.

Jacobsen, Jens, T. Schlenker, & L. Edwards. *Implementing a Digital Asset Management System*. Focal Press.

Kahn, Rashid N. *Understanding Workflow Automation*. Prentice Hall.

Kobielus, James G. *Workflow Strategies*. Hungry Minds.

Kochan, Stephen and Patrick Wood. *UNIX Shell Programming*. Hayden Books, 1990.

Korpela, Jukka K *Unicode Explained*. O'Reilly, 2006.

Latham, Lance. *Standard C Date/Time Library*. R & D Books, 1998.

Manjunath, B.S., Phillippe Salambier and Thomas Sikora. *Introduction to MPEG-7*. Wiley, 2002.

Marinescu, Dan C. *Internet-Based Workflow Management*. John Wiley & Sons.

Martelli, Alex (Ed). *Python Cookbook*. O'Reilly, 2002.

Neuberg, Matt. *AppleScript—The Definitive Guide*. O'Reilly, 2006.

Newham, Cameron, and Bill Rosenblatt. *Learning the bash Shell*. O'Reilly, 1998.

Poyssick, Gary. *Managing Digital Workflow*. Prentice Hall.

Poyssick, Gary and Steve Hannaford. *Workflow Reengineering*. Adobe.

Rimmer, Steve. *Bit-Mapped Graphics 2nd Edition*. Windcrest/McGraw Hill, 1993.

Romano, Frank J. *PDF Printing and Workflow*. Prentice Hall.

Rule, Keith. *3D Graphics File Formats*. Addison Wesley, 1996.

Sharp, Alec and Patrick McDermott. *Workflow Modeling*. Artech House Publishers.

Simon, Alan R. and William Marion. *Workflow, Groupware, and Messaging*. McGraw-Hill.

Snyder, J.P. *Map Projections—A Working Manual*, USGS Professional Paper 1395. USGPO, 1987.

Sobel, Mark A. *Practical Guide to the UNIX System*. Benjamin Cummings, 1989.

Tannenbaum, Adrienne. *Metadata Solutions*. Addison Wesley, 2002.

Thompson, Roy. *Grammar of the Edit*. Focal Press, 1993.

van der Aalst, Wil and Kees van Hee. *Workflow Management: Models, Methods, and Systems*. B&T.

Williams, Mark. *ANSI C—A Lexical Guide*. Mark Williams Company, 1988.

Wilson, Greg. *Data Crunching*. O'Reilly, 2005.

Internet RFC Documents

RFC documents are available from the IETF web site. Here is an example URL for RFC 2413: *http://www.ietf.org/rfc/rfc2413.txt*

Substitute the RFC number you need to access other RFC documents, or refer to the contents listing at: *http://www.ietf.org/rfc/*

RFC	Description
RFC 2822	Internet Message Format
RFC 2821	The Simple Mail Transfer Protocol
RFC 1870	SMTP Extension for Message Size Declaration
RFC 2554	SMTP Extension for Authentication
RFC 2920	SMTP Extension for Command Pipelining
RFC 3030	SMTP Extensions for Large Binary MIME Messages
RFC 3207	SMTP Extension for Secure SMTP over Transport Layer Security
RFC 3461	SMTP Extension for Delivery Status Notifications
RFC 3463	Enhanced Status Codes for SMTP
RFC 2387	MIME Multipart/Related Content-type
RFC 2045	MIME Part One: Format of Internet Message Bodies
RFC 2046	MIME Part Two: Media Types
RFC 2047	MIME Part Three: Message Header Extensions
RFC 4288	MIME Part Four: Media Type Specifications
RFC 4289	MIME Part Four: Registration Procedures
RFC 2049	MIME Part Five: Conformance Criteria and Examples
RFC 2231	MIME Parameter Value and Encoded Word Extensions
RFC 1847	MIME Security Multiparts
RFC 1766	Tags for the Identification of Languages
RFC 2396	Uniform Resource Identifiers (URI): Generic Syntax
RFC 2413	Dublin Core Metadata for Resource Discovery
RFC 3462	Mail System Administrative Messages
RFC 3464	An Extensible Message Format for Delivery Status Notifications
RFC 3552	Guidelines for Writing RFC Text on Security Considerations
RFC 3834	Recommendations for Automatic Responses to Electronic Mail
RFC 4409	Message Submission for Mail
RFC 3966	The `tel:` URI for telephone numbers
RFC 4519	LDAP User Applications
RFC 4514	LDAP Distinguished Names
RFC 4515	LDAP Search Filters

Webliography

Standards Related Organizations

Name	URL
EBU	http://www.ebu.ch/
SMPTE	http://www.smpte.org/
NAB	http://www.nab.org/
AES	http://www.aes.org/
DIN	http://www2.din.de/index.php?lang=en
ISO	http://www.iso.org/
IFPI	http://www.ifpi.org/
BSI	http://www.bsi-global.com/
ANSI	http://www.ansi.org/
IRMA	http://www.recordingmedia.org/
Cable Labs	http://www.cablelabs.org/
IETF	http://www.ietf.org/
TPEG	http://www.tpeg.org/default.htm
TV-Anytime Forum	http://www.tv-anytime.org/
SMPTE Registration Authority	http://www.smpte-ra.org
XML cover pages	http://www.oasis-open.org/cover/schemas.html
G-FORS	http://www.g-fors.com
Multimedia Wiki	http://wiki.multimedia.cx/index.php?title=Main_Page
Forum for Metadata Schema Implementers	http://www.schemas-forum.org
P/Meta home page	http://www.ebu.ch/en/technical/metadata/specifications/ notes_on_tech3295.php.
EBU/SMPTE Task Force	http://www.ebu.ch/pmc_es_tf.html
DOI	http://www.doi.org/
AAF Association	http://aafassociation.org/

Metadata Philosophy

Name	URL
BCS articles	http://archive.bcs.org/BCS/review04/articles/
ETSI glossary	http://portal.etsi.org/edithelp/abbrev/e.asp
Data model	http://www.free-definition.com/Data-model.html

File Formats and Protocols

Name	URL
AAF Home Page	http://www.aafassociation.org/
File ext .com	http://filext.com/detaillist.php?extdetail=GXF
Material Exchange Format	http://www,mxfig.org/
Wiki page on SMTP	http://en.wikipedia.org/wiki/Simple_Mail_Transfer_Protocol

See also:

- P/META
- MXF

Code Sets

Name	URL
Unicode encodings	http://en.wikipedia.org/wiki/Comparison_of_Unicode_encodings
Unicode mapping	http://en.wikipedia.org/wiki/Mapping_of_Unicode_characters
Windows code pages	http://en.wikipedia.org/wiki/Windows_code_pages
Windows code pages	http://www.microsoft.com/globaldev/reference/sbcs/874.mspx
Windows code pages	http://www.microsoft.com/globaldev/dis_v1/html/S24CB.asp?TOC=Y
Internationalisation	http://en.wikipedia.org/wiki/Internationalization_and_localization
Byte order marks	http://en.wikipedia.org/wiki/Byte_Order_Mark
Unicode and e-mail	http://en.wikipedia.org/wiki/Unicode_and_e-mail
Unicode and HTML	http://en.wikipedia.org/wiki/Unicode_and_HTML

Date and Time

Name	*URL*
ISO date and time	*http://www.uic.edu/depts/accc/software/isodates/index.html*
EB XML	*http://lists.ebxml.org/archives/ebxml-core/200104/pdf00005.pdf*
Date formats	*http://www.merlyn.demon.co.uk/datefmts.htm#8601*
ISO 8601	*http://www.probabilityof.com/ISO8601.shtml*
ISO date and time	*http://www.uic.edu/depts/accc/software/isodates/isocontents.html*
ISO 8601	*http://www.mcs.vuw.ac.nz/technical/software/SGML/doc/iso8601/ISO8601.html*
ISO 8601	*http://www.cs.tut.fi/~jkorpela/iso8601.html*
ISO 8601	*http://en.wikipedia.org/wiki/ISO_8601*
Date and time	*http://www.iso.org/iso/en/prods-services/popstds/datesandtime.html*
ISO 8601	*http://www.iso.org/iso/en/CatalogueDetailPage.CatalogueDetail?CSNUMBER= 40874*
vCalendars	*http://www.imc.org/pdi/vcaloverview.html*
vCalendars in Java	*https://vcalendar.dev.java.net/*
vCalender	*http://en.wikipedia.org/wiki/VCalendar*
vCalender org	*http://www.vcalendar.org/site/*
W3C date and	*http://www.w3.org/TR/NOTE-datetime* time formats

Directory Mechanisms

Name	*URL*
vCard	*http://en.wikipedia.org/wiki/VCard*
Open LDAP	*http://en.wikipedia.org/wiki/OpenLDAP*
LDAP DIF	*http://en.wikipedia.org/wiki/LDAP_Data_Interchange_Format*
LDAP User Applications:	*http://tools.ietf.org/html/rfc4519*
LDAP Distinguished Names	*http://tools.ietf.org/html/rfc4514*
LDAP Search Filters	*http://tools.ietf.org/html/rfc4515*

Geographical Reference

Name	URL
Country codes	*http://www.unc.edu/~rowlett/units/codes/country.htm*
Countries and flags	*http://www.statoids.com/wab.html*
Country codes	*http://en.wikipedia.org/wiki/Country_codes*
ISO 3166 2-letter	*http://en.wikipedia.org/wiki/ISO_3166-1_alpha-2*
ISO 3166 3-letter	*http://en.wikipedia.org/wiki/ISO_3166-1_alpha-3*
ISO 4217	*http://en.wikipedia.org/wiki/ISO_4217*
ISO 3166 numeric	*http://en.wikipedia.org/wiki/ISO_3166-1_numeric*
Getty Thesaurus of Geographic Names	*http://www.getty.edu/research/tools/vocabulary/tgn/index.html*
ISO 639-2: Names of languages	*http://lcweb.loc.gov/standards/iso639-2/*
Names of countries	*http://www.din.de/gremien/nas/nabd/iso3166ma/index.html*
ISO 3166	*http://www.iso.org/iso/en/catsupport/maralist.html).*
ISO Country codes	*http://www.iso.org/iso/en/prods-services/iso3166ma/02iso-3166-code-lists/index.html*

Networking Protocols

Name	URL
Internet TLDs	*http://en.wikipedia.org/wiki/List_of_Internet_TLDs*
Internet TLDs	*http://en.wikipedia.org/wiki/Top-level_domain*
ISO 4217	*http://en.wikipedia.org/wiki/ISO_4217*

See also:

- RFC documents

Telephone Related

Name	URL
Phone numbers	*http://en.wikipedia.org/wiki/Telephone_number*
Numbering plans	*http://en.wikipedia.org/wiki/Telephone_numbering_plan*
Country codes	*http://en.wikipedia.org/wiki/List_of_country_calling_codes*

See also:

- ITU-T Recommendation E.123: Notation for telephone numbers, e-mail and Web
- RFC 3966 The `tel:` URI for telephone numbers

Name and Address Info

Name	URL
Postal codes	*http://en.wikipedia.org/wiki/Postcode*
USA ZIP codes	*http://en.wikipedia.org/wiki/Zip_code*
USA ZIP codes list	*http://en.wikipedia.org/wiki/List_of_Zip_Codes*
UK post codes	*http://en.wikipedia.org/wiki/Uk_postcodes*
UK post code areas	*http://en.wikipedia.org/wiki/List_of_postal_areas_in_the_United_Kingdom*

EBU Standards

Description	URL
BPN 027	*http://www.ebu.ch/en/technical/projects/b_tpeg.php*
ESCORT	*http://www.ebu.ch/CMSimages/en/tec_EBU_escort2-4_tcm6-11889.pdf*
Facility codes	*http://www.ebu.ch/CMSimages/en/tec_EBU_facility_codes_tcm6-11891.pdf*
Media type codes	*http://www.ebu.ch/en/technical/metadata/specifications/media_types_publication_notes.php*
Members standards	*http://www.ebu.ch/en/technical/metadata/members_specs/index.php*
Metadata entities	*http://www.ebu.ch/metadata/*
NES	*http://www.ebu.ch/metadata/nes/*
Network ID codes	*http://www.ebu.ch/CMSimages/en/tec_info_tr231-2006_tcm6-41792.pdf*
P/Meta v1.2 specification	*http://www.ebu.ch/CMSimages/en/tec_doc_t3295_v0102_tcm6-40957.pdf*

R99-1999	*http://www.ebu.ch/CMSimages/en/tec_text_r99-1999_tcm6-4689.pdf*
RDS Country codes	*http://www.ebu.ch/en/technical/metadata/specifications/rds_country_codes.php*
Role codes	*http://www.ebu.ch/en/technical/metadata/specifications/role_codes.php*
Roles in broadcasting	*http://www.ebu.ch/tech_info_roles.html*
Storage media codes	*http://www.ebu.ch/en/technical/metadata/specifications/storage_media_ codes.php*
Storage media	*http://www.ebu.ch/tech_info_store.html*
Tech 3279	*http://www.ebu.ch/CMSimages/en/tec_doc_t3279-2004_tcm6-15016.pdf*
Tech 3293	*http://www.ebu.ch/CMSimages/en/tec_doc_t3293_tcm6-10494.pdf*
Tech 3295	*http://www.ebu.ch/CMSimages/en/tec_doc_t3295_v0102_tcm6-40957.pdf*
Tech 3301	*http://www.ebu.ch/CMSimages/en/tec_doc_t3301_tcm6-40955.pdf*
Tech 3303	*http://www.ebu.ch/CMSimages/en/tec_doc_t3303-1_tcm6-43109.pdf*
Type of resource	*http://www.ebu.ch/tech_info_media.html*
XTRADIO DTD	*http://www.ebu.ch/metadata/xtradio/v10/xml/dtd/dc_archive.dtd*
P/Meta tools	*http://www.crit.rai.it/attivita/pmetatools/*

Dublin Core Metadata Initiative

Description	*URL*
Dublin Core	*http://dublincore.org/*
Box Encoding Scheme	*http://dublincore.org/documents/dcmi-box/*
Element Set	*http://dublincore.org/documents/dces/*
Period Encoding Scheme	*http://dublincore.org/documents/dcmi-period/*
Point Encoding Scheme	*http://dublincore.org/documents/dcmi-point/*
Qualifiers	*http://dublincore.org/documents/dcmes-qualifiers/*
Type Vocabulary	*http://dublincore.org/documents/dcmi-type-vocabulary/*
Using DCMI	*http://dublincore.org/documents/usageguide/*

Other Metadata Standards and Usage

Description	URL
News Management System	*http://ebupop1/support/docu/NMS-XML_eng.html (suspect URL)*
LCC – Library of Congress Classification	*http://lcweb.loc.gov/catdir/cpso/lcco/lcco.html*
LCSH – Library of Congress Subject Heading	*http://lcweb.loc.gov/cds/lcsh.html*
SMEF	*http://www.bbc.co.uk/guidelines/smef/*
VOD Metadata	*http://www.cablelabs.org/projects/metadata/*
MPEG-7	*http://www.chiariglione.org/mpeg/standards/mpeg-7/mpeg-7.htm*
UML	*http://www.uml.org/*
V-ISAN	*http://www.collectionscanada.ca/iso/tc46sc9/15706-2.htm*
DDV Metamodel	*http://www.dedigitalevoorziening.nl/wwwdata/documenten/dc_31.pdf*
DR Metadata Standard	*http://www.dr.dk/metadata*
ISRC	*http://www.ifpi.org/isrc/*
BMF	*http://www.irt.de/IRT/home/indexbmf.htm*
ISAN	*http://www.isan.org/*
Internet Media Types	*http://www.isi.edu/in-notes/iana/assignments/media-types/media-types*
Metaglue Diffuser	*http://www.metaglue.tv/smpte-ra/mg-diffuser.php*
ISAN – International Standard Audiovisual Number	*http://www.nlc-bnc.ca/iso/tc46sc9/15706.htm*
ISRC – International Standard Recording Code	*http://www.nlc-bnc.ca/iso/tc46sc9/3901.htm*
MeSH – Medical Subject Headings	*http://www.nlm.nih.gov/mesh/meshhome.html*
DDC – Dewey Decimal Classification	*http://www.oclc.org/dewey/index.htm*
RDS PTY display terms	*http://www.rds.org.uk/rds98/pty_languages.htm*
SMPTE Metadata Registration Authority	*http://www.smpte-ra.org/*
SMPTE Metadata Dictionary	*http://www.smpte-ra.org/mdd/index.html*
TV – Anytime	*http://www.tv-anytime.org/*
UDC – Universal Decimal Classification	*http://www.udcc.org/*
ebXML	*http://www.ebxml.org/geninfo.htm ebXML*

Media Asset Management Systems

Company	URL
Adam Systems Group of ASR, Inc.	http://www.adamsystems.com/
AEM Technology Inc	http://www.aemtechnology.com/
Alienbrain (NxN Software)	http://www.alienbrain.com/
Ancept	http://www.ancept.com/ancept_main.html
Ardendo (Vizrt)	http://www.ardendo.com/
Artesia Digital Media Group	http://www.artesia.com/
Atempo	http://www.atempo.com/
Blue Order	http://www.blue-order.com/
Blueline Technology Inc	http://www.bluelinetech.com/
Broadcast Communications	http://www.boxer.co.uk/
Canto Software (Cumulus)	http://www.canto.com/
Cinegy	http://www.cinegy.com/
Ciprico	http://www.ciprico.com/
CIS Technology Co Ltd	http://www.cistech.co.kr/
ClearStory Systems	http://www.clearstorysystems.com/
Dalet Digital Media Systems	http://www.dalet.com/
DiskStream Incorporated	http://www.diskstream.com/
eMotion Inc	http://www.emotion.com/
Etere Automation	http://www.etere.com/
Extensis	http://www.extensis.com/
Focus Enhancements	http://www.focusinfo.com/
Graphic Detail	http://www.graphicdetail.com/
Hardata S.A	http://www.hardata.com/
High-End systems (Catalyst)	http://www.highend.com/
Hot Banana	http://www.hotbanana.com/
Intrinet Systems Inc	http://www.intrinetsystems.com/
Konan Digital, Inc	http://www.konandigital.com/
Masstech Group Inc	http://www.masstechgroup.com/
Metus (Library)	http://www.metus.com/
MSO	http://www.mso.net/
mSoft Inc	http://www.msoftinc.com/
North Plains Systems (Telescope)	http://www.northplains.com/
Pathfire	http://www.pathfire.com/
Pebble Beach Systems	http://www.pebble.tv/

Pharos Communications	*http://www.pharos-comms.com/*
Picdar – Media Mogul	*http://www.picdar.com/*
Pictron Inc	*http://www.pictron.com/*
Plone	*http://plone.org/*
PLU	*http://www.plu.edu/~dmc/dam/index.html*
Proximity Corporation	*http://www.proximitygroup.com/*
QPict	*http://www.qpict.net/*
SGI	*http://www.sgi.com/*
SIGNUM Bildtechnik GmbH	*http://www.signumbt.com/*
Square Box Systems, Ltd	*http://www.squarebox.co.uk/*
Stipkomedia	*http://www.stipkomedia.com/*
Streamtel	*http://www.streamtel.com/*
Synergy Broadcast Systems	*http://www.synergybroadcast.com/*
Tedial	*http://www.tedial.com/*
Thomson (NETg LCMS)	*http://www.netg.com/*
Transmedia Dynamics Ltd	*http://www.tmd.tv/*
Unisys	*http://www.unisys.com/*
Venaca Inc	*http://www.venaca.com/*
V-Finity	*http://www.vfinity.com/*
VideoBank	*http://www.videobankdigital.com/*
Virage Inc	*http://www.virage.com/*
Vizrt	*http://www.vizrt.com/*
XenData	*http://www.xendata.com/*
Xytech Systems Corporation	*http://www.xytechsystems.com/*

Index